Make No Mistake!

Make No Mistake!

An Outcome-Based Approach to Mistake-Proofing

C. Martin Hinckley

CRC Press
Taylor & Francis Group
Boca Raton London New York

CRC Press is an imprint of the
Taylor & Francis Group, an informa business

The author and Productivity Press would like to acknowledge and thank the following organizations for the permission to adapt their mistake-proofing principles and examples for this book.

Kaneka Corporation. *Sochi-gata Shokuba-no Poka-yoke Katsudo*. Copyright 1991 by Kaneka Corporation. Published by JMA Management Center, Inc.:

Pages 124–125, 130–131,137–138,140, 149, 154–155,189, 192, 203–204, 209, 217, 222, 239–240, 302, 306 & 315.

Nikkan Kogyo Shinbunsha. *Poka-yoke Daizukan*, Japanese version published 1986 by Nikkan Kogyo Shinbunsha; *Poka-yoke*, English version published 1986 by Productivity, Inc.:

Pages 111–112, 133, 139, 141–142, 144, 150–151, 158, 167–168, 170–171,173, 176–177, 184, 186, 188, 190–191, 193–195, 199, 206, 208, 211–212, 220, 224–225, 228, 235, 237, 241, 242, 245, 248–251,257–258, 262, 264, 267–268, 273–274, 278–279, 285, 288, 291, 293–294, 296–297, 304–305, 312–313, 317, 319–320, 325, 328, 330, 334–336, 338 & 342.

Yamaha Motor Co. Ltd.:

Pages 129, 174, 269, 299, & 343.

Yamato Kogyo Co.:

Pages 143, 153, 158, 233, 244, 256, 265, 318, & 341.

Cover Design: Stephen Scates
Production Editor: Michael Ryder
Page Composition: William H. Brunson Typography Services
Illustrations: Guy Boster
Printed in the United States of America

Library of Congress Cataloging-in-Publication Data

Hinckley, C. Martin.
    Make no mistake : an outcome-based approach to mistake-proofing / C. Martin Hinckley.
       p.   cm.
    Includes bibliographical references and index.
    ISBN 978-1-56327-227-1
    1. Quality control.   2. Total quality management.   I. Title

TS156 .H535   2001
    658.5′62—dc21

                                                            2001031736

07 06   6 5 4 3

Contents

ACKNOWLEDGMENTS

Professor Phil Barkan, my former dissertation advisor at Stanford, was the inspiration for this book. Our initial goal simply was to determine which elements of design have the greatest influence on product quality. We were frustrated by the fact that we could not find a reasonable relationship between product defect rates and tolerance studies, process capability indices, or other variation-based parameters. The breakthrough occurred when Professor Barkan discovered an article by Motorola that suggested a potential link between defect rates and design for assembly parameters. We subsequently demonstrated that defect rates were strongly linked to a simple function of assembly time and the number of assembly operations. This relationship has proven to be remarkably sound over a wide range of industries, product complexities, manufacturers, and production volumes. These strong correlations demonstrated that the dominant source of defects in production today could not be variation—a conclusion that was initially troubling. This lead to our examination of the role of mistakes in product quality, and eventually to the concepts presented here.

Interactions with education and industry leaders like Stanford University, Caterpillar, GE Aircraft Engines, and the American Society of Quality (ASQ), helped refine our approach to mistake-proofing. Kosuke Ishii, who took over Professor Barkan's teaching assignments at Stanford upon his retirement, has been a strong supporter. Continuing research in this field under his leadership has repeatedly validated and reinforced the underlying premise of this work. Professor Ishii has opened doors to interactions with quality leaders from around the world, enabling the sharing of examples and experiences. Continuing interactions with graduate students at Stanford and participation in the lectures have helped refine and clarify mistake-proofing approaches. Peder Fitch, Steve Kmenta, and Brent Cheldelin are among the researchers at Stanford whose help and support is greatly appreciated.

Gene Wiggs, at GE Aircraft Engines, has also played a key role in the evolution of this work. Prompted by our observations, this organization—under Gene's leadership—set out to apply and test the basic concepts. They not only have had remarkable success in this effort, but also have expanded upon the ideas and demonstrated that they apply in a variety of new ways. GE provided nearly 30 mistake-proofing examples for this effort. Of these, roughly a dozen have been used in this book. In addition, their experience has identified approximately 15 of the mistake-proofing principles contained in the Appendix A. Gene has also been kind enough to review this work. His concepts and encouragement have been invaluable.

This work would have little substance without the foundation in mistake-proofing laid by Shigeo Shingo and Hiroyuki Hirano, Chairman of the JIT Management Laboratory Co., in

Japan. Sandia National Laboratories has been another major source of new mistake-proofing examples. While mistake-proofing is normally thought of as a volume production tool, teams at Sandia have shown that it is remarkably effective even for prototype development.

Among the organizations that have contributed mistake-proofing concepts are: Kanebuchi, Yamaha, Yamato Kogyo, Canon, Alexander Ogilvy, and Lawson Mardon Packaging USA.

This work could not have moved forward without the continued support and attention of Maura May and Michael Ryder at Productivity Press.

Finally, I want to acknowledge the help and support of my family. Each of the children have participated in some way by looking up supplier and product data, sorting through the examples, entering mistake-proofing data, and mailing the letters and packages necessary to keep this work moving forward. My wife, Karen, has been my most constant friend and advocate. Without her help, the task could not have been completed.

FOREWORD

If your business is like ours (and I bet it is), 60 to 90 percent of all defects created in production—and a similar percentage of defects escaping to customers—are due to mistakes, either human or technological (mechanical) in origin.

We find that the overwhelming majority of our designs are Six Sigma-capable, and our processes have consistently high capability indices ($C_{pk}s$). Nevertheless, our manufacturing and assembly processes still produce nonconformances. Once we recognized that mistakes were the culprit, we had the breakthrough that allowed us to focus on error prevention rather than our historical "blame-and-train" corrective action cycle. Manufacturers all over the world, in a wide variety of industries, have had the same "A-ha!" experience and are now realizing that dramatic improvements in conformance quality can be achieved by mistake-proofing.

Of course, mistakes are pervasive in all human activities—design, accounting, health care, customer service, and thousands more. To improve customer satisfaction dramatically, we have to eliminate errors from *all* of our business processes.

Martin's new book is a must-read for everyone concerned with improving customer satisfaction. This is an excellent addition to the small but growing body of literature on mistake reduction. Eliminating human and technological errors may be the most difficult job we face in producing defect-free products and services. Martin's approach will help us all learn how to give our customers the quality they deserve.

Gene E. Wiggs
GE Aircraft Engines
Evendale, Ohio

INTRODUCTION

Traditionally, mistake-proofing has been learned by experience. Like musicians, designers develop a repertoire of skills as they practice mistake-proofing, and they observe a wide variety of mistake-proofing devices. Novices, however, struggle with mistake-proofing. They have difficulty finding examples relevant to their problems, and when they do find them, they have difficulty translating the concepts from one product to another. Consequently, novices frequently revert to solving problems using traditional quality methods.

This book provides a structured approach to mistake-proofing that allows individuals to classify mistakes quickly, identify pertinent examples rapidly, and understand the relevant mistake-proofing principles. This facilitates the development of a variety of mistake-proofing concepts for each problem. A simple matrix for benchmarking and comparing concepts can readily identify those that potentially are most effective. This structured approach helps novices quickly develop confidence and skill in mistake-proofing, while increasing the efficiency of experienced designers.

Yet there are fundamental reasons why a methodology alone is not sufficient to assure successful mistake-proofing. Although many books have been written on the subject of mistakes and their control, very few organizations have aggressively sought to eliminate mistakes and their consequences. Individuals often fail to implement mistake-proofing simply because they fail to recognize the frequency and significance of mistakes. More importantly, many individuals just don't believe that mistakes can be prevented. In yet other instances, efforts to control mistakes are based on a wide range of ineffective methods. And even when highly effective methods are used, significant results rarely result when mistake-proofing is no more than a token effort that addresses only a few problems. Finally, mistake-proofing efforts flounder when leaders fail to recognize that mistake-proofing requires a cultural change more profound than a mere change in technology.

One possible reason that mistake-proofing efforts fail is that existing books on mistake-proofing do not adequately address all of the following fundamental issues in a single text:

- Why mistake-proofing is essential and must be extensive;
- How effective mistake-proofing is in improving productivity and eliminating waste;
- What mistake-proofing methods are most effective; and
- How the culture must be changed to facilitate mistake-proofing.

To illustrate, some outstanding books on mistake-proofing techniques do not explain fully why traditional statistical methods are inadequate. Consequently, the reader may fail to grasp the urgency and importance of mistake-proofing.

Although this book cannot provide a complete description of *every* aspect of mistake-proofing, our goal is to address the critical elements noted here in a way that inspires and motivates individuals and organizations to take action. In Chapter 1, we will address the role of mistakes in defects. The next four chapters review the techniques essential to eliminating or controlling mistakes, and the last chapter characterizes the cultural changes that facilitate mistake-proofing.

CHAPTER 1

THE ROLE OF MISTAKES IN PRODUCT QUALITY

NO WATER

You're running late for work. You had intended to take a shower, but there's only a drip of water coming from your faucet and it's brown at that. So you call the Water Department.

LOCATING THE BREAK IN THE WATER MAIN

The Water Department says they have been aware of the problem for a couple of hours, but haven't yet located the break in the water main. Actually, they did find and fix one small leak, but afterward there was still low pressure and dirty water. They think there must be a larger break at some other location. You're thinking, "Why are they having so much trouble finding the source of the problem?"

THE WATER DEPARTMENT'S EQUIPMENT AND TOOLS

This problem is particularly annoying in light of the City Council's recent decision to postpone appropriation of money for new tools and equipment for the Water Department. Even when the real problem is found, it may take hours to repair it and prevent it from happening again, given the department's current equipment.

DEFECTS CONTAMINATE THE PRODUCT

Leaks reduce the quantity of water that can be delivered by a supply line. Leaks also degrade water quality by allowing the introduction of contaminates. When gross leaks result in discolored water or dramatic flow reductions, we expect immediate corrective action. However, because of a false sense of security, leaks can be most harmful when water appears to be clear and pure but is contaminated with minute amounts of hazardous material. Even trace amounts of toxins or bacteria can pose an unacceptable health risk.

Just as leaks reduce water output and quality, defects reduce production output and product quality. Unfortunately, many companies view their moderate product quality like a deceptively clear glass of water that may really have serious quality problems. Because their defect rates seem to be low, they do not perceive the potential threat of competitors who may achieve world-class product quality.

CONFORMANCE QUALITY

We define conformance quality as product yield, or the fraction of non-defective parts generated during the manufacturing process. We measure the deviation from the ideal conformance quality in terms of noncon-forming (defective) parts per million (ppm).

Our goal is to help organizations achieve world-class conformance quality and economic advantage through *efficiently* eliminating or con-trolling the cause of defects. More specifically, we seek to:

- Clarify the root cause of defects,
- Identify the techniques for efficiently eliminating defects,
- Identify when to apply each existing quality control method, and
- Provide a framework for defining a quality control strategy based on continuous improvement.

THE STATUS OF QUALITY CONTROL IN AMERICA

QUALITY CONTROL EFFORT AND DEFECT RATE

U.S. quality control performance generally lags behind world-class standards, even though many companies have initiated aggressive quality control efforts. A benchmarking study by a major corporation showed that quality leaders in the United States, including those aggressively pursuing Six Sigma goals, rarely achieved defect rates below 1,000 parts per million. The scrap, rework, repair, warranty, and quality control costs among these U.S. quality leaders consumed 6 to 24 percent of their production budget. In contrast, world-class pacesetters, such as Toyota, maintain defect rates below 50 ppm while spending less than 3 percent of their production budget on the same quality losses, as illustrated in Figure 1-1. The clear economic leverage of high-quality manufacturing inspires a sense of urgency in achieving a real reduction in defects in an increasingly competitive global market.

While traditional quality control levels may seem adequate, the con-sequences of "pretty-good" quality are staggering. Table 1.1 summarizes the expected frequency of a few significant events given traditional quality control levels. At first glance, the projected frequency of such

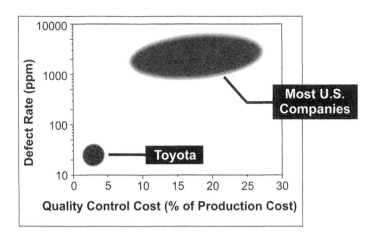

FIGURE 1-1
Relative quality control performance for quality leaders based on a benchmarking study by a major corporation. Toyota consistently maintains defect rates below 50 ppm while spending less on quality control than competitors.

serious consequences may seem unreasonably high. However, the data in some cases suggests that the error rates are actually much higher than projected in the table. For example, one doctor told the author that on the average two babies were dropped in their hospital each month. Given roughly 6,000 hospitals in the United States, this suggests that roughly 12,000 babies may be dropped each month in hospitals. In addition, the Institute of Medicine's report (Kohn, Corrigan, and Donaldson 2000, 26) estimated that 44,000 to 98,000 people die as a result of hospital mistakes each year in the United States.

If we settle for a 99.9% conformance quality (1,000 ppm defect rate), we get:	
2	Unsafe landings at O'Hare per day
10	Gallons of unsafe drinking water per person per month
300	Newborn babies dropped in the hospital per month
2,100	Incorrect surgical operations per month
20,000	Wrong medical prescriptions per year
1,000,000	Incorrect phone bills per year
193,000,000	Checks deducted from the wrong account per year

TABLE 1-1
Expected frequency of a few quality lapses based on traditional quality control levels.

VARIATION—A MAJOR SOURCE OF DEFECTS

With the advent of mass production in the early 1900s, part-to-part variation was identified as the major source of assembly problems and product defects. Owing to the inherent inconsistency of production during this time, it is not surprising that variation was the first defect source identified. The quality problems caused by uncontrolled variation can be compared to major leaks in a water supply line caused by a broken pipe like the one illustrated in Figure 1-2, which are the easiest to locate and demand the most urgent corrective measures.

FIGURE 1-2

Uncontrolled variation is like a major leak in a water supply line.

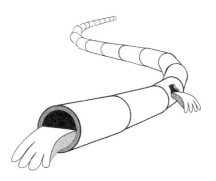

From this historical context, it is natural that the most commonly accepted concept in quality control is that "variation is *the* enemy." Based on this perspective, statistical quality control (SQC) is viewed as an adequate means of controlling defects. This approach, however, has fundamental limitations that must be understood to achieve world-class quality.

THE SQC PARADIGM

The SQC paradigm is based on the observation that the outcome of every repeated action follows a distribution, like that shown in the histogram in Figure 1-3. In a histogram, frequencies are plotted in dimensional increments or bins. Lower magnitude values, such as time, quantity, size, and distance are plotted on the left, and those of higher magnitude on the right.

FIGURE 1-3.

A histogram showing observations grouped into bins or increments.

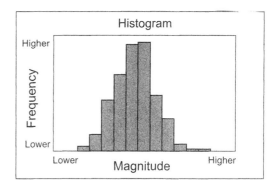

A mathematical model that matches the data is then selected to describe the observed distribution, as shown in Figure 1-4. We also use

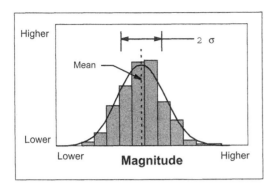

FIGURE 1-4
A mathematical model that "fits" the data is selected.

commonly computed properties like the *mean* (μ) and the *variance* (σ), which describe the "average" value and dispersion of a sample, respectively.

Because sample sizes are generally small, we can only predict the fraction of the distribution falling in the tails beyond specified limits by extrapolation using the selected mathematical model as illustrated in Figure 1-5. If the defects estimated by the fraction below the lower specification limit (LSL) or above the upper specification limit (USL) exceed a desired value, we try to improve process control to reduce variation, or adjust the mean or limits until acceptable conditions are achieved.

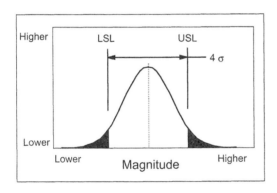

FIGURE 1.5
Extrapolation of the model to predict events above or below defined limits.

LIMITATIONS OF SQC AS A GUIDE FOR QUALITY CONTROL

Just as accurate maps showing water line locations are essential for locating and repairing leaks, an accurate understanding of the cause of defects is essential in the journey to ever-higher quality. Thus, the success of SQC in achieving world-class quality depends upon its ability to accurately predict and control the tails of a distribution.

Unfortunately, traditional statistical methods are inadequate quality tools because they consistently underestimate the frequency and magnitude of events falling in the tails. This weakness of SQC can be traced to several factors:

- Sample sizes are generally small, and consequently inadequate to characterize the tails of a distribution. Furthermore, since only a portion of the product is sampled, many defects pass through production undetected.
- Typically, two or three readings are averaged to provide a single data point for fitting the distribution of manufacturing processes (Juran and Gryna 1988, 24.6) (Ishikawa 1990, 65). This practice obscures the skewness, or unsymmetrical characteristics, of a distribution.
- Outliers, or oddball observations that do not appear to fit the population, are arbitrarily discarded. Consequently, events that suggest that the tails are "heavier" than predicted generally are ignored.
- Traditional inspection methods are not perfectly reliable (Tavormina and Buckley 1992). There is generally a significant probability that defective parts will not be detected even when inspected. Thus, defects always tend to exceed the number observed by inspection.
- Defect rates are predicted by assuming the population faithfully follows a selected model far beyond the range of collected data. These models, particularly the normal distribution, are frequently assumed without evaluation. Juran, one of the champions of SQC, stated: "The Pareto principle would lead us to believe that most distributions of quality characteristics would not quite be normal. Both Shewhart's and the authors' experience confirm this" (Juran and Gryna 1988, 24.6).

Evidence Illustrating the Limitations of SQC

An example drawn from production experience clearly illustrates the limitations of statistical methods. The dashed line in Figure 1-6 is the distribution of time required for operators to perform a "standard" operation in a production environment. The data are plotted as a probability density function (PDF), showing the probability on the vertical axis that a random observation has the value plotted on the horizontal axis. For comparison, the familiar bell-shaped curve associated with the normal distribution is also a PDF plot. This distribution is derived from work rate studies of roughly 9,000 employees over a 10-year period, wherein each employee was evaluated four times a year, as published by Ralph Barnes (Barnes 1980, 323). Thus, the data reflects over 360,000 observations, an exceptionally large sample. Note the long thin tail extending to the right.

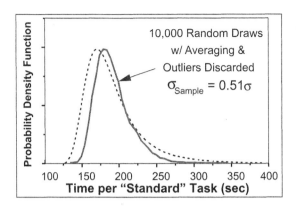

FIGURE 1-6
Probability density functions (PDFs) for a large population (dashed line) and 10,000 averaged random draws from the distribution (solid line). Curves are not plotted to the same vertical scale.

Given this distribution, we can simulate random samples to assess the effectiveness of traditional sampling methods. The distribution shown as a solid line in the figure was obtained using 10,000 random draws from the larger sample. Outliers, or those readings more than four standard deviations from the mean, were discarded. Remaining readings were averaged in sets of 3 to produce about 3,300 observations. The "averaged" distribution is overlaid on the original population using different vertical scales for comparison. The estimated variance based on discarding outliers and averaging is roughly half the true population variance (σ) in this example. The figure also shows that the traditional sampling methods result in poor approximations for the tails of the distribution.

IMPACT OF SMALL SAMPLE SIZES

A small sample size further degrades the accuracy of predicting the tails. A typical histogram based on 300 random draws from the time per task distribution, with outliers discarded and averaging, is plotted in Figure 1-7. Note that the resulting histogram appears to follow a normal distribution,

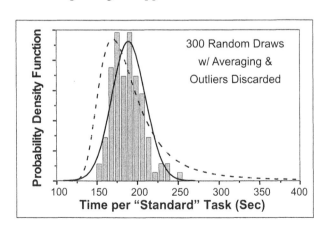

FIGURE 1-7
Probability density functions (PDFs) for a large population (dashed line) and 300 averaged random draws from the distribution (solid line). Curves are not plotted to the same vertical scale. In most cases, a normal distribution appears to be a good model for such small samples.

which is plotted as a solid line but deviates significantly from the population plotted as a dashed line. In 7 out of 10 such samples, the best statistical tests would not reject the normal distribution as an inappropriate model! In other words, 70 percent of the time most researchers would conclude that this population follows a normal distribution using traditional sampling methods.

In a study of 23 distributions of human performance that have been traditionally modeled with the normal distribution, we have observed that the frequency and magnitude of events more than three standard deviations from the mean *consistently* are underestimated (Hinckley 1993, 136). One case illustrating this pattern is shown in Figure 1-8. This suggests that statistical methods by themselves will never be a complete quality control solution.

FIGURE 1-8

Fraction of the distribution in the tail as a function of the distance from the mean measured in standard deviations, with a normal distribution and an accurate model of the work rate study by Barnes (Barnes 1980, 323). Note that the normal distribution consistently underestimates the fraction in the tail.

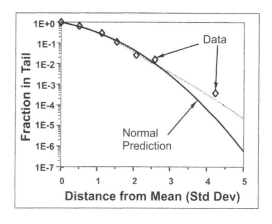

INADEQUACIES OF STATISTICS AS A
MAP FOR WORLD-CLASS QUALITY CONTROL

- **It cannot take us to the highest quality levels.**
  As we seek the highest level of quality conformance (defect rates below 50 ppm), we are forced to address even the extremely rare events that impact quality, not just those near the mean that are most frequent.

- **We may ignore the important few while controlling the trivial many.**
  The variation paradigm can lead us to focus on controlling many small variations while ignoring the control of gross variations. The gross variations are extremely rare, but actually have a more devastating effect on quality. Several studies have shown that the rare extreme events actually account for the major portion of the quality control problems.

- **It underestimates the probability of extreme events.**
  Our studies show that extreme events occur much more frequently in manufacturing operations than statistical methods would predict.

- **It focuses on feedback control from downstream observations.**
  Because the control mechanism is downstream of the process execution, many defects may occur, even in a "controlled" process.

THE WATER IS ON!

Returning home from work, you head to the sink to get a drink of water. Today has been a scorcher, and the cool water is a welcome relief. You suddenly realize that the water line must have been repaired—and you're reminded of the shower you missed this morning.

THE PROBLEM IS FIXED

After working all night to fix the problem, the crew chief slaps the backhoe operator on the back, telling him to go home and get some rest. He calls to the team and yells, "Great job, lets take tomorrow off."

THEN AGAIN, MAYBE IT'S NOT

The next day, the city engineer decides to test the line just to be sure that everything is fine. He's disturbed by what he finds. There's too much bacteria in the water, and the pressure is only two-thirds what it should be. Puzzled, the engineer reviews the construction drawings and realizes that the wrong joint gaskets were specified by mistake. As a result, the entire water line is leaking a little at each joint. Although the leak at each joint is almost imperceptible, collectively the water loss exceeds that observed for the recently repaired break. After a couple of restless nights, the engineer tells the city manager that their diagnostic tools and equipment aren't useful in solving the current problem.

BEYOND SQC

Mistakes impact quality the same way that many trivial leaks reduce a water supply. Independently each mistake seems negligible; but collectively, mistakes can be a major barrier to achieving world-class quality standards. To achieve the highest levels of quality control, we must understand how to control mistakes.

MISTAKES

In the assembly of the simple products like the box shown in Figure 1-9, an operator may occasionally forget to install a screw. In the assembly, each screw is either missing or present. A mistake occurs when:

- A required action is not performed,
- A prohibited action is executed,
- Information essential for an action is misinterpreted, or
- An error is made in selecting among alternatives.

Rook found that 1 in 10,000 to 1 in 100,000 manufacturing operations will be omitted without detection (Rook 1962). *In other words, omission errors alone will result in defect rates as high as 100 ppm.*

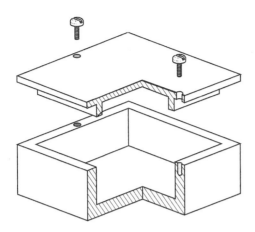

FIGURE 1-9
Many errors can be made in the fabrication and assembly of this box, which is cut away for visibility. A bolt may be omitted, a hole may not be drilled, or a bolt may not be tightened.

Omissions are only one type of mistake. Other types of mistakes that have been identified (Poka-yoke 1988, 12–14) include:

- Processing mistakes
- Mistakes setting up workpieces, equipment, tools, and jigs
- Missing or wrong parts
- Processing the wrong workpiece
- Misoperation or adjustment mistakes

Although each specific type of mistake occurs rarely, collectively defect rates resulting from many types of mistakes typically exceed 1 mistake per 1,000 actions (1,000 ppm). Such error rates lead us to wonder what fraction of defects in production environments are caused by mistakes versus excessive variation. The results of studies that have attempted to answer this question are rather surprising.

Harris (Harris 1969, 9) concluded that 80 percent of the defects in complex systems could be attributed to human error. In an examination of 23,000 production defects, Rook (Rook 1962) found that 82 percent of all defects were caused by human errors. His tabulation revealed that most errors occurred during assembly. A study of front end automotive headlamps produced by a major manufacturer (Student 1992) also showed that more than 70 percent of 6,600 observed defects were caused by assembly or handling errors. Finally, the National Aeronautics & Space Administration (NASA) (Associated Press 1993) reported that most space shuttle mishaps are the result of human error based on a study of mishaps occurring since October 1990. In fact, human error is identified as the dominant cause of defects in modern production and human activity in virtually every study where this source of problems has been examined.

Mistakes in the News

The outcomes resulting from mistakes are generally more severe and dramatic than would be expected for excessive variation. Mistakes are often the source of major catastrophes reported in the news on a nearly daily basis. The following are just a few examples.

- On September 14, 1997 an F117 stealth fighter airplane crashed, destroying the $42 million aircraft. Investigation revealed that four of five one-inch diameter fasteners that attached the wing to the fuselage were missing. The pilot had complained to the maintenance crew about unusual wing vibrations, but inspection did not reveal the missing bolts because a stiffener plate that concealed the missing bolts was not removed during inspection (Pemberton 1997).
- In the Saturn automobile startup, fluids were incorrectly labeled. As a result, thousands of cars were shipped with fluids that eventually would have caused critical engine seals to fail. Saturn realized that their reputation was on the line. Rather than fixing the cars, Saturn's management elected to replace the vehicles by taking replacement vehicles to the owners regardless of the remoteness of the destination. GM's loss for this simple labeling error was estimated to be in the multibillion-dollar range.
- On September 23, 1999 the Mars Climate Orbiter was lost because it was 50 to 60 miles off course when it entered the Martian atmosphere. The flight path error occurred because the contractor supplied the performance data for orbiter rocket motors in English units instead of the requested metric units used by the orbiter flight control software. The error was not detected until the failure occurred. The $125 million dollar mission was a complete failure (Sawyer 1999, A1).
- On September 30, 1999 a mixture of uranium exploded in a blue flash that spread radiation near Tokyo, Japan. Workers, with management consent, willfully avoided using equipment and procedures put in place to prevent criticality of enriched uranium (French 1999, A1).

CONSEQUENCES OF MISTAKES

Although seemingly simple mistakes can result in staggering economic losses as noted above, the real cost of mistakes should be measured in terms of human suffering. Illustrating this loss, on March 7, 1998 "The

Record" published an article about Daniel Garza, a 10-year-old boy who had just passed away. Sadly, medical mistakes contributed to his suffering. The paper reported that "The boy's life turned into a chain of medical visits . . . that . . . led to one mistake after another . . . One error cost him several ribs that were mistakenly removed during surgery . . . Daniel had to go under the knife again to have the correct ribs removed" (The Associated Press 1998).

We would like to think that mistakes are rare events that are not likely to affect us. However, in November 1999, the Institute of Medicine estimated that between 44,000 to 98,000 people die in hospitals each year due to mistakes, and that medical mistakes are the eighth top killer in the nation. Hospital errors alone have been estimated to cost the nation $8.8 billion a year (Kohn, Corrigan, and Donaldson 2000, 70).

SQC Does Not Prevent Mistakes

Just as a part is either assembled or not assembled into a product, mistakes either occur or do not occur. Thus, mistakes are best described in terms of *probability* rather than variation. Distributions describing variation can be expressed in terms of probabilities, but the converse is not always true. *Consequently, the only universal method for describing both variation and mistakes is probability.*

Mistakes, though rare, occur more frequently—and with more profound consequences—than SQC predicts. A *joint*, or combined, distribution of hole diameters, which addresses occasionally omitted drilling operations, is illustrated in Figure 1-10 (the familiar bell-shaped curve plots as a parabola when the vertical scale is logarithmic). Note that the hole diameter for an omitted drilling operation falls completely outside

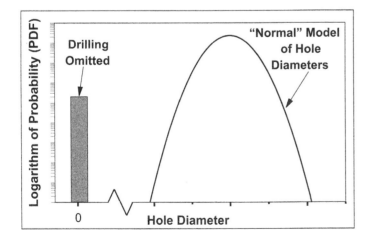

FIGURE 1-10

The probability density function for normally distributed hole diameters that plots as a parabola on a logarithmic vertical scale. Omitted hole drilling operations result in outcomes exceeding statistical predictions.

of the traditionally accepted model describing the distribution of hole diameters. In other words, SQC methods predict that hole drilling omissions will *never* occur.

SQC is useless in preventing most mistakes. Sampling 1 operation in 100, 99 percent of the defects resulting from mistakes would never be detected or corrected. Even if SQC accurately predicted the frequency of mistakes, it cannot be used to predict *when* these rare events will occur. Thus, world-class quality can only be achieved through control of virtually every mistake rather than by prediction of their frequency.

CONTROLLING DEFECTS USING MISTAKE-PROOFING

Although mistakes are inevitable, defects are not. To prevent defects caused by mistakes, our approach to quality control must include several new elements. First, to avoid wasted product, mistakes must be detected and corrected *before* they result in defects. To achieve this goal, inspection must be upstream of the process. Shigeo Shingo perfected these upstream or *source inspection* methods (Shingo 1986). Secondly, since mistakes must be detected to be corrected, they can only be blocked using reliable *100 percent inspection*. Finally, inspections must be *autonomous* to prevent inadvertent omission of the inspection operation.

100 Percent Inspections

The high cost of inspection, combined with Deming's view that quality cannot be "inspected into" a product, have discouraged 100 percent inspections. However, Shingo demonstrated that new techniques based on *poka-yoke* (mistake-proofing) enable 100 percent inspections at a fraction of the cost of SQC (Shingo 1986). More importantly, these inspections are fundamentally different than those that Deming characterized as ineffective. Unlike traditional inspection that tries to detect defects, mistake-proofing and source inspection generally detect the conditions that could cause defects and enable corrective action before the defect occurs.

EVIDENCE SUPPORTING THE NEW INSTRUMENTS OF QUALITY CONTROL

Because mistakes are the dominant source of today's defects, and SQC is not an adequate tool for controlling mistakes, it follows that the SQC approach to quality control cannot by itself assure world-class quality performance. The experiences reflected in the following observations support this conclusion.

- **Shigeo Shingo (Toyota's QC guru):** "We should recognize that people are, after all, only human and as such, they will, on rare occasions, inadvertently forget things. It is more effective to incorporate a checklist—i.e., a poka-yoke—into the operation so that if a worker forgets something, the device will signal that fact, thereby preventing defects from occurring. This, I think, is the quickest road leading to attainment of zero defects" (Shingo 1986, 45).
- **Bill Smith (Motorola):** "Motorola elected to enter this market (electronic ballast) and set a quality goal of Six Sigma for initial delivery. *But it became evident early in the project that achieving a* C_p *greater than 2* (a measure of variation control) *would go only part of the way. Mistake-proofing the design would also be required . . . Mistake-proofing the design is an essential factor in achieving the TDU* (total defect per unit) *goal. The design team is forced to investigate any opportunities for errors during manufacture and assembly, and to eliminate them*" (Smith 1993, 43-47).
- **Shawn Buckley (CogniSense):** "Defect rates in the automated manufacturing of bolts typically were in the range of 5,000 ppm for one automotive manufacturer. The user charged back several thousand dollars for each bad bolt because of the high cost of shutting down the production line for defective bolts. A common source of problems was bolt blanks of the wrong size left in trays during the cleaning process that became mixed with the subsequent batches. Only 100 percent inspection methods made it possible to reduce defect rates to 9 ppm" (Buckley 1994).

COMPLEXITY—ANOTHER DEFECT SOURCE

Product complexity is the root cause of mistakes and excessive variation that result in defects. For example, we can reduce the probability of omitting a screw or interference due to excessive variation if we change the design to require fewer screws. In other words, as the complexity of a product decreases, the probability that it contains a defect will drop. Consequently, complexity is the root cause or foundation of defects arising from the more familiar and accepted sources.

A NEW WATER LINE

The city council just approved a new subdivision. Now it's the engineer's job to figure out a way to supply water for the area. He has just a few weeks to sort through several options and make a recommendation to the city council.

SELECTING A WATER LINE THAT DELIGHTS CUSTOMERS

Although the engineer knows that leaks are the most common customer complaint, and that repairs are a major factor in life cycle cost, he's wondering how the various water line options will impact the frequency and magnitude of leaks that will occur.

SIMPLE IS BEAUTIFUL

The engineer realizes that straight water lines are generally less likely to break than meandering water lines because of less exposure to tree roots, uneven settlement, and excavation. In addition, water losses at the joints will be lower for the straight line because it has fewer joints. "If we use longer pipe sections for the project," he exclaims, "we could cut the number of joints and potential water losses even more!" What's really exciting is that design changes that make the task easier and less expensive generally improve the throughput and product quality.

Many researchers have observed that mistakes and defects increase with the difficulty and duration of tasks. This link between complexity and defects is intuitively sound; however, it has never been previously quantified. The difficulty in linking defect rates to complexity can be attributed to three factors:

- Overly simplistic measures of complexity
- Large variations in quality control between manufacturers
- Small sample sizes

DFA—A Measure of Complexity

A sound measure of complexity must address two factors: 1) the number of elements contributing to complexity, and 2) the difficulty of each activity. For example, a bolt and an engine block both count as one part, but the engine block is much more difficult to make. Complexity can take the form of:

- The number of assembly operations
- The difficulty of each assembly operation
- The number of parts in an assembly
- The complexity of the parts in an assembly

Modern Design for Assembly (DFA) introduced a new means of assessing assembly complexity (Boothroyd and Dewhurst 1985) (Assembly View 1989). These methods provide a variety of potential standards for assessing complexity. Among other potential complexity measures, the estimated time to manually perform each assembly operation in a product can be extracted from DFA databases based on factors relating to the difficulty of the operation. In general, the execution times in these databases are a function of the task complexity, more difficult tasks take longer to complete. In our study of roughly 250 products, we examined over 50 combinations of complexity factors to assess product complexity. We concluded that the total number of operations (TOP) and total assembly time (TAT), as illustrated for the box in Figure 1-11, is the best cumulative estimate of the overall product assembly complexity.

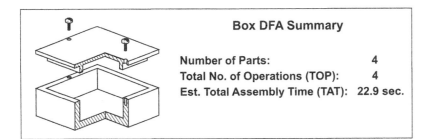

Box DFA Summary

Number of Parts: 4
Total No. of Operations (TOP):   4
Est. Total Assembly Time (TAT):   22.9 sec.

FIGURE 1-11

Summary of the results obtained from a design for assembly analysis of a box.

Reinforcing this conclusion, General Electric initiated a study based on this research to characterize part complexity. They set out to determine which of roughly 75 different complexity measures were related to part complexity (Wiggs 1997). Their research again concluded that the fabrication time and number of operations were by far the most robust and simple measures of part complexity.

THE LINK BETWEEN COMPLEXITY AND DEFECTS

Assured Quality has demonstrated that product defect rates are strongly related to assembly complexity. As illustrated in Figure 1-12, each point represents the average defect rate for a product reflecting the results of millions of assembly operations. Note that the assembly complexity is a function of the total assembly time (TAT), a constant (c), and the total number of operations (TOP). *This link between defects and DFA measured complexity is more accurate and consistent than any model based on variation or mistakes alone.*

FIGURE 1-12

Defects per unit versus complexity for three different manufacturers. The lines through the three data sets are the least squares fits to the data, and all have virtually the same slope.

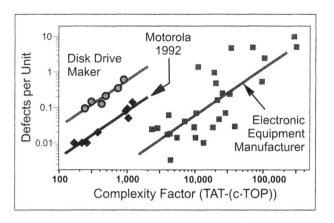

PRODUCT CONCEPTS IMPACT QUALITY

Traditionally, quality has been viewed as a production problem. The Six Sigma and Taguchi techniques have shown that tolerances assigned during development can also impact quality. The new relationship is profoundly important because it shows that the product concept is also a key quality factor.

Generally, the complexity of a product concept is accepted as having some relatively fixed value. However, DFA methods have typically been able to cut the part count and assembly complexity in half (Hinckley 1993, 88). Simplification of the product concept must occur in the earliest stage of design because it is extremely difficult to change the product concept after committing to development. Thus, simplifying product concepts with a focus on eliminating mistakes represents the ultimate method of controlling defects at their source.

Toyota's Experience

Based on the link between complexity and defect rates, it is not surprising that Toyota is recognized both as a leader in quality and as having the most easily manufactured products as judged by their peers (Womack, Jones, and Roos 1990, 97). They also have the highest efficiency auto assembly plants in the world. The manufacturability of Toyota's designs and their outstanding manufacturing skills clearly contribute to their world-class conformance quality.

Reinforcing this link, a Boothroyd Dewhurst study showed that product defect rates were reduced roughly in proportion to the improvements achieved in assembly efficiency (Boothroyd Dewhurst 1993).

PARADIGMS IN THE QUEST FOR QUALITY

The levels of conformance quality we seek lie along the pathway of a continual and perhaps never-ending journey. Progress, as in any other journey, requires accurate maps or guidelines for the way that we view quality.

PARADIGMS: WHERE ARE THE REAL SOURCES OF DEFECTS?

Fundamental changes in the way that we think about quality control must occur to achieve defect rates below 50 ppm. This represents a shift in our paradigms—the theories and models that we use to think about quality. Toward this goal, we have shown that there are three fundamentally different sources of defects: variation, mistakes, and complexity.

Historically, key concepts for controlling these defect sources have evolved in the same order as that listed above. The first major quality developments focused on controlling variation. Shewhart developed control charts in 1924—a key step in the evolution of statistical process control (SPC) (AT&T 2000). In 1962 Genichi Taguchi published his work on the design of experiments (DOE) (ASQ 2000). The techniques for eliminating adjustments and associated variations were developed at Toyota, as described in their method for single-minute exchange of dies (SMED) between 1950 and 1969 (Shingo 1985). Studying world-class products, Motorola concluded that extremely low defect rates were being achieved by tighter statistical process control and developed Six Sigma concepts in the 1990s (Harry and Stewart 1988). The chronological evolution of quality paradigms and the resulting impact on quality is illustrated in Figure 1-13.

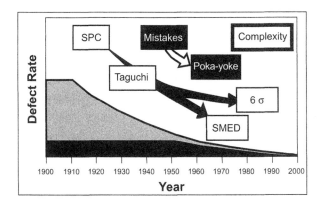

FIGURE 1-13

The chronology of evolving quality paradigms and the trend in defect rates among world-class quality leaders. The dark band at the bottom of the figure reflects the portion of the total defect rate attributable to mistakes. As the control of variation improved, the relative fraction of defects caused by mistakes increased.

The earnest study of mistakes appears to have started during the 1950s in connection with the effort to avoid catastrophic nuclear power plant failures. Although many methods of characterizing and controlling mistakes have been defined and proposed, none of the approaches has proven more effective or efficient than the poka-yoke and source inspection concepts developed by Shigeo Shingo in the 1960s.

The link between defects and product complexity long has been suspected; however, the relationship between complexity and quality was the last of the three major defect sources to be quantified in the 1990s. The strong link between assembly complexity and defect rates suggests that mistakes are a dominant source of product defects, and that simplifying products reduces defect rates.

CONTROLLING MISTAKES IS *THE* CENTRAL THEME

The highest levels of quality control are achieved only when teams recognize that mistakes are the dominant source of defects *and that the best methods of controlling complexity, mistakes, and variation are all forms of mistake-proofing*. When a product is simplified, opportunities for mistakes are eliminated. Mistake-proofing intervenes to assure that mistakes do not become defects. Finally, when traditional manufacturing adjustments are converted to "settings" using Shingo's SMED (Shingo 1985), numerous mistakes made during typical adjustments are virtually eliminated, dramatically reducing the tails of the variation distributions that statistical methods can not control.

AN ORDERLY QUALITY IMPROVEMENT PROCESS

Although quality control techniques were discovered first for variation, then mistakes, and finally complexity, the most efficient method of achieving world-class quality is to approach product development in the reverse order. The first goal should be to eliminate mistakes by simplifying the product or process. Why should simplification be the first step? If we first mistake-proof a product, and then simplify it, we discover that simplification eliminates the need for many mistake-proofing devices and concepts. Spending time developing unnecessary mistake-proofing concepts is a wasted effort that can be eliminated by focusing on simplification first.

Traditional control of variation requires data collection, analysis, decisions, and process control activities. These actions consume resources and contribute to production inefficiencies. In contrast, mistake-proofing can virtually eliminate the need for quality related documentation activities on the factory floor while achieving superior results at lower cost. Thus, whenever possible, we should first seek to control processes with mistake-proofing rather than SPC. For similar reasons, when mistake-proofing is inadequate, we should first try to convert adjustments to settings using SMED, using SPC only as the last resort.

This pattern of quality improvement can be applied to the product and its use and repair, the manufacturing processes, and the tools, fixtures, and manufacturing equipment. The priority and order for these improvement activities is shown in Figure 1-14.

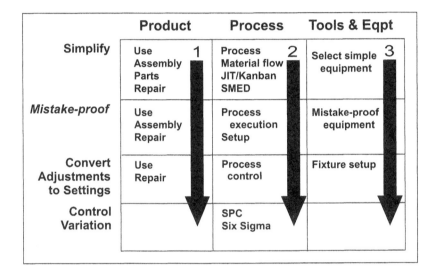

FIGURE 1-14
For the most efficient quality control, the priority in applying quality paradigms should proceed from top to bottom and then right to left in the order shown in this chart.

This chapter establishes the limitations of traditional quality control, identifies complexity, mistakes, and variation as the principle sources of defects, and reveals that the best methods for controlling each defect source is a form of mistake-proofing. We have shown that the order for addressing these defect sources is important for efficient and effective quality control. In the next chapter, we present the tools that are most effective in characterizing the source of quality problems. Subsequent chapters address key concepts that have proven to be effective in reducing complexity; mistake-proofing; and controlling variation.

CHAPTER 2

MISTAKE-PROOFING SUPPORT TOOLBOX

THE GOAL

Most of time, the city engineer feels like he is just running around "putting out brush fires." The construction of the new water line adds to his already heavy schedule. "We need to find ways of doing our job more efficiently, or we'll never get the work done," he muses.

LOCATING AND FIXING LEAKS

Recognizing that leaks can result from broken pipes, assembly mistakes, or unnecessary complexity helps the city engineer accurately identify the cause of leaks, but that is only part of the problem. He must also isolate the location of the leak before the repair process can begin. Finding the leaks is often the most difficult and time-consuming part of the process.

BETTER TOOLS AND METHODS

Perhaps better tools and methods exist for finding leaks. However, it isn't likely that the city will be willing to spend a lot more money for new tools—they would have to be both inexpensive and effective.

FINDING THE LEAKS

The first indication of mistakes or excessive variation is typically a defective part or product, and it is not always clear whether the cause of the problem is unnecessary complexity, a mistake, or uncontrolled variation. In terms of the water supply analogy, this can be equated to locating and characterizing the leaks. To find leaks in water lines, engineers use a variety of tools including pressure gages, flow meters, and television cameras. Similarly, many tools have been developed to isolate and prevent defects. While all of the quality tools that have been developed are useful, they are not equally effective. The best tools for preventing defects are those that most accurately and *efficiently* isolate the source of problems. In this chapter we present the tools that facilitate and support mistake-proofing.

EFFICIENT PROBLEM SOLVING

One of the simplest yet most effective problem-solving methods adapted from Toyota is outlined in the wheel pattern shown Figure 2-1. This pattern is an evolution of Deming's four-step process, shown at the center of the wheel. It has the advantage of being graphical and easy to remember.

FIGURE 2-1

A cycle for rapid and efficient problem solving.

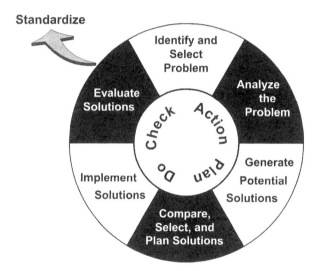

In most organizations, quality improvement is a problem-rich environment, meaning that there are more problems than possibly can be addressed in the near term. The first step, therefore, is to identify and select those problems that will be solved. The next step requires an analysis of each problem. To eliminate a problem, we must first correctly characterize and understand its source. Without this step, corrective action may be misdirected.

When the problem is understood, the next step is to generate *solutions*. Please note the emphasis on the plural! A common error in addressing problems is that individuals and teams tend to focus on point solutions too quickly. Taking a little time to identify alternatives improves creativity and produces better remedies that can be implemented more quickly and at a lower cost.

The next step is to compare proposed alternatives, select the best solutions, and plan for their deployment. The comparison process reveals the relative strengths and weaknesses of the alternatives. Often, the best solution evolves from an effort to find a concept that combines the best attributes of many of the alternatives.

The solution then is implemented, and after implementation it is evaluated as the last step of the process. If the solution proves effective, the goal is to standardize its use throughout the organization.

IDENTIFYING AND SELECTING PROBLEMS

The process of identifying and selecting quality problems for correction should be as quick and efficient as possible. Unfortunately, many quality improvement efforts never get beyond this point because available resources are consumed in an effort to quantify quality problems. This waste of resources is a particular concern with regard to mistake-proofing.

The cumulative impact of 10 different mistakes that each occur only once in 10,000 operations will result in a product defect rate of 1,000 ppm, well above world-class standards. To characterize how frequently the most common mistakes are occurring, we would need a sample with at least 15 repetitions of each error. Given a sampling inspection method where 1 part in 100 is inspected on a production line, over 15,000,000 operations would have to be performed to yield the 150,000 samples necessary to accurately characterize the frequency of a single mistake! Most products do not even have a production volume this large. Thus, by the time accurate data is collected, the opportunity for action has already passed.

Even when data is collected over relatively long time periods, such as a three-month production period, large swings in the relative significance and frequency of various mistakes occur from one period to the next, or from one setting to another. Mistake rates may jump dramatically during a period when demand is high, or when many new employees are hired.

Thus, the traditional approach—identifying quality problems through sampling and data collection—is accurate only when defect rates are quite high. Massive efforts to collect data are likely to be inaccurate at best, and may in fact consume resources better used in actual mistake-proofing.

MAKE MISTAKES OBVIOUS

Our tendency is to conceal mistakes. Yet when this happens, the root cause of a problem is never identified and corrected. One of the keys to getting to the root cause of problems is to involve everyone; key insights often are obtained from the comments and suggestions of others. One powerful but simple technique that makes mistakes obvious, and identifies problems that deserve attention, is to display current defects where everyone in the factory will see them. These displays should be located in high-traffic areas, near the entrance or by the cafeteria, where everyone can consider the consequences of defects and the opportunities for preventing them. A simple defect display board like the one pictured in Figure 2-2 can be used when the quality has improved to the point that the defects will fit on the board. By displaying *all* defects, rather than a single example, factory workers can readily grasp the scope of quality problems.

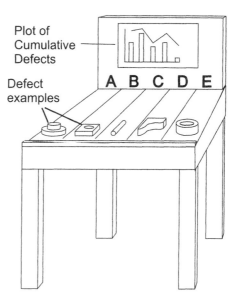

FIGURE 2-2

A defect display board (adapted from Hirano 1994, 265).

PRIORITIZE MISTAKE-PROOFING

In most cases, the major sources of mistakes can be identified readily in brief discussions with workers on the factory floor. In a problem-rich environment, the difficulty is in choosing which problem to address first. Three key attributes of a mistake influence the urgency of corrective actions:

1. The frequency of occurrence,
2. The impact on production process, and
3. The potential impact on the company.

Based on these attributes, Hiroyuki Hirano proposed a simple formula for prioritizing the problems that should be mistake-proofed first

(Hirano 1994, 160–162). For each type of defect, a score ranging from 1 to 3 is determined for each attribute. Higher scores indicate problems of greater concern. For each attribute, the scores are determined as follows:

Problem frequency score:

1. Never occurs
2. Occurs infrequently
3. Occurs frequently

Production process impact score:

1. Does not disrupt production processes
2. Some effect on processes, but the problem can be corrected with some modifications
3. Defect throws downstream production into confusion; product or equipment cannot be recovered

Company impact score:

1. No influence
2. Possible complaints, but the product can be repaired
3. Defect poses a safety concern; leads to lawsuits, severely injures the confidence of the customers, or causes other disasters

An overall score is determined by multiplying the frequency score (f), times the process impact score (p), times the company impact score (c). A sample calculation is shown in Table 2-1 using the same format as appears in the "Mistake-Proofing Worksheet" in Appendix B. Any defect with an overall rating of 4 or higher should be mistake-proofed, and any defect with an overall score of 12 or higher requires immediate corrective action. In general, it is best to mistake-proof the defects with the highest scores first. Applying limited resources to do so produces immediate defect reductions and benefits. In contrast, merely collecting data about mistakes produces no immediate result.

Problem Urgency			
Frequency	Process Impact	Corporate Impact	Product

$$1 \times 3 \times 2 = 6$$

Rate 1 to 3, 3 = Worst

TABLE 2-1

Problem urgency calculation for a low-frequency, high process impact, and moderate corporate impact problem.

ANALYZE THE PROBLEM

Once the problem has been selected, the next step is to analyze it. The most important part of this analysis is to characterize correctly the root cause of the defect. If the cause of the problem is misunderstood, then the control methods are not likely to be effective.

Among the various methods for identifying the cause of defects, we have found two techniques to be remarkably easy to learn, yet highly effective.

4 M'S AND AN I

One way of classifying the source of defects is according to "4 M's and an I" (Poka-yoke 1988, 13–14), as shown in Figure 2-3.

FIGURE 2-3

The sources of defects classified by the process element.

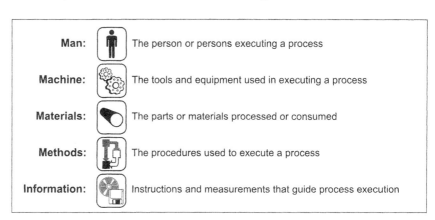

The 4 M's and an I classify defects according to the process element that causes a defect, in contrast with classifying defects according to the type of event—namely variation, mistakes, or complexity. Both classification schemes provide useful insights. Figure 2-4 illustrates the relationship between the 4 M's and an I and complexity, mistakes, and variation (CMV) with a few illustrative examples for intersections between the classification schemes.

The 4 M's and an I/CMV matrix chart is intended to be used as an aid in "discovering" the true source of defects. Whenever a problem is discovered, teams working to solve it identify potential root causes and write them on a matrix worksheet at the appropriate intersections between the production elements and variation, mistakes, and complexity. Blank areas of the chart may reveal key root causes that have been overlooked, prompting a more thorough examination of the problem.

After enumerating and classifying possible root causes, those that are most probable and will be addressed are circled or highlighted on the

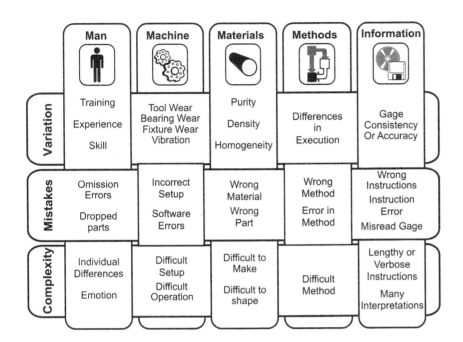

FIGURE 2-4

4 M's and an I/CMV matrix chart illustrating classification of several general defect sources.

chart. (A blank worksheet similar to Figure 2-4 is provided in Appendix B to facilitate the defect source discovery process.)

Typically, there are many potential defect root causes. Those most familiar with the process are likely to be among the best judges of the probable root cause. Naturally, in some cases it may be necessary to implement more than one control to assure that a mistake is not repeated.

5 WHYS AND A HOW

The search for the source of—and the solution to—a quality problem is facilitated further by "5 Whys and a How" (Poka-yoke 1988, 25). Investigators first ask why the problem occurred. When the reason for the defect is identified, investigators then ask why this defect-causing condition occurred. This process is repeated until the question, "Why?" has been answered five times. The purpose of this method is to identify the root cause of defects.

When the root cause of a defect is identified, investigators then ask, "How can the root cause be *eliminated* or controlled?" (Subsequent chapters address the best control methods once the root cause has been identified.)

An Example of 5 Why's and a How

The following example comes from a problem encountered in a component development. The same hole on five pressure vessels was incorrectly machined on a computer-controlled lathe, ruining all available parts on a critical development path.

1. Why did the defects occur?
   Answer: The machinist did not have the correct tool to machine the hole. He recognized the problem but attempted to machine the parts with the wrong tool because of pressure to meet the schedule.
2. Why didn't the machinist have the correct tool?
   Answer: A special tool was required to do the machining. This tool had a long lead time, which had not been considered in planning.
3. Why wasn't the tool ordered on time?
   Answer: The shop did not review the drawings soon enough to order the tool in a timely fashion.
4. Why didn't the shop review the drawings soon enough to initiate a timely tool order?
   Answer: The shop/production team is not required to review drawings.
5. Why hasn't manufacturing review of the drawings been required?
   Answer: The design team has not used concurrent engineering methods.
6. How will the problem be solved?
   Answer: An expert on machining processes will participate on the design team. Drawings will be reviewed regularly to assess manufacturability and tooling requirements. Changes in the design that simplify tooling and shorten tool lead times will be recommended. Where these changes are not possible, design details must be solidified consistent with the schedule, and required tooling will be ordered to meet the delivery date.

MISTAKE-PROOFING—A FORM OF INSPECTION

Mistake-proofing shares many of the attributes of an inspection process. For example, it may be used to detect out-of-tolerance parts or confirm that a previous operation has been completed before allowing the next process to proceed. Although mistake-proofing is a form of inspection, it is important to understand how it differs from traditional inspection methods that Deming characterized as ineffective. The following section describes the various types of inspection and how they differ.

WASTED EFFORT

After working overtime to repair three leaks in one week, the crew chief is tired and frustrated. He tells the engineer, "We can fix the leaks, but we waste a lot of time fixing problems that could have been avoided."

AN OUNCE OF PREVENTION IS WORTH A POUND OF CURE

Because of the crew chief's comment, the engineer goes back through the repair records and finds that the same types of problems occur repeatedly. The water department is spending lots of money to repair leaks, but very little to prevent them.

PREVENTION—A COST SAVER

A little research shows that the city would save money if crewmembers marked waterline locations before excavation rather than fixing leaks after waterlines are damaged. The engineer's plan is presented to the city manager, who is pleased by the potential cost savings.

THE ROLE OF INSPECTION IN QUALITY CONTROL

Inevitably, defect-causing conditions will occur in every process. Whether or not these conditions result in a defect strongly depends upon the type and timing of inspection used to control the process. As a consequence, some types of inspection can reduce but not eliminate defects. We cannot achieve world-class quality by detecting every defect and removing or repairing the defective product. Such an approach simply increases scrap without changing the total number of defects generated. Rather, the goal of quality control should be to prevent all defects from occurring. Eliminating defects requires a clear understanding of the inspection methods.

JUDGMENT INSPECTIONS

Shingo observed that there are three different types of inspection: 1) judgment, 2) SQC, and 3) source inspection (Shingo 1986, 41–50). The process for a judgment inspection is illustrated in Figure 2-5. As shown in the figure, processes result in outputs or products. The product can be inspected after the process is completed. Information from the inspection is used to "judge" whether or not the product is acceptable. For example, a "go" or "no go" functional test of electronic components is a judgment inspection. From the figure we note that the information obtained from judgment inspections is generally not useful in controlling the upstream process.

Judgment Inspections

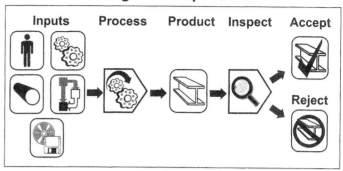

SQC and Downstream Inspection

Compared to judgment inspections, SQC provides a significant advancement in quality control because feedback from inspection can be used to guide upstream processes, as reflected in Figure 2-6. This makes it possible to adjust the process to reduce the probability of a defective part before the process is "out of control."

SQC Inspections

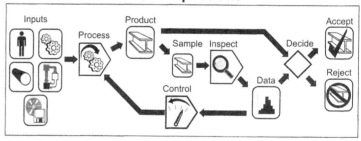

However, SQC inspections are performed downstream of the process execution (Ishikawa 1988, 5, 109). Consequently, if a problem occurs in a process it may not be detected until some process deviation has occurred. In addition, since SQC is based on sampling inspection, many defects may be generated before a problem is detected. Thus, because SQC inspections are downstream of the process, they can reduce but not eliminate defects.

Frequently, sampled parts are taken to remote locations for SQC inspections. In such cases, transportation and handling time can delay the process feedback, potentially contributing to increased defect rates.

SOURCE INSPECTION

Just as it is easier to dam a river at its source, the most efficient quality control method is to prevent rather than to correct defects. In progressing toward this goal, we can catch virtually every mistake by inspecting the inputs before processing, as illustrated in the sequence in Figure 2-7.

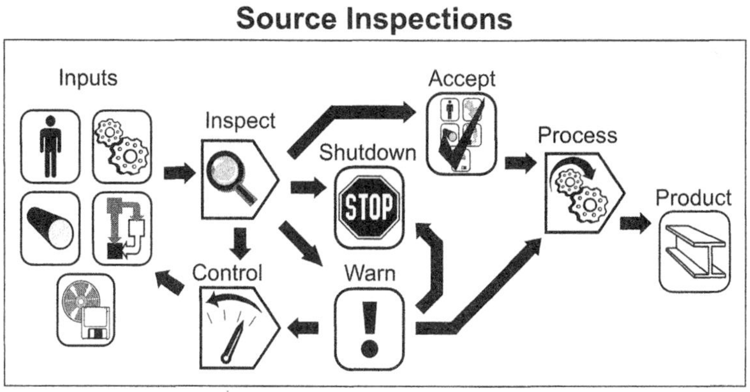

Source Inspections

FIGURE 2-7

Source inspection that verifies all inputs are in acceptable order before the process is allowed to proceed—controlling defects at their source.

Because source inspection, which was developed by Shingo (Shingo 1986, 50), checks all inputs before executing the process, it can detect conditions that are likely to cause a defect before it is generated, allowing the operator to correct problems and eliminate defects. Thus, source inspection can result in a fundamentally lower defect rate than SQC. Mistake-proofing is a form of source inspection.

Some things that source inspections can check for:

• Wrong or missing parts
• Tools or equipment out of adjustment
• Missing or incorrect information
• Human error

SUCCESSIVE CHECKS

Some processes can't be easily or completely controlled by mistake-proofing or source inspection. For example, mistake-proofing can be used to assure that an adequate number of bolts are drawn from a bin for installation; however, assuring that every bolt is properly tightened poses a more difficult problem. If, for example, a sensor detected the number of times a wrench reached a desired torque, the results could be misleading if the operator tightened one bolt twice but missed tightening another bolt in the pattern. In such instances, mistake-proofing and other quality control techniques can be complemented by successive checks (Shingo 1986, 47). Before proceeding with the next process, the operator checks to verify that the upstream process has been properly executed. These inspections may be repeated through several successive steps to assure that a specific operation is inspected frequently, as illustrated in Figure 2-8.

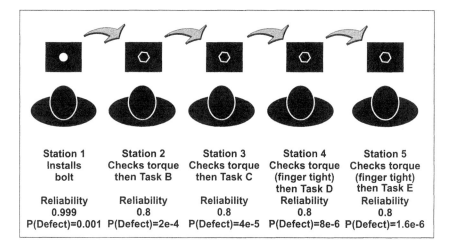

Station 1 Installs bolt	Station 2 Checks torque then Task B	Station 3 Checks torque then Task C	Station 4 Checks torque (finger tight) then Task D	Station 5 Checks torque (finger tight) then Task E
Reliability 0.999	Reliability 0.8	Reliability 0.8	Reliability 0.8	Reliability 0.8
P(Defect)=0.001	P(Defect)=2e-4	P(Defect)=4e-5	P(Defect)=8e-6	P(Defect)=1.6e-6

This same example can be used to illustrate the effectiveness of successive checks. In a series of successive checks, where each inspection has only an 80 percent chance of catching a loose bolt, 2 successive checks would allow 4 percent of the loose bolts to pass undetected. However, 4 successive checks would catch all but 0.16 percent of the loose bolts. If the probability of a not tightening a bolt is 0.001 for the initial process, then the probability that a bolt is not tightened in the final product after 4 successive checks is 1.6 per million. One additional successive check would drop this probability to 0.32 per million bolts.

In traditional quality control efforts, "careful" inspections that have the goal of being thorough are common. This is true particularly in high-value, low-volume production, such as encountered in the aerospace industry. However, no amount of care can overcome the fact that inspection methods are imperfect. As a result, a series of simple, successive checks can generally achieve lower defect rates than sophisticated one-time inspections.

This chapter has armed the reader with a simple, easy-to-remember sequence for solving problems that consistently produces superior results. In addition, it outlines the tools we need to quickly and clearly identify the source of quality problems, and introduces Shingo's source inspection. These tools are an essential foundation for all quality improvement efforts because they help correctly characterize problems, guide efficient problem solving, and provide a new vision of the inspection control methods. In the following three chapters, specific techniques are provided for reducing complexity, eliminating or controlling mistakes, and controlling variation.

CHAPTER 3

CONTROLLING COMPLEXITY

WHICH ROUTE?

The water department has identified two possible routes for a new waterline. "To make sure that the water delivery downstream is adequate," muses the city engineer, "I'd really like to know how much leakage I should expect from each line. Perhaps more importantly, to make the best route selection, I would really like to know which line would have the lowest potential water loss."

CHARACTERIZE PRESENT PERFORMANCE

To estimate the losses in a new waterline, the water department must first know the leak rates of similar water lines in the area. In assessing the leak rates of existing lines, they have to be careful not to just count joints or pipe sections. After all, one would expect more leakage from a 48-inch diameter pipe than a 12-inch diameter pipe.

COMPARING THE ROUTES

Once a sound basis for estimating losses from each line has been established, the comparison should be pretty easy. Of course, route selection cannot be based on water losses alone. Sometimes the department has to pick the route with the highest potential losses because that line just gets the water line closer to the customers.

THE LINK BETWEEN DEFECTS AND ASSEMBLY COMPLEXITY

It just seems logical that defect rates must be linked to complexity. For example, we would expect a product with 10,000 parts to have more defects on the average than products with just 5 parts. This intuitive relationship does not explain, however, why assembly complexity determined by the estimated assembly time should be linked to defect rates. In the following sections we examine the connection between assembly complexity and defect rates.

THE LINK BETWEEN MISTAKES AND ASSEMBLY TIME

The frequency of mistakes has often been linked with the difficulty of executing a task. For example, typical laboratory experiments for assessing mistake frequencies are made deliberately difficult to increase mistake rates to reduce the required sample size for statistical convenience (Swain & Guttmann 1983, 7–5). Listed in the left hand column of Table 3-1 are factors that have been shown by Seidenstein to increase the difficulty of a task *and* mistake rates (Seidenstein). On the right-hand side of the table are listed similar factors that increase estimated assembly time for products. By comparison, we can observe that those factors that increase mistake rates are virtually identical to those factors that increase the estimated execution or assembly time per operation. Naturally, Table 3-1 is not a complete list of factors that increase mistakes or assembly time. Many other factors, such as a complex ordering of assembly operations, also can increase stress and mistakes.

TABLE 3-1

Comparison of high-stress factors that have been shown to increase mistakes (Seidenstein) with factors associated with increased assembly time.

High-Stress Factors Increasing Mistakes	Factors Increasing Assembly Time
Individual steps must be coordinated	Two hands or holding down required
Difficult discrimination (of displays)	Subtle alignment features
Feedback is inadequate	Obstructed access or restricted vision
Long task sequence	Complex assembly process
Comparison of displays required	Alignment/orientation (feature comparison)
Decisions based on several inputs	Mental processes, adjustments
Nature and timing of inputs unanticipated	Jumbled part presentation

Data Linking Mistakes to Task Duration

Numerous studies that support the general relationship between mistake rates and process execution times have been identified. In just one of many possible examples, Figure 3-1 shows the percentage of pointing errors as a function of the execution times for a study of various computer pointing devices (Card, English, and Burr 1978, 601–613). As shown, mistakes generally are more frequent for devices that take longer to operate. An independent study examined the impact of holding down a button while moving the pointing devices. Compared to simple pointing operations, the "click and drag" actions also consistently took longer and

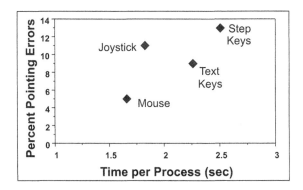

FIGURE 3-1

Pointing error rates versus time to complete the pointing task for four computer input methods (Card, English, and Burr 1978, 601–613).

resulted in more mistakes, regardless of the pointing device used (MacKenzie, Sellen, and Buxton 1991, 161–166).

Collectively, the data—covering a broad range of conditions—clearly shows that task complexity and execution times are linked with mistake rates. *As task complexity increases, both execution time and mistake frequencies increase.*

THE LINK BETWEEN PART AND ASSEMBLY COMPLEXITY

Many product defects are the result of defective parts rather than assembly mistakes. Consequently, the observed relationship between assembly time and defect rates is stronger than initially expected. However, increased assembly time also implies increased part complexity. To illustrate, several assembly interfaces were examined to assess how the number of dimensions in the interface compared with the estimated assembly time. Figure 3-2 shows that there is a general increase in assembly time as the dimensional degrees of freedom (i.e., part complexity) increase. Furthermore, long assembly times suggest more parts, and as the part count increases, the product is more likely to contain a complex part. Thus, it is reasonable to conclude that part defect rates in addition to assembly error rates are related in some way to assembly complexity. This conclusion is supported by General Electric's study of part complexity, which showed that fabrication time was the best measure of part complexity (Wiggs 1997).

Supporting this conclusion, other research has shown that the ability to detect a defect decreases as the complexity of the inspected object increases. Since an assembly is always more complex than any individual part in the assembly, part defects are more likely to be detected and eliminated than assembly defects. These patterns reinforce the strong observed relationship between DFA estimated assembly time and defect rates.

FIGURE 3-2

The relationship between the time to assemble a part and part complexity as determined by the number of dimensional degrees of freedom. Parts of increasing complexity generally take longer to assemble.

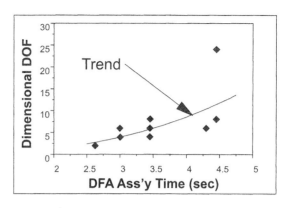

TIME—A MEASURE OF COMPLEXITY

Every change that reduces product or process complexity also reduces the total *time* required to procure materials, fabricate parts, or assemble products. Thus, time is a remarkably useful standard of complexity because it is fungible, or, in other words, an interchangeable standard useful in measuring and comparing the complexity of dissimilar product attributes. As a result, we can use time to compare the difficulty of installing a bolt to an alternative assembly method based on a snap-fit assembly. In addition, time has a common international value that is universally recognized and easily understood.

Care must be exercised, however, to achieve consistency when using time to measure complexity. Worker skill, training, and work pace strongly influence the time it takes different individuals to perform similar tasks. Moreover, the time to complete an operation on automated equipment is generally a small fraction of the time required to complete the same operation manually. To measure complexity separately from performance, a standard method of interpreting work rate is essential. Without a work rate standard, measuring complexity with time would be like measuring distance by the transit time of randomly selected individuals. Some individuals may choose to run the distance; others would choose to walk it.

A key consideration is that the time to complete a task must be reduced by reducing the complexity of the task rather than by urging the worker to work faster. Rushing workers can dramatically increase error rates and defects. Similarly, when workers are bored, their attention wanders and errors increase. Thus, there must always be a strong distinction between assessments of complexity and work rates.

Techniques for defining standard work rates have evolved from time and motion studies (Barnes 1980, 12–21). The standard work rate reflects the average time required for an experienced worker to complete tasks at a sustained, self-paced rate. Eventually a variety of predetermined time systems (PTS), or databases of time per task, evolved (Barnes, 1980, 361–388). Similar work rates have been used to develop design for assembly (DFA) databases.

INTRODUCTION TO QUALITY BY CONTROL OF COMPLEXITY

A variety of DFA methods evolved in the early 1980s to help designers simplify products by making assembly easier. The methodologies provided assembly guidelines that helped evaluate the difficulty of each assembly and opportunities for improvement. Bob Sturges, who is now at Virginia Tech, created one of these tools, originally described as a "design for assembly calculator," for the Westinghouse Electric Corporation (Sturges 1989, 237).

Examining a variety of DFA methodologies, a pattern was discovered that made it possible to substantially reduce the size of the databases and the difficulty of assembly analysis. A modification of the Westinghouse method, called quality by control of complexity (QCC), has been adapted here for use in simplifying product assembly to eliminate mistake opportunities. Kosuke Ishii and his associates at Stanford University provided suggestions for improving our approach and developed the assembly diagramming method used here (Ishii 1997, 6.1–4).

ASSEMBLY SEQUENCE DIAGRAM

The first step in a QCC analysis is to select the product that will be simplified. The analysis of the existing product begins by preparing a diagram that describes the sequence of assembly operations required for a product or subassembly. An assembly diagram for a computer floppy disk in Figure 3-3 is illustrated in Figure 3-4. The diagram begins at the top with the base part, or first part set down in the assembly sequence. Part insertions and other operations are represented by a descriptor and a connecting arrow. The assembly diagram helps to organize the order of assembly operations for subsequent QCC analysis.

FIGURE 3-3

Exploded view of the parts in a floppy disk assembly.

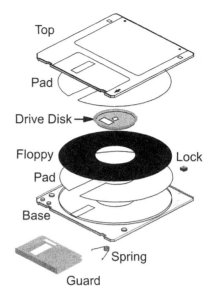

FIGURE 3-4

A tree diagram illustrating the sequence of operations required to assemble a floppy disk.

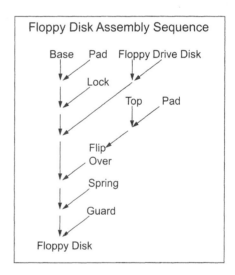

LISTING THE OPERATIONS

The next step in performing a QCC analysis is to list the parts and assembly operations on a QCC worksheet in the sequence obtained from the assembly sequence diagram (readers will find blank a QCC worksheet in Appendix B). This is illustrated in Table 3-2 for the floppy disk from the previous example.

Ass'y/Subass'y Name
Floppy Disk (3.5")

No.	Part/Op. Description	A End to End Orientation	B Rotational Alignment	C Part Size	D Part Thickness	E Insertion Clearance	F Insertion Direction	G Insertion Condition	H Fastening	I Fastening Process	J Handling Condition	K Time/Each Operation (T$_{op}$)	L Number of Repetitions (N$_{rep}$)	M Repetition Time (K*L) (T$_{rep}$)	N Insert Part (1=Yes;0=No)
1	Base	1.8	1.0				0.6					3.4	1	3.4	1
2	Pad	1.3	1.0		1.0		0.6	7.4		5.0	1.0	17.3	1	17.3	1
3	Lock	1.8	1.0				0.6			1.0		4.4	1	4.4	1
4	Floppy	1.3	0.5		0.5		0.6	7.5			1.0	11.4	1	11.4	1
5	Drive Disk	1.8	0.5			0.9	0.6			11.0		14.8	1	14.8	1
6	Top	1.8	1.0				0.6					3.4	1	3.4	1
7	Pad	1.3	1.0		1.0		0.6	7.4		5.0	1.0	17.3	1	17.3	1
8	Apply Adhesive									11.0		11.0	4	44.0	0
9	Flip Top Over							2.3				2.3	1	2.3	0
10	Join Top Ass'y to Base	1.8	1.0				0.6			11.0		14.4	1	14.4	0
11	Spring	1.8	0.5	0.1	0.4		1.4	7.4		1.0	4.5	17.1	1	17.1	1
12	Guard	1.8	1.5			0.3	1.4	2.7		3.0	1.5	12.2	1	12.2	1
												15	162.0	9
												TOP	**TAT**	**NUP**

Step 1: Identify assembly sequence

Step 2: List parts & assembly operations in order of execution in top row of table

Step 3: Enter part/fastening times from DFA Operation Chart

Step 4: Enter sum of ass'y times A–J in column K

Step 5: Enter number of times each operation is repeated in column L. Enter T$_{op}$ x N$_{rep}$ in row M.

Step 6: Enter a 1 in column N if a part is inserted, a 0 otherwise

Step 7: Calculate summary statistics

NUP	= Number of unique parts (sum of column N)
TOP	= Total number of operations (sum of column L)
TAT	= Total assembly time (sum of column M)
NP	= Number of parts = sumproduct (L,N)
C	= Assembly complexity = **TAT** – (2.4* **TOP**)
OR	= Operation difficulty rating = **TAT** / (2.4* **TOP**)

NP	9
C	126.0
OR	4.50

Estimating Assembly Time

The time required to insert each part or complete each assembly operation is estimated. The time required to complete each operation is influenced by part attributes such as size, shape, symmetry, weight, and flexibility. Insertion and fastening conditions also influence assembly time. The time penalty for each attribute of an operation is extracted from the QCC database and summed to give the total assembly time for the operation. QCC assembly times for common part and assembly operation attributes are given in Tables 3-3 through 3-12.

TABLE 3-2
QCC worksheet example for a floppy disk.

TABLE 3-3
End-to-end alignment.

Condition	1 Subtle Feature	1 Obvious Feature	2 or More Orientations	Preoriented
Number of acceptable end to end alignments during assembly	Asymmetry of offset ring is not easily noticed		Either end of part can be inserted due to symmetry	
QCC Times	2.3 seconds	1.8 seconds	1.3 seconds	0.8 seconds

TABLE 3-4
Orientation about insertion axis.

Condition	1 Subtle Orientation	2 or More Subtle Orientations	1 Obvious Orientation	2 or More Obvious Orientations	Part Preoriented
Number of rotational alignments about the axis of insertion allowing proper assembly					
QCC Times	1.5 seconds	1.0 seconds	1.0 seconds	0.5 seconds	0.0 seconds

TABLE 3-5
Part dimension—size.

Note: Double QCC times for size if the part has less than 4 possible orientations about the insertion axis.

Condition	< 2 mm	2 to 6 mm	6 to 12 mm	> 12 mm
Size is the largest dimention of a rectangular box enclosing the part	Size / Thickness	Size / Thickness	Size / Thickness	Size / Thickness
QCC Times	0.6 seconds	0.4 seconds	0.1 seconds	0 seconds

Condition	< .2 mm	0.5 to 2 mm	> 2 mm
		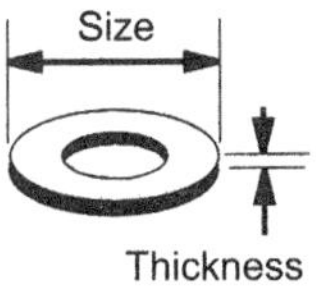 Size / Thickness	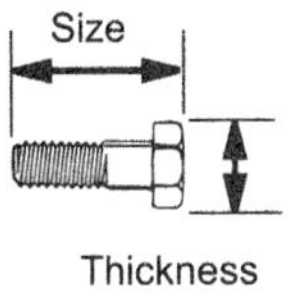 Size / Thickness
QCC Times	0.5 seconds	0.2 seconds	0 seconds

TABLE 3-6

Part dimension—thickness.

Note: Double QCC times for thickness if the part has less than 4 possible orientations about the insertion axis.

Condition	Very Small Clearance	Small Clearance	Large Clearance	Very Large Clearance
	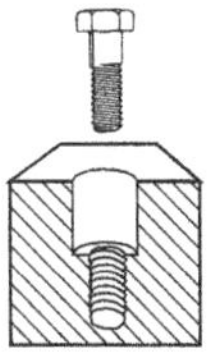	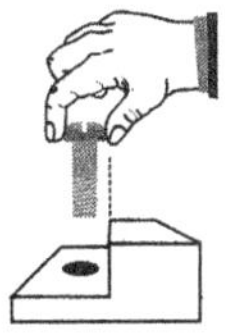	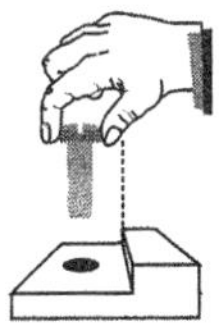	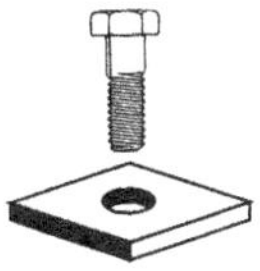
QCC Times	1.6 seconds	0.9 seconds	0.3 seconds	0.0 seconds

TABLE 3-7

Insertion clearances.

Condition	Bottom Up	Diagonally	From Side	Top Down
			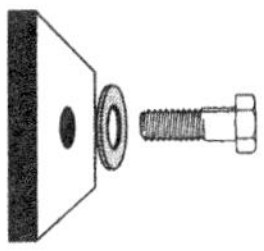	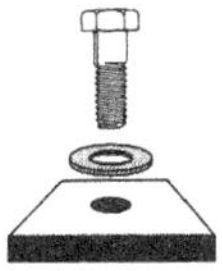
QCC Times	2.0 seconds	1.7 seconds	1.4 seconds	0.6 seconds

TABLE 3-8

Insertion directions.

Condition	Flexible	Rotate or Fixture	Two Hands	Temporary Hold Down	Constrained Motion	No Constraint
				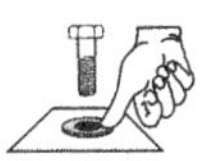	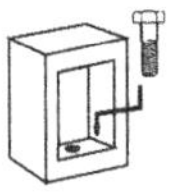	
QCC Times	6.0 seconds	2.3 seconds	1.5 seconds	1.4 seconds	1.3 seconds	0.0 seconds

TABLE 3-9

Insertion conditions.

TABLE 3-10
Fasteners.

Fastener Type	Rivet	Nut	Screw or Bolt	Retaining Ring	Pin	Washer
QCC Times	6.0 seconds	5.0 seconds	4 seconds	2.5 seconds	1.0 seconds	0.0 seconds

TABLE 3-11
Fastening process.

Condition	Adhesive	Weld	Solder	Polymer Stake of Weld	Screwing	Bend or Crimp	Snap or Press Fit
QCC Times	11 seconds	9.0 seconds	7.0 seconds	5.0 seconds	4.0 seconds	3.0 seconds	1.0 seconds

TABLE 3-12
Handling conditions.

Condition	Nest or Tangle	Tools Required	Delicate	Heavy > 4.5 kg	None
Handling conditions for special cases, times for conditions are additive	Poor Better				
QCC Times	1.5 seconds 6.0 seconds Severe Tangle	2.5 seconds Tweezer 3.5 seconds Other Tool	1.0 seconds	0.5 seconds	0 seconds

EVALUATING REPEATED OPERATIONS

For repeated identical operations, we multiply the assembly time by the number of repetitions. As the final step, we total the number of assembly operations and the assembly time for all operations.

LIMITATIONS OF QCC METHODS

Anyone performing an assembly evaluation using QCC methods will immediately recognize that the database is incomplete. For example, it does not include time factors for operations like sewing, as encountered in the fabrication of car seats or airbags. One approach to improving the methodology would be to add time factors as previously undefined operations are encountered. However, the value of the methodology lies in its simplicity. If every possible operation were added, it would soon become so cumbersome to use that it would lose much of its attractiveness. Still others may feel that the "assembly" oriented factors have little application to the work that they do.

The beauty of the methodology is that it can be adapted easily to any task. For example, without any prior data, a manufacturer of car seats might consider time factors that could be defined for sewing operations. He or she might conclude that the time it takes to sew a linear inch of edging is different than the time it takes to sew a linear inch of seam, which is different than the time per linear inch of zipper. The time required to sew a buttonhole would be different than any of these operations. Also, significant time may be required to reorient fabric to sew along a different path. With a few observations on the factory floor, very reasonable conclusions about the time factors and estimates for the relative time per task could be determined in just a few hours. For most purposes, this is adequate without being cumbersome. Armed with data, the manufacturer can quickly estimate which method of sewing a car seat is likely to be easiest and least defect prone.

The key principle is that the goal of the methodology is simplifying the task by reducing the number of operations and the time it takes to execute the complete task. The methodology should be adapted to each specific problem. The same principles that are applied to evaluating assembly complexity can be applied to reducing complexity of any task, including the fabrication or machining of parts, or equipment operation.

MISTAKES ARE LINKED TO QCC TIME FACTORS

As noted previously, the frequency of mistakes increases with increasing assembly complexity. Note that both mistake frequencies and assembly times decrease from right to left in each of these tables.

To illustrate the link between assembly time and mistake rates, the QCC time for inserting a part from a bottom-up direction adds 2.0 seconds, as illustrated in the left column of Table 3-8. By comparison, insertion in a top-down assembly direction only adds 0.6 seconds, as shown in the right column of the same table. We are more likely to omit a part using the more time-consuming bottom-up assembly direction compared to the top-down direction because there are no visual reminders that a part needs to be inserted, and if an omission occurs it is less visible. Similarly, misalignment errors are more likely during a bottom-up part insertion because there are fewer visual clues to aid in alignment. As illustrated, there are consistently more opportunities for mistakes as the duration of the operation increases.

Many of the mistake-proofing examples introduced in this book are based on simplifying the product or process following the principles enumerated in the QCC tables. Familiarity with QCC principles provides additional insight into alternative mistake-proofing choices when development or production problems are encountered. Naturally, the QCC guidance for better design should never be interpreted rigidly. For example, even though a threaded fastener may take longer and introduce more opportunities for error than other alternatives, it may be the only choice that has adequate strength or meets other criteria, such as accommodating disassembly.

After completing a QCC analysis of a prior product or the preliminary product concept, designers should use the results of the QCC analysis to search for better designs. In particular, the goal of QCC analysis is to eliminate unnecessary parts and assembly operations and make the most difficult assembly operations less difficult.

ESTIMATING THE RELATIVE QUALITY OF DESIGN ALTERNATIVES

The level of quality control differs significantly from one organization to another. For example, Motorola and Ford would have different defect rates producing identical products. Because of these differences, accurate estimates of defect rates for specific products cannot be made without careful review of each company's product and defect data. Such data is often difficult to obtain. Furthermore, since quality control can improve or degrade from one product cycle to the next, the best projections are often inaccurate for the next product cycle.

For most applications, all that is really needed is a relative comparison of potential defect rates for alternative product concepts. The power of QCC is that it provides a simple method for making such comparisons. The first step is to perform a QCC analysis of the existing product and the most attractive alternatives that are being considered to replace the product. For each alternative, the total assembly time (TAT) and total number of assembly operations (TOP) are determined. Then, for each product concept, the complexity factor (CF) is calculated using the following formula:

$$\mathbf{CF_i = TAT_i} - t_0 \times \mathbf{TOP_i} \qquad\qquad (3.1)$$

In this equation, "i" is a subscript for the ith product concept and t_0 is the threshold assembly time, or time required to perform the simplest possible assembly operation. Correlation with data shows that t_0 can be treated as a constant with a value of 2.4 seconds per operation. Notice that both TAT and t_0 times the number of operations have values expressed in units of time. Thus, the product CF value is also in units of time.

To illustrate the application of this equation, TAT is estimated to be 30.6 seconds, and 6 assembly operations are required for the baseline design in Table 3-13. The complexity factor for this product is therefore calculated to be 16.2 seconds (30.6 seconds minus 2.4 seconds per operation times 6 operations).

Based on the correlations previously illustrated in Figure 1-14, it can be shown that the relative defect rates of two products manufactured within the same company will have the following approximate relationship:

$$\frac{DPU_i}{DPU_m} = \left(\frac{CF_i}{CF_m}\right)^k \tag{3.2}$$

Here, **DPU** equals the defects per unit, "i" and "m" are subscripts for the ith and mth alternatives, and *k* is a constant that has a value of 1.3. The value of *k* is the slope of DPU versus CF plot on a log-log plot, and has been shown to have the same value in every company examined. Note that both sides of the equation are dimensionless.

Comparing Product Defects Per Unit—an Example

A simple example illustrates the simplicity, effectiveness, and value of the QCC comparison. Table 3-13 shows four alternative concepts for assembling a simple box. A corner of each box has been cut away to make it easier to visualize internal features. For the purpose of this example, let us assume that the manufacturer currently is producing the box with two screws and has developed the three new alternatives as potential replacement products. Which of the four alternatives is likely to have the lowest defect rate? The answer to this question is not obvious.

Table 3-13 lists the results of a QCC analysis for each alternative concept. For each, there is one operation to set the base in place and one operation to insert the lid. Each pin and screw insertion also requires an assembly operation. Each screw requires an additional screwing operation. The QCC analysis shows that it will take four to five times longer to install the lid with two screws than the snap fit lid. However, the estimated "complexity" for the original concept with two screws is eight times greater than for the snap-fit concept!

TABLE 3-13

Relative estimates of the defects per unit (DPU) for four alternative concepts for assembling a box.

Description	Baseline Design 2 screws	Option A: 1 screw	Option B: 2 Press Fit Pins	Option C: Snap Fit Lid
TAT (seconds)	30.6	17.2	12.5	6.8
TOP	6	4	4	2
CF (seconds)	16.2	7.6	2.9	2
$\dfrac{\text{DPU}_{\text{Option}}}{\text{DPU}_{\text{Baseline}}} =$	1	0.37	0.11	0.07

Referring again to Table 3-13, given a complexity factor for Option A of 7.6 seconds and baseline design of 16.2 seconds, we would first divide 7.6 seconds by 16.2 seconds, to give a complexity ratio of 0.469. In other words, the assembly of Option A is roughly half as complex as the assembly of the Baseline Design. The complexity ratio raised to the exponential power of 1.3 ($0.469^{1.3}$) equals 0.37, the ratio of defects per unit for Option A divided by the defects per unit for the baseline design. In other words, the estimated DPU for Option A would be 37 percent of the DPU for the baseline design.

When we compare the expected defect rates of the various alternatives, the conclusions are truly stunning. Just changing from two screws to one screw will cut the defect rate by roughly 60 percent. The lid that is held on with press-fit pins has a projected defect rate that is only 11 percent of the current baseline. *Given the same level of quality control, the defect rate for the baseline design is 14 times greater than that projected for the snap-fit lid concept.* If the manufacturer had a current defect rate of 2,400 defects per million units, he could expect to achieve a defect rate of 170 defects per million units for the snap-fit lid design without any improvement in quality control. This change is achieved principally through eliminating mistake opportunities by simplifying the product.

In this example, the six-step development pattern previously described has been followed. The problem was selected and analyzed. Alternative solutions were generated and compared. The next steps would be to select, plan, and implement the best concept. Although defect rates and assembly times are very important considerations, there may be other factors that need to be addressed, such as structural strength, sensitivity to vibration, the ability to seal, disassembly, maintenance, disposal, development cost, and so forth. In selecting a concept, assembly complexity and projected defect rates should not dominate the decision process, but should be an important part of those considerations.

Although QCC can lead to significant product improvements, QCC guidelines should never be viewed as rigid rules. They must be applied with judgment. Ease of assembly must be balanced against other desirable attributes such as functionality, reliability, and manufacturability.

THE BENEFITS OF QCC ANALYSIS

Given the more complex products typically encountered in most companies, QCC analysis will generally not improve the product as much as illustrated in the previous box assembly example. Typically, the number of parts in a product can be reduced to half the number in the initial concept. The shipping container concepts developed by Sandia National Laboratories illustrated in Figure 3-5 demonstrate the effectiveness of the QCC analysis. The initial design, derived from previous products, required 37 major parts. Many of the parts in the initial design were complex, custom shapes. In addition, the initial container concept required over 500 linear inches of weld per assembly.

Original Concept   **Simplified Concept**

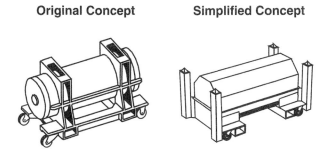

FIGURE 3-5

Two shipping-container designs for carrying the same aerospace product. The original design is more complex and less functional than the new design.

The improved design concept can be made from standard bar, tube, and plate stock using just 24 major pieces that are simple shapes. The new design saves roughly 300 linear inches of weld per product. The detailed design can be completed more quickly and at a lower cost than its predecessor. In addition, the new design is lighter in weight, more stable, and easier to open, repair, and stack. Mistakes and defects are estimated to be less than a third as great as for the original concept. As this example illustrates, QCC analysis can have a profound influence on product complexity.

PRODUCT VERSUS PROCESS COMPLEXITY

There are two fundamentally different aspects of complexity in every activity: the complexity of *what* is to be done, and *how* it is accomplished. In terms of manufacturing, this can be described as the difference between product complexity and the manufacturing process complexity. A task requiring the insertion of four bolts is illustrated in Figure 3-6. The product would be less complex if the design could be changed from four bolts to three. Decreasing the number of bolts in the pattern eliminates a hole in the plate, a part, and assembly operations. Such a change alters the manufacturing objective (i.e., what is to be done).

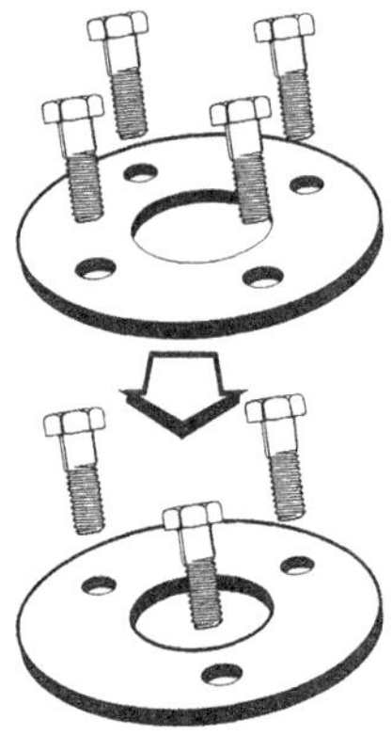

FIGURE 3-6

Eliminating a fastener reduces the complexity of that task that must be done.

In contrast, the complexity of the assembly process can be reduced even if the product design is not changed. As illustrated in Figure 3-7, if bolts for an assembly task are randomly oriented in a bin, the assembler must decide how to pick up the bolt and orient it for insertion. On the other hand, presenting the bolts one at a time in a position oriented for easy grasping reduces the difficulty of handling the bolt. Assembly is also easier if the bolt is oriented in a position that aligns with the direction of

FIGURE 3-7

Changing the complexity of how the task is executed. When the bolts are organized and presented with the head of the bolt upright, they are easier to pick up and handle than when they come randomly oriented in a box.

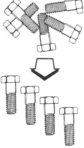

insertion. If the reach distances between the bolts and insertion points are reduced, operator strain decreases. None of these changes alter the objective of installing a specified number of bolts. However, the changes do reduce the complexity of the assembly process (i.e., how the task is accomplished).

Our primary focus in this section has been on reducing product complexity. However, the same principles that apply to reducing product complexity apply to process complexity.

REDUCING PROCESS COMPLEXITY

Reducing the complexity of the how the task is executed is equally as important as reducing the task complexity. The following list briefly introduces a few key concepts that world-class manufacturers use to reduce process complexity.

- Where possible, divide the work into tasks that can be completed in one to two minutes (takt time) (Adler and Cole 1993, 85–94). Many repetitions of simple tasks promote rapid learning and easy recall of the required actions, helping the factory rapidly achieve low defect rates when new products are introduced or when new workers are trained. Rotation of work assignments and multi-process equipment operation minimizes boredom.
- Define operating standards and establish standard operations. Let the experts of production—-the workers on the factory floor—define and refine the work cycles in conjunction with designers. The documents defining the work on the shop floor are the operating standards. The teams defining these standards should constantly seek to make the task easier while reducing stress and strain. The team should regularly observe the best worker's methods and identify opportunities for improvement. When the team selects the best method, all workers performing the same task must learn and use the method. In other words, the best production methods become the standard operations. Industrial engineers should support, rather than direct, the work teams (Adler 1993, 103–104) (Hirano 1994, 226–241).
- Design or arrange the factory so that materials "flow" through the production plant (Hirano, 1988, 64–101). Minimize the distance that parts must travel during fabrication and assembly. Organizations striving to meet these goals avoid large, expensive, multipurpose machines, function-based factory layouts, and single-function operations. U-shaped rather than linear produc-

tion flow is used because workers needn't travel from the end of the production line to the beginning at the conclusion of each work cycle. The goal is to eliminate all non-value–added activities. Eliminating non-value-added activities eliminates the mistakes and defects occurring during these activities.

- Multiprocess manned production is emphasized. In traditional factories, an operator may control the operations at a single machine or a variety of similar machines, such as several different drilling machines (Hirano 1994, 214–225). In such cases the worker is frequently idle while the machine is working, and the machine is idle while the man is working. In efficient factories, each worker operates a variety of different machines arranged in a production sequence, such as a drill, a punch, and a press. These workers leave one machine to complete its work while they move material to the next machine in the production cycle. Production is naturally more efficient if workers stand rather than sit. In multiprocess manned production where there is virtually no inventory in the work cycle, defects are immediately obvious, promoting prompt action.
- Simplify the methods used to control material flow. Where possible, material flow should be controlled locally on the factory floor using methods such as kanban rather than MRP methods (Stalk and Hout 1990, 120–122), (Hirano 1988, 168–173). These techniques eliminate many of the instruction errors in production.
- Use single minute exchange of dies (SMED) to rapidly change the setups of production fixtures. This approach simplifies the tooling setup and teardown. SMED enables increased variety and productivity. It makes it possible to produce small batches economically while reducing setup mistakes (Shingo 1985).
- Apply the 5S strategy. The 5S strategy consists of: 1) clearing up (seiri), 2) organizing (seiton), 3) cleaning (seiso), 4) standardizing (seiketsu), and 5) training and discipline (shitsuke) (Hirano 1988, 28–63). The 5S strategy is an essential part of keeping the factory in order so that clutter and debris do not distract or confuse workers during production.
- Full participation productive maintenance (Hirano 1994, 250–256) dramatically reduces work interruptions due to equipment and tooling breakdowns, as well as the frequent errors that occur when production is restarted after a breakdown. Except

for equipment that would greatly impede production if broken down, equipment operators become responsible for the clean up and maintenance of the equipment they operate. Checklists guide equipment inspection and maintenance. Naturally, training and direction from the production engineer and maintenance specialist are needed to establish the what, when, how, and why of maintenance procedures. Using these techniques, small problems that would otherwise be overlooked are detected and corrected before defective products are generated.

- Use visual controls to make the difference between necessary and unnecessary items obvious (Hirano, 1994, 257–266). Traditional factories put the production guidelines in printed instructions. Visual controls move the instructions from a paper format to highly visible elements of the production process, eliminating a substantial portion of written instructions and the associated reading errors.

Although this book does not contain a detailed discussion of techniques for simplifying the execution of a task, many excellent books are available on this topic, as referenced throughout this section. However, a few practices and procedures do have a direct bearing on mistake-proofing and deserve further explanation, because references to these techniques in the Appendix may not be understood otherwise.

The Red Tag Tactic

Unnecessary inventory and equipment can accumulate on the production line. This material confuses operators, clutters the work area, and expands the size of the factory floor, making material movement more difficult. The red tag tactic, which is part of the 5S strategy for clearing up, is used to identify and eliminate unnecessary parts on the work floor.

In the months preceding the activity, participants are instructed in the techniques and employees are instructed not to hide any items. Leadership identifies the red tag targets, which should include excessive stock, unused tools and equipment, and unused space like floors and shelves. The guidelines for red tag activities also need to be defined in advance. For example, one criterion for attaching a red tag could be that the item will not be needed on the work floor within the next month. Red tags are normally printed on letter size sheets in a color that cannot be easily overlooked or ignored (Figure 3-8).

Personnel from other departments apply tags to assure objectivity. The tagging operation should be completed in a short time period—a

FIGURE 3-8

Illustration of a red tag (adapted from Hirano 1994, 184).

RED TAG

Item Name:		
Material Type:	☐ Inventory ☐ Work-in-process ☐ Part ☐ Finished goods	☐ Equipment ☐ Fixture ☐ Tool ☐ Other
No. of Items:		
Reason for Tagging:	☐ No longer needed ☐ Defective	☐ Used infrequently ☐ Other
Action:	☐ Dispose ☐ Send to reclamation ☐ Return to owner ☐ Place in storage ☐ Remove tag	☐ Closeout
Action Dates	Tag Date: _____	Closeout Date: _____

week or so. Product information, key dates, and the reason for placing the tag on the item are recorded on the tag.

Following the tagging activities, red tagged items are evaluated to determine if they will not be used again, are "dead stock," or will be used infrequently ("sleeping stock"). A schedule is created to dispose of dead stock and transfer sleeping stock to a storage location.

Sign Strategies

Errors in retrieving the wrong part, or placing a fixture in the wrong storage location, do happen. If there is a delay in getting the right part, or the wrong part is delivered to the factory floor, production can be shut down, or incorrect parts may be used in assembly. Thus, no discussion of mistake-proofing would be complete without reviewing fundamental principles of signs and signboards (Hirano 1994, 257–266). Traditionally, signs for storage areas may contain the description of an item, such as "Press Fixture," if there are any signs at all. Since there may be a variety of press fixtures, the label does not provide sufficiently clear information to assure that a part has been placed in the proper storage location or that an item retrieved from a location is the desired part. Signs like this are similar to parking lot signs that designate a space for a Vice President or General Manager. When there is a car in the space, there may be no way of knowing whether or not the car belongs to the designated person, unless individuals recognize the owner's car or the owner complains when the space is taken. Unfortunately, tools and equipment cannot complain when they are put in the wrong place or when their storage place is occupied.

The first characteristic of well-marked storage is that each storage location is uniquely identified and easy to find. To achieve this, a unique designator, typically a letter of the alphabet, is used for each storage area, and a separate designator is used for each storage subsystem within the area. The person responsible for the storage area should be designated on the sign for the area. Next, each storage location within the storage area is given a unique designator. For example, each row and column on a shelf can be assigned a row and column number, assigned sequentially top to bottom and left to right. For example, a storage location BG-23 identifies a storage space in area "B," shelf system "G," column 2, row 3. Note that columns should always be designated before rows as a matter of common practice. Large items that do not fit in shelves still need proper storage location markings. White lines created with tape or paint can demarcate the storage location for such items and keep the storage area well organized.

The second characteristic of well-marked storage is that there is a unique matching label or sign on the item (or tray holding the item) and the storage location. For example, a sign at location BG-23 could indicate that this was the proper place to store "Fixture 12698." Now, if the fixture has a matching sign, operators can quickly determine whether or not the part is stored in the proper location by comparing the sign on the shelf and the sign on the part. Naturally, signs should be easy to read from a distance, and there should never be any doors covering stored items. A storage area with proper signs is illustrated in Figure 3-9.

Red Lines and Storage Quantity Indicators

The third attribute of the best storage signs is that they provide an easily recognized indication of the correct quantities, which is particularly important for items stocked for production. These indicators show the maximum allowed quantities and the point at which the material should be reordered or replenished.

Without upper limits on stored quantities, the amount of material on hand can accumulate beyond useful limits, wasting resources. Naturally, the best technique for controlling the upper limit of stock on-hand is to limit the quantity by the available storage volume. Since this is not always possible, simple indicators like a red line (Hirano 1994, 258) at the upper limit of the storage level can achieve similar results.

FIGURE 3-9

Properly marked storage bins, with designators for the storage area and shelving system.

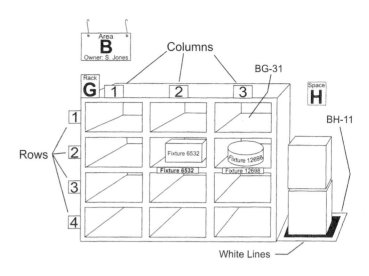

On the other hand, in the absence of clear indicators that show when material should be ordered or replenished, supplies may drop so low that production may be impeded. A white line can be used to indicate the order point or replenishment point, or a kanban card or other visual indicator can be placed in a stack of material at the order point. Red lines and order lines are illustrated in Figure 3-10. Sensors can also be used to detect the order point and excessive material supply.

FIGURE 3-10

The stack of material should not exceed the red-line limit, and new material should be ordered when the stack drops to the order point or replenishment line. The maximum quantity in the tank is volume limited, but a refill point indicator is needed.

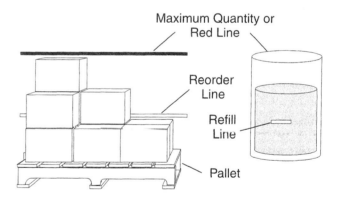

Signboards and Lights

During production, the supply of a specific material on the factory floor will drop to the point that the material needs to be replenished. Traditionally, the operator communicates these needs to "runners" on the materials-handling team who retrieve stock from storage. Many errors occur because of delays in communication. Lights and signboards can be used in several ways to overcome such problems (Figure 3-11).

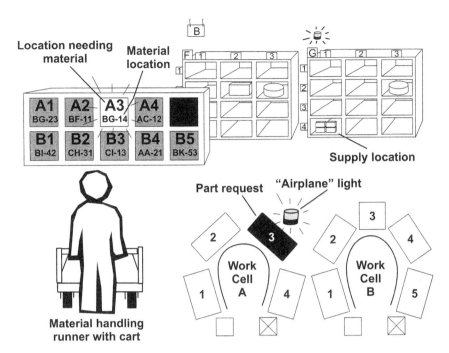

FIGURE 3-11
Signboards and lights like airplane call lights alert material handlers to what material is needed and where it is located (adapted from Hirano 1994, 258–259).

When an operator detects that it is time to replenish materials or retrieve a fixture from storage, he or she can flip a switch to signal the need. Sensors that detect low material supplies can perform the same function. Like call buttons and call lights in an airplane, this action turns on a light above the workstation, alerting material-handling runners where attention is needed. In conjunction with the "airplane lights," signboards can be located in central locations. Signboards also can be used in conjunction with sensors that detect low supply quantities in storage to alert workers that materials need to be ordered.

Modern technology can enhance communication. For example, signboards can display the workstation where stock or fixtures are needed and the storage location and quantity of the needed material. This allows the runners to retrieve and deliver the needed supplies without having to go to the workstation to determine what is needed. In addition, modern communication techniques can literally place a "signboard" at the fingertips of each runner, communicating the information even more efficiently.

In summary, a key to eradicating and controlling mistakes is to reduce complexity, since this eliminates many of the unnecessary actions that often are the source of mistakes. Mistakes are eliminated by simplifying the use of a product, parts, assembly, maintenance, repair, and manufacturing processes. Both the complexity of the task and how it is performed must be addressed. Time is the most useful measure in assessing complexity and is strongly correlated with defect rates. Modest efforts to reduce product and process complexity during the early stages of product design have, perhaps, the highest return on investment in terms of improving quality and productivity. Typically, reducing complexity will cut costs and defect rates in half or more, and will reduce development time. Mistake-proofing should begin only after opportunities for reducing complexity have been explored, since the need for mistake-proofing is often eliminated by simplification. In the following chapter, we will examine techniques for the next step in achieving profound improvements in product quality—mistake-proofing.

CHAPTER 4

MISTAKE-PROOFING

FRUSTRATION

The water department has faced tough challenges before, but dealing with hundreds of little leaks in the water line is one of their toughest. They can't afford to dig up every water line in the city to fix tiny leaks, yet they must stop them to meet the increasing demand for water. The task just seems overwhelming.

HOPE

The general contractor on the waterline construction for the new subdivision is grinning from ear to ear the next time she stops by the office. She blurts out: "I've heard your waterline joints are leaking like a sieve, and I think we can help! I just heard about a new product at a contractor's convention that might save your bacon."

THE RIGHT TOOL

"They have a new plug, or 'pig,' that can be pulled by a cable through the water lines. It's equipped to detect leaks, and when it finds one, it stops and pumps a little sealant into each crack or joint. Virtually every leak can be completely sealed without tearing up the waterline. The best part is that it is so inexpensive that it will make the city council smile. Mike says he can have someone here next Thursday to show us how it works."

QUALITY CONTROL

The purpose of locating leaks in a water line is to repair them and correct the problem that caused them. Similarly, when the condition that results in defects is identified, the goal should be to control or eliminate it. Each source of defects requires different control methods. Methods that reduce the complexity of a product are proactive, eliminating the opportunity for mistakes before they even occur. In many situations, mistakes and excessive variation can also be anticipated and prevented by proactive product and process design.

However, the best of the proactive quality control methods is imperfect, and defects will be discovered in production requiring a reactive response to quality breaches. Typically, by the time a breach in quality control is discovered the opportunity to improve quality by reducing complexity has passed. Therefore, corrective action at this point focuses on controlling mistakes or variations. This chapter describes the proactive and reactive techniques most useful in controlling mistakes.

CONTROLLING MISTAKES

Controlling mistakes is like plugging leaks at each joint in a water supply line. No single patch or repair will plug every leak. The control of any single mistake may result in a nearly imperceptible improvement in conformance quality, but the collective control of many types of mistakes has a profound impact on quality. Illustrating the need for many mistake controls, each operation has an average of 12 mistake-proofing devices at Toyota (Chase & Stewart 1994, 35–44).

Poka-yoke, which was developed by Shigeo Shingo at Toyota, is the most effective method for controlling mistakes (Shingo 1986). Mistake-proofing is the English translation of *poka-yoke*. Since there are many types of mistakes, mistake-proofing devices must generally be custom designed for each specific condition. Thus, mistake-proofing should be viewed as a general approach to understanding and controlling mistakes rather than a well-defined methodology.

Regardless of the implementation, effective mistake-proofing techniques share the following attributes:

- They are like checklists that verify correct procedures or conditions.
- They are based on 100 percent inspection, since mistakes are so rare that they cannot be detected and corrected by any other means.
- Inspection methods must be very reliable.
- Inspections are autonomous, where possible, to avoid omission of the inspection operation.
- Since they control rare events, devices must be inexpensive to design, implement, and operate.

MISTAKE-PROOFING THE DESIGN CONCEPT

To effectively control mistakes, design teams cannot wait until they are discovered in production—control of mistakes begins at the earliest stage of product design. Design teams must identify the mistakes that are most likely to occur and implement techniques that minimize or eliminate them. For example, many parts can be redesigned so that they can only be assembled in the correct location and orientation. In some cases the parts can be designed so that assembly can't proceed if parts are missing.

Often, simple changes can have an important influence on eliminating mistakes. For example, if all bolts installed at a single workstation are identical, the probability of installing the wrong bolt is virtually eliminated.

CLASSIFYING MISTAKES

Although the underlying principles for mistake-proofing are remarkably simple, a large fraction of mistake-proofing solutions require unique adaptations to specific problems. Thus, mistake-proofing is a skill that improves through familiarity with a variety of solutions. To find solutions to current problems rapidly, examples of mistake-proofing need to be organized in a clear, consistent manner.

As stated earlier, mistakes can be classified in many ways. Some classification methods previously used in the study of mistakes include:

- Causal factors (fatigue, noise, poor lighting, urgency, interruption)
- Project phase (design, fabrication, assembly)
- Ergonomic factors (perception, decision, action, skill, training)
- Human error probability (error frequency, human performance)
- Stress factors (workload, occupational change, or frustration)
- Mistake consequences (injury, loss, damage)
- Function or task (welding, milling, detailing, inspecting)
- Behavioral factors (communication, motor processes, perception)
- Corrective action (rework, repair, scrap)

These classification schemes have each led to a better understanding of mistakes and human limitations; however, they are not particularly useful for mistake-proofing. This is true because the best mistake-proofing techniques do not control the root causes of mistakes, such as errors in psychological reasoning or anomalies in human behavior. The great value of mistake-proofing is that, independent of the cause, psychological factor, production stage, or potential consequences it blocks or warns about an undesired outcome at a point in the process when the consequences can be minimized. Finding the best solution for mistakes is strongly influenced by the way we think about and classify problems. Understanding that mistake-proofing is really an *outcome intervention* method points to a better way of thinking about and classifying mistakes for mistake-proofing.

MISTAKE-PROOFING BLOCKS UNDESIRABLE OUTCOMES

Some types of undesirable outcomes resulting from mistakes include:

- Omitted parts
- Omitted processes
- Parts placed in the wrong orientation
- Parts placed in the wrong location
- Misadjustment

Described in terms of outcome, each type of mistake can occur at virtually any project or production phase. Most importantly, regardless of the process, phase, or root cause, techniques that prevent specific outcomes—such as omitted parts—share similar attributes (Figure 4-1). However, mistake-proofing techniques that eliminate incorrectly oriented parts are distinctly different from techniques that prevent part omissions.

As a result, when mistake-proofing examples are sorted according to the outcome they control, there is more similarity in the problems as well as the control methods than when organized by any other approach. Thus, this method of arranging the mistakes provides the fastest and easiest means for identifying alternative mistake-proofing concepts.

FIGURE 4-1

Mistake-proofing blocks undesirable outcomes.

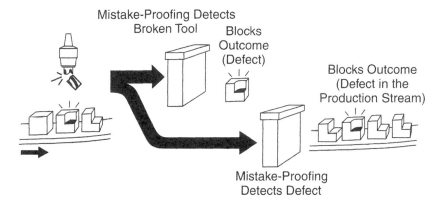

An Outcome-Based Mistake Classification Scheme

An outcome-based classification for mistake-proofing follows, with a brief definition of terms and examples.

Defective Material (DM)

The material *entering* a process is defective or inadequate for the intended function, process, or purpose. Note that the root cause of defective materials may be traced to mistakes or excessive variation in earlier processes. However, in many cases companies may not be able to directly control supply quality, or the process may not be adequately understood to establish better control. In such cases, mistake-proofing may be useful in detecting and removing defective material entering a process.

Information Errors

Ambiguous information (IA): Information can be interpreted many ways, and some interpretations may be incorrect. *Example: A reference letter states, "You will be really lucky if you can get this person to work for you."*

Incorrect information (II): Information is provided, but is incorrect. *Example: The operator performs the correct action based on a gage that is read correctly, but the gage is faulty.*

Misread, mismeasure, misinterpret (IM): Gage reading errors, errors in measuring, or errors in understanding correct information.

Omitted information (IO): Information essential for the correct execution of a process or operation is not available or has never been prepared.

Inadequate warning (IW): A warning is sent or readily available, but the method of warning is not adequate to attract the operator's attention.

Misalignments, Misadjustments, and Mistiming

A correct operation is performed, but the accuracy of the motion control or timing is not adequate to result in the desired outcome.

Misaligned parts (MA): Parts or tooling are in the proper general location and orientation, but the alignment is not sufficiently accurate for fit, function, or the correct execution of an operation (Figure 4-2).

FIGURE 4-2

Two examples of misalignment errors.

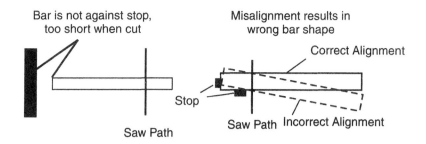

Misadjustment (MD): An incorrect adjustment of an operation, either before or during execution, which is not the result of information errors. This generally includes incomplete operations.

Mistimed or rushed (MT): The operator does not have sufficient time to execute a process correctly, or does not respond at the appropriate time.

Omission or Commission Errors

Failure to perform a required action or the execution of a prohibited action.

Added material or part (OA): The failure to remove materials or parts—such as protective coverings, temporary fixtures, or parts from a mold—or the addition of extra parts—such as dropping a bolt into a cavity—resulting from causes other than counting errors.

Commit prohibited actions (OC): Performing an action that is not allowed or desired. *Examples: dropping a part, or turning on power to an electrical panel where another person is working.*

Omitted operations (OO): Failure to perform a required operation.

Omitted parts and counting errors (OP): A missing part, or the wrong number of parts resulting from a counting error.

Selection Errors

An incorrect selection from available alternatives.

Wrong concept or material (WC): Design decision errors resulting in incompatible materials, hazardous products, nonfunctional products, or any one of a wide range of problems. Such errors can also result in products that are subject to excessive wear, are not robust, are unreliable, or are unsatisfactory to the customers.

Wrong destination (WD): After completing an operation, the product is sent to the wrong address or destination. *Examples: A good part is put in the "bad" bin, or HIV test results are sent to the wrong patient.*

Wrong location (WL): Part insertion or process execution in an incorrect location that is not the result of incorrectly orienting parts. An example of selecting the wrong location is illustrated in Figure 4-3.

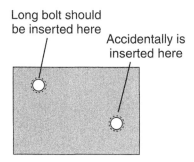

Long bolt should
be inserted here

Accidentally is
inserted here

FIGURE 4-3

Putting a bolt in the wrong hole is an example of picking the wrong location (WL).

Wrong operation (WO): An operation is executed, but the wrong operation is used. *Example: a right-hand process is used on a left-hand part.*

Wrong part (WP): A part is selected, but it is the wrong part. Examples: a red part is selected when green is required, or a 1″ bolt is selected when a 2″ bolt is required.

Wrong orientation (WR): A part is inserted in the correct location, but the part has the wrong orientation. See the example shown in Figure 4-4.

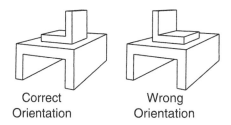

Correct
Orientation

Wrong
Orientation

FIGURE 4-4

A part in the wrong orientation has been flipped end-to-end or rotated incorrectly about the axis of insertion, as illustrated here.

Appendix A contains 200 examples that have been sorted according to this outcome-based mistake-proofing classification scheme. Although the examples emphasize solutions for industrial production, mistake-proofing concepts have been selected from a wide range of environments to illustrate the broad applicability of mistake-proofing. Among many other applications, concepts that control mistakes are provided for maintenance, clinical chemistry, sports, assembly, fabrication, documentation, information systems, and home applications.

FREQUENT MISTAKES

Some types of mistakes occur more frequently than others. The frequency of each type of mistake differs for each task, organization, and individual. Common mistakes are given in the following list in the approximate order of frequency in production environments, with the most frequent listed first. This list is particularly useful for anticipating mistakes and mistake-proofing the product design and production process.

1. Omitted operations
2. Omitted parts
3. Select wrong orientation
4. Misaligned parts
5. Select wrong location
6. Select wrong parts
7. Misadjustments
8. Commit prohibited actions
9. Added material or parts
10. Misread or mismeasure

CHALLENGES IN CLASSIFYING MISTAKES

In an ideal mistake classification scheme, the categories would be mutually exclusive and collectively exhaustive. In such a classification scheme, there would be a classification for every mistake, but each mistake would only fit in a single classification. Unfortunately, because many factors can contribute to a particular mistake, each mistake can often be classified in a variety of ways, and the correct classification is a matter of interpretation. In general, there is little value in agonizing over the precise classification of a mistake. Where more than one classification seems to describe a particular mistake, significant insight may be obtained by examining examples in each of the various ways the problem can be classified.

Table 4-1 illustrates the relationships between the classifications and is helpful in finding alternative approaches to solving a problem. If, for example, a mistake is classified in the category of the Wrong Destination, we can read across Table 4-1 and determine that this class of mistake is strongly associated with Incorrect Information, Wrong Location, and Wrong Part. Thus, if we do not find good examples under Wrong Destination, it may be useful to search some of the other classifications that are strongly related.

Legend:
- ⊙ Strong Connection
- ○ Connection
- Blank Weak or no connection

		Information					Misadjust			Omission				Selection Error					
	DM	IA	II	IM	IO	IW	MA	MD	MT	OA	OC	OO	OP	WC	WD	WL	WO	WP	WR
Defective Material (DM)	▓						○	⊙	⊙		○	⊙	⊙				⊙	⊙	⊙
Ambiguous (IA)		▓		⊙			⊙	⊙			○					○	⊙	⊙	○
Incorrect (II)			▓	⊙				⊙	⊙		⊙			○	⊙		⊙		
Mismeasure, interpret (IM)	○	⊙	⊙	▓			⊙	⊙	⊙					⊙		○			○
Omitted Information (IO)					▓		○	○			⊙	○	○	⊙		○	○	○	○
Inadequate Warning (IW)						▓	⊙	⊙	⊙										
Misalign (MA)	○	⊙		⊙	○	⊙	▓	⊙	⊙			○	○			⊙			⊙
Misadjust (MD)	⊙	⊙	⊙	⊙	○	⊙	⊙	▓	⊙		○					○			○
Mistimed or Rushed (MT)	⊙		⊙	⊙		⊙	⊙	⊙	▓		○	⊙	⊙		○	○	○	○	○
Added Parts (OA)										▓	⊙		○					○	
Commit Prohibited (OC)	○		⊙		⊙			○	○	⊙	▓			○					
Omitted Operation (OO)	⊙	○			○		○		⊙			▓	⊙	⊙			⊙		
Omitted Parts (OP)	⊙				○		○		⊙	○		⊙	▓			○	○	○	
Concept or Material (WC)		○		⊙	⊙						○	⊙		▓			⊙	⊙	
Destination (WD)		⊙							○						▓	⊙	⊙		
Location (WL)		○		○	○		⊙	○	○				○		⊙	▓	○	○	⊙
Operation (WO)	⊙	⊙	⊙		○				○			⊙	○	⊙		○	▓	⊙	⊙
Parts (WP)	⊙	⊙			○				○	○			○	⊙	⊙	○	⊙	▓	○
Orientation (WR)	⊙	○		○	○		⊙	○	○								⊙	⊙	▓

THE BASIC FUNCTIONS OF MISTAKE-PROOFING

In addition to outcome-based classification, there are other attributes of mistake-proofing that need to be considered. A mistake exists in one of three states:

- It is about to occur,
- It has already occurred but has not yet resulted in a defect, or
- The mistake has already caused a defect.

TABLE 4-1

Interrelationships between mistake classifications. Correlations are strong when mistakes in the two classes are similar, or when mistakes could reasonably be placed in either of the related categories.

A mistake is about to occur when an operator reaches toward the wrong bin to draw a part. Pulling a wrong part from a bin illustrates a case where a mistake has occurred; but the defect does not exist until the wrong part is inserted into the product.

Mistake-proofing methods have three basic functions to use against mistakes—control, shutdown, and warning. Control prevents mistakes, defects, or the flow of defective items to the next process. Shutdown stops normal functions when mistakes or defects are detected or predicted. Warnings signal that an abnormality, mistake, or defect has been detected. Recognizing that a mistake is about to occur is "prediction," and recognizing that a mistake or defect has already occurred is "detection." Figure 4-5 shows the relationship of the three possible states of mistakes with the three functions of *poka-yoke*.

FIGURE 4-5

The basic functions of mistake-proofing that eliminate defects from the production stream begin with the prevention, detection, or prediction of mistakes or defects. The undesirable outcome is blocked by prevention, shutdown, or warnings.

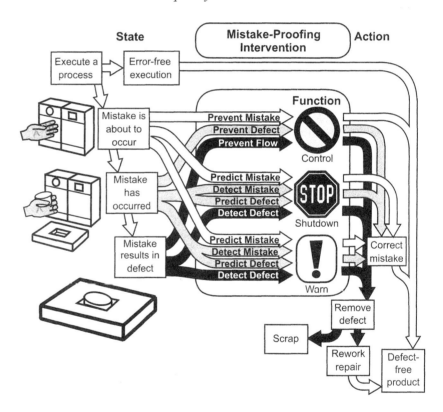

IDENTIFYING THE BEST MISTAKE-PROOFING CONCEPTS

Applying the concept of source inspection, the best techniques eliminate quality problems at their source. If the quality control method detects rather than prevents defects, the result will be unnecessary scrap, rework, and repair even if mistake-proofing is the type of detection method used. Thus, it is generally better to detect and correct mistakes before defects are generated, whenever possible.

Where practical, it is better still to assure that mistakes and subsequent defects never occur. When mistakes are prevented rather than detected, productivity is generally improved. For example, production workers generally spend a significant portion of their time making decisions: selecting correct parts, selecting correct insertion positions and orientations, or checking their work after the process has been completed. In cases where mistakes are frequent or decision processes constitute a large fraction of the process time, preventing mistakes will often dramatically improve productivity by eliminating these nonproductive activities. In summary, preventing mistakes is generally better than detecting mistakes, which, in turn, is better than detecting defects (Figure 4-6).

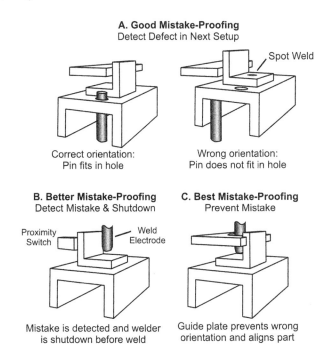

A. Good Mistake-Proofing
Detect Defect in Next Setup

Spot Weld

Correct orientation:
Pin fits in hole

Wrong orientation:
Pin does not fit in hole

B. Better Mistake-Proofing
Detect Mistake & Shutdown

Proximity
Switch

Weld
Electrode

Mistake is detected and welder
is shutdown before weld

C. Best Mistake-Proofing
Prevent Mistake

Guide plate prevents wrong
orientation and aligns part

FIGURE 4-6

Three concepts that eliminate orientation defects in the production stream. It is better to prevent a defect (Concept B) than to detect a defect (Concept A). The best concepts, however, prevent mistakes (Concept C) rather than detect them (Concept B) because they eliminate the wasted time spent correcting mistakes.

THE MISTAKE-PROOFING EFFECTIVENESS MATRIX (MEM)

Because operators can ignore warnings, either intentionally or unintentionally, shutting down an operation is better than warning that an abnormal condition may exist. Similarly, controls that make mistakes impossible without interrupting the production flow are better than shutdowns.

Table 4-2 captures the relationships between mistake states and control functions. The letters "A," "B," and "C" reflect the control concepts shown as "Good," "Better," and "Best," respectively, in Figure 4-6. As mistake-proofing concepts are developed, this table helps identify potentially better alternatives, encouraging a more thorough exploration of mistake-proofing opportunities. The three major control functions in the MEMs table are: a) control of variation, represented by a sine shaped curve; b) control of mistakes, representated by *poka-yoke*; and c) the control of complexity, achieved by simplification.

TABLE 4-2

The mistake-proofing effectiveness matrix (MEM). Generally, mistake-proofing alternatives that map into the chart further to the right and closer to the top are more effective in eliminating defects.

State	Adjustment	Setting	Warn	Shutdown	Control	Tools & Eqpt.	Process	Product
	\~		Poka-yoke			Simplify		
Complex								
Prevent Mistake					C			
Detect Mistake				B				
Detect Defect			A					
Variation								

Control Function

Better →

Although mistake-proofing is essential, it alone will not achieve world-class conformance quality. To address a global spectrum of quality control concepts, the matrix also addresses control functions for variation and complexity. As reflected in the table, changes that simplify the product typically eliminate many opportunities for mistakes and excessive variation. The best product simplification incorporates mistake-proofing in the product design, frequently eliminating the need for separate mistake-proofing devices. Thus, simplifying product concepts is one of the most effective quality methods.

Within each classification, the mistake-proofing examples in this book are presented from most to least effective. In other words, techniques that prevent and control mistakes are presented first, while those that provide a warning when a defect is detected are presented last.

MISTAKE-PROOFING PRINCIPLES

The Most Useful Mistake-Proofing Devices

Although there are many mistake-proofing devices, they are not equally effective or as widely applicable. Figure 4-7 summarizes the most useful mistake-proofing devices (Hirano 1988, 71–72). These devices should be thought of as solution principles rather than physical descriptions.

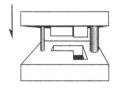

Guide Pins of Different Sizes
Guide pins of different sizes or ribs, blocks, guides and slots assure that parts can only be assembled in the intended location and orientation. Ideally, guides should align parts before critical features mate.

Limit Switches
Limit switches or other sensors detect mistakes, or the absence of mistakes. These sensors trigger warnings, shutdown or enable an operation, or are interlocked with other processing equipment.

Specialized Mistake-Proofing Jigs
Most of these specialized mistake-proofing devices detect defects created just upstream in the previous production process or step. This allows the defects to be removed from the production flow as quickly as possible.

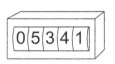

Counters
Counters, and counting devices are used to verify the proper number of parts or operations, and may be linked to warning devices or equipment interlocks. Timers verify the duration of a task in the same way.

Checklists
Checklists remind operators of required tasks that may otherwise be forgotten. While written checklists are imperfect mistake-proofing aids, kanban, shadowboxes, kits, and similar devices are extremely effective forms of checklists.

FIGURE 4-7

The five best mistake-proofing devices are guide pins of different sizes, limit switches, specialized mistake-proofing jigs, counters, and checklists.

The following techniques demonstrate that there are a variety of ways to perform operations that require counting. The height of a stack of quarters can be compared against a gage to count quarters because they have a relatively uniform thickness. Bolts for assembly could be counted by pre-filling a tray with the correct number of cavities. If a cavity in the tray is empty during setup, the wrong number has been collected. If a bolt is left in the tray at the end of the assembly process, a part is omitted. On a drill press, a mechanical or electrical counter connected to a limit switch may be used to count the number of holes that have been drilled. Each of these approaches, while physically quite different, provides a counting function.

Principle-Based Concept Development

The principles that control one class of mistakes are generally quite different from those that control other classes of mistakes. To illustrate, to prevent inadequate warning, a warning light or alarm may be needed. On the other hand, to prevent the insertion of a part in the wrong location, unnecessary features, such as extra holes, may need to be eliminated. The principles that overcome inadequate warning are quite different from those that prevent insertion of a part in the wrong location.

In Appendix A, at the beginning of each classification category, the mistake-proofing principles that are most useful in controlling that specific type of problem are listed. The principles listed have been gleaned from hundreds of mistake-proofing examples and are generally organized from most to least effective.

The principles listed in Appendix A are substantially more comprehensive than any previously published, and are helpful in developing mistake-proofing concepts. When faced with a particular problem, reviewing the applicable mistake-proofing principles at the beginning of the section can prompt new ideas that are often more effective than could be otherwise achieved.

For example, selecting the wrong part is a common problem. This can occur during assembly, the execution of a process, or during setup. Three characteristics could be used to assure that parts are properly sorted before selection (Poka-yoke 1988, 17): weight, dimensions, and shape. However, a variety of other useful principles prevent selection of the wrong part, including the use of a first-in first-out rack for parts used in a repeated sequence, or smart part bins that prevent the operator from reaching for the wrong part. By reviewing these applicable principles, we may be reminded that smart part bins may be an easier or more appropriate solution than using a first-in first-out rack for a specific problem.

The principles enumerated with the examples in Appendix A encompass the traditional mistake-proofing techniques. The search for solution principles and concepts using the new classification approach is more efficient, however, because users need not search through as many examples or sort through as many irrelevant principles to find applicable solutions. Table 4-3 shows the relationship between traditional mistake-proofing concepts and the new mistake-proofing classifications.

Key:
⊙ Related Mistake-Proofing

Traditional Mistake-Proofing Approach

	Mistake-Proofing by New Classification																		
		Information Errors					Misalign, Adjust, Time			Omission or Commission				Selection Errors					
	Defective Materials	Ambiguous Information	Incorrect Information	Misread, Measure, Interpret	Omitted Information	Inadequate Warning	Misaligned Parts	Misadjustments	Mis-timed or Rushed	Added Material or Part	Commit Prohibited Action	Omitted Operations	Omitted Parts, Counting Err.	Wrong Concept or Material	Select Wrong Destination	Select Wrong Location	Select Wrong Operation	Select Wrong Part	Select Wrong Orientation
Process Sequence Control — Intra-process									⊙	⊙		⊙	⊙				⊙	⊙	
Process Sequence Control — Inter-process									⊙	⊙		⊙	⊙				⊙	⊙	
Material & Part Distinctions — Shape — Dimensions							⊙	⊙		⊙		⊙				⊙		⊙	⊙
Shape — Feature characteristics							⊙	⊙		⊙		⊙				⊙		⊙	⊙
Shape — Feature relationship & shape							⊙	⊙		⊙		⊙				⊙		⊙	⊙
Weight	⊙			⊙														⊙	
Impurity	⊙																		
Labeling, marking, color		⊙	⊙	⊙	⊙		⊙												
Identification & product data				⊙	⊙														
Quantity or Duration Control — Duration									⊙										
Repetitions (counter method)										⊙		⊙	⊙						
Remainder or ejected parts										⊙			⊙						
Fixed number calculation										⊙		⊙	⊙						
Motion or Position Control — Position & displacement				⊙			⊙	⊙										⊙	
Proximity & registration				⊙			⊙	⊙										⊙	
Acceleration or velocity				⊙				⊙			⊙							⊙	
Dynamics, shock, vibration								⊙			⊙								
Mishandling											⊙								
Environment Control Error Detection											⊙								

Although the mistake-proofing principles have been extracted from hundreds of examples, the list of principles in Appendix A is incomplete; readers may identify new principles that should be added to these lists.

TABLE 4-3

Relationship between traditional mistake-proofing techniques and the new mistake-proofing classifications.

BUILDING YOUR OWN MISTAKE-PROOFING CATALOG

Most individuals have difficulty recognizing how a mistake-proofing concept developed for one industry can apply to another. Individuals in the medical industry, for example, may not be able to visualize how industrial mistake-proofing examples fit their problems. Consequently, companies and organizations may want to create industry-specific catalogs by adding their own mistake-proofing examples. To add a mistake-proofing example, first determine which classification best describes the mistake. Fill out a mistake-proofing form to describe the mistake (a blank form is provided in the Appendix B for this purpose).

If you find a mistake that doesn't seem to fit anywhere, adding to or adapting the classification scheme is appropriate. Just be careful that added classifications are outcomes: if they are not, classifying mistakes and finding solutions will become more confusing and difficult.

QCM—AN EFFICIENT APPROACH TO MISTAKE-PROOFING

By combining an efficient problem-solving procedure, an outcome-based classification scheme, examples sorted by classification, mistake-proofing principles, and a technique for selecting the best mistake-proofing ideas, a new methodology has been defined for rapidly developing superior mistake-proofing concepts. This methodology is called quality by control of mistakes (QCM), which is outlined as follows:

Step 1. Identify and select the problem.

Step 2. Analyze the problem:
    A. Assess the urgency of solving the problem (see Hirano's method in Chapter 2).
    B. Identify the root cause of observed or anticipated defects using the 5 Whys and a How and the 4Ms and an I/CMV tools.
    C. If the anticipated problem or root cause is a mistake, classify the mistake according to the outcome-based mistake classification scheme.

Step 3. Generate solutions for mistake-proofing:
    A. Review relevant mistake-proofing examples with the same classification as the problem.
    B. Review the principles useful in mistake-proofing this class of problem.
    C. If the examples or principles are not a good match for the problem, identify and review related mistake-proofing examples and principles (see Table 4.1).
    D. Identify several principles that may be most useful in solving this problem.
    E. Quickly generate a few alternative concepts for mistake-proofing this problem.

Step 4. Compare, select, and plan the solution:
   A. Compare the potential effectiveness of the alternative solutions using mistake-proofing effectiveness matrix (MEM). If none of the generated alternatives prevents mistakes, some key opportunities may have been overlooked, suggesting that additional, more effective alternatives may exist.
   B. Compare alternative solutions based on additional decision factors such as cost, difficulty of implementation, and the potential speed of implementation.
   C. Select the best alternative based on effectiveness and other considerations.
   D. Refine the design of the device, making sure that the workers on the factory floor concur with the implementation and use of the device.
   E. Plan and schedule the deployment to minimize the impact on production.

Step 5. Implement the solution:
   A. Procure the mistake-proofing device hardware.
   B. When practical, set up and evaluate functionality and utility offline before insertion in the production process.
   C. Familiarize and train operators regarding the operation of the device and the appropriate responses to alarms or shutdown.
   D. Deploy on the production line.

Step 6. Evaluate:
   A. Determine if the problem has been solved.
   B. If the solution is ineffective or incomplete, identify other actions that need to be taken.
   C. Publish the results to communicate mistake-proofing opportunities within the organization (use the one-page mistake-proofing form).
   D. Where the solution has broad application, the company should work to standardize implementation across the company.

Naturally, the deployment of the mistake-proofing devices depends upon the cooperative support of product engineering, production engineering, and the workers on the factory floor. Consequently, the implementation of mistake-proofing devices will proceed most readily if they all participate in the process outlined.

When it comes to mistake-proofing, the importance of low-cost solutions can't be overemphasized. If either the devices or process of mistake-proofing becomes too expensive, the mistake-proofing process will not succeed. The process of classifying a mistake, generating several good mistake-proofing alternatives, and comparing those alternatives should take no more than a few hours except for the most difficult problems or the most inexperienced teams. Scrap bins and junkyards may be useful sources of raw materials for making mistake-proofing devices. The agility of the organization in producing mistake-proofing devices is greatly enhanced by a small Kaizen shop staffed with individuals familiar with basic fabrication skills and a fundamental understanding of electronics.

In summary, three new mistake-proofing tools are introduced in this book: a) an outcome-based classification scheme, b) the mistake-proofing effectiveness matrix (the MEM, which is also included in each example in the Appendix), and c) an enumeration of mistake-proofing principles effective for each type of mistake. Collectively these tools facilitate mistake-proofing by making it easier to find relevant mistake-proofing examples. In addition, the mistake-proofing principles and design examples lead to better mistake-proofing concepts. Finally, the mistake-proofing effectiveness matrix enables rapid comparison and selection of the best mistake-proofing concepts.

The Benefits of Mistake-Proofing

Properly implemented, mistake-proofing provides many benefits for production. First, it can dramatically reduce the amount of scrap material produced. As a result, the amount of material ordered from suppliers can be reduced, cutting material and procurement costs. Eliminating scrap has the added benefit of reducing the cost of disposing of the scrap material.

Mistake-proofing can dramatically cut the cost of rework and repair. As recently as a few years ago, a major German automotive manufacturer had skilled teams examine each vehicle coming off the production line and correct any defects that could be found. This activity required many highly trained personnel and a very large floor space within the factory. In contrast, Toyota achieves lower defect rates and has virtually no rework at the end of the production line, substantially reducing the cost of production. The reduced floor space is a contributing factor in the ability to have two or three production lines in factories, such as NUMMI, that previously contained only one production line.

Perhaps more importantly, when defect rates are extremely low, interruptions in the production process are minimized. Furthermore, mistake-proofing simplifies activities that formerly required longer decision times for operators, providing an acceleration in the production. Some companies, like SpeasTech, have observed that productivity doubled with mistake-proofing (Frye 1997).

When defect rates are high, operators need spare parts between processes so that they can pick a "good" part from the factory floor inventory if a "bad" part shows up. Mistake-proofing can virtually eliminate the need for inventory between workstations, allowing a compression of the factory floor, and cleaner workspaces, with fewer resources tied up in inventory.

Repairing defects that reach the customer has been estimated to cost roughly 10 times the cost of fixing defects found in the factory. As the defect rates decline, the number of defects escaping the factory and reaching the customer drops. Thus mistake-proofing can also dramatically cut warranty costs.

Traditional quality control requires extensive documentation. Recently, when an ISO 9000 audit team visited a manufacturer that achieved a defect rate of one part per million using mistake-proofing, the auditors asked to see the company's quality documentation. They presented minimal data collected on quality and quality control. Unsatisfied, the auditors pressed for more data. Only when they demonstrated the mistake-proofing for the auditors were the auditors able to understand how high quality could be achieved without extensive documentation. Quality is in the product, not in the reports. Mistake-proofing eliminates many wasteful documentation activities.

Although the need for mistake-proofing is often recognized and the techniques for mistake-proofing are well-documented, inexperienced individuals generally have difficulty developing effective mistake-proofing concepts. Combined with the examples and principles in Appendix A, this chapter introduces the first mistake-proofing procedure that helps the user quickly find the best mistake-proofing solutions. Because novices using this procedure can deliver concepts comparable to those experienced in mistake-proofing, it accomplishes results that would otherwise take many years to develop. In the next chapter, we will turn our attention to mistake-proofing the control of variation using the concept of settings rather than adjustments.

CHAPTER 5

CONTROLLING VARIATION WITH SETTINGS

WHERE IS THE PRESSURE?

The new water line is installed, and everything seems fine until the new manufacturing plant comes on line. Twice a day, the demand for water is so large at the plant that the pressure drops in the supply line. The water department has already had five complaints today from residents around the plant who say they are having difficulty watering their lawns.

ADJUSTING THE VALVES

"We've tried to control the water pressure by adjusting the valve openings," complains the crew chief, "but every time we think we've got the valves adjusted properly, the usage at the plant changes and we're back to square one. We've adjusted the valves six times in three days, and we're not any better off than when we started! There is plenty of water, it is just that we can't keep up with the swings in the demand."

CONVERTING ADJUSTMENTS TO SETTINGS

By locating a water tank at the manufacturing plant that is filled at a constant rate throughout the day, the plant demand can be supplied from the tank without causing large pressure fluctuations in the water supply line. With less variation in the supply-line pressure, a pressure relief valve in the residential line will assure that water is delivered at a constant pressure of 80 pounds per square inch (psi). The pressure in the residential line is controlled now by settings, rather than adjustments, and everybody benefits with more consistent and predictable results.

CONTROLLING VARIATION

Many methods and techniques exist for reducing defects arising from excessive variation. Traditional techniques are generally well known, and excellent training for these techniques is available from a wide range of reputable organizations. Consequently, this work does not focus on traditional methods and our discussion of this topic will be limited to a very brief description of the following common methods.

STATISTICAL PROCESS CONTROL (SPC)

SPC is a manufacturing tool based on statistical evaluation of inspection data. In volume production, a small fraction of the product is selected for inspection. Feedback from the inspection is used to adjust and control a process to assure that the mean, or average value, is centered within the control limits and that variation is not excessive. The goal of traditional SPC is to limit variation measured in standard deviations to one-third the difference between the specification limit and the mean (Juran and Gryna 1988, 24.3) (Ishikawa 1990, 79–83).

MOTOROLA'S SIX SIGMA

Motorola's Six Sigma method seeks to achieve a thousandfold reduction in defects compared to traditional SPC by: 1) allocating tolerances during design based on statistical methods, and 2) reducing process variation during production. The goal is to achieve a process control where the process limits are six standard deviations from the mean, hence the name Six Sigma (Harry & Stewart 1988).

TAGUCHI METHOD

The Taguchi method seeks to reduce defects (and improve reliability) by reducing the sensitivity to variation. It is largely an experimental method based on statistics and design of experiments (DOE). It can be used to identify the variables that have the strongest influence on variation and define the nominal values and limits for these factors (Ross 1988).

CONTROLLING VARIATION WITH SETTINGS

World-class leaders in quality are eliminating SPC from the factory floor by controlling variation with settings rather than adjustments. The setting control methods developed by Shigeo Shingo are generally simpler, less expensive, and more effective than adjustment methods.

TRADITIONAL ADJUSTMENTS

An example is useful in clarifying the difference in settings and adjustments. Consider a case where a milling machine repeatedly is used to machine a groove in a series of identical parts. The machining process causes the tool tip to wear. As a result, the depths of the grooves in the workpieces change from part to part as additional workpieces are machined. Traditionally, to compensate for tool wear on the milling machine, the milling head is advanced, as illustrated in Figure 5-1. For clarity, the tool wear is exaggerated. Advancing the mill head to compensate for wear is an adjustment. On a numerically controlled milling machine, the programming is complicated by the need to track multiple adjustments that are necessary for complex parts.

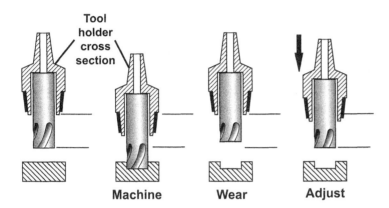

Machine   **Wear**   **Adjust**

FIGURE 5-1

Traditional manufacturing controls variation through a sequence of adjustments such as the one illustrated above, where the mill head is "adjusted" to compensate for tool wear.

The timing of adjustments like the one just described are typically determined using SPC. The depth of the groove is measured periodically and plotted on a control chart. When the process approaches an "out of control" condition based on a variety of rules, the mill head will be adjusted downward or the milling tool will be replaced.

Each milling tool has a slightly different length, and tools are not placed in the tool holder in exactly the same axial position every time. As a result, when the milling tool is replaced, the relationship between the milling tool tip, the mill head, and the workpiece are unknown. Consequently, the operator must spend time adjusting the fixtures and the tools to reestablish the proper relationship between tool tip, mill, fixture, and workpiece.

State-of-the-Art Adjustments

A modern approach to controlling variation is based on automated adjustments. Automation can be used to:

- Improve and eliminate errors in data collection,
- Reduce the delay between data collection and the adjustment using feedback control techniques, and
- Minimize errors in the adjustments.

Consequently, automation is frequently viewed as a key to achieving less variation. However, automating adjustments often just speeds up processes that are fundamentally inefficient.

SETTING TOOL POSITIONS

Variation can be controlled using a different approach developed as a key element of SMED (Shingo 1985). The milling tool can be spring-loaded into the tool holder. Periodically, between machining cycles, the tool holder and tool are removed from the milling machine and placed in a fixture. The grip on the mill tool is released, allowing the spring to push the tool forward to a fixed precision stop; then the grip on the tool is retightened, setting precisely the relationship between the tool tip and tool holder mounting points, as shown in Figure 5-2. Now, every time the tool holder is placed back on the milling machine after these setting operations, the tip of the tool is always in precisely the same position relative to the mill head. Thus, the operator can begin machining immediately without any adjustment of the mill head position. Having eliminated adjustments, programming for numerical control is also much easier because there is no need to track and correct for adjustments. When tools or fixtures are replaced, the same precision alignment is maintained without the need for adjusting the mill head for wear or changes in setups.

FIGURE 5-2

To change a mill tool position from an adjustment to a setting, a spring is put behind the tool. At regular intervals, the tool holder is taken off the machine and the tool grip released. The spring forces the tool to a fixed precision stop, setting the position of the tool tip relative to the tool holder.

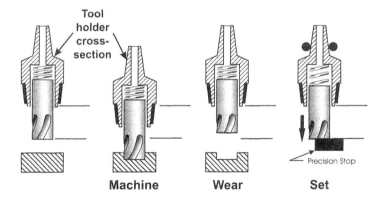

Having converted adjustments to settings, SPC can be eliminated. Trials with a few tools can be used to characterize how rapidly the mill tool wears for the particular task and how long it will last. A simple counter is then used with mistake-proofing to assure that the mill tool position is set at the proper interval, and that the tool is replaced long before dimensional tolerances are exceeded. A sensor is used to detect unexpected tool failure.

FIXTURE SETUP USING ADJUSTMENTS

Changing fixtures that hold workpieces on the mill is a substantially more complex operation than changing a milling tool. Most of the setup time during fixture changes is spent reestablishing the correct relationship between the fixture and the production equipment. Accurate fixture changes traditionally require substantial skill and experience. The traditional process is also prone to mistakes because of the complexity of the task.

Figure 5-3 shows a simplified, two-dimensional view of a fixture change as viewed from the ceiling looking downward on the mill bed. The top view illustrates the first L-shaped fixture that will be removed. When the new fixture is placed on the mill, as shown in the second view, the fixture is not square with the bed or directions of travel. Adjustments square the fixture with the bed and align the origin of the mill head (illustrated by the circle) with the origin of the fixture (illustrated by the cross).

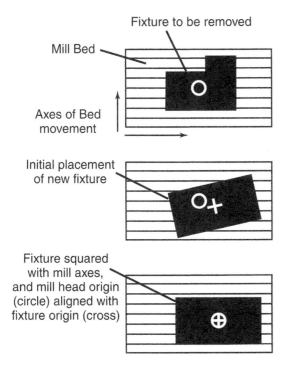

Mill Bed

Fixture to be removed

Axes of Bed movement

Initial placement of new fixture

Fixture squared with mill axes, and mill head origin (circle) aligned with fixture origin (cross)

FIGURE 5-3

Three views of a traditional fixture change out on a mill bed or way. All three views look down from the ceiling toward the mill bed. When the first fixture is removed, considerable time is spent aligning the new fixture with the travel of the bed. These adjustments are time consuming and error prone.

The bed of a typical milling machine can move in three basic directions: up and down, right and left, and away from or toward the operator. For flexibility, the bed is flat with T-slots running the width of the bed. Fixtures are held in place on the bed by fasteners that fit in the T-slots. Because the bed is flat and without distinct locating features, the location of every fixture placed on the bed is random. Since the bed is not perfectly flat, the random location of the fixture can also cause variations in the vertical level and position of the fixture.

As the machinist aligns one axis of the fixture with an axis of mill travel, the adjustment may move an orthogonal axis out of alignment. Just loosening or tightening a fastener can shift the position and alignment of the fixture. After the proper alignment with the horizontal axes of the mill is achieved, the origin of the mill head must be adjusted to match the origin of the fixture. For precision parts, the accuracy of the alignment must be within 0.0001 inches in every direction! On complex parts it can take up to two weeks to setup a fixture, complete the adjustments, and change the tools.

FIXTURE SETUP USING SETTINGS

Fortunately, adjustments during fixture changes can be virtually eliminated. For a mill, a guide bar must first be permanently attached to the far side of the mill bed where it does not interfere with the operation of the mill. This bar is accurately aligned with the mill axes and has a V-shaped extension. *Every* fixture placed on the mill has a base plate with a V-notch that matches this extension on the guide bar.

A simplified, two-dimensional illustration of the fixture change-out using settings is shown in Figure 5-4. In this figure, the same top-down view of the mill bed is used as employed in the previous example. The top view shows the fixture to be removed on a standard fixture base plate. After the first fixture is removed, a new fixture, also attached to a standard base plate, is set on the mill bed. The machinist simply slides the fixture and base plate until the base plate makes contact with two points on the guide, and then fastens the fixture in this position as shown in the bottom view. The base plate can only make contact with both points on the guide when the V-notch is properly centered on the guide bar. Furthermore, the V-shaped notch and matching extension on the guide bar help to move the base plate into the proper position during the setup. With two points in contact with the guide, the fixture is precisely aligned with the mill.

Using this technique, fixtures can be repeatedly positioned within 0.0001 inches without any adjustments. Because the fixture sets in precisely the same location every time it is placed on the mill, variations in the vertical level of the fixture are eliminated. Equally as important, the origin of the mill head and the fixture are aligned as soon as the fixture is set in place. The machinist never needs to adjust the mill head origin to align with any fixture!

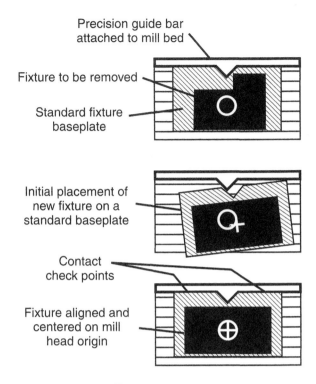

Precision guide bar attached to mill bed

Fixture to be removed

Standard fixture baseplate

Initial placement of new fixture on a standard baseplate

Contact check points

Fixture aligned and centered on mill head origin

FIGURE 5-4

The positioning of a fixture on the mill can be changed from an adjustment to a setting. The V-notch guides the new fixture into the same position each time it is placed on the mill. When the fixture makes contact with two points on the alignment bar, it is accurately positioned and machining can begin almost immediately. All three views look down from the ceiling toward the mill bed.

SETTINGS IN PROCESS CONTROL

Although the concept of settings has been illustrated for a fabrication process, it can generally be used in a wide range of fabrication, assembly, and process-execution activities. One process application is injection molding. Injection molds must be warm enough to allow the plastic to flow smoothly into the mold, but cool enough to let the plastic solidify at the conclusion of the mold-filling process. Proper mold temperatures must be controlled and stabilized during production. Typically this cannot be achieved until a continuous production rate and constant cycle time are reached.

In the traditional approach, molds are stored at room temperature. They must be accurately positioned to function properly, traditionally requiring many adjustments. The cool mold temperature allows the operator to safely touch the mold—an essential part of traditional adjustments. After installation on the injection-molding machine, heating and cooling lines are connected and a controller adjusts them until the operational temperature is reached. Even with heating, the massive molds generally have undesirable temperature gradients. As a consequence, hundreds of parts generally are scrapped before the injection process is running smoothly. Setups using this process can typically take four to eight hours or more (Figure 5-5).

FIGURE 5-5

Traditionally, injection molds are heated (an adjustment) after insertion on the molding machine. By keeping the molds stored at operating temperatures and quickly installing them hot, the temperature is "set" rather than adjusted, saving time and eliminating scrap.

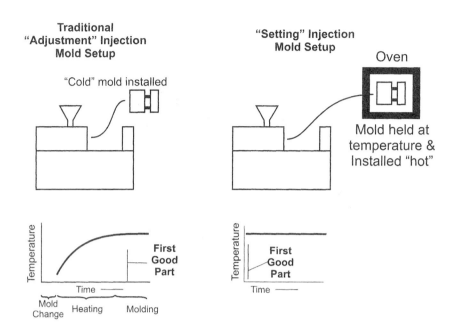

In contrast to this approach, molds that are in storage can be placed in an oven at a set temperature. Typically, waste energy from the plant can be used to keep the molds warm. Using settings rather than adjustments, the mold can be positioned precisely on the injection-molding machine without the operator having to touch the hot mold. Without the ability to position the mold using settings, it would be nearly impossible to install the mold on the machine while it is hot. Furthermore, traditional adjustment delays would allow the mold to cool to the point that there would be little value in keeping the mold preheated prior to installation on the injection molding machine.

The heating and cooling line connections are attached next. With the mold at a uniform temperature, the molding process can begin immediately. Typically, only a few parts are scrapped during startup transients and production is back on-line within a few minutes.

Shingo's book on SMED contains dozens of examples illustrating the techniques of converting adjustments to settings (Shingo 1985).

BENEFITS OF CONTROLLING VARIATION WITH SETTINGS

IMPROVED PRODUCTIVITY AND FLEXIBILITY

Techniques that control variation by settings have many major advantages over those that control variation with adjustments, one of the most significant being that they are key enablers in dramatically reducing the setup times of fixtures. Some of the most difficult die set changes in the automotive industry are the multi-ton dies used to stamp auto body parts. The top and bottom die must be aligned precisely, or the sheet metal will not be smooth. Generally, each body part must be struck three to five times by different dies to form a part. As a result, multiple die sets must be changed to switch the production from one sheet metal part to another. NUMMI completes all die changes in 20 minutes, according to conversations with the plant manager. Using traditional methods, such die set changes require one to two weeks.

In conjunction with other SMED techniques (Shingo 1985), *setup times and fixture changes using settings take about one-fortieth to one-hundredth the time of adjustment-based setups*. Such dramatic improvements seem incredible, but in their first attempt to implement SMED, a Department of Energy pressure vessel manufacturer reduced a setup time from over four hours to roughly six minutes. Results like these are typical, and they dramatically impact production flexibility. For example, NUMMI produces Toyota Corollas and Chevrolet Prisms on the same production line, rapidly switching back and forth from one product to the other. Other manufacturers in Japan switch from producing one washing machine product to another in as little as eight minutes. Such short product changeover times dramatically reduce the cost-effective size of batches, allowing factories to be more responsive to the market. Equally as important, the rapid die and fixture changes make it possible to do prototype development on production equipment.

In industries that have small production quantities, setup changes are frequent. As a result, production equipment actually may be idle most of the time to accommodate die changes. In such industries, settings can improve productivity even more dramatically than occurs in industries with large production volumes.

STANDARDIZATION AND SIMPLIFICATION

Building all fixtures for a production machine on standard base plates simplifies the fixture design; thus, fixtures can be completed more quickly. In addition, virtually all of the fixtures that are placed on any individual production machine easily can be designed to have common tie-down locations to the production equipment. Since many of the setup operations are then similar, it is easier to mistake-proof them.

With settings, it is often possible to make superior products on less sophisticated production equipment than would be required using adjustments. Reflecting this difference, when one engineer from Motorola spent a year in Japan in an exchange with Sharp Electronics, he commented that the Sharp equipment making competing products was "disappointingly unsophisticated" (Gebala 1996). This type of response is not uncommon and is consistent with production planning that focuses on "smaller, slower, and cheaper equipment" (Hirano 1994, 218). The less sophisticated production equipment is less expensive to buy and can be procured more quickly, improving profit margins and reducing the time to market.

In a production environment there will always be a need for skilled workers. The setup operations, however, can become so simple with settings that the work can be done by individuals with less skill or training than required when adjustments are needed. In this environment, workers have the opportunity of learning and performing a wider variety of jobs, reducing boredom. Workers can also be trained more quickly because they can focus on the operation of the equipment rather than the setup. Thus, settings increase the flexibility and adaptability of the workforce.

IMPACT OF SETTINGS ON QUALITY

In the traditional approach to controlling variation, a measurement is made. A decision regarding the appropriate actions is determined based on the measurement, and if required, an adjustment is made. Note in this process that action depends upon a measurement that must always be made downstream of the process execution. As a result, regardless of how much improvement is made in adjustment cycles or how extensively the adjustments are automated, there will always be instances when this approach results in defects. Furthermore, the ability to catch mistakes and correct process adjustments always depends on measurements that are error prone. In contrast, settings control variation upstream of the process execution rather than downstream. In most cases, settings eliminate the need for measurements. Thus, settings are superior to adjustments in the same way that source inspection is superior to SPC, contributing to defect prevention rather than defect detection.

Settings dramatically reduce the need to collect, record, and analyze quality data on the production floor. Because settings are almost always faster and easier to perform than adjustments, they can be completed more frequently with less disruption to the production process. As a result, settings almost always lead to a tighter control of variation than can be achieved by adjustments!

QCV—A KEY MISTAKE-PROOFING TOOL

Many years ago, at the point when Toyota had just reached a 2.5 percent defect rate, engineers from Japan visited a German factory. After proudly explaining their accomplishments, they were shocked when the German officials told them that they had achieved a defect rate roughly eight times lower—0.3 percent. They studied what this German company was doing to reduce defects and discovered that they had a second individual check each setup before they started production with that setup (Shingo 1986, 50–51).

This has a number of profound implications. First, it suggests that a large fraction of production defects can be traced to setup errors! Consequently, simplifying the product design and mistake-proofing the product and production processes is not enough to achieve world-class quality. As has been previously demonstrated, simplifying the task eliminates opportunities for mistakes. Settings in conjunction with other SMED techniques will cut die change times forty-fold; in other words, a setup using settings can be completed in 2.5 percent of the time required to complete the same setup using adjustments. *The previous correlations between defect rates and complexity demonstrate that this reduction in setup time eliminates more than 97 percent of setup mistake opportunities.* The major quality contribution of settings compared to adjustments may be reduced mistake rates rather than improved control of variation.

Settings control variation, as opposed to adjustments, which strive to continually compensate for variation. Consequently, settings are the only means of achieving quality by control of variation (QCV).

Settings can eliminate most errors in misreading gages, recording data, and interpreting data. In changing dies, it is easy to forget to check a cross axis alignment that may have been disturbed in subsequent adjustments. Settings avoid the need for these repetitive cross checks and prevent the omission errors that commonly occur in these circumstances. Tasks are easier and can be remembered more readily; thus reducing the likelihood of an omitted operation. In short, converting adjustments to settings does more than control variation; it is one of the very best mistake-proofing tools.

FUTURE OPPORTUNITY FOR DEVELOPING A QCV METHODOLOGY

Like mistake-proofing, the ability to convert adjustments to settings is a skill that improves with experience. Unlike mistake-proofing, the number and variety of examples describing the conversion from adjustments to settings that have been published are quite limited. If an effort were made to collect and classify setting examples, it might be possible to develop a setting methodology that would be particularly helpful to novices.

Experience suggests that more than 80 percent of traditional adjustments in any process can be replaced with settings, as described in this chapter. Thus, in conjunction with reducing complexity and mistake-proofing, settings nearly eliminate the need for dependence upon traditional quality control methods. Each of the tools introduced to this point requires less effort and documentation than traditional quality control while delivering superior results and improved productivity. However, knowing that changes are needed, what must be done to make the changes, and how to change is not a sufficient motivation to make changes. The greatest barriers to implementing these new quality tools are cultural. In the following chapter, the cultural changes essential to implementing mistake-proofing are enumerated.

CHAPTER 6

THE CULTURAL ELEMENTS OF WORLD-CLASS QUALITY

PRESSURE

You walk into the office and you can feel the tension. No one looks you in the eye, and everyone is busy without any of the normal business chatter. When you reach your desk, your secretary tells you that the city manager wants to see you as soon as you arrive. When you ask what this is all about, she says, "I can't say."

HEAT

When you reach the city manager's office, his back is to the door. You can't hear what he is saying on the phone, but you can tell he's angry. When he sees you, he hangs up abruptly and, jabbing his finger toward a chair, commands you to sit down.

FIRE

"Someone screwed up on the Sequoia Park bid. Instead of the needed 10,000 feet of pipe, the contract called for 1,000 feet by mistake. The contractor is charging us double the price for the 9,000 feet not listed in the contract and the legal department says we have to pay. That's $1,000,000 over the amount we should have paid for this work. Find the person who made the mistake and fire them—or your job is on the line, mister."

ELIMINATING MISTAKES—A CULTURAL CHANGE

A comprehensive understanding of quality control principles and management commitment to improvement are not sufficient to evoke a dramatic defect reduction. The reason that most quality efforts fail is that quality improvement is a cultural change more than a change in technology. True cultural changes require more than catchy slogans or outward lip service promoting a stated goal.

In practice, it seems as though we want to have quality without really changing how the organization functions. Achieving change in organizational behavior often requires a restructuring of the organization's fundamental goals and values. This is difficult at best and virtually impossible if the leadership is not solidly behind the changes or is unwilling to accept the associated consequences of quality improvement.

In the following sections, the key cultural barriers to mistake-proofing will be identified, along with the actions that help to break them down.

I Am Responsible for Quality

We each recognize mistakes and product defects that we receive from upstream workers. For example, production floor workers often identify errors in drawings and production instructions that engineers and industrial designers overlook. Such problems can be very difficult to work around or correct. In addition, defective parts from upstream sources are frequently identified by the problems they cause in assembly. However, we rarely perceive the frequency of our own errors because we feel that we are detecting and correcting most of our own mistakes, not realizing that many of our errors escape our work area undetected.

Because of such problems, production workers blame poor quality on design flaws, designers view quality as a production problem, and managers wonder why the progress in quality improvement is so slow. Each individual tends to view quality as somebody else's problem.

To make effective changes in conformance quality, each person must first recognize his or her role in eliminating defects and then measure up to his or her responsibility in preventing defects.

The Factory Floor Worker's Role in Conformance Quality

Factory floor workers are key players. They can help every individual recognize his or her responsibility for quality. They are the eyes of the organization, often being the first to see clearly excessive variation, mistakes in drawings and specifications, mistakes in upstream manufacturing, and operations that are unnecessarily complex. Thus, to bring quality awareness home, the role of the factory floor worker needs to be elevated.

Factory floor workers want to do their best. They want to produce a quality product. However, they are often viewed as the most expendable or interchangeable members of the organization. Consequently, under the pressure of production schedules many of the quality breaches that they observe are never addressed by engineers or management. Furthermore, they are often unable to get necessary upstream problems corrected because they lack sufficient influence in the organization.

One of the key opportunities for correcting individual indifference to quality problems and raising everyone's awareness of their own contributions to quality improvement is to make factory floor workers team leaders on quality improvement efforts. Just as the factory is accountable to designers for meeting design intent, everyone in the organization needs to be accountable to factory floor workers for meeting quality standards. This change has the added value of building the confidence and esteem of those workers.

In order for factory floor workers to become leaders on quality improvement teams, appropriate preparation and guidance are required. Naturally, they will need to understand quality principles to fill this role. In this way, they will be able to identify and implement the right quality control methods in their own work areas. With training and experience they will be able to articulate and communicate their quality needs more clearly to engineers, suppliers, and upstream work areas.

For factory floor workers to be effective quality team leaders, management must provide support that holds the organization accountable to the quality concerns of the factory floor.

The Engineer's Role in Conformance Quality

As engineers become accountable to factory floor workers for quality, their awareness of design errors that create problems on the factory floor increases. With a greater appreciation for their role in quality, they are likely to work more diligently to detect or prevent concept and drawing errors at their source. In addition, a better understanding of factory floor quality problems helps engineers develop more mistake-proof product concepts and process plans. This in turn can lead to superior specifications for production equipment. More and more problems are thus prevented before they even occur.

Although factory floor workers are the ones to see quality problems, it is the engineers who become the champions of the quality effort. With experience they begin to anticipate and prevent most opportunities for mistakes and defects before production starts. The technical skills of engineers also can be used to design quality control devices. In addition, engineers may have a more direct line to upper management that facilitates the allocation of resources for quality improvement.

Management's Role in Conformance Quality

Management is at the heart of the quality improvement effort. Managers teach best by example—by mistake-proofing their own work and striving to reduce the complexity of communication and information flow. They continually teach and demonstrate that zero defects are possible. They also play a key role in selecting the quality tools and techniques that will be used, as well as the champions that will implement required changes.

Management holds the organization accountable for tracking quality performance and achieving results, and furthermore sustains this focus. Far too often, quality efforts are merely slogan campaigns with little or no lasting improvement. Management must instill in the organization that quality is in the product, not the documentation. Rather than promoting extensive documentation of poor quality, management demonstrates that dramatic defect reductions can be achieved while reducing the amount of paperwork and quality tracking.

Management also has the responsibility to define and direct quality training. Caution, however, must be exercised in setting quality training requirements and goals. Many organizations have measured the success of their conformance quality effort by tracking the number of people trained or the number of quality teams formed, only to discover that high performance relative to these metrics has not contributed to any measurable improvement in product quality. Keeping the focus on results can eliminate unnecessary or excessive training expenses.

TRADITIONALLY, MISTAKES ARE PUNISHED OR REWARDED

The way that most managers deal with mistakes reveals the impact of culture on quality. The traditional view in the United States is that mistakes are the result of negligence and that negligence should be punished. Indeed, our entire legal system is based on this premise. If an individual makes a mistake, he or she is likely to be punished, particularly if the mistake is a costly one. Even when an individual is not dismissed, he or she is likely to get a lecture. When we know that this will be the outcome, we are likely to conceal rather than reveal mistakes. Furthermore, we are likely to conceal the mistakes of coworkers because we don't want to get them in trouble. The consequence of this cultural attitude is that the role of mistakes is never fully appreciated, and the same mistakes are repeated over and over.

Reflecting this attitude toward mistakes, a vice president at one company recently issued a directive that anyone injured on the job would be immediately fired, because such an injury clearly demonstrated that the worker was not doing the task safely according to company policy. Naturally, under these circumstances individuals would conceal minor injuries so that they would not lose their jobs. Outwardly it may appear that the directive reduces injuries, because fewer are being reported; but secretly the injury rate may actually be increasing because problems are not communicated and similar mishaps are not prevented.

Perhaps a more serious problem is that mistakes are sometimes rewarded. In one instance reported to the author, a worker on an assembly was installing rivets with a defective rivet tool. Even though the operator knew the tool was defective, the individual did not stop to fix the riveting machine because fixing it would have reduced the number of times the rivet tool trigger could be pressed, which was the basis for determining how the worker would be paid. In this case, the worker was being paid more for repeating known errors than for intervening to prevent mistakes.

Creating a Mistake-Prevention Environment

To eliminate mistakes, the organization's attitude toward them must change. This is difficult, because punishing and rewarding mistakes is common in our culture. The following key actions can be taken to change the culture.

- *Stop punishing or rewarding unintentional mistakes.* No one must feel threatened when revealing mistakes if they are to be eliminated. Management sets the example by not punishing subordinates for unintentional mistakes, and holds all subordinates to the same standard. This must be true even when the consequence is serious—a mistake is still a mistake. Each new policy should be reviewed to assure that it doesn't establish punishment for mistakes, but rather encourages prevention of repeated errors. Similarly, policies should be reviewed to assure they are not rewarding mistakes.
- *Provide small rewards for mistake-proofing suggestions.* To change the focus from mistake punishment to mistake prevention, provide a small reward, perhaps in the range of $25 to $50, for each mistake-proofing suggestion. Even the person who makes an unintentional mistake should be eligible for such rewards.
- *Implement mistake-proofing.* Most suggestion programs fail because no one acts on the suggestions. Let the team closest to the problem determine if the suggested mistake-proofing is likely to work and whether or not it is cost effective. Implement most suggestions.
- *Reward successful mistake-proofing.* When mistake-proofing has been implemented, provide a small reward for those methods that have proven to be real cost savers. The rewards for successful

implementation should be larger than for suggestions, but generally need not exceed a few hundred dollars, even when the cost savings are very large.

- *Put pressure on management to teach and apply mistake-proofing.* When mistakes occur, recognize that the most likely problem is that management has not provided adequate training or support for implementing mistake-proofing. Pressure middle-level management and factory floor supervisors to teach and apply mistake-proofing.

NOTHING CAN BE DONE

In major hospitals, doctors usually meet on a weekly basis to discuss mistakes that have occurred in the medical practice. These sessions are called Morbidity and Mortality Conferences. Many of the mistakes reviewed in these sessions have resulted in serious injury or death to patients. One landmark study published in 1991 estimated that, nationwide, 120,000 patients die each year at least partly as a result of errors in care (Guwande 1999, 44). These sessions help doctors to become aware of mistakes, with the goal of preventing the repetition of the errors in the future. In spite of these meetings, error rates are often unchanged because needed action is not taken.

In one example described in *The New Yorker* (Guwande 1999, 51–53), errors in the administration of anesthesia were known for several decades to be a leading cause of death during operations. Between the 1960s and 1980s, the death rate attributed to anesthesia errors stabilized at one to two per 10,000 operations. If a knob was inadvertently turned the wrong way, a patient could have his oxygen supply cut to the point it would damage the brain, or the patient could be given too much medication, shutting down the heart. Compounding these problems, manufacturers each set their own standards. Turning a knob clockwise on one controller increased the supply of anesthetics, but decreased the supply of anesthetics on equipment produced by another manufacturer.

Although many recognized the frequency of anesthesia administration mistakes and the resulting human suffering, dramatic reductions in these errors did not result from the physicians' weekly review of the mistakes until a champion and leader at a national level, Ellison (Jeep) Pierce, insisted that changes must and could be made. His leadership defined consistent standards for equipment manufacturers and introduced mistake-proofing type elements to the administration of anesthesia. As a result of this work, deaths from the administration of anesthesia dropped over twentyfold in the space of a decade.

The key point is that recognizing the frequency and consequences of mistakes is different than acting to prevent them. Too often we recognize the scope of the quality problems, but have the sense that we can to nothing to change the problem.

Act Now*!*

When defects or mistakes are discovered, many alternative courses of action exist, including: ignoring the problem, discussing the problem, identifying the root cause, implementing administrative controls, or increasing inspection. None of these actions change the fundamental error and defect rates. Organizations that have eliminated defects place the emphasis on acting swiftly to block repetition of the problem, preferably with mistake-proofing methods. If there is a 60 percent probability that a solution might solve the problem and it can be done inexpensively, implement it immediately.

The distinction between the traditional and "act now" approach is easiest to recognize in factory startups. Traditionally, in schedule-driven factories, the urgent startup schedule dominates behavior, and quality problems are passed along with the attitude that they'll be fixed when time allows. In such factories production is commonly behind schedule, and quality does not return to a low steady state level for a year or more after the production startup.

Shigeo Shingo reversed the priority in the factory startup, placing the rapid implementation of controls that prevent repetition of observed quality problems as a higher priority than meeting the production schedule. The results were dramatic. In less than one week, the factory was meeting the production goals not expected until the end of the month. In addition, the steady state product quality goals were met within a month.

Kaizen shops can be particularly effective in facilitating rapid response. These shops fabricate and modify simple devices that mistake-proof a process more quickly than can be accomplished by any other method.

CULTURAL VALUES

Just as punishing mistakes blocks the effective implementation of mistake-proofing, incorrect quality goals based on cultural values lead to inefficient and ineffective quality improvement efforts.

To illustrate, consider a company that is expending extensive resources to develop on-machine inspection by combining coordinate measurement machines with production equipment like lathes and mills. The consequences of such an approach can be anticipated. First, this type of production equipment will be more complex and more expensive, and it will take longer to procure. Preparing to make a part on the equipment will also take longer because inspection tool paths must be planned sequentially with machining tool paths. The part processing time on the equipment is likely to increase because of the additional inspection, resulting in lower productivity. Furthermore, the combined inspection and machining task is more complex than either alone, suggesting that mistakes for this type of equipment are likely to be more frequent than those resulting from traditional machining.

In fact, the first two batches processed on this type of equipment were scrapped because operators first used the wrong drawing revision to program the part (a more likely problem when production preparation takes longer) and then used an incorrect tool.

Although team members on this project are familiar with mistake-proofing, they strongly resist using it. The organization has a strong commitment to research, and basic mistake-proofing measures—which have proven to be both inexpensive and highly effective—are viewed as being too simple and unworthy of publication as research in technical journals. In this case, the cultural values of technology and research are a higher priority than the goal of eliminating defects as efficiently as possible.

Establish Clear and Consistent Goals

Values in organizations are most productive when: a) everyone shares a clear vision of where the company is headed; b) leaders focus on results rather than the means; and c) priorities are consistently interpreted.

Begin by establishing a quality vision that is daring but that the team still believes is achievable. A vision of "zero defects" often fails to motivate team members because many of them feel they have tried to reach this goal already—and failed—using other approaches. A better goal may be to cut the average number of product defects in half in each product cycle, or cut the defect rate in half each year of production. While pushing the team to perform, such goals are realistic enough that they can't be easily dismissed or ignored.

When focusing on results, remember that quality is in the product, not in the documentation of poor quality. Never confuse results with "gee-whiz" technology. The most elegant solution is the one that is simple, effective, inexpensive, and can be implemented most quickly.

Give the design and development teams a clear list of priorities, and then follow those priorities when faced with decisions. If you tell the team that low defect rates are a priority, and then make decisions that constantly place "lower priorities" ahead of quality, the organization can become confused and dysfunctional.

ADDING VALUE BY FINDING DEFECTS

Each day, pharmacists in large hospitals produce a list of the prescription errors made by doctors that they have caught and prevented. Because of this approach to defect tracking, pharmacists perceive that catching these mistakes and preventing patient injury is a key element of the value they add to the process. Thus, the longer the list, the more successful they feel they have been in performing their work. If errors in prescriptions as received from doctors could somehow be eliminated upstream of the pharmacy, pharmacists might fear that their jobs could be performed by less qualified individuals. Quality inspectors in production environments who catch product defects, like the pharmacist, also believe that they contribute value to the organization by catching defects. Because of these perspectives, such professionals are likely to resist changes that appear to reduce their value to the organization.

The flaw in this logic is that the human ability to detect defects after they enter the product stream is imperfect. Consequently, the longer the list of detected defects, the more likely it is that an undetected defect has slipped through the inspection process. Hence, long lists of detected mistakes or defects are actually evidence that the product quality is very poor.

Define New Measures of Personal Value

As long as an individual's perceived worth to the organization is linked to catching defects and preventing near misses, mistakes will never be eliminated and mistake-proofing will not succeed. The key to making a change in this situation is to redefine the measures of performance and educate team members on opportunities for increasing their value to the organization.

For the pharmacist and the quality inspector, the focus must shift from the number of errors or defects detected to reducing the number of errors passed down to the customer or the next stage in the production process. It must be clear that the most valuable employees are not the ones with the most saves, but those with the fewest defects or mistakes that are passed downstream through their process. This change can help shift the focus from finding mistakes to preventing them.

Education is also important in changing cultural values such as these. Team members need to learn that there is little value in performing a task that can be completed more efficiently with fewer errors by moving the control closer to the source.

MISTAKE-PROOFING NEEDS TO BE HUMANE

When seatbelts were introduced, many cars came equipped with alarms that would sound until there was some indication that the seat belts were fastened. In spite of the fact that everyone knew that seatbelts saved lives, some people didn't want to wear them; they felt seatbelts were too constraining or uncomfortable. Other drivers who were constantly getting in and out of their vehicles felt that they were too inconvenient. Still others did not like having their car telling them what to do. People would pull out one strap until the alarm shut off, then tuck it under their leg to hold the belt in an extended position while driving without fastening it. Many individuals simply cut the wiring to the seat belt sensors.

In these cases, seatbelt mistake-proofing was circumvented. So many people were irritated by the alarms that manufacturers began using quieter alarms that turned off after a brief period even if the seatbelts were unfastened. On current models a small light may remain lit if seatbelts aren't fastened.

This seatbelt example illustrates the natural aversion to some types of mistake-proofing. Improper implementation will aggravate and alienate the workers whose support of mistake-proofing is so essential to its success. Alarms can be a particular problem in mistake-proofing. Wherever practical, use shutdown or control techniques instead of alarms, which tend to annoy workers. Alarms can be used to attract helpers for time urgent tasks, but may also send a message that one particular worker is not doing his or her job well—a message that can be embarrassing and intimidating. Where alarms are essential they should be adequate to attract attention without grating on the nerves. Alarms that are occurring frequently may indicate significant problems upstream that must be corrected. Get input from the workers who must live with the devices every day, and implement their suggestions whenever possible. Mistake-proofing should also complement and follow ergonomic and safety considerations.

MISTAKE-PROOFING IS AN ONGOING EFFORT

One company preparing assembly kits for automobile companies achieved dramatic improvement with mistake-proofing for the first two years. Then they found that the defect rate leveled off. Puzzled by the change, management began talking to the workers on the factory floor. They found that some workers felt that they had "learned" everything they needed to know from mistake-proofing and that it was no longer necessary to use the mistake-proofing devices, so they began to turn them off. When management showed the workers the results of their performance with and without the devices, the workers were quite surprised at how much difference the devices actually made. As a consequence, they became more committed to using the devices and defect rates continued to decline.

Because we humans are fallible, we will never reach the point where we have learned enough from mistake-proofing that we can stop doing it. Individuals become committed to mistake-proofing when they recognize that it really makes a difference. Thus, a continuous dialog regarding performance relative to mistake-proofing is essential. Everyone wants to produce defect-free products, and when people really understand that these devices make a difference they employ them enthusiastically.

SUCCESS BREEDS RESISTANCE

It seems that the successful deployment of mistake-proofing or complexity-reduction methods should lead to increased use and popularity of the methods. Unfortunately, success is often the reason that improvements are resisted.

To understand such resistance, we must first understand the consequences of improvement. What would happen if defects dropped from a few thousand parts per million to virtually zero in a one- or two-year period? There would be less scrap and fewer parts would need to be made. Rework would be eliminated. Without defects in the production stream, the average time to complete a task would drop, resulting in higher productivity. There might be a dramatic drop in customer service demands and warranty work. In most organizations this means that someone will lose their job. Other things remaining equal, this level of quality improvement would typically result in a 6 to 15 percent reduction in the workforce!

Everyone wants to produce a quality product, but people may be afraid to make improvements if their job or a friend's job might get eliminated. The bottom line is that job security is more valued than quality improvement.

Real improvements in quality are frequently accompanied by additional changes in the organization. Quality teams often improve communication between work areas. Some managers view this as a threat to their power and control. Similarly, union leaders may feel threatened by improvements in the working relationship between management and employees that results from improved quality.

As these examples illustrate, many individuals find substantive quality improvements threatening, resulting in subtle yet powerful resistance to the implementation of quality methods even when the value of those methods is widely recognized.

Overcoming Resistance

Overcoming resistance to quality and productivity improvement is easy: remove the penalties for improvement and replace them with rewards. *The first step in this change is to establish a policy that no one will lose their job or be demoted as the result of quality or productivity improvements.* Naturally, this policy will have value only if it is rigorously and continually followed. To assure this, management must prepare for changes in the organization that result from quality improvement. Some of the ways that job security can be achieved are as follows:

- *Implement quality improvement during expansion.* When product demand is increasing, quality improvements allow output to increase more rapidly than growth in employees. Quality improvements during such periods reduce the pressure on hiring and the cost of company growth. Unfortunately, the external pressure to improve quality and productivity generally is not very strong when business is booming.
- *Increase market share.* When defects drop, the workforce can remain stable if the company gains in market share. Management should explore opportunities to capture and maintain increased market share to utilize the improvements in productivity without laying off employees.
- *Expand into new markets.* In cases where it may be difficult to increase market share, the company can explore opportunities for developing new markets. At NUMMI, when productivity improved, the company added a truck line to its existing auto production line, with a minimal increase in the workforce.
- *Reduce dependency on suppliers.* Companies that are eliminating defects often learn that they can perform some tasks more efficiently and with fewer defects than existing suppliers can. Companies may explore manufacturing parts previously purchased from suppliers. NUMMI, for example, began to make rather than buy tires as the production line became more efficient.
- *Reward success.* Those team members who excel in mistake-proofing efforts should be designated as change agents who teach, guide, and implement quality improvements throughout the

organization. Give these individuals increased status within the organization.

No Excuses!

Lawrence D. Miles identified a variety of excuses used for resisting the implementation of value analysis/value engineering at the General Electric Corporation (Hirano 1994, 24–25). These excuses are basically the same ones frequently expressed by those who resist quality improvement efforts. They include:

- Mistake-proofing is a nice idea, but it will not work in our situation.
- We do not like being told what to do by outsiders.
- We're the best judge of that kind of thing.
- It's no good, we tried that 20 years ago.
- Costs cannot be reduced any further.
- If you reduce costs, quality will suffer.
- We always do that anyway.
- Everything is going good—why change it?

The first four excuses imply that employees know their work better than outsiders do, and reflect a misplaced pride in their work. The next two excuses, based on cost arguments, may reflect a fear of job security if quality is improved. Those that claim they "always do that anyway" may believe that the token mistake-proofing efforts of the past are sufficient. Finally, those that are satisfied with how things are going may have difficulty perceiving the enormous cost and waste resulting from "pretty good" quality.

Many of these excuses have their roots in a bad past experience. Many workers have been involved in quality initiatives or other improvement efforts that just have not made a difference. One study showed that 60 percent of the companies implementing total quality management (TQM) realized less then a 10 percent reduction in defect rates (Shaffer 1992, 80–89). Naturally, mistake-proofing efforts can fail, and will without a sustained effort. Rather than a slogan for a season, mistake-proofing must become a regular part of every activity.

One technique for addressing excuses is to post in every conference room and meeting place a list of positive statements that defuse excuses and address the way individuals are to respond to specific issues. This list can include statements such as:

- Act *now*!
- Focus energy on solving problems, not on reasons it can't be done.
- If it has a 60 percent chance of working, do it.
- No excuses.
- Spend more time doing than thinking.

When an excuse is raised, simply point to the correct attitude that the company is trying to instill.

Negative attitudes towards mistake-proofing must be overcome. This process begins by raising awareness. In most cases, workers, designers, and managers simply do not appreciate how important mistakes are in causing defects and degrading quality and productivity. Furthermore, even when they appreciate the role of mistakes, most people feel relatively helpless in controlling them. In general, this sense of helplessness is a consequence of not understanding the techniques that control mistakes effectively. Thus, there must be a continuing effort to raise the awareness of the role of mistakes and mistake-proofing methods with numerous examples of results that have been achieved through use of the methodology.

The second step on the road to world-class quality is to strive aggressively for dramatic improvement in production efficiency by eliminating waste at every turn. It may seem unusual to pursue efficiency as a means of improving quality, but this is an essential element of achieving mistake-proofing. We would like to think that quality improvement is motivated by a desire to satisfy the customer, or by the desire of workers to produce a great product. As noble as these goals may be, they do not drive world-class quality.

When a lot of inventory exists and a bad part is identified, it is easy to grab another part and continue with production. As production becomes efficient, though, inventory in the factory drops. In an efficient factory, if a part is bad there is no spare part available, so the entire production line is shut down until a replacement part can be found. Because bad parts shut down production in efficient manufacturing facilities, everyone becomes more aware of the role of mistakes and the impact of poor quality on production. In efficient factories, this sense of urgency to correct production flow problems is the major driving force behind defect elimination and mistake-proofing.

Once workers realize the extent of the problems caused by mistakes, and understand how to respond to them, active mistake-proofing becomes an attractive, natural solution to the factory team. In this environment, mistake-proofing becomes a natural part of every individual's work.

TOOLS TO GO THE FULL DISTANCE

Each year companies spend millions of dollars to control variation. To reduce defects these companies perform tolerance studies, apply SQC, and conduct many expensive experiments. Although such efforts are essential to achieving low defect rates, these efforts alone will never achieve world-class quality control. In today's competitive environment, controlling mistakes and product complexity are just as important as controlling variation.

Naturally, a hammer would be the wrong tool to select for cutting a board, yet decisions like this happen frequently in the quality arena when individuals only see variation as the enemy.

We have introduced concepts that will help individuals correctly identify the root cause of defects, and the best tools for controlling problems at their source. These concepts and tools will take companies to the highest achievable levels of quality control while minimizing the resources and investment required to reach them.

A clear understanding of product defect sources reveals new opportunities for achieving world-class conformance quality. Understanding the root cause of defects enables selection of the best tools for each particular quality problem. This can lead to an entirely new approach to defining quality strategies.

Most importantly, the greatest opportunities for efficiently eliminating defects can be determined at the earliest stages of product development when changes can be made most easily. In many cases, dramatic reductions in defect rates and improved productivity can be achieved for a fraction of the cost of traditional quality control methods. The ability to define efficient quality improvement strategies represents a breakthrough in the quality technology.

WHAT WILL *YOU* DO?

In this book we have brought together a wide range of world-class quality concepts that have never before been summarized in a single source. We have demonstrated that the very best methods of controlling variation and complexity are each, in reality, different approaches to controlling mistakes—the dominant source of defects in modern production. The best methodologies and control principles for eliminating defects have been briefly outlined. Novel new concepts for simplifying the mistake-proofing process and for comparing and selecting the best mistake-proofing concepts have been presented. Finally, the key elements of cultural change essential for effective implementation of mistake-proofing were defined.

The principles presented herein have proven effective time and again in a wide range of industries and services. It isn't a question of whether or not they will work. The question is: "What will *you* do?" Will you work to change your organization, to achieve the extremely low defect rates that are possible? If so, it is our sincere hope that the concepts we have presented will help you achieve your quest.

APPENDIX A

MISTAKE-PROOFING PRINCIPLES AND EXAMPLES

DEFECTIVE MATERIALS (DM)

The material *entering* a process is defective, or inadequate for the intended function, process, or purpose. Note that the root cause of defective materials may be traced to mistakes or excessive variation in earlier processes. However, in many cases companies may not be able to directly control supply quality, or the process may not be adequately understood to establish better control. In such cases, mistake-proofing may be useful in detecting and removing defective material entering a process.

Principles that Eliminate Defective Materials	Examples
1. Use source inspection of raw stock to identify and eliminate material flaws:	
a. Remove ingot surface blemishes.	DM-1
2. Tag out material use until an evaluation demonstrates it is adequate.	*OO-8*
3. Use interference between fixtures and defective material based on shape or dimensions to:	
a. Prevent setup, or	OO-17, OO-18, WR-17
b. Provide a warning.	
4. Detect defective material (excessive variation, wrong weight, debris, etc.) and:	
a. Remove defective material,	DM-4
b. Shut down a continuous process: (surface "follower" or sensors at feed source), or	DM-2
c. Provide a warning.	DM-7
5. Make defective material unusable or obvious as soon as discovered.	OO-16
a. Mutilate.	
b. Mark or paint.	
6. For materials that may degrade or fail during processing:	
a. Provide continuous performance monitoring.	DM-5
b. Check the condition at regular intervals.	DM-3
7. Use a checklist to verify critical material properties at the source.	DM-6

Defective Material

Process Pressure-forming rivets from wire stock

Problem Seams on finished rivets

Solution Defects caused by blemishes on ingot, control surface finish

Product Rivets

Parts Rivet, wire stock

Stage 1-Fabrication
2-Forming rivets

	Control Function							
	∿	Poka-yoke			Simplify			
State	Adjustment	Setting	Warn	Shutdown	Control	Tools/Eqpt	Process	Product
Complexity								
Prevent Mistakes					X			
Detect Mistakes								
Detect Defects								
Variation								

Description of Problem: Rivets are pressure-formed from wire stock.

Before Improvement

Numerous rivets had seams in them, rendering them defective and unusable. Sorting the rivets visually after pressure-forming did not solve the problem, and some defective parts were always overlooked.

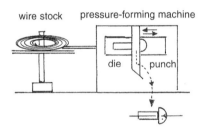

wire stock   pressure-forming machine

die   punch

ingot (300 kg) or more)

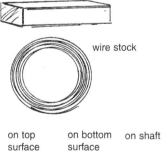

wire stock

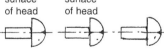

on top   on bottom   on shaft
surface   surface
of head   of head

After Improvement

The cause of the seams was determined to be scratches in the ingots used as raw material for the wire stock. These scratches are not removed completely before the ingots are rolled and drawn, and so turn up as seams in the wire stock.

The acceptance standards for the wire stock were upgraded. Defects are completely eliminated by thorough implementation of acceptance inspections, which allows no acceptance of wire stock with seams. This is a good example of source inspection.

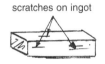

scratches on ingot

wire stock with seams completely removed

wire stock with seams remaining

111

Defective Material

Process	Processing wire stock
Problem	Foreign matter, variations in wire dimensions
Solution	Stopper on wire feeder stops process if out of dimension
Product	
Parts	Wire stock
Stage	1-Fabrication 2-Wire forming

Control Function								
	∿		Poka-yoke			Simplify		
State	Adjustment	Setting	Warn	Shutdown	Control	Tools/Eqpt	Process	Product
Complexity								
Prevent Mistakes				X				
Detect Mistakes								
Detect Defects				X				
Variation								

Description of Problem: Wire stock is sometimes produced with shape or dimensional variations or with foreign matter stuck to the stock. When this defective stock is processed, these variations must be detected to prevent defective products.

Before Improvement
Deposits of foreign matter or variations of the wire stock dimensions made the motor stall when the wire stock entered the processing machine.

After Improvement
If there is any foreign matter, or a shape or dimensional variation on the wire, a stopper on the feed device catches on the wire at that place and moves along with the wire. The machine stops automatically when the stopper strikes a limit switch inside the machine.

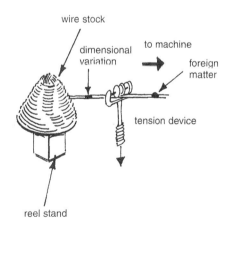

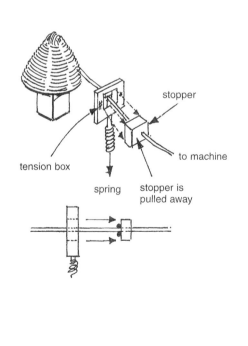

Defective Material, Misadjust, Wrong Part

Process	Machining
Problem	Tools are broken or worn
Solution	Gages measure tool length and diameters
Product	Aircraft engines
Parts	Tool verification gages, various machining tools
Stage	1-Fabrication 2-Machining

	Control Function							
	∿	Poka-yoke				Simplify		
State	Adjustment	Setting	Warn	Shutdown	Control	Tools/Eqpt	Process	Product
Complexity								
Prevent Mistakes								
Detect Mistakes				X				
Detect Defects				X				
Variation	X							

Description of Problem: Sophisticated machining equipment cycles through a variety of tools to perform complex machining operations.

Before Improvement

Tool conditions sometimes degrade unpredictably. Undetectable microscopic imperfections in brittle machining materials, such as ceramic inserts, can result in unexpected wear or degradation of the tool condition. In addition, the wrong tool could be loaded on the machining equipment, or the equipment may need to adjust the tool path to compensate for tool wear.

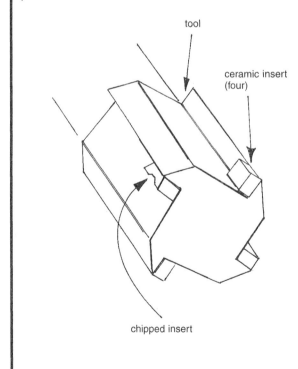

tool

ceramic insert (four)

chipped insert

After Improvement

Tool Verification Gages (TVGs) that are capable of measuring tool lengths and diameters are integrated with the machine tool control. These infrared optical devices can assess tool condition, detect when an incorrect tool is loaded, and measure tool wear. When the tool condition is degraded, the equipment can shut down and warn the operator that a tool change is needed. Tool wear information can be used to update tool-offset paths to achieve more consistent and accurate product dimensions.

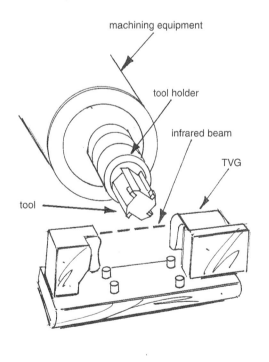

machining equipment

tool holder

infrared beam

TVG

tool

Process   Thread rolling

Problem   Bolts have checks or splits

Solution   Source inspection of incoming bolt blanks

Product   Bolt

Parts   Bolt

Stage   1-Fabrication
2-Cold forming and thread rolling

Control Function							
∿		Poka-yoke			Simplify		
Adjustment	Setting	Warn	Shutdown	Control	Tools/Eqpt	Process	Product
State							
Complexity							
Prevent Mistakes							
Detect Mistakes							
Detect Defects				X			
Variation							

Description of Problem: Bolts are used in automated automotive engine assembly. A single bad bolt shuts down the assembly equipment, and it typically takes an hour to correct the problem and restart production.

Before Improvement

The bolt manufacturer is charged back thousands of dollars for each bad bolt in the supply. To eliminate defective bolts, the bolt manufacturer uses an ultra-sonic technique to do a 100 percent inspection of every bolt at the rate of hundreds of bolts per minute. Although defective bolts are virtually eliminated, many bad blanks are processed, potentially damaging equipment.

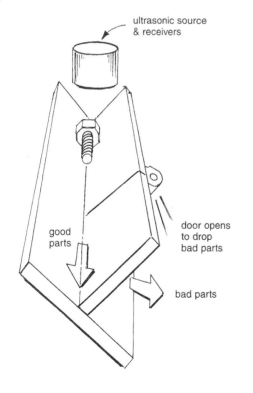

ultrasonic source & receivers

good parts

door opens to drop bad parts

bad parts

After Improvement

Defective bolts are traced to defective blanks and blanks with the wrong size or shape that have been accidentally mixed in the supply stream. Upstream ultrasonic inspection of the blanks eliminates defective material before processing.

Using mechanical sorting to remove incorrect blanks and source inspection of the raw material to eliminate defective blanks would be a better approach that is likely to be less expensive than ultrasonic inspection.

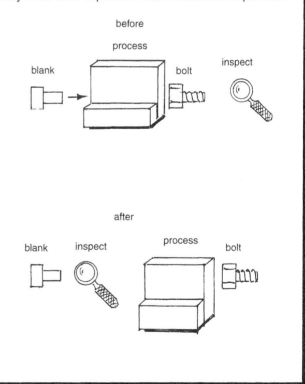

before

blank   process   bolt   inspect

after

blank   inspect   process   bolt

Defective Material

Process Drilling, boring

Problem Tool breakage, excess wear

Solution Power change signals problem

Product Aircraft engines

Parts Hole-forming processes

Stage 1-Fabrication
2-Drilling and boring

State	Adjustment	Setting	Warn	Shutdown	Control	Tools/Eqpt	Process	Product
			Poka-yoke			Simplify		
Complexity								
Prevent Mistakes								
Detect Mistakes								
Detect Defects				X				
Variation								

Description of Problem: Many holes are machined in a variety of parts.

Before Improvement
Occasionally a drill or boring tool may have an unobservable material flaw, or may not be heat-treated appropriately. These tools may fail suddenly or may wear excessively, damaging expensive parts.

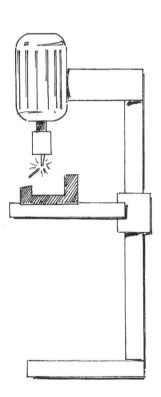

After Improvement
In critical hole-forming applications, the power is monitored throughout the machining process and compared to application-specific limits. If the limit is exceeded, the machine is immediately interrupted to change the tool.

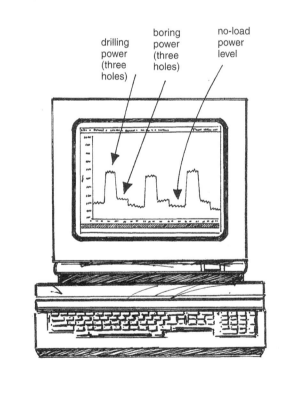

drilling power (three holes)

boring power (three holes)

no-load power level

Defective Material, Incorrect Information

Process	Casting
Problem	Part was the wrong density
Solution	Create a mass properties checklist
Product	Aerospace product
Parts	Prototype test hardware
Stage	1-Product development 2-Prototype qualification

Control Function							
∿		Poka-yoke			Simplify		
Adjustment	Setting	Warn	Shutdown	Control	Tools/Eqpt	Process	Product
State							
Complexity							
Prevent Mistakes							
Detect Mistakes							
Detect Defects		X					
Variation							

Description of Problem: For structural testing, a resin product replaces a hazardous material. By changing the additives in the resin mixture, the density of the simulant can be altered to accurately match the density of the hazardous material. Matching mass properties is critical for this project.

Before Improvement

The designer mistakenly specified a density that was too low. Compounding the problem, the cast billet of the simulant had a density lower than that specified by the designer. After extensive machining, the parts were weighed, but no one compared the measured weights with predictions. The completed parts were bonded into a complex assembly.

Mass property measurements of a major sub-assembly revealed that the assembly was substantially lighter than desired, and the problem was traced to the low simulant density. Because the assembly could not be disassembled without destroying expensive parts, complex modifications requiring additional structural tests were required.

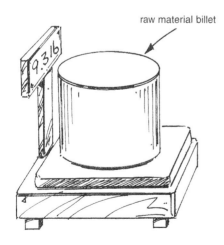

raw material billet

After Improvement

A comparison of predicted and measured density and weight is added to the assembly checklist for all parts that can be made from materials of variable density. Assembly cannot proceed until these checks have been completed. Potential problems can now be detected and corrected early in the prototype build.

Naturally, it would be better to catch the problem earlier by comparing the predicted and as-cast density as soon as parts are cast, or by mistake-proofing the formulation of the resin.

Defective Material, Omitted Information

Example DM-7

		Control Function						
Process	Press assembly and insert snapring							

Process   Press assembly and insert snapring

Problem   Stack height too great

Solution   Excess stack height triggers alarm

Product   Automotive product

Parts   Snapring, bearing assembly

Stage   1-Assembly
2-Press and insert part

		Control Function						
	∿		Poka-yoke			Simplify		
State	Adjustment	Setting	Warn	Shutdown	Control	Tools/Eqpt	Process	Product
Complexity							X	
Prevent Mistakes								
Detect Mistakes								
Detect Defects			X					
Variation								

Description of Problem: After installing a bearing, a snapring is installed. The assembly is flipped over and a second bearing is installed, followed by the another snapring.

Before Improvement
Because of variability in the stack height, the second snapring sometimes does not seat properly. In most cases, the press used to insert the bearings can be recycled and the snapring will set properly. However, when the snapring does not seat properly and is not detected, the bearing assembly can come apart during use, resulting in a potentially dangerous situation for the user.

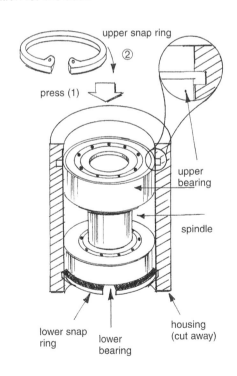

After Improvement
A limit switch is attached to the press. If the stack height is not adequate to allow clearance for assembling the snapring, the press stroke will be too short, sounding an alarm. The operator can immediately recycle the press to see if the problem is corrected. If the stack height is still excessive, the part can be removed for rework, or if the snapring can be installed, the operator is aware that particular care must be paid to the snapring assembly.

To obtain an accurate measurement of stack height, special gages such as capacitance or hall effect sensors could be used in place of traditional limit switches.

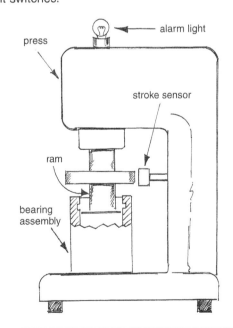

AMBIGUOUS INFORMATION (IA)

Information can be interpreted many ways, and some interpretations may be incorrect. *Example: A reference letter states, "You will be really lucky if you can get this person to work for you."*

Principles that Eliminate Ambiguous Information	**Examples**
1. Where possible, simplify the task, instruction, or specification.	
a. Minimize the number and similarity of parts and tools at each workstation.	WL-4
b. Identify and remove unnecessary material from the work floor using red tags.	
c. Minimize the number and complexity of operations at each workstation.	
d. Make instruction brief and graphic.	
e. Minimize or eliminate the need to add up dimensions and tolerances to fabricate parts.	IA-1
2. Provide, where practical, visual access and clearance for hands and tools.	
3. Make labels, switches, switch settings, and controls easy to see, read, and reach.	WC-1, MD-9
4. Make relationships between the controls, instruments, functions, and equipment obvious.	IA-4
a. Visual Control signs and signboards make the location of supply material obvious.	
b. Airplane lights (light turns on adjacent to the equipment that "triggered" the warning).	
5. Eliminate translation steps (worksheet to setup table to setup).	IA-2
6. Provide summary warning signals that "roll up" information next to the control point. (One summary signal is red if any one of "n" gauges indicates an out of "spec" condition)	IA-5
a. Interlock operation with the "roll-up" signal.	
7. Limit the amount of information available.	
a. Instruction for only one process step is visible at a time.	IA-3, WO-4
b. Nonessential information and controls are covered or hidden.	IA-4, IA-6
8. Make various types of information distinctly different.	
a. Visual—group related items and distinguish by color.	IA-8, IA-5
b. Tactile—use different shapes to distinguish products or processes.	IA-8, WO-6
c. Audio—use different sounds, notes, or melodies to distinguish messages.	IA-7

9. Make subtle product and process distinctions obvious with organization and information.

    a. Use 5S, kanban, and white lines.   WP-6

10. Use pictures, videos, graphics, or drawings to identify complex parts and clarify complex operations.   IA-2, IA-3

11. Have several individuals with diverse backgrounds review instructions and specifications to identify and eliminate potential ambiguity.

12. Look-alike parts must have drawing numbers that differ in the last two digits.

		Control Function							
		∿		Poka-yoke			Simplify		
State		Adjustment	Setting	Warn	Shutdown	Control	Tools/Eqpt	Process	Product
Complexity									
Prevent Mistakes						X			
Detect Mistakes									
Detect Defects									
Variation									

Process   Parting tube from raw stock

Problem   Tube cut too short due to misinterpretation

Solution   Change drawing

Product   Pressure vessel cylinder

Parts   Tube

Stage   1-Fabrication
2-Turning

Description of Problem: A cylinder for a pressure vessel is cut from bar stock.

Before Improvement
Cylinders were fabricated for a low-volume production run. The machinist interpreted dimension "A" in the figure below as the overall length of the tube. After cutting the tube to length, he machined the lip indicated as dimension "B." Because the total tube length is equal to "A" plus "B," the machined parts were too short, and the lot was scrapped.

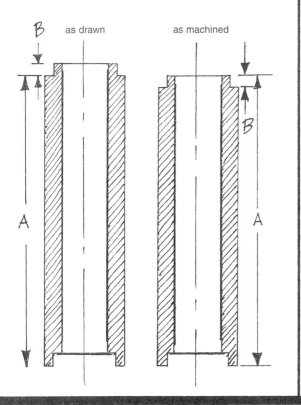

After Improvement
The dimensioning is changed so that the maximum dimension corresponds with the total part length. Parts cut to this dimension will never be too short.

As illustrated, the "best" dimensioning practices may not be covered adequately by dimensioning and tolerancing standards. A checklist can reduce the likelihood that this problem is repeated.

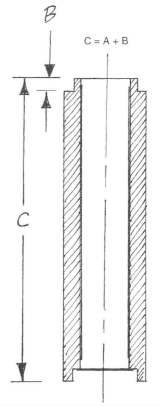

Ambiguous Information, Wrong Orientation

Process	Print on rolled sheet, film, or foil
Problem	Printing press setup errors
Solution	Simplify instructions to eliminate confusion
Product	Printed foil or film wrapped on cores
Parts	Foil or film and core
Stage	1-Setup 2-Print press

	Control Function							
	∿		Poka-yoke			Simplify		
State	Adjustment	Setting	Warn	Shutdown	Control	Tools/Eqpt	Process	Product
Complexity							X	
Prevent Mistakes					X			
Detect Mistakes								
Detect Defects								
Variation								

Description of Problem: Printing can be done in many unwind, rewind, and print configurations.

Before Improvement
The unwind, rewind, and print orientation setup is given as a number on the order form that the operator matches with a configuration on a chart "near" the machine. Errors in the setup are common because of confusion in selecting the correct setup configuration. Errors in the setup can scrap large press runs.

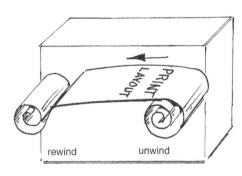

After Improvement
The chart near the machine is eliminated, and a graphical representation of the setup is printed on each order. The operator can take the order form to the machine to verify the setup, eliminating errors and avoiding confusion.

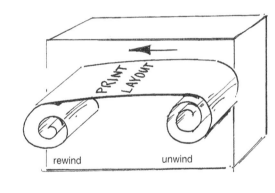

Process   Infrequent assembly operations

Problem   Instructions are misunderstood

Solution   Pictures and movies clarify complex operations

Product   Aerospace equipment

Parts   Various

Stage   1-Development
2-Assembly instructions

| | Control Function ||||||||
| | ∿ || Poka-yoke ||| Simplify |||
State	Adjustment	Setting	Warn	Shutdown	Control	Tools/Eqpt	Process	Product
Complexity					X		X	
Prevent Mistakes					X			
Detect Mistakes								
Detect Defects								
Variation								

Description of Problem: Traditional assembly instructions have been based on text and drawings.

Before Improvement

Text can be confusing. To illustrate, an instruction to "Insert the forward support into the aft housing cover using the forward support guide" does not make sense without drawings or pictures.

Even with drawings, some operations are difficult to understand. Novices make many mistakes because they do not understand the correct process.

Drawings help clarify the process, but drawings can be very expensive to create.

Step 6: Insert the forward support into the aft housing cover using the forward support guide.

After Improvement

Using a digital camera, several views of the correct parts for a process can be linked quickly to electronic assembly instructions. Part selection errors are virtually eliminated.

For complex operations, a movie of the assembly replaces traditional drawings. Operators can quickly understand exactly what is meant by the instructions, and novices learn the process more quickly.

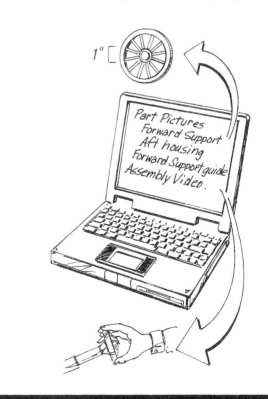

Part Pictures
Forward Support
Aft housing
Forward Support guide
Assembly Video.

Process	Selecting the right control switch or knob		
Problem	The wrong switch is pressed or turned		
Solution	Intuitive control panel layouts		
Product	Control panels		
Parts	Switches, remote controlled devices		
Stage	1-Material production		
	2-Adjust or set controls		

Control Function

State	∿ Adjustment	∿ Setting	Poka-yoke Warn	Poka-yoke Shutdown	Poka-yoke Control	Simplify Tools/Eqpt	Simplify Process	Simplify Product
Complexity								
Prevent Mistakes					X			
Detect Mistakes								
Detect Defects								
Variation								

Description of Problem: Operators in a control room turn a variety of remote devices on or off and adjust settings.

Before Improvement

Control panels often have a complex array of switches, gages, and control knobs that are not intuitively arranged. As the complexity of control panels increases, there is an increased likelihood that operators will commit control errors even with training. In addition, during high-stress situations such as emergencies, error rates increase dramatically. Panel layouts that may seem adequate for day-to-day operations can be a disaster in an emergency.

After Improvement

Change the panel layouts to be intuitive wherever possible. Computer-based controls can simplify the task by limiting the scope of the displayed material to critical functions and graphically illustrating the functional relationships, device status, and interactions.

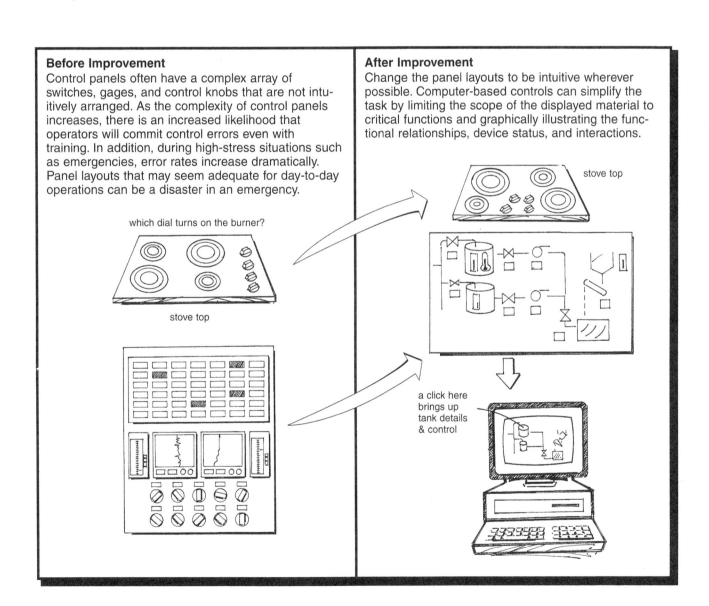

which dial turns on the burner?

stove top

stove top

a click here brings up tank details & control

Ambiguous Information

Process   Operation startup

Problem   Start with warning lights on

Solution   Group and color-code lights

Product   Process control

Parts   Control panel

Stage   1-Process control
                2-Control room operation

| | | Control Function | | | | | | |
| | | ∿ | | Poka-yoke | | Simplify | | |
State	Adjustment	Setting	Warn	Shutdown	Control	Tools/Eqpt	Process	Product
Complexity							X	
Prevent Mistakes				X	X			
Detect Mistakes								
Detect Defects								
Variation								

Description of Problem: When starting the operation of a machine, the operator pushes the start button in a control room after checking the various temperature conditions.

Before Improvement
After checking various temperature conditions, operators in a control room push a start button for a machine. Operators should confirm that all warning lights are off, but sometimes the start button is pushed while some warning lights are still on. These warning lights indicate that some instruments essential for the process are not ready for production to begin. The warning lights are not arranged systematically.

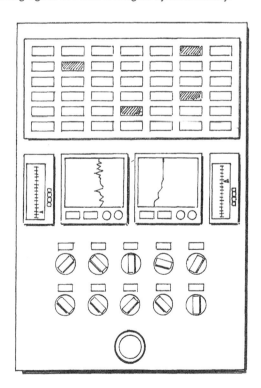

After Improvement
Warning lights are arranged by instrument type. Color coding is used to display similar information, making critical information easier to distinguish.

An additional improvement would be to place a "master" light for each group of instruments next to the start switch. If any critical warning lights are on within a class of instruments, the master light also goes on, and the operator can then quickly identify the problem. Better yet, the start button could be interlocked with the master lights.

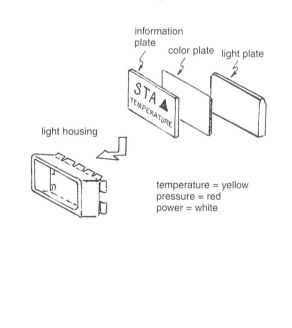

temperature = yellow
pressure = red
power = white

Ambiguous Information

Process   Production

Problem   Emergency lights overlooked

Solution   Cover lights that do not require action

Product   Chemicals

Parts   Warning lights

Stage   1-Product change-over
               2-Set controls

State	Adjustment	Setting	Warn	Shutdown	Control	Tools/Eqpt	Process	Product
Control Function			Poka-yoke			Simplify		
Complexity							X	
Prevent Mistakes			X					
Detect Mistakes								
Detect Defects								
Variation								

Description of Problem: When switching to a different product type, processes change and several warning lights turn on in response. These warning lights indicate expected equipment stoppages and temperature changes.

Before Improvement

Because many warning lights are on during production changeover, operators sometimes overlook emergency lamps that are difficult to distinguish from other warning lights. There is too much information; as a result, operators have difficulty concentrating on the important information and translating that information into correct actions.

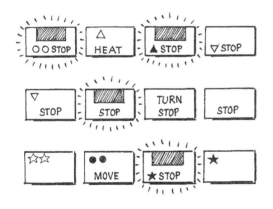

After Improvement

During the changeover, emergency lamps are distinguished from other warning lights by hanging a signboard over the warning lights that do not require action. The operators can then easily translate the information into appropriate action.

An improvement on this concept would be to use a "smoked" plastic cover instead of a signboard. The operator would still be able to see all warning lights, but emergency lights would be clearly distinguished.

sign board covers non-critical functions during setup change

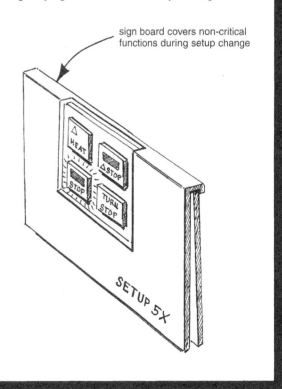

Ambiguous Information

Process   Assembly

Problem   Undifferentiated warning for multiple locations

Solution   Distinct warnings for each station

Product   Electromechanical equipment

Parts   Automated assembly equipment

Stage   1-Process control
2-Equipment reset

	Control Function							
	∿		Poka-yoke			Simplify		
State	Adjustment	Setting	Warn	Shutdown	Control	Tools/Eqpt	Process	Product
Complexity							X	
Prevent Mistakes			X					
Detect Mistakes								
Detect Defects								
Variation								

Description of Problem: When a problem is detected in the operation of automated assembly equipment, music is played to warn the operators of the problem.

Before Improvement

The music is broadcast from a single point, and there is only one type of music for multiple assembly stations and a variety of assembly equipment. Because the location of the problem is not always obvious, the operators restore or reset the wrong station without correcting the real problem.

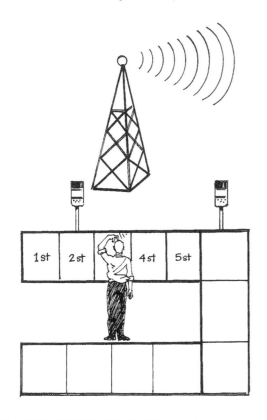

After Improvement

The number of musical tunes is increased, and each station is assigned a single, unique tune. Thus, when the alarm sounds, the operator knows immediately which station needs to be reset.

To train new workers, the specific tune for a station can be played by pressing a button at each work station.

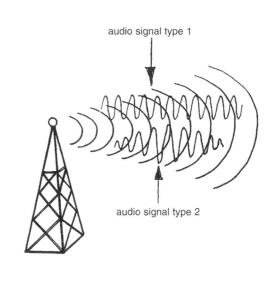

audio signal type 1

audio signal type 2

Process	Inject medication
Problem	Medication types are confused
Solution	Modify bottles for distinction
Product	Insulin for diabetics
Parts	Insulin bottles
Stage	1-Use 2-Select and inject medication

State	Control Function — $\cap$ Adjustment	Setting	Poka-yoke — Warn	Shutdown	Control	Simplify — Tools/Eqpt	Process	Product
Complexity								
Prevent Mistakes								
Detect Mistakes			X					
Detect Defects								
Variation								

Description of Problem: Many diabetics use a fast-acting insulin in conjunction with insulin that acts over a broader time period. The fast-acting (regular) insulin is used before meals, while the NPH insulin is used once or twice a day to keep the glucose level stable. To properly control blood sugars, they must select the right medication.

Before Improvement

The regular and NPH insulin are packaged in identical bottles. The only distinction is the labels. Since a common side effect of diabetes is vision problems, this distinction is inadequate. If a diabetic takes regular insulin at bedtime, a hypoglycemic reaction could occur at night, causing a particularly dangerous situation.

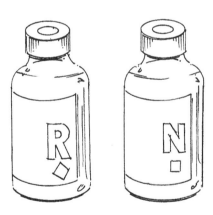

After Improvement

Using distinctly different bottles or caps is prohibitively expensive, since new bottling equipment would be required. A nonremovable snap-on plastic ring that fits around the cap is added to the NPH insulin after the insulin is bottled. Since this ring, which is a different color than the regular insulin cap, must be held by the diabetic to fill the syringe, the contents of the bottle are immediately recognized.

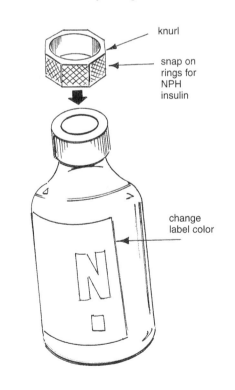

knurl

snap on rings for NPH insulin

change label color

INCORRECT INFORMATION (II)

The information provided is incorrect. *Example: The operator performs the correct action based on a gauge that is read correctly, but the gauge is faulty.*

Principles that Eliminate Incorrect Information	Examples
1. Prevent spurious information.	II-1
2. Change faceplates of instruments to read directly in the units needed.	II-2, II-3
3. Assure that instructions cannot be skipped or repeated (computer linked).	*IO-6*
4. Use visual control signs and signboards to make the location of supplies accurate and obvious.	
5. Automate checks of data entry.	
a. Check for correct measurement "units."	II-4
b. Check for compliance to specification limits.	II-4
6. Redundant gauges warn when one gauge is unreliable.	II-5
7. Use a checklist to verify that results match predictions or requirements.	*DM-6*
8. Review instructions and information for accuracy.	

Incorrect Information *Example II-1*

Process	Set neutral gear position
Problem	Wrong message from accidental electrical contact
Solution	Protect lead wire
Product	Motorcycle engine
Parts	Lead wire
Stage	1-Inspection

Control Function							
∿		Poka-yoke			Simplify		
Adjustment	Setting	Warn	Shutdown	Control	Tools/Eqpt	Process	Product
State							
Complexity							
Prevent Mistakes				X			
Detect Mistakes							
Detect Defects							
Variation							

Description of Problem: During the assembly of an engine, the operator sets the neutral position of the gears using a gear change lever. To verify the setting, electrical contact is made with an output connector on the engine. When the engine is in neutral, this electrical contact turns on an "OK" light.

Before Improvement
The tip of the lead wire on the test stand is unprotected. If this lead wire touches any conductive part on the engine or the test stand, the "OK" light turns on, even if the engine is not in the neutral position. The operator may think the engine is OK when it is not, producing a defect.

After Improvement
A nylon cover is placed around the tip of the electrical connector on the test stand. With the protective cover in place, the lead can only make contact with the output terminal of the engine, and spurious signals indicating that the engine is OK when it is not are eliminated.

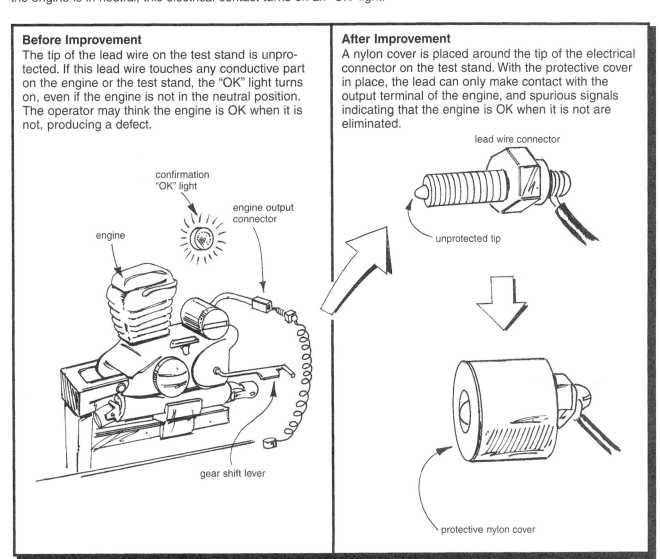

confirmation "OK" light

engine output connector

engine

gear shift lever

lead wire connector

unprotected tip

protective nylon cover

Incorrect Information

Example II-2

Process	Reading a gage
Problem	Mistakes in interpreting gage readings
Solution	Change scale for direct readings
Product	Chemicals
Parts	Gage
Stage	1-Data management 2-Read instruments

	Control Function							
	∿	Poka-yoke				Simplify		
State	Adjustment	Setting	Warn	Shutdown	Control	Tools/Eqpt	Process	Product
Complexity							X	
Prevent Mistakes					X			
Detect Mistakes								
Detect Defects								
Variation								

Description of Problem: The operator reads a measurement instrument.

Before Improvement
The measurement scale of the instrument ranges from 0 to 100 percent. The operator must multiply the gage reading by a constant to convert the percentage reading to the correct units needed. Mistakes occur when operators forget to multiply the readings or make an error in the calculations.

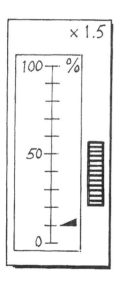

After Improvement
The scale of the measurement instrument is changed so that the operator can read the correct measurement directly from the scale.

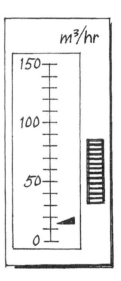

Incorrect Information

Example II-3

Process	Production
Problem	Misread scale
Solution	Enlarge lettering and change units
Product	Chemicals
Parts	Gage
Stage	1-Measure 2-Weight

Control Function								
	〜		Poka-yoke		Simplify		
State	Adjustment	Setting	Warn	Shutdown	Control	Tools/Eqpt	Process	Product
Complexity								
Prevent Mistakes					X			
Detect Mistakes								
Detect Defects								
Variation								

Description of Problem: The operator reads a scale to determine the amount of material received for a process.

Before Improvement

The face of the scale is large, but it is placed above eye level, making it difficult to read. In addition, the scale face is marked in kilograms (kg), but the needed quantity must be determined in tons. The operator misreads the scale and accepts more than the regulated amount of material.

After Improvement

The graduations on the scale face are changed from kg to ton. The lettering for the numbers is enlarged so that they can be read more easily.

Marks are placed on the scale face for common measurements.

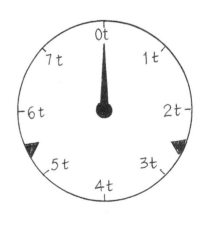

131

Process	Data submission
Problem	Spacecraft lost due to English rather than metric units
Solution	Automatic conversion to proper units
Product	Mars Climate Orbiter satellite
Parts	Satellite, thrusters, thrust data table
Stage	1-Data management 2-Entry and validation

Control Function

State	Adjustment	Setting	Warn	Shutdown	Control	Tools/Eqpt	Process	Product
Complexity							X	
Prevent Mistakes								
Detect Mistakes			X	X				
Detect Defects								
Variation								

(Control Function column groups: Adjustment/Setting under ∿; Warn/Shutdown/Control under Poka-yoke; Tools/Eqpt/Process/Product under Simplify)

Description of Problem: Performance parameters for all hardware on a spacecraft are requested in metric units for consistency.

Before Improvement

A contractor supplied the performance characteristics of their hardware in English units. The English units were entered into the spacecraft control algorithms as metric units. The error was not detected. As a result, the Mars Climate Orbiter maneuvered incorrectly, and the $125M mission failed when the spacecraft was lost.

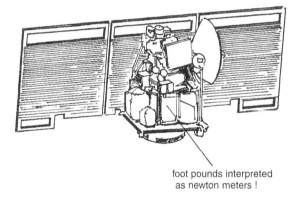

foot pounds interpreted
as newton meters !

After Improvement

A password-protected site is created where contractors log on to enter product performance data. The password allows contractors to enter data for their product. Contractors select the units for the data from a selection list. The performance data is automatically converted to metric units, checked against allowable limits, and stored in the algorithm if within tolerance.

If the data is not within acceptable limits, an alarm warns the operator and data entry is prevented.

Data entry and conversion errors are virtually eliminated.

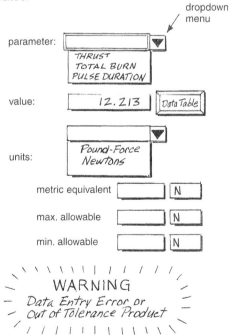

Incorrect Information

Example II-5

Process	Casting operation control using gage setting
Problem	Unreliable pressure gages result in setting errors
Solution	Redundant gages
Product	
Parts	Control gage
Stage	1-Measure 2-Pressure

	Control Function							
	∿	Poka-yoke			Simplify			
State	Adjustment	Setting	Warn	Shutdown	Control	Tools/Eqpt	Process	Product
Complexity								
Prevent Mistakes								
Detect Mistakes								
Detect Defects					X			
Variation								

Description of Problem: When casting products with a large casting machine, undesired changes in machine conditions can result in blowholes and other defects. Pressure gages are installed at key locations to monitor the casting process and the state of the machine.

Before Improvement
One pressure gage was installed at each measuring site, but if a gage was reading a nonstandard condition, it was difficult to determine whether it was the process or the gage at fault.

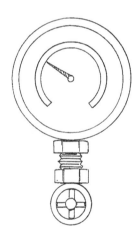

After Improvement
Two pressure gages are installed on the same outlet at each measuring site. The operator can quickly determine the reliability of the readings on the gages by comparing them. Calibration detects the defective gage, which is replaced.

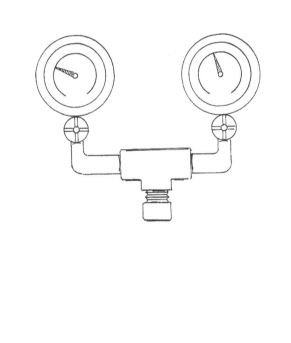

MISREAD, MISMEASURE, OR MISINTERPRET (IM)

Gauge-reading errors, errors in measuring, or errors in understanding correct information.

Principles that Eliminate Misreading, Mismeasuring, or Misinterpreting	Examples
1. Use fixed dimension guides or stops instead of scales and gauges.	IM-6, IM-7, IM-8
2. Make interpretation easy:	
a. Drawings, pictures, or videos illustrate complex parts, concepts, or operations.	IA-3
b. Visual Control signboards makes the location of supplies obvious.	WP-6
3. Print a required dimension guide on the worksheet.	IM-1
4. Use check boxes, radio buttons, selection lists, and formatted fields for data entry.	II-4
5. Use rules for and tests on data entry to assure consistency. (Example: warn if child's date of birth is before parent's during data entry.)	
6. Detect the gauge pointer position and	
a. Shut down or release the operation, or	
b. Warn (when fill is completed).	IM-9
7. Convert gauge readings and settings from adjustments to settings.	
a. Design measurements at a workstation to have the single common value and mark.	IM-2
i. (Salt box + 75 gm salt = 120 gm, Sugar box + 35 gm sugar = 120 gm)	

b. Provide visual indicators of correct settings adjacent to gauge and scales.   IM-4

  i. (Use interchangeable templates for multiple process settings)

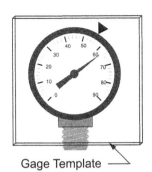

Gage Template

FIGURE IM-1

A visual indicator of the correct gauge reading on replaceable cover glass

8. Cover confusing information.   IA-6, IM-3

  a. Limit the number of digits displayed and recorded.   IM-5

9. Compare entered data to specifications and warn if a mismatch exists.   II-4, *WL-13*

Misread, Mismeasure, Misinterpret

Process	Wind printed sheet, film, or foil on cores
Problem	Printed material wound on the wrong core size
Solution	Visual indicators on order forms eliminate core selection errors
Product	Printed foil or film wrapped on cores
Parts	Foil or film and core
Stage	1-Setup 2-Printing

	Control Function							
	$\sim$		Poka-yoke			Simplify		
State	Adjustment	Setting	Warn	Shutdown	Control	Tools/Eqpt	Process	Product
Complexity								
Prevent Mistakes					X			
Detect Mistakes					X			
Detect Defects								
Variation								

Description of Problem: Customers use different machines to process printed film or foil, requiring various core sizes.

Before Improvement
Operators make errors in selecting core sizes. The core size is printed as a number on the sheet, but errors in selecting the core size can easily occur. Although some errors are discovered before shipment, significant time is wasted rewinding material even when discovered before shipment. Customers are unhappy and return products that must be rewound at substantial cost and delay.

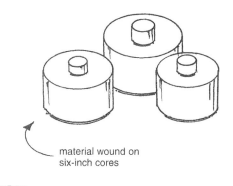

material wound on six-inch cores

After Improvement
A circle is printed on the order that makes it obvious which core size should be selected. A bar printed along the side of the order form makes it easy to check the core size, eliminating selection errors while providing a selection gage.

printed order graphically illustrates core size

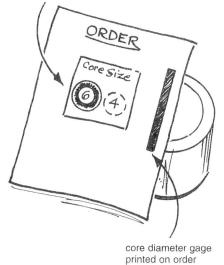

core diameter gage printed on order

Misread, Mismeasure, and Misinterpret

Example IM-2

		Control Function						
		∿	Poka-yoke			Simplify		
State		Adjustment	Setting	Warn	Shutdown	Control	Tools/Eqpt	Process	Product
Complexity								
Prevent Mistakes						X		
Detect Mistakes								
Detect Defects								
Variation								

Process	Weighing
Problem	Mismeasure raw material
Solution	Separate scales for each material
Product	Chemicals
Parts	Raw material in sacks, weight scale
Stage	1-Measure
	2-Weigh raw materials

Description of Problem: Operators use the same scale to divide a variety of materials into smaller portions. The daily report specified the number of portions for each type of material.

Before Improvement

Operators had to remember the weight to be measured out for each material. In addition to opportunities for misreading the weight scale, operators could become confused on the correct weight for a specific material. One operator mistakenly measured 1450g instead of the required 1350g.

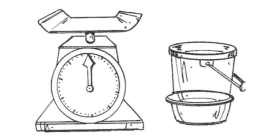

After Improvement

Use a separate scale for each material, with a mark on each scale for the correct amount of that material. Use separate containers for weighing each type of material. With this change, operators easily see the correct quantity for each material.

As an alternative, use separate containers to weigh out each material, adding permanent weights to the containers so that the combined weight of material and container has the same total weight for each material type. Now a single scale with a single mark can be used to weigh all materials.

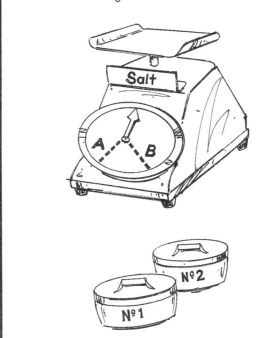

Misread, Mismeasure, and Misinterpret

Example IM-3

	Process	Reading instructions
	Problem	Misread table
	Solution	Mask unnecessary information
	Product	Chemicals
	Parts	Operation sheet
	Stage	1-Data management 2-Read worksheet

| | Control Function | | | | | | | |
| | | ∿ | | Poka-yoke | | Simplify | | |
State	Adjustment	Setting	Warn	Shutdown	Control	Tools/Eqpt	Process	Product
Complexity								
Prevent Mistakes					X			
Detect Mistakes								
Detect Defects								
Variation								

Description of Problem: A variety of instructions and conditions are written on a single sheet. Operators select the necessary numbers from the sheet for their operations.

Before Improvement
It is easy to misread the information from the sheet. In particular, operators can easily read the information from the wrong rows or columns in a table.

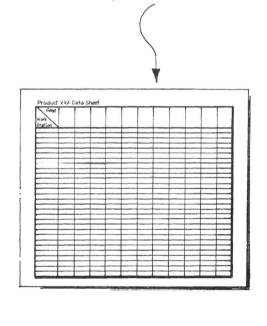

product data sheet

Product XXX Data Sheet

After Improvement
A masking card is made for every workstation. With the table located in the proper position, each operator can only see the information that he needs.

Care must be used to mistake-proof the alignment between the table and the masking card. Note that the worksheet below is only aligned properly when the black dot appears in the round window of the mask.

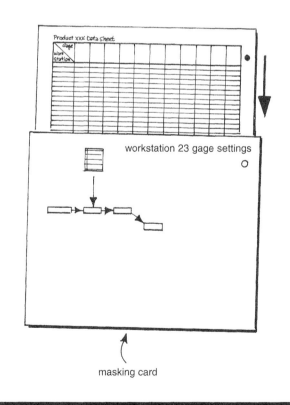

Product XXX Data Sheet

workstation 23 gage settings

masking card

Misread, Mismeasure, Misinterpret

Example IM-4

Process — Setup gage settings to test plastics

Problem — Setup – errors on testing machines (wrong settings)

Solution — Setup templates for gages for each type of plastic tested

Product

Parts — Plastics

Stage — 1-Inspection
2-Setup process test conditions

	Control Function							
State	∿	Poka-yoke				Simplify		
State	Adjustment	Setting	Warn	Shutdown	Control	Tools/Eqpt	Process	Product
Complexity					X		X	
Prevent Mistakes					X			
Detect Mistakes								
Detect Defects								
Variation								

Description of Problem: A number of different types of plastic batches are tested using a testing machine. It is necessary to set up the conditions, such as temperature, time, and pressure, differently for each type of plastic.

Before Improvement
Errors sometimes occurred when the operators misread the scales or the instruction documents. Therefore, deviations sometimes occurred in the tests, and it was often necessary to repeat the tests to confirm the results.

After Improvement
Transparent templates for setting the conditions were prepared for each different type of plastic. When beginning operations, the operator first checks the type of plastic to be tested, then takes the appropriate template out of the case and attaches it to instrument panel. The template is marked with the correct settings for each of the dials and instruments on the instrument panel, ensuring that testing is done according to the proper procedures.

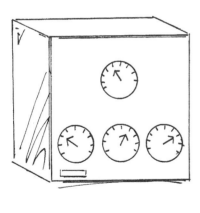

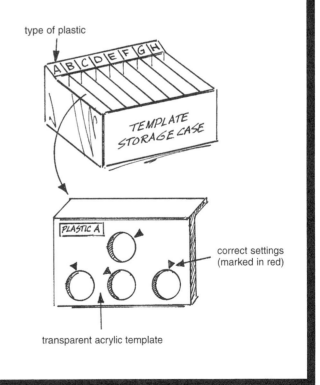

type of plastic

TEMPLATE STORAGE CASE

PLASTIC A

correct settings (marked in red)

transparent acrylic template

Misread, Mismeasure, Misinterpret

Example IM-5

Process	Fluid metering	
Problem	Wrong volume measured due to misread Numbers	
Solution	Cover unnecessary digits	
Product	Water	
Parts	Water and meter	
Stage	1-Measure 2-Volume	

	Control Function							
	$\curvearrowright$		Poka-yoke			Simplify		
State	Adjustment	Setting	Warn	Shutdown	Control	Tools/Eqpt	Process	Product
Complexity								
Prevent Mistakes					X			
Detect Mistakes								
Detect Defects								
Variation								

Description of Problem: A semi-automatic meter is used to measure the quantity of water used for a process.

Before Improvement
The digital gage has nine digits. It is easy to misread the gage when there are many digits or numbers to read.

After Improvement
Unnecessary digits are covered with tape, decreasing the number of digits visible from nine to five. Mistakes in misreading the gage are dramatically reduced.

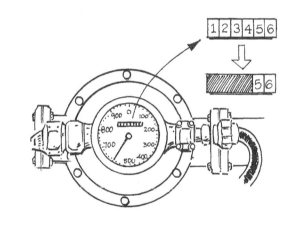

140

Process	Cut fabric using various patterns
Problem	Worn pattern templates
Solution	Mark templates for easy visual inspection
Product	Garment
Parts	Templates, fabric
Stage	1-Assembly 2-Setup

Control Function

State	Adjustment	Setting	Warn	Shutdown	Control	Tools/Eqpt	Process	Product
			Poka-yoke			Simplify		
Complexity					X	X		
Prevent Mistakes					X			
Detect Mistakes								
Detect Defects								
Variation								

Description of Problem: Sheet metal pattern templates for cutting garment pieces sometimes become damaged during use. It is important to maintain accurate templates so the garments will fit properly when assembled.

Before Improvement

It was difficult to determine whether the template was worn and needed repairing, and inaccurate garment pieces were cut as a result.

After Improvement

Using a guide, a stylus is used to inscribe a line 1mm in from the edge of the template when the template is new. After the template is used, the worker visually inspects this margin. Any variations, especially nicks and dents, are easy to detect. If there is any damage (if the interval is less than 1mm), the template is repaired. This method is fast and easy because it uses visual inspection and is simple to understand.

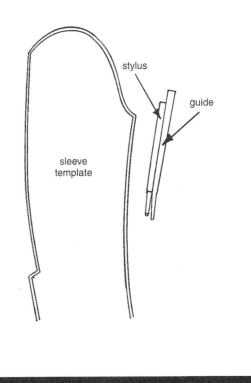

stylus

guide

sleeve template

Misread, Mismeasure, Misinterpret

Example IM-7

Process   Sew buttons onto suit jacket sleeves

Problem   Buttons unevenly spaced

Solution   Button positioning jig

Product   Garment (suit cuff)

Parts   Buttons, suit sleeves

Stage   1-Measure
2-Position buttons

| | Control Function | | | | | | | |
State	Adjustment	Setting	Warn	Shutdown	Control	Tools/Eqpt	Process	Product
Complexity					X		X	
Prevent Mistakes					X			
Detect Mistakes								
Detect Defects								
Variation								

(Poka-yoke spans Warn, Shutdown, Control; Simplify spans Tools/Eqpt, Process, Product)

Description of Problem: Some jacket cuffs have two buttons, others have three, and still others have four, depending on the design. The buttons are sewn on the cuffs one at a time using a large sewing machine.

Before Improvement
The operator made marks at each button position and then sewed the buttons on, following the marks. However, partly because of problems with the sewing machine mechanism, and also due to the viewing angle, buttons were not sewn exactly at the right positions, resulting in uneven spaces between them.

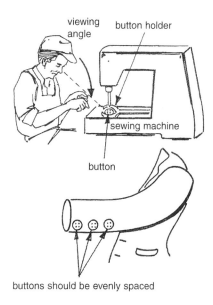

After Improvement
A positioning jig was developed for sewing buttons. Now cuffs are positioned for buttons merely by putting the cuff end against the jig mounted on the sewing machine. This positions the cuff accurately for the required number of buttons, and they come out neatly in a row.

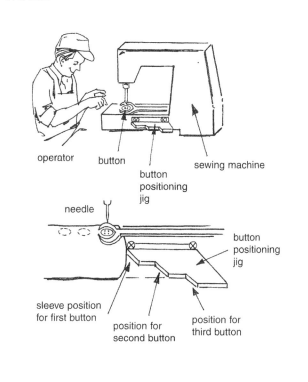

142

Process	Production
Problem	Defective cylinders not detected
Solution	Plate checks dimensions
Product	Control cylinder
Parts	Cylinder with rod
Stage	1-Inspection 2-Measure length

	Control Function							
	∿		Poka-yoke			Simplify		
State	Adjustment	Setting	Warn	Shutdown	Control	Tools/Eqpt	Process	Product
Complexity								
Prevent Mistakes					X			
Detect Mistakes								
Detect Defects			X					
Variation								

Description of Problem: Operators check the cylinder length and rod position, and they count the quantity of finished cylinders.

Before Improvement

Operators use a scale to check the cylinder length and rod position. Defects can be passed along if the operator makes an error in positioning the tube or reading the scale during this measurement. After measuring the cylinders, the operator counts out the finished products one by one, with occasional counting errors.

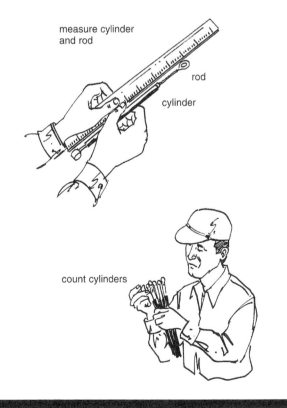

measure cylinder and rod

rod

cylinder

count cylinders

After Improvement

A mistake-proofing board is made that can hold exactly 50 cylinders. A ring on one end of each cylinder slides onto a bar attached to the mistake-proofing board. One end of the bar lifts for easy insertion and removal of parts. The length of each cylinder and rod extension can be visually compared with red and black lines on the boards. If the cylinder and rod extension fall within the black bands, they are acceptable. Unacceptable parts are quickly recognized, and the units are accurately counted.

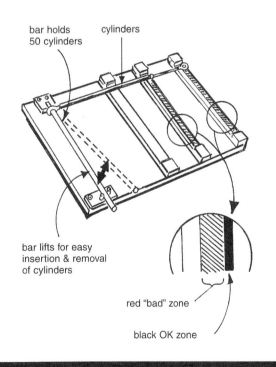

bar holds 50 cylinders

cylinders

bar lifts for easy insertion & removal of cylinders

red "bad" zone

black OK zone

Misread, Mismeasure, Misinterpret

Example IM-9

Process Measure liquid product installed by weighing

Problem Weighing errors

Solution Sensor on scale trips alarm when container is full

Product

Parts Liquid

Stage 1-Measure
2-Weigh liquid

	Control Function							
			Poka-yoke			Simplify		
State	Adjustment	Setting	Warn	Shutdown	Control	Tools/Eqpt	Process	Product
Complexity								X
Prevent Mistakes			X					
Detect Mistakes								
Detect Defects								
Variation								

Description of Problem: Workers pack a pigment solution into cans by setting the cans on a scale and pouring in the product until the can has the proper amount of product.

Before Improvement
Workers watched the scale to determine when the can was full. After filling several hundred cans, the workers would tire and weighing errors would result, slowing down the work.

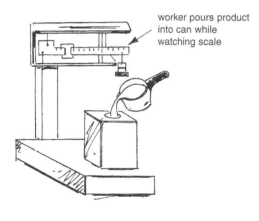

worker pours product into can while watching scale

After Improvement
A photoelectric detector was installed to monitor the movement of the scale, activating a buzzer when the scale reaches the correct weight. Much less vigilance is required, resulting in less worker fatigue. Weighing errors are substantially reduced, and the operating efficiency (per can) is improved.

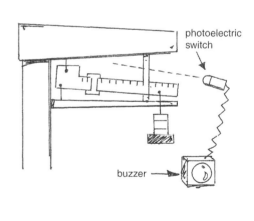

photoelectric switch

buzzer

144

Omitted Information (IO)

Information essential for the correct execution of a process or operation is not available or has never been prepared.

Principles that Eliminate Omitted Information	Examples
1. Make information nonremovable.	IO-1
a. Mark raw stock so that marking is not lost when material is partially consumed.	IO-4
b. Mark all parts for easy identification, where possible.	
2. Take the information out of files and move it to the location of the work.	
a. Create a manual or standard procedures chart.	IO-3
b. Put setup instructions on the fixtures.	
c. Put assembly procedures on a tool.	
3. Use a video or animation where a series of drawings or figures is incomplete.	*IA-3*
4. Add signals or indicators that make the information obvious.	*MA-10*
5. Add sensors to detect and warn about things that are difficult to observe.	IO-7, IO-9, *DM-7*
6. Define inventory, ordering, and replenishment rules:	
a. Define the maximum supply or inventory of a product or material.	
b. Define the supply level that will trigger product orders or replenishment.	IO-5, IO-8, IO-9
c. Define the rules for ordering and replenishment (responsibility, action, etc.).	IO-5, IO-8, IO-9
7. Make the inventory action points obvious:	
a. Red line indicates maximum inventory level.	
b. Make a low material supply obvious (cut out in wire coils).	IO-8, IO-9
8. Detect excess or low material supply conditions:	
a. Automatically halt upstream production if supply exceeds the limit,	
b. Automatically order or replenish material if the supply drops below inventory point, or	
c. Warn of the need to order or replenish material.	IO-5, IO-7

Principles that Eliminate Omitted Information   **Examples**

9. Prevent advancement to the next step until all required information is entered.   IO-6

10. Use cleanup and organization (5S) to make omitted information obvious.   IO-8

11. Use kanban to guide the selection of the next operation.

12. Defect display boards make mistakes that occurred obvious.

13. Create and use a checklist to identify and gather needed information.   IO-2

Process Print on rolled sheet, film, or foil

Problem Lost material specification sheets results in selection errors

Solution Put material markings on core

Product Printed foil or film

Parts Foil or film and core

Stage 1-Stock management
2-Marking

	Control Function							
	∿		Poka-yoke			Simplify		
State	Adjustment	Setting	Warn	Shutdown	Control	Tools/Eqpt	Process	Product
Complexity								
Prevent Mistakes					X			
Detect Mistakes								
Detect Defects								
Variation								

Description of Problem: Many different and difficult to distinguish materials are used for printing.

Before Improvement
Documentation describing the print stock is typically "wrapped" on the material as received. When removed for printing, the documentation is sometimes misplaced, or the operator forgets to put it back with the stock when the print run does not consume the entire roll. Print runs are subsequently ruined when the wrong material is selected due to missing material specifications.

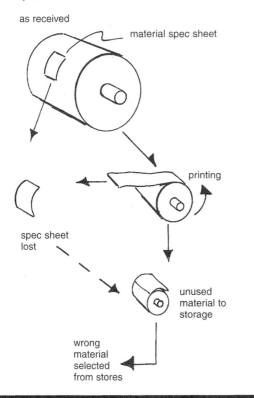

as received
material spec sheet
spec sheet lost
printing
unused material to storage
wrong material selected from stores

After Improvement
Upon receipt, a label describing the raw material is printed and attached to the core. The material specifications remain with the raw stock until it is consumed. Simple visual guides facilitate material identification. The best "source" inspection would be to persuade suppliers to label cores.

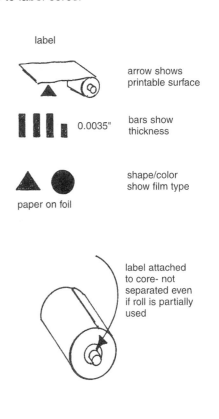

label
arrow shows printable surface
0.0035" bars show thickness
shape/color show film type
paper on foil
label attached to core- not separated even if roll is partially used

Process	Strain gage mounting
Problem	The wrong strain gages were mounted
Solution	Add the gage properties to the data list
Product	Aerospace development unit
Parts	Strain gages
Stage	1-Stock management 2-Order parts

Control Function

State	Adjustment	Setting	Warn	Shutdown	Control	Tools/Eqpt	Process	Product
			Poka-yoke			Simplify		
Complexity								
Prevent Mistakes					X			
Detect Mistakes								
Detect Defects								
Variation								

Description of Problem: Strain gages are mounted to units for qualification during testing.

Before Improvement

For increased sensitivity and reduced power consumption, 1000Ω strain gages were selected for a project. Although this was verbally communicated, the group responsible for the strain gages ordered readily available 350Ω gages because the original guidance was probably forgotten.

The incorrect gages were not discovered until the gages were installed. Either new custom gages had to be ordered, or the signal-conditioning boards had to be redesigned or rebuilt. Either alternative was expensive and would cause a delay of several weeks.

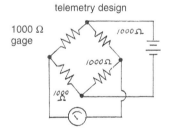

telemetry design

1000 Ω gage

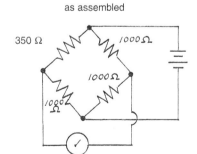

as assembled

350 Ω

After Improvement

Strain gage attributes and other sensor attributes are now a required part of a data list. This data list is used as a checklist when ordering gages and sensors for testing. Verification of the strain gage resistance prior to assembly has been added to the assembly checklist.

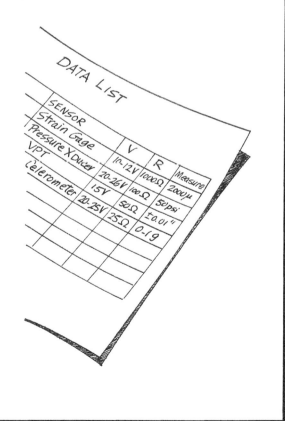

	Control Function						
	∿		Poka-yoke			Simplify		
State	Adjustment	Setting	Warn	Shutdown	Control	Tools/Eqpt	Process	Product
Complexity							X	
Prevent Mistakes					X			
Detect Mistakes								
Detect Defects								
Variation								

Process   Complex operation with valve settings

Problem   Valve setting error during a complex operation

Solution   Shopfloor manual with a checklist

Product   Chemicals

Parts   Valves

Stage   1-Material production
2-Valve operation

Description of Problem: Operators perform complex operations, such as opening and closing an array of valves, for infrequent production activities.

Before Improvement
Because the instructions are not available, operators depend on their memory for the correct execution of the task. Errors occur frequently under these conditions.

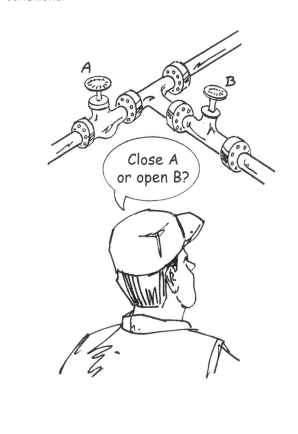

After Improvement
An easy-to-read manual is created and placed on the shop floor. The manual has a checklist, and a new strip of tape is applied at the edge of the instructions each time the process is initiated. The operator can then use a pencil to check the operations, one-by-one on the clean tape, as they are completed. Operations are no longer omitted, and the operator knows exactly what steps should be performed and the correct order of execution.

Note: This type of solution is not the most appropriate for operations that are repeated frequently.

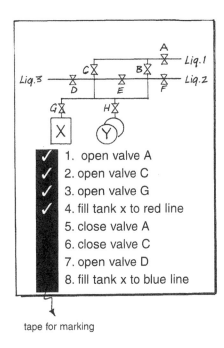

Omitted Information

Example IO-4

Process — Marking raw stock for handling and storage

Problem — Scrap because of lost material identification

Solution — Paint in several places on receipt

Product

Parts — Bar and wire stock

Stage —
1-Stock management
2-Mark material

Control Function							
∿		Poka-yoke			Simplify		
Adjustment	Setting	Warn	Shutdown	Control	Tools/Eqpt	Process	Product
State							
Complexity				X		X	
Prevent Mistakes				X			
Detect Mistakes							
Detect Defects							
Variation							

Description of Problem: Various processes use different types of metal stock and wire.

Before Improvement
Different types of metal stock and wire (alloy steel, soft steel, etc.) were identified by colored marks painted on before use. However, many leftover materials were not identifiable after processing because the colored marks had to be cut off and the new ends were not repainted. As a result, the wrong materials were sometimes used in processing.

round bar

hexagonal or square bar

wire
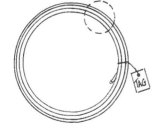

After Improvement
Instead of having to repaint identifying colors after the material is used, material is painted directly in several places after it has been received and inspected. Identifying colors are placed on both ends of the bar stock, and in two places around the circumference of wire coils. This eliminates unidentifiable leftovers and ensures that products are not manufactured with the wrong materials.

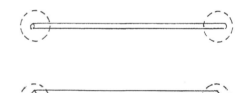

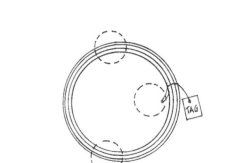

Omitted information

Process   Storage of parts for assembly line

Problem   Commonly used parts out of stock

Solution   Automatic parts bin with low stock detectors

Product

Parts   Pins

Stage   1-Stock management
2-Order to replenish

		Control Function					
∿		Poka-yoke			Simplify		
Adjustment	Setting	Warn	Shutdown	Control	Tools/Eqpt	Process	Product
State							
Complexity					X		X	
Prevent Mistakes			X		X			
Detect Mistakes								
Detect Defects								
Variation								

Description of Problem: Everyone is always careful to ensure a constant stock of special parts needed in assembly, but supplies used in common and general-purpose supplies tend to be overlooked. However, these are necessary parts for assembly, and work will stop without them.

Before Improvement
Different sizes of straight pins and tapered pins were used in a workplace. The pins were arranged by size and stored in a cabinet, from which they were taken when needed. Sometimes certain pins were out of stock, and this held up assembly. In addition, the pins at the bottoms of the drawers had been lying there a long time, and they sometimes became rusty. Stocking the pins was neglected because there was no particular person who monitored the stock.

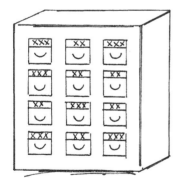

After Improvement
A storage cabinet was built with boxes containing various sizes and shapes of pins. Each box is equipped with a switch that detects when the pins are in low supply and lights a red lamp for that box on the display panel. This makes it possible to notify the acquisitions department immediately, eliminating the rush and confusion that were the rule in the past.

New pins are put in the boxes from the back and pins are taken out from the front. This "first-in, first-out" arrangement makes it possible to avoid backlogs of old pins remaining a long time and rusting.

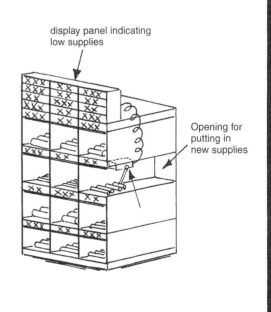

display panel indicating low supplies

Opening for putting in new supplies

Omitted, Incorrect Information

Process Low-volume assembly operations

Problem Operations omitted when assembly starts at wrong point

Solution Electronic aid guides assembly

Product Aerospace systems

Parts Various

Stage 1-Assembly
2-Insert part, fasten, and join

Control Function							
∿		Poka-yoke			Simplify		
Adjustment	Setting	Warn	Shutdown	Control	Tools/Eqpt	Process	Product
State							
Complexity							
Prevent Mistakes		X					
Detect Mistakes							
Detect Defects							
Variation							

Description of Problem: During complex assembly of low-volume units, such as prototypes and satellites, assembly operations continue for many work shifts.

Before Improvement

Assemblers may be confused about the exact state of assembly when interrupted by events such as power outages, personal emergencies, or shift changes. Hand-off errors to other assemblers can easily occur when the new assemblers are confused about the progress of the previous shift. Assembly may resume at a later step than appropriate, resulting in omitted operations and system failures or expensive rework. Occasionally, essential connections will not be made, or parts may be left out, because of the confusion.

connector not mated

After Improvement

A software package guides assembly. The instructions cannot advance to the next step until all required data for a step has been collected and entered and the step has been "checked-off" as being completed. Regardless of the state of the assembly process or distractions, the precise state of the assembly is known whenever assembly is interrupted and resumes.

Omitted Information, Inadequate Warning

Process	Assembly
Problem	Ungreased parts due to empty grease container
Solution	Magnetic sensor detects low grease supply
Product	Greased inserts
Parts	Grease, parts
Stage	1-Assembly 2-Lubricate

	Control Function							
	∿		Poka-yoke			Simplify		
State	Adjustment	Setting	Warn	Shutdown	Control	Tools/Eqpt	Process	Product
Complexity							X	
Prevent Mistakes			X					
Detect Mistakes								
Detect Defects								
Variation								

Description of Problem: Custom equipment applies grease to parts.

Before Improvement
If the grease supply becomes depleted, parts that are not greased enter the production stream, causing defects. Because the grease is black, it is difficult for the operators to see the quantity of grease remaining in the supply cylinder. Thus, even though operators diligently checked the amount of grease in the injection instrument, occasionally the machine would ran out of grease, producing unanticipated defects.

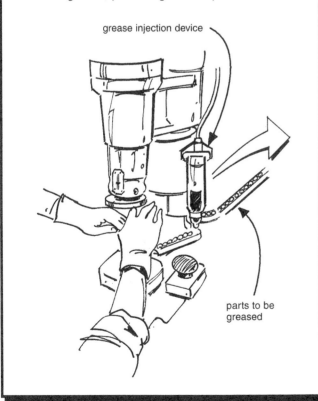

grease injection device

parts to be greased

After Improvement
A magnetic sensor is attached to the supply cylinder that detects when the grease supply is depleted. When the grease supply is low, the sensor triggers an alarm that warns the operator to refill the cylinder before defects are produced.

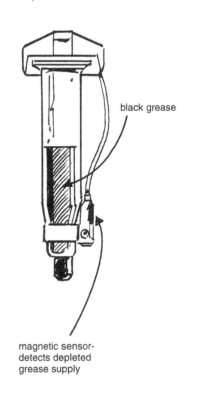

black grease

magnetic sensor-detects depleted grease supply

Omitted Information

Process   Production

Problem   Depleted flange supply halts product delivery

Solution   Provide a low-supply warning

Product   Chemicals

Parts   Flange packing

Stage   1-Stock management
            2-Order and replenish flange packings

Control Function							
∿		Poka-yoke			Simplify		
Adjustment	Setting	Warn	Shutdown	Control	Tools/Eqpt	Process	Product
State							
Complexity						X	
Prevent Mistakes		X					
Detect Mistakes							
Detect Defects							
Variation							

Description of Problem: Various flange packings are used in packaging chemical products.

Before Improvement
The flange packing seals are stored with other materials. It is difficult to see when the supply of flange packings is low. When the stock unexpectedly ran out, more packings were ordered immediately, but the operation was delayed until the packings were delivered.

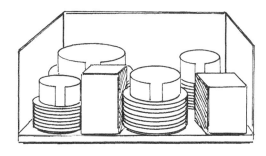

After Improvement
The 5S method is used to create a unique storage location for each type of flange packing. Each size of packing is stored in a separate location. A colored packing is placed in the stack as an indicator. An order for new packings is made whenever this packing is removed from the stack. A system is developed making it possible for anyone to place an order when necessary.

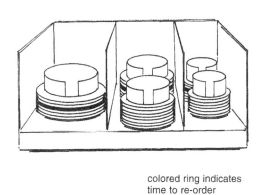

colored ring indicates time to re-order

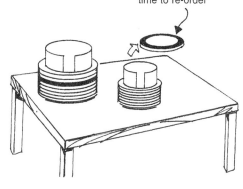

Omitted Information, Inadequate Warning

Process   Refill tank

Problem   The tank is not refilled because no one notices it is empty

Solution   Warn the operator when the supply is depleted

Product   Chemicals

Parts   Liquid in a tank

Stage   1-Stock management
2-Replenish liquid

	Control Function						
	∿	Poka-yoke			Simplify		
State	Adjustment	Setting	Warn	Shutdown	Control	Tools/Eqpt	Process	Product
Complexity							X	
Prevent Mistakes			X					
Detect Mistakes								
Detect Defects								
Variation								

Description of Problem: A supply tank is filled with a clear liquid. The operator must refill the tank before the liquid in the tank is depleted.

Before Improvement
It is difficult to see the inside of the tank. As a result, the operator often fails to notice that the tank is empty. Furthermore, there are no clear guidelines regarding when the tank should be refilled.

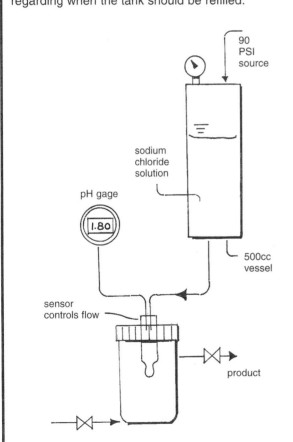

90 PSI source

sodium chloride solution

pH gage

1.80

sensor controls flow

500cc vessel

product

After Improvement
A small, fluorescent buoy is placed inside the tank so that the operator can easily see the liquid level. In addition, a scale is placed outside the tank. If the fluid level in the tank drops below a red line on the scale, the tank is refilled.

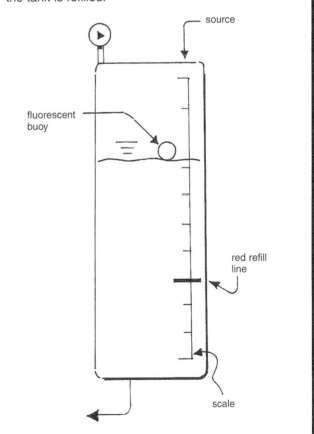

source

fluorescent buoy

red refill line

scale

INADEQUATE WARNING (IW)

A warning is sent or readily available, but the method of warning is not adequate to attract or hold the operator's attention.

Principles that Eliminate Inadequate Warning   **Examples**

1. Create warning signals as needed (lights, alarms, vibrators, or barriers).   IW-5

2. Supplement existing warnings with signals in remote or isolated locations.
   a. Provide warnings for workers in a utility chase.   IW-4

3. Use sensors to detect warning conditions:
   a. When detection can be inadvertently missed (distraction, inattention, etc.).
   b. When the range of human perception is inadequate.   IW-6, IO-7
   c. When hazardous conditions exist.   IW-6
   d. For data entry that indicates specification limits are exceeded.   IW-3

4. Make it easy to observe conditions that warrant warnings.
   a. Facilitate visual access for hard-to-see places (fluorescent colors, mirrors).   IO-9
   b. Increase sensitivity to problems (pin alignment on snapring tool).   IW-2
   c. Create a visual indicator of changes that can't be perceived (centrifuged blood).   OO-16
   d. Use magnification or amplification.

5. Select the right warning method for the environment and conditions.
   a. Visual signals (suits most situations, particularly noisy places).   IW-1
   b. Sound signals (use where visibility is poor; limit use in noisy places).
   c. Tactile or vibratory signals (best individual warning, use in dim and noisy places).   IW-4
   d. Barriers to block action (use where actions must be prevented).   IW-3

6. Establish the correct warning attributes.

   a. Warnings should not be irritating, particularly if they are frequent.

   b. Warning intensity, size, or level should be sufficient to attract attention.

   c. Warnings should be continuous enough that they cannot be easily ignored.

   d. Warnings should be located for easy perception and association with corrective action.

7. Mistake-proof the setting of timers.   MT-3

Inadequate Warning

Process   Electrostatic painting

Problem   Loss of air pressure

Solution   Improve warning—visible from paint booth

Product   Fuel tank

Parts   Fuel tank

Stage   1-Fabrication
2-Painting

	Control Function							
	∿		Poka-yoke			Simplify		
State	Adjustment	Setting	Warn	Shutdown	Control	Tools/Eqpt	Process	Product
Complexity								
Prevent Mistakes			X					
Detect Mistakes								
Detect Defects								
Variation								

Description of Problem: An operator working inside a paint booth paints fuel tanks with an electrostatic painting machine. To prevent defects, it is important that the operator know if the electrostatic machine loses its high air pressure.

Before Improvement

A buzzer sounded when pressure dropped below a certain level. However, it was so noisy in the paint booth that the operator often did not hear the buzzer and did not realize that the pressure had been lost. A warning lamp could not be used due to the fire hazard of a light bulb in the paint booth.

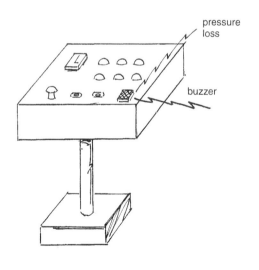

After Improvement

The electric signal indicating a pressure drop now sends a mechanical visual warning to the operator in addition to the buzzer. The operator can see the signal flag when it pops out and can take prompt action to prevent defects. A better alternative would be to put a vibrator in the handle of the paint gun that vibrates when the pressure is low.

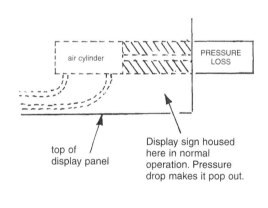

Inadequate Warning

Process	Insert snaprings to hold bearing assembly
Problem	Snapring does not seat
Solution	Modified pliers reveal unseated snaprings
Product	Automotive product
Parts	Snapring, bearing assembly, snapring pliers
Stage	1-Assembly 2-Insert part

Control Function

State	Adjustment	Setting	Warn	Shutdown	Control	Tools/Eqpt	Process	Product
			Poka-yoke			Simplify		
Complexity							X	
Prevent Mistakes								
Detect Mistakes			X					
Detect Defects								
Variation								

Description of Problem: After installing a bearing, a snapring is installed. The assembly is flipped over, and a second bearing is installed followed by another snapring. Snaprings are manually assembled using 90-degree snapring pliers.

Before Improvement

Because of variability in the stack height or errors in assembly, the second snapring sometimes does not seat properly. Sometimes it is difficult to see that the snapring is not seated properly. When the snapring does not seat properly and is not detected, the bearing assembly can come apart during use, resulting in a potentially dangerous situation for the user.

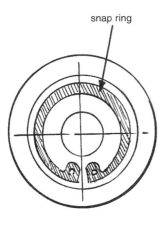

snap ring

After Improvement

The holes in the snapring will be too close together if it is not properly seated in its retaining groove. By putting a pin and clearance hole in the snapring tool, the operator can quickly see if the snapring is properly seated before removing the tool. For better resolution and warning, a leaf spring could be placed over the tool hole. When the pin touches the spring, it completes an electrical path and turns on an LED that is only extinguished if the snapring is seated when the grip is released.

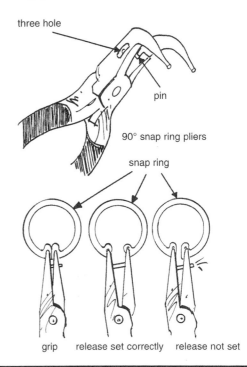

three hole

pin

90° snap ring pliers

snap ring

grip　　release set correctly　　release not set

Inadequate Warning

Example IW-3

Process	Low-volume assembly operations
Problem	Out-of-tolerance condition not detected
Solution	Entry of out-of-tolerance data triggers warning
Product	Aerospace product
Parts	Various
Stage	1-Assembly 2-Various

Control Function								
	∿		Poka-yoke			Simplify		
State	Adjustment	Setting	Warn	Shutdown	Control	Tools/Eqpt	Process	Product
Complexity								
Prevent Mistakes								
Detect Mistakes			X					
Detect Defects								
Variation								

Description of Problem: During complex assembly of low-volume units, such as prototypes, key data is recorded to confirm appropriate assembly and facilitate root cause analysis if the unit does not function as intended.

Before Improvement

During assembly, operators occasionally record out-of-tolerance conditions but proceed with the assembly without recognizing that the assembly conditions are incorrect. For example, operators may set a torque wrench for too low a value and record the value correctly as set, but proceed with the assembly using a torque setting that can result in a product failure. Data from numerous assemblies demonstrates that this type of error is not uncommon.

instructions

After Improvement

A software package guides assembly. Acceptable ranges of values for such characteristics as torque, weight, tolerance, or other performance-related characteristics are entered with assembly instructions. Operators enter the values for these parameters at the time of assembly. If any value exceeds acceptable ranges, an alarm sounds and the assembly instructions cannot advance until the operator corrects the out-of-tolerance conditions. Similarly, data entry of such attributes as part and drawing numbers are linked to templates so that incomplete data entry, or entering the wrong type of character in any column, is detected. Thus, most data-entry errors are eliminated, and out-of-tolerance conditions are detected when it is easy to change the assembly.

display flashes
alarm sounds

laptop computer

Inadequate Warning

Example IW-4

Process	Building maintenance in confined spaces	
Problem	Workers do not hear fire alarms in confined spaces	
Solution	Vibrating pagers provide warning	
Product	Maintenance worker warning system	
Parts	Pager	
Stage	1-Maintenance 2-Hazard alarm	

Control Function

State	∿		Poka-yoke			Simplify		
	Adjustment	Setting	Warn	Shutdown	Control	Tools/Eqpt	Process	Product
Complexity								
Prevent Mistakes								
Detect Mistakes			X					
Detect Defects								
Variation								

Description of Problem: Maintenance workers in buildings often work in confined spaces, such as maintenance raceways and above false ceiling tiles.

Before Improvement

In addition to working in confined spaces, maintenance workers are frequently using noisy tools. As a result, fire and other alarms cannot be heard as they perform their work. Other workers in the building may be completely unaware that these individuals are in the building. Consequently, when an alarm sounds to evacuate the building, maintenance workers may not have any warning, putting them at a very high safety risk.

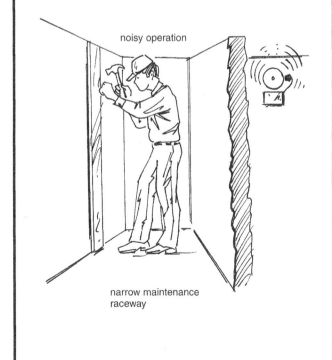

narrow maintenance raceway

noisy operation

After Improvement

Maintenance workers pick up special pagers as they enter confined spaces and replace them as they exit. An automatic dialer is linked to the building alarm system. If an alarm sounds, the special pagers are called and a vibratory warning is felt regardless of the noise level. Maintenance workers can then evacuate the building safely.

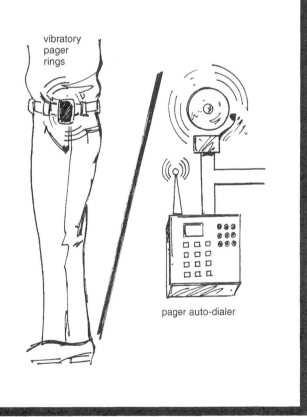

vibratory pager rings

pager auto-dialer

161

Inadequate Warning

Process	Centrifuge mixture to separate blood products	
Problem	Centrifuge shuts down without warning due to imbalance	
Solution	Alarm warns of shutdown due to imbalance	
Product	Separation process for chemical analysis of blood	
Parts	Specimen vials, centrifuge	
Stage	1-Use 2-Setup centrifuge balance	

Control Function

State	Adjustment	Setting	Warn	Shutdown	Control	Tools/Eqpt	Process	Product
	∿		Poka-yoke			Simplify		
Complexity								
Prevent Mistakes								
Detect Mistakes			X					
Detect Defects								
Variation								

Description of Problem: Clinical chemists execute other tasks while blood products are being centrifuged.

Before Improvement
Precious time in life-or-death situations is lost when the centrifuge shuts down prematurely due to imbalance. Operators do not realize that the centrifuge has shut down until they check at the expected completion of the operation. They must rebalance the load and start the centrifuge for another cycle, wasting a full production cycle.

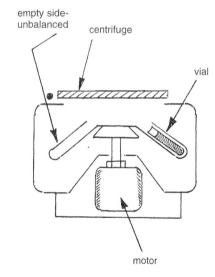

After Improvement
A sensor detects the premature shutdown due to imbalance, and a warning light or alarm alerts the operator as soon as it occurs. The operator can correct imbalance problems immediately.

A better solution would be to check the balance before the operator closes the lid. Sensors that detect "empty" positions may be used to predict an imbalance condition before or as the lid is closed.

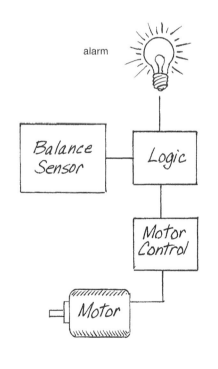

Inadequate Warning, Omitted Operation

Process	Inspect operation of the cooling air fans
Problem	Manual inspection is inaccurate and dangerous
Solution	Power used by fans verifies operation
Product	Electromechanical product
Parts	Nine ventilation fans for cooling
Stage	1-Inspection 2-Airflow

Control Function

State	Adjustment	Setting	Warn	Shutdown	Control	Tools/Eqpt	Process	Product
Complexity								X
Prevent Mistakes								
Detect Mistakes								
Detect Defects			X					
Variation								

(Control Function columns: Adjustment/Setting under ∿; Warn/Shutdown/Control under Poka-yoke; Tools/Eqpt/Process/Product under Simplify)

Description of Problem: Nine fans are used to feed and exhaust cooling air in a product. After verifying operation of the fans, a cover is attached that prevents subsequent functional tests of the fans.

Before Improvement

Initially, operators held their hands in front of the fans to check their operation. It was especially difficult to check the fans that draw air into the box where the airflow cannot be easily felt. These checks were not safe, and fingers could get caught in the fans. Operators had to move around the product to check all of the fans. Occasionally operators would forget to check a fan or fail to detect a fan that was not working.

Since the operation of the fans could not be checked after attaching a protective cover, defects that were not detected during this inspection were always passed along to the customer.

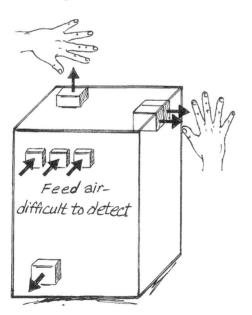

After Improvement

A tester was developed that verifies the electrical voltage and current for each fan simultaneously, allowing all nine fans to be checked at once. Software in the tester integrates the information and shows the fans that are and are not working. Checking the fans is reliable and safe, and can now be completed more efficiently. Errors in accidentally failing to check a fan operation are eliminated.

MISALIGNED PARTS (MA)

Parts or tooling are in the proper general location and orientation, but the alignment is not sufficiently accurate for fit, function, or the correct execution of an operation.

Principles that Eliminate Misaligned Parts	Examples
1. Make alignment easy.	
a. Insert parts top-down or from the side, whenever practical.	MA-1
b. Make alignment features obvious.	
c. Eliminate the need for bending, twisting, and deformation to achieve alignment.	MA-1
2. Design parts to be self-guiding and self-aligning.	
a. Design parts to align before mating.	MA-4
b. Make the correct alignment the only stable condition.	
c. Eliminate steps in mating parts where "hang-ups" occur (insertion and removal).	MA-7
d. Replace steps in mating parts with tapers (insertion and removal).	MA-2
3. Control alignment with settings rather than adjustments.	MA-4, MA-5, MA-10, *WL-9*
a. A notch on the part or carrier "sets" the location for drilling holes (or other process).	WL-11
4. Automate alignment and positioning (especially when precision exceeds human skill).	MA-8
5. Eliminate the need to temporarily hold parts to maintain alignment (washers).	
6. Detect correct or incorrect alignment.	
a. Interlock the associated operation.	MA-11, MA-12
b. Warn about incorrect alignments.	MA-13

7. Provide temporary alignment guides or fixtures.
   a. Constrain to the correct alignment and orientation.   MA-5
   b. Create a guide to align splines.   MA-6

8. Provide visual alignment references:
   a. To show the location of correct alignment.   MA-10
   b. To align parts vertically, straight, or parallel.   MA-9

9. Provide barriers to prevent cross-alignment connection (solder bridges).   MA-3

Misaligned Parts, Commit Prohibited Action

Example MA-1

Process   Tubing assembly

Problem   Tubing damaged during insertion, leaks in seals

Solution   Change insertion direction

Product   Aerospace product

Parts   Valve and tubing

Stage   1-Assembly
2-Insert part

	Control Function							
	∿		Poka-yoke			Simplify		
State	Adjustment	Setting	Warn	Shutdown	Control	Tools/Eqpt	Process	Product
Complexity					X		X	X
Prevent Mistakes					X			
Detect Mistakes								
Detect Defects								
Variation								

Description of Problem: High-pressure tubes routed from opposite directions must be inserted into a valve.

Before Improvement

Late in the assembly process, tubes connected to deeply buried internal parts must be inserted into a valve. Just before insertion into the valve, special fixtures are used to bend the tubes to the desired configuration. Then, tubes must be flexed to insert the tubes into the valves. Tubes can be damaged easily in either process because they are difficult to align, but the damage is not easy to detect. Consequently, leaks may occur. When tubes are damaged, the complex assembly must be completely dismantled, and many bonded components are destroyed.

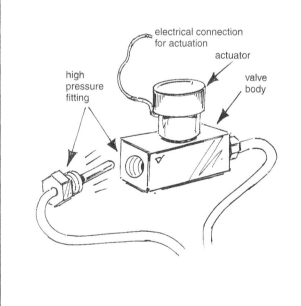

After Improvement

The valve is redesigned so that the tubes can enter from the same direction. Now the tubing can be pre-bent easily before installation, and opportunities for damaging tubes during insertion into the valve are virtually eliminated. The tubing is designed to allow modest axial and radial movement, so that alignment with valve features during assembly is very easy. This is a good example of mistake-proofing the design concept using top-down assembly.

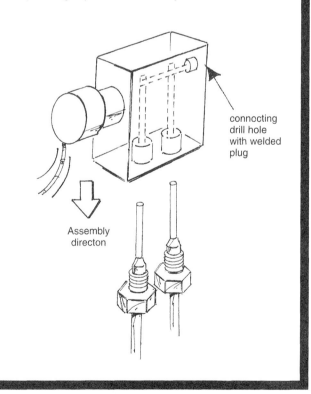

Misaligned Parts

Process	Insert decorative screws
Problem	Screws difficult to set properly
Solution	Change shaft of screw to make positioning easy
Product	
Parts	Decorative screws
Stage	1-Assembly
	2-Fasten

	Control Function							
	∿		Poka-yoke			Simplify		
State	Adjustment	Setting	Warn	Shutdown	Control	Tools/Eqpt	Process	Product
Complexity					X			X
Prevent Mistakes					X			
Detect Mistakes								
Detect Defects								
Variation								

Description of Problem: Decorative screws are installed on workpieces.

Before Improvement

The screws were difficult to seat properly. Improperly seated screws could be discovered only during packing, at which time it was necessary to loosen and tighten the screw repeatedly to get it to seat properly. This process became a bottleneck on the assembly line.

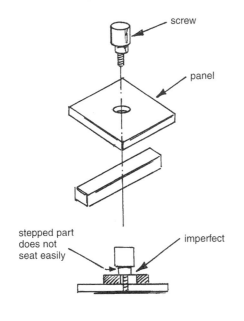

After Improvement

The shape of the screw was altered. The stepped part on the screw was changed to a taper. This made it possible to tighten the screw correctly in the hole in one operation.

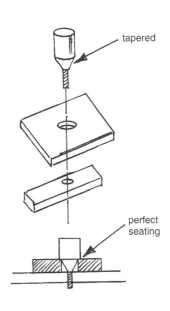

Misaligned Parts

Process	Solder electrical parts to wires from motor and power unit
Problem	Solder bridges
Solution	Provide barriers in molded part
Product	Motors
Parts	Electric parts
Stage	1-Assembly 2-Join by soldering

Control Function							
	∿		Poka-yoke		Simplify		
State	Adjustment	Setting	Warn	Shutdown	Control	Tools/Eqpt	Process	Product
Complexity					X		X	X
Prevent Mistakes					X			
Detect Mistakes								
Detect Defects								
Variation								

Description of Problem: Certain motor components have electrical leads soldered to five places on a molded insulator.

Before Improvement
The spaces between the solder pads were narrow, and solder bridges occurred if operators lacked skill or forgot to be careful.

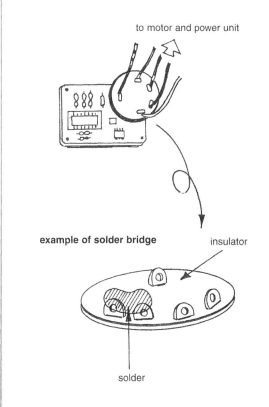

example of solder bridge

insulator

solder

to motor and power unit

After Improvement
The insulator was improved (the molding dies were modified) to provide partitions between the solder pads. These now act as barriers to the solder, so it cannot run from one pad to the next. Solder bridges were completely eliminated.

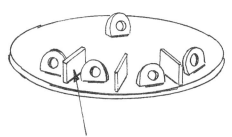

insulator improved with barriers

	Adjustment	Setting	Warn	Shutdown	Control	Tools/Eqpt	Process	Product
Control Function	⌣		Poka-yoke			Simplify		
State								
Complexity								
Prevent Mistakes					X			
Detect Mistakes								
Detect Defects								
Variation								

Process	Assembly	
Problem	Parts are cross-threaded	
Solution	Use bolts with unthreaded tip	
Product	Automotive part	
Parts	Threaded fasteners	
Stage	1-Assembly 2-Insert part and fasten	

Description of Problem: Operators manually position an automated bolt-insertion device to attach parts in a light truck. The bolts are installed on the interior floor of the truck.

Before Improvement
Access is restricted, and it is difficult to properly align the equipment during the insertion process. Consequently, roughly one out of four bolts is stripped. This creates problems in repair, wastes precious time, and results in buckets of scrapped bolts.

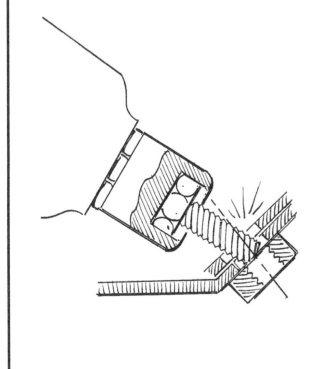

After Improvement
Although a solution was quickly identified, it took more than two years to implement because it required the concurrence of design engineers. The standard bolt is replaced with a dog-point bolt that does not have any threads on the leading end of the bolt. The tip aligns the bolts with the nut before the threads are engaged, eliminating defects.

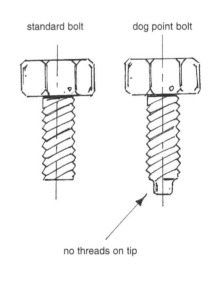

standard bolt   dog point bolt

no threads on tip

Process   Drill and tap holes in cylinder welded to tube

Problem   Tubes incorrectly positioned

Solution   Additional restraint on jig

Product

Parts   Cylinder on tube

Stage   1-Fabrication
                2-Insert workpiece and drill

State	Control Function							
	〜	Poka-yoke				Simplify		
	Adjustment	Setting	Warn	Shutdown	Control	Tools/Eqpt	Process	Product
Complexity					X		X	
Prevent Mistakes					X			
Detect Mistakes								
Detect Defects								
Variation								

Description of Problem: Cylinder tubes are set into a jig on a drill press and clamped in place against a target so holes can be drilled in the tap seats.

Before Improvement

Although there was one positioning clamp on the jig, it was possible to clamp the workpiece so the tube was out of position, resulting in hole misalignment and eccentric holes.

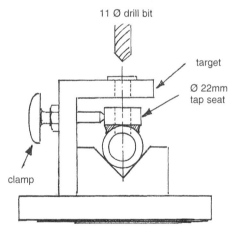

11 Ø drill bit

target

Ø 22mm tap seat

clamp

the tap seat side of the cylinder is put up against the target and held in place by a screw-tightened clamp

After Improvement

A second clamp was provided to prevent incorrect positioning of the workpiece. This now regulates alignment of the workpiece and completely eliminates defects.

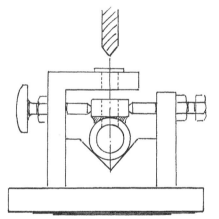

a second clamp is installed to prevent misalignment

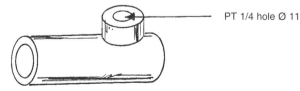

PT 1/4 hole Ø 11

Misaligned Parts

		Control Function						

Process   Mount asymmetric gear to shaft

Problem   Gear and shaft aligned incorrectly

Solution   Jig assures correct alignment

Product   Transmission, rice-planting vehicle

Parts   Gear, partial segment

Stage   1-Assembly
2-Insert part

	Control Function						
	$\curvearrowright$	Poka-yoke			Simplify		
State	Adjustment	Setting	Warn	Shutdown	Control	Tools/Eqpt	Process	Product
Complexity					X		X	
Prevent Mistakes					X			
Detect Mistakes								
Detect Defects								
Variation								

Description of Problem: A gear is mounted on a shaft and plate assembly inside the transmission case of a rice-planting vehicle. Alignment marks are punched on the shaft assembly and the gear and then must be properly aligned during assembly.

Before Improvement

On a number of occasions mistakes occurred in aligning the marks. It was necessary to dismantle the units after they had been completed in these cases.

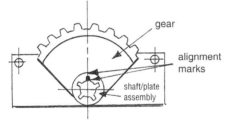

correct

gear

alignment marks

shaft/plate assembly

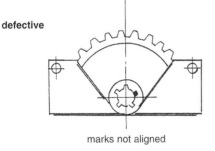

defective

marks not aligned

After Improvement

A jig was made to ensure that the gear and shaft assemblies were properly aligned when assembled. The jig is now set over the shaft and positioned using one of the holes in the plate. The long rod on the jig (shown in diagram) then guides the gear along the shaft in the correct orientation.

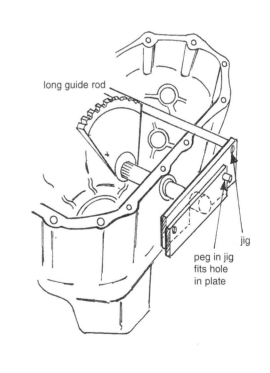

long guide rod

jig

peg in jig fits hole in plate

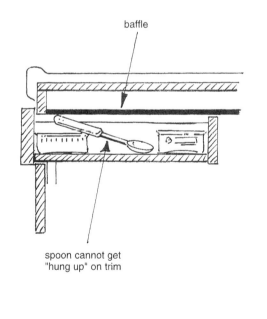

Misaligned Parts, Commit Prohibited Action

Process	Open drawer
Problem	Drawer cannot be opened
Solution	Barrier keeps loose items from locking drawer
Product	Kitchen drawer
Parts	Drawer, cabinet, utensils
Stage	1-Use 2-Store and retrieve

Control Function							
∿		Poka-yoke			Simplify		
Adjustment	Setting	Warn	Shutdown	Control	Tools/Eqpt	Process	Product
State							
Complexity							
Prevent Mistakes				X			
Detect Mistakes							
Detect Defects							
Variation							

Description of Problem: A variety of kitchen utensils are put in a drawer for storage after washing.

Before Improvement
When the drawer is closed, the items shift. Occasionally an item might wedge itself in a position that is hard to remove. In some situations the items can become so tightly wedged, and the drawer opening is so small, that it is almost impossible to open the drawer without taking the drawer apart.

After Improvement
Organization of the drawer contents with trays help to keep items from shifting when the drawer is closed. This reduces, but does not eliminate, the possibility that the drawer can be wedged shut. A better solution is to put a baffle in the cabinet over the drawer. Now, even if the items shift, they cannot become caught and wedge the drawer shut.

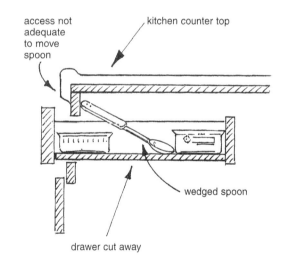

access not adequate to move spoon

kitchen counter top

wedged spoon

drawer cut away

baffle

spoon cannot get "hung up" on trim

Misaligned Parts

Process	Roll form threads in plate
Problem	Omitted operations, defective operations, and power interruptions
Solution	Limit switch detects omission, better part fixturing
Product	
Parts	Plate
Stage	1-Fabrication 2-Setup thread forming

	Control Function							
	∿	Poka-yoke				Simplify		
State	Adjustment	Setting	Warn	Shutdown	Control	Tools/Eqpt	Process	Product
Complexity								
Prevent Mistakes				X	X			
Detect Mistakes								
Detect Defects				X	X			
Variation								

Description of Problem: A two-spindle roll-forming machine is used to cut threads in a certain part.

Before Improvement

Products with defective threads were produced because the guide had enough clearance that the workpiece could shift during forming. In addition, when the machine was started up after an emergency shutdown or a power loss, unthreaded parts were ejected at first. Items with faulty threads and items with no threads cut were sorted out by the workers, but some defects got by.

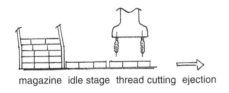

magazine   idle stage   thread cutting   ejection

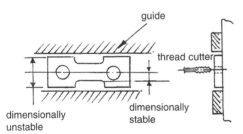

guide

thread cutter

dimensionally unstable

dimensionally stable

After Improvement

Correctly threaded items, unthreaded items, and items with faulty taps all have different hole diameters. A device that checks the inner diameter of the holes and a limit switch circuit to shut off the threading operation are used together to eliminate defective items at the beginning of work.

1. Hole diameter before threading Ø 7.3
   Hole diameter if threading ID faulty Ø 7.5
   Hole diameter if threading is good Ø 6.8
   Check pin diameter Ø 7.0

limit switch

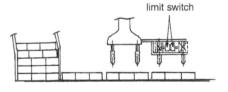

2. A limit switch circuit is added to detect omitted or faulty threading.

3. The guide is revised, adding blocks to hold the workpiece in a stable position for threading.

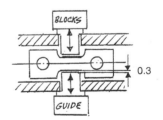

BLOCKS

0.3

GUIDE

Process	Tapping
Problem	Manual tap is often aslant
Solution	Level attached to tapping tool
Product	Motorcycle
Parts	Engine
Stage	1-Fabrication 2-Tapping (manual)

	Control Function							
	∿	Poka-yoke				Simplify		
State	Adjustment	Setting	Warn	Shutdown	Control	Tools/Eqpt	Process	Product
Complexity							X	
Prevent Mistakes			X					
Detect Mistakes								
Detect Defects								
Variation								

Description of Problem: The operator must manually tap a product during production.

Before Improvement
The operator made a square to align the tap vertically before tapping. After checking the alignment. the hole was tapped, but the alignment guide could not be held in place or checked during the tapping process. Misalignment of the tap sometimes resulted.

After Improvement
The operator attached a leveling instrument to the tap handle. The operator can now verify the vertical alignment while tapping the part. The level can rotate about the handle because it is held in place by a bearing.

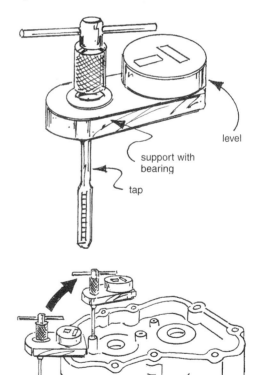

level

support with bearing

tap

part to be tapped

Misaligned Parts

Process   Parking

Problem   Vehicle positioned improperly

Solution   Position indicator

Product   Automobile parking

Parts   Garage and vehicle

Stage   1-Use
2-Park vehicle

State	Adjustment	Setting	Warn	Shutdown	Control	Tools/Eqpt	Process	Product
			Poka-yoke			Simplify		
Complexity								
Prevent Mistakes			X					
Detect Mistakes								
Detect Defects								
Variation								

Description of Problem: Vehicles are parked in the garage after an excursion.

Before Improvement

The available parking space may be limited, requiring accurate positioning of the vehicle. With a sloping hood on the vehicle, it is difficult to accurately judge the position of the bumper. Drivers may bump into walls or cabinets if they pull in too far, or the garage door may hit the car if they do not pull in far enough.

After Improvement

A tennis ball can be hung from the ceiling and adjusted so that the car is in the proper position when the ball touches the windshield.

A variety of electrical sensors provide alternative solutions that are equally as effective, but more expensive.

Misaligned Parts

		Control Function						
		∿		Poka-yoke		Simplify		
State		Adjustment	Setting	Warn	Shutdown	Control	Tools/Eqpt	Process	Product
Complexity									
Prevent Mistakes									
Detect Mistakes					X			
Detect Defects									
Variation									

Process   Drill high-precision holes in the sidewall of a cylinder

Problem   Chips cause misaligned part during drilling

Solution   A microswitch detects proper part placement

Product

Parts   Tube side hole

Stage   1-Fabrication
2-Insert workpiece and drill

Description of Problem: A special drilling machine is used to drill reference position holes for a process in which small, high precision parts are assembled. The pinholes are used for positioning references when assembling the parts. It is important that the pinholes be accurately positioned. Since the parts have threads tapped on their inner diameters, the pinholes are positioned by screwing the parts into a reference jig (as shown in the drawing). Foreign matter such as chips or shavings adhere to the contacting surface at times, and the positioning can be incorrect as a result.

Before Improvement
It was not possible to detect small variations in positioning when drilling, so if foreign matter had interfered with the part on the jig, entire lots had to be rejected when the parts arrived at assembly.

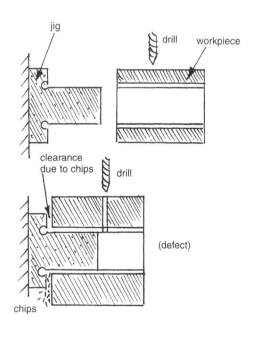

After Improvement
A notch was made on part of the contacting surface of the jig, and a microswitch was mounted there to detect whether the workpiece and the jig were fitting snugly. The switch is now connected to a red lamp, which lights when the switch is open, and a blue lamp, which lights when the switch is closed, and to the power switch of the drilling machine. The switch is adjusted so that it does not close if there are chips on the jig, so drilling cannot begin unless there is nothing caught on the jig. Setting errors have been completely eliminated.

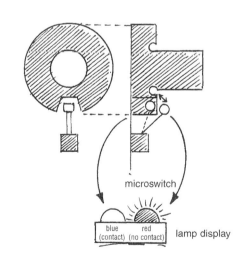

Misaligned, Omitted Parts

Process — Mount nuts to workpiece

Problem — Omitted or mispositioned

Solution — Limit switch detector

Product

Parts — Nuts, multipiece channel

Stage — 1-Assembly
2-Join

	Control Function							
	∿		Poka-yoke			Simplify		
State	Adjustment	Setting	Warn	Shutdown	Control	Tools/Eqpt	Process	Product
Complexity								
Prevent Mistakes								
Detect Mistakes								
Detect Defects				X				
Variation								

Description of Problem: A dedicated machine is used for mounting nuts onto parts for a wide variety of different models.

Before Improvement

Omission of nuts or faulty centering of nuts occurred and caused trouble during later assembly. A clamp was used to check for missing nuts, but faulty nut centering could not be detected.

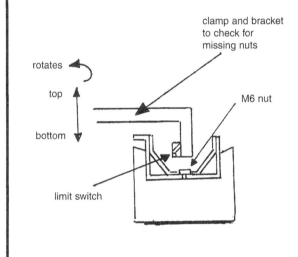

rotates
top
bottom

clamp and bracket to check for missing nuts

M6 nut

limit switch

After Improvement

The machine power was connected to a limit switch that is actuated by a spring-mounted rod. If the nut is missing, the rod goes through the hole and the limit switch remains off. On the other hand, if the nut is off-center, the rod cannot rise at all, and the limit switch also stays off. If the nut is positioned correctly, the rod raises enough to turn on the limit switch, but no further. Selection switches are used to change the settings for different models.

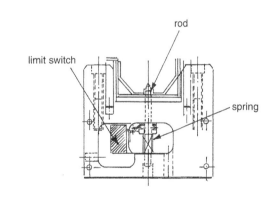

rod

limit switch

spring

Misaligned Parts

	Process	Injection molding

Process Injection molding

Problem Difficulty detecting small misalignment

Solution Air venting detects misalignment

Product Injection molded plastic parts

Parts Injection mold

Stage 1-Fabrication
2-Molding

	Control Function							
	⌒⌒		Poka-yoke			Simplify		
State	Adjustment	Setting	Warn	Shutdown	Control	Tools/Eqpt	Process	Product
Complexity								
Prevent Mistakes								
Detect Mistakes								
Detect Defects			X					
Variation								

Description of Problem: In the operation of an injection mold for small plastic parts, the faces of the mold halves must fit tightly without gaps to form the product correctly.

Before Improvement

Small gaps between the flat mating surfaces of the right and left mold halves are difficult to detect. If molding is started before a tight alignment is achieved, plastic can be forced out of the mold, creating a difficult clean-up problem. In addition, because the resin is not adequately constrained during injection, the parts are defective if the mold does not seal.

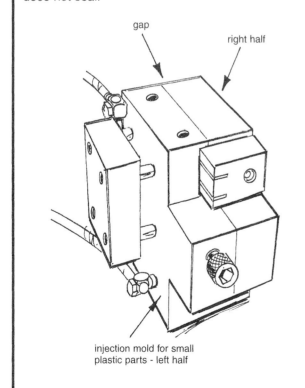

injection mold for small plastic parts - left half

After Improvement

Air holes are machined on one of the two mold halves. Air pressure is applied to the air holes. If the two halves do not mate properly, air will leak out when pressure is applied. By measuring the pressure loss, gaps as small as 0.05 mm (0.002") can be quickly identified.

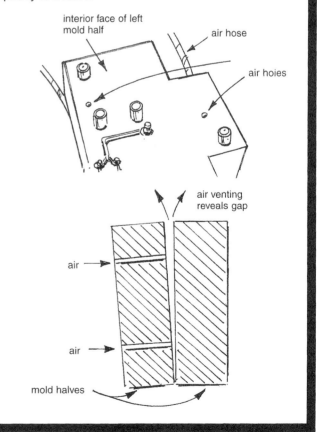

178

MISADJUSTMENTS (MD)

An incorrect adjustment of an operation, either before or during execution, that is not the result of information errors. This generally includes incomplete operations.

Principles that Eliminate Misadjustments	Examples
1. Convert adjustments to setting.	
a. Use self-limiting settings (drive slips at preset torque).	MD-1
b. Set gaps.	MD-2
c. Coolant routing eliminates adjustments.	MD-3
d. Redesigning a fastener prevents tool from slipping during insertion.	MD-4
e. Set timer duration with one touch.	*MT-3*
2. Automate adjustments.	
a. Control travel or stroke with a limit switch.	MD-5, MD-6
b. Detect and compensate for tool wear.	*DM-3*
c. Automate adjustments requiring continuous attention.	
d. Prevent overstroke by shutting down the process.	
3. Prevent damage due to misadjustments with protective barriers.	
a. Plastic shim protects cutting tool.	MD-7
4. Detect misadjustments, and:	
a. Shut down the line if adjustment is not correct (pneumatic pressure).	MD-13
b. Warn if the travel or stroke is not adequate.	MD-8, MD-10, MD-11
5. Make the results of an adjustment error obvious.	MD-9
6. Product cannot be removed from a fixture until the part insertion stroke is adequate.	MD-14

Principles that Eliminate Misadjustments   **Examples**

7. Detect part deviations from the ideal (shape, dimension, weight) due to misadjustment:
   a. Diameters.   MD-15, MD-16

8. Automatically mark the part if the adjustment performed to the part is correct
   or incorrect.

9. Place the adjustment information next to the adjustment controls.
   a. Magnetic signs.   MD-12

10. Use mechanical stops to limit the motion of controls.

Misadjustment, Omitted Part, Commit Prohibited Action

Example MD-1

Process	Refueling
Problem	Gas cap overtightened
Solution	Ratchet prevents excess torque
Product	Automobile
Parts	Gas cap, gas tank fill stem
Stage	1-Stock management 2-Replenish fuel

Control Function							
		Poka-yoke			Simplify		
Adjustment	Setting	Warn	Shutdown	Control	Tools/Eqpt	Process	Product

State	Adjustment	Setting	Warn	Shutdown	Control	Tools/Eqpt	Process	Product
Complexity								
Prevent Mistakes					X			
Detect Mistakes								
Detect Defects								
Variation		X						

Description of Problem: Automobiles need to be refueled at regular intervals.

Before Improvement

If the gas cap is overtightened, the tank will not vent properly. The gas caps can also be lost during refueling. In the past, fuels containing lead could have been introduced into cars that can only use unleaded gasoline.

gas cap

After Improvement

A "ratchet" cap action signals that the cap has been tightened adequately but "slips" to prevent excess torque. Connecting the gas cap to the vehicle with a cord assures that the gas cap will not be accidentally lost. Inserts in the fuel fill stems of unleaded vehicles are too small to allow insertion of the nozzles for gasoline containing lead. This example graphically illustrates that even simple tasks require multiple mistake-proofing devices to achieve extremely low defect rates.

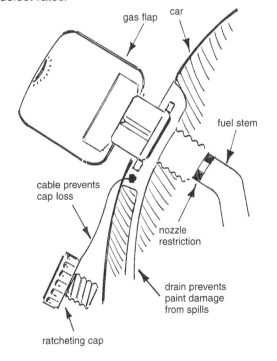

gas flap — car — fuel stem — cable prevents cap loss — nozzle restriction — drain prevents paint damage from spills — ratcheting cap

181

Process   Gap adjustment

Problem   Incorrect gap setting

Solution   Spring load sensor

Product   Robot motor

Parts   Motor encoding wheel and sensor

Stage   1-Assembly
2-Sensor adjustment

	Control Function						
	∿		Poka-yoke			Simplify	
State	Adjustment	Setting	Warn	Shutdown	Control	Tools/Eqpt	Process	Product
Complexity							X	
Prevent Mistakes					X			
Detect Mistakes								
Detect Defects								
Variation	X							

Description of Problem: The gap between an encoder wheel and sensor must be set accurately. The sensor is attached to the housing, and the encoder wheel is connected to the motor shaft. The gap between the encoder wheel and sensor are adjusted by manually moving the encoder wheel.

Before Improvement

To set the gap, the operator holds the motor housing, inserts a gapping tool, moves the encoder wheel, and secures the assembly when the gap is correct. This is a very difficult process, since the motor, gapping tool, and Allen wrench must all be held at the same time. Frequently, the gapping tool falls out during the process, and the process must be started over. Many errors occur in the adjustment, requiring disassembly of the motor for repair.

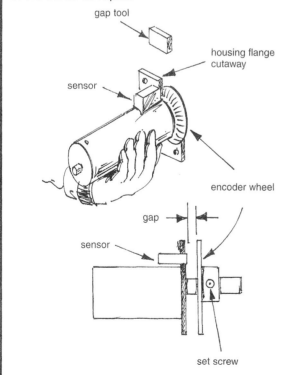

After Improvement

The operation is converted from an adjustment to a setting. The encoder wheel is fixed to the shaft when assembled. The sensor is spring-loaded on the housing and can slide axially. Installing the gapping tool sets the correct gap, and the sensor spring force holds the gap tool in place until the attachment screws are tightened, locking the sensor in the correct position.

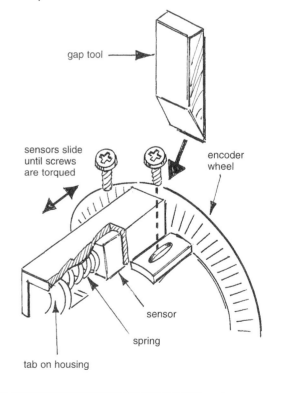

Misadjustment

Process	Various machining operations
Problem	Flexible coolant hoses are damaged or deflected
Solution	"Showerhead" curtain coolant delivery
Product	Aircraft engines
Parts	Milling, boring, drilling machines
Stage	1-Fabrication 2-Machining

Control Function							
∿	Poka-yoke				Simplify		
Adjustment	Setting	Warn	Shutdown	Control	Tools/Eqpt	Process	Product
State							
Complexity							
Prevent Mistakes				X			
Detect Mistakes							
Detect Defects							
Variation	X						

Description of Problem: During machining operations, coolant must be delivered continuously to the tool tip to control wear and achieve accurate machining.

Before Improvement

Traditionally, flexible hoses have been used to deliver coolant to the tool tip. These coolant hoses must be repositioned when tools of different lengths are used. The hoses are prone to misadjustments, deflection, and damage. Tool chips have even pulled off coolant hoses. Any of these conditions can result in excessive tool wear, poor surface finish quality, out-of-tolerance parts, and premature tool wear or failure.

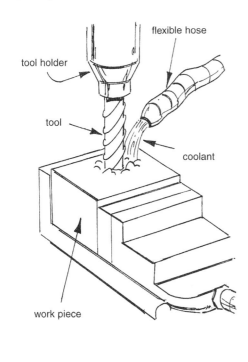

After Improvement

A "showerhead" coolant delivery system directs a cylindrical "wall" of coolant flow along the axis of the machining tool, assuring the coolant reaches the tool from every side. The operator does not need to adjust flexible hoses, eliminating adjustment errors. Because the "showerhead" is rigidly mounted to the machining head, unexpected deflections are completely eliminated.

This type of coolant delivery is also useful in containing dust, which may be hazardous, when machining some types of material. It does, however, reduce visual access to the machining process, which may be important on some manually controlled machine operations.

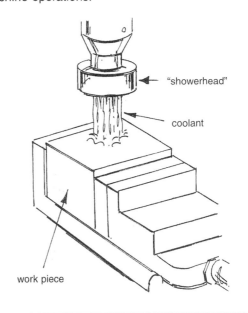

Misadjustment

Example MD-4

Process	Torque screws to attach cassette transport covers
Problem	Damaged covers when screwdriver slips from slot
Solution	Slot captures screwdriver tip
Product	Cassette transport covers
Parts	Screw, cassette transport
Stage	1-Assembly 2-Fasten

Control Function							
∿		Poka-yoke			Simplify		
State	Adjustment	Setting	Warn	Shutdown	Control	Tools/Eqpt	Process	Product
Complexity								
Prevent Mistakes					X			
Detect Mistakes								
Detect Defects								
Variation		X						

Description of Problem: Plastic cassette transport covers are assembled with screws.

Before Improvement
Cassette covers were frequently scratched when the screwdriver slipped out of the screw slot and slid against the plastic covers.

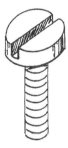

After Improvement
The cause of the trouble was scrutinized and a change was made in the shape of the screw slot to prevent the screwdriver from slipping. Scratches caused by the screwdriver slipping have been completely eliminated.

Misadjustment

Process	Move equipment frames using forklifts

Process   Move equipment frames using forklifts

Problem   Forklift is raised too high, running frame into the ceiling

Solution   "Limit switches" on forklift limits lift and tilt

Product   Precision electronic manufacturing equipment

Parts   Equipment frames

Stage   1-Transportation and handling
2-Forklift assembly

	Control Function							
	∿	Poka-yoke			Simplify		
State	Adjustment	Setting	Warn	Shutdown	Control	Tools/Eqpt	Process	Product
Complexity								
Prevent Mistakes					X			
Detect Mistakes								
Detect Defects								
Variation								

Description of Problem: Precision electronic manufacturing equipment is built in large frames where clearance with the ceiling is limited.

Before Improvement
Precision equipment can be easily damaged during movement when forklift operators lift the frame for movement. Paying careful attention to avoid hitting objects that are easily seen, forklift operators, particularly recently hired individuals, occasionally raise the frames too high or tilt the frames too far, unintentionally hitting the ceiling or door frames.

After Improvement
"Limit switches" are mounted to the forklift. If the operator tries to raise the forklift too high or tilt the frame too much, further movement is prevented.

relief value prevents excessive tip

switch relieves lift pressure if forks are raised too high

Process Transport goods with overhead crane

Problem Sudden stop at end of travel results in dangerous swinging loads

Solution Limit switch shuts down crane before reaching end of travel

Product

Parts Overhead crane

Stage 1-Transportation and handling
2-Crane operation

	Control Function							
	$\bigwedge$		Poka-yoke			Simplify		
State	Adjustment	Setting	Warn	Shutdown	Control	Tools/Eqpt	Process	Product
Complexity								
Prevent Mistakes					X			
Detect Mistakes								
Detect Defects								
Variation								

Description of Problem: A suspended overhead crane is used to transport goods throughout a section of the factory.

Before Improvement

Mechanical stoppers are mounted at the ends of the rails on which the crane travels. Sometimes when the crane was traveling at a fast speed or had traveled only a short distance, it would strike against the stoppers rather violently. This caused the loads to swing, resulting in dangerous situations.

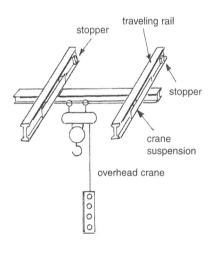

After Improvement

A limit switch was mounted on the crane and contacting fixtures were mounted on the traveling rails just before the stoppers. Now, when the limit switch on the crane hits the contacting fixtures, the crane motor is stopped, and the crane continues to move only under inertial force. The crane no longer stops suddenly after moving at high speed. This mitigates shocks and prevents swinging of loads without any vigilance on the part of the crane operator.

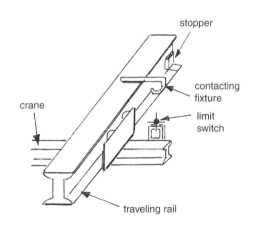

Process   Set up lathe tools

Problem   Tool chipped during setting

Solution   Plastic shims used in setup

Product   Aircraft engines

Parts   "Set rings," shim, lathe tools

Stage   1-Setup
2-Set lathe tool position

	Control Function						
	∿	Poka-yoke			Simplify		
State	Adjustment	Setting	Warn	Shutdown	Control	Tools/Eqpt	Process	Product
Complexity								
Prevent Mistakes					X			
Detect Mistakes				X				
Detect Defects								
Variation								

Description of Problem: To avoid adjustments during lathe setup operations, the relationship between the tool tip and tool holder is set using a work holding fixture and "set rings," which have accurately measured precision diameters and flats.

Before Improvement
When setting the tool tip position, operation errors can chip the lathe inserts. In addition, the "set rings" can also be damaged.

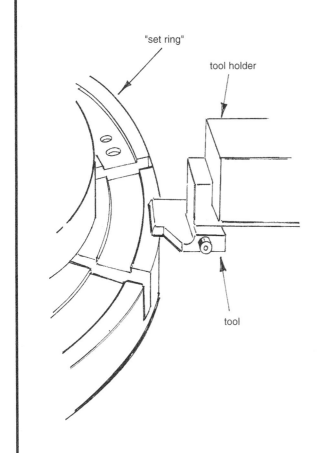

After Improvement
Precision plastic shims are used to set the lathe tool position. The precision tool setting is achieved, but the "set rings" and tools are protected and never have to make direct contact. The problem with chipped lathe inserts is eliminated.

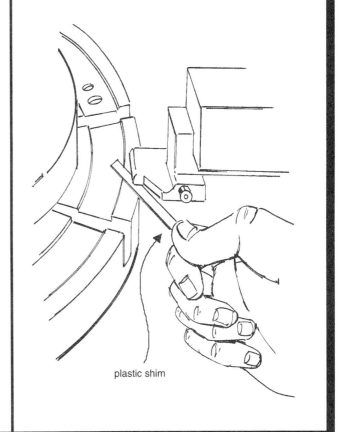

Process Press-fit steering wheel spoke reinforcement plates

Problem Plates not pressed to proper position

Solution Switch detects faulty positioning

Product Steering wheel

Parts Spoke reinforcement plate, steering wheel

Stage 1-Assembly
2-Insert part and press fit

Control Function							
∿		Poka-yoke			Simplify		
Adjustment	Setting	Warn	Shutdown	Control	Tools/Eqpt	Process	Product
State							
Complexity							
Prevent Mistakes		X					
Detect Mistakes							
Detect Defects							
Variation							

Description of Problem: Reinforcement plates are press-fitted into steering wheel spokes.

Before Improvement
The reinforcement plates sometimes were not pressed into the proper position, and thus the spokes could not be mounted correctly.

After Improvement
The end of the spoke was mounted on a jig equipped with a contact switch at the proper final position of the reinforcement plate. A buzzer sounds and a light goes on to show when the plate has been pressed all the way to the proper position. Faulty positioning is completely eliminated.

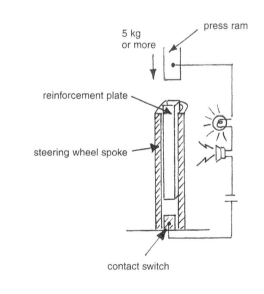

5 kg or more

press ram

reinforcement plate

steering wheel spoke

contact switch

Process   Switch setting

Problem   Switch set incorrectly

Solution   Improve switch position indicators

Product   Chemicals

Parts   Automatic valve switch

Stage   1-Material production
2-Valve operation

State		Adjustment	Setting	Warn	Shutdown	Control	Tools/Eqpt	Process	Product
Control Function				Poka-yoke			Simplify		
Complexity								X	
Prevent Mistakes			X						
Detect Mistakes									
Detect Defects									
Variation									

Description of Problem: The operator sets a switch to control the operation of an automatic valve.

Before Improvement
It is difficult to see the switch position indicator. As a result, the operator sets the valve in the wrong position.

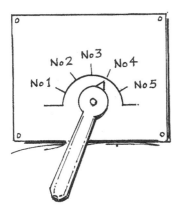

After Improvement
The handle on the switch is replaced. The new handle has a long pointer. Larger numbers are used to indicate the switch position. The switch position can now be easily seen at a glance.

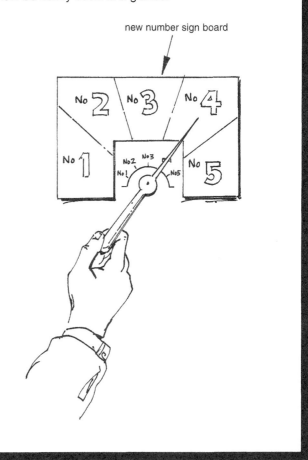

new number sign board

Process   Plate

Problem   Holes not to depth

Solution   Limit switches determine start of drilling and
                proper depth

Product

Parts   Plate

Stage   1-Fabrication
                2-Drilling

State	Control Function							
	$\cap$		Poka-yoke			Simplify		
	Adjustment	Setting	Warn	Shutdown	Control	Tools/Eqpt	Process	Product
Complexity								
Prevent Mistakes								
Detect Mistakes			X					
Detect Defects								
Variation								

Description of Problem: A series of holes are drilled in a plate.

Before Improvement
The operator's skill was relied on to determine whether the hole was drilled to the correct depth. However, the drill was sometimes retracted before it had gone in all the way, resulting in faulty drilling. Troubles resulted during assembly.

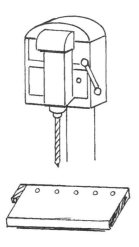

After Improvement
Two limit switches were mounted on the drill press. Faulty drilling now is indicated if limit switch 1 is released before limit switch 2 has been tripped. A buzzer is sounded to alert the operator.

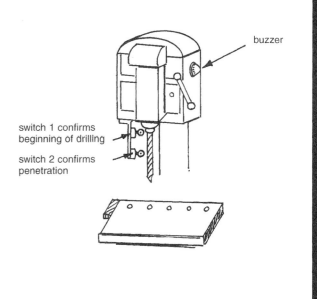

buzzer

switch 1 confirms beginning of drilling

switch 2 confirms penetration

Misadjustment

Example MD-11

Process	Tap through holes	
Problem	Tap depth not sufficient	
Solution	Microswitch detects adequate tap penetration	
Product		
Parts		
Stage	1-Fabrication 2-Tapping	

Control Function							
	∿	Poka-yoke			Simplify		
State	Adjustment	Setting	Warn	Shutdown	Control	Tools/Eqpt	Process	Product
Complexity								
Prevent Mistakes								
Detect Mistakes			X					
Detect Defects								
Variation								

Description of Problem: Holes are drilled and tapped in aluminum flange.

Before Improvement

Tapping was checked with a screw gage after the holes were threaded. However, items with insufficient tapping depth often resulted due to errors in setting the tap.

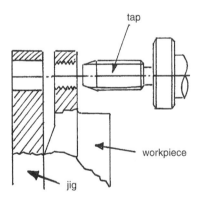

After Improvement

A microswitch for checking tap penetration was installed on the jig. Tap breakage and errors in setting the tap are both detected by this means.

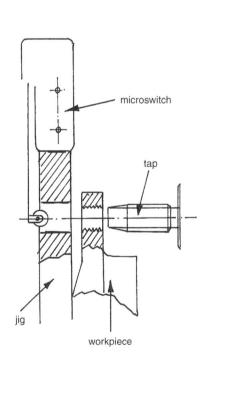

Misadjustment, Omitted Information

Example MD-12

	Process	Control adjustment

Process   Control adjustment

Problem   Undetected adjustment error during production change

Solution   Put correct setting information near controls

Product   Chemicals

Parts   Operation controller

Stage   1-Material production
2-Set controls

	Control Function							
	∿		Poka-yoke			Simplify		
State	Adjustment	Setting	Warn	Shutdown	Control	Tools/Eqpt	Process	Product
Complexity							X	
Prevent Mistakes								
Detect Mistakes			X					
Detect Defects								
Variation								

Description of Problem: When changing the production type, the control settings for measurement instruments are changed according to instructions on the daily report.

Before Improvement

Operators read the daily report and memorize the settings for the current production. One operator set the instrument control points incorrectly when changing the production type and left the room, taking the daily report. Other operators in the control room watched process measurements to assure that measured values were between the established control points. However, because they did not have a copy of the daily report, they could not recognize that the control points were set incorrectly.

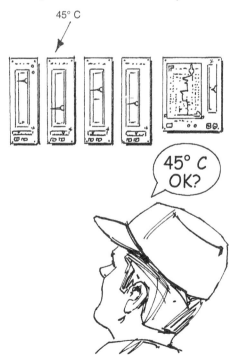

After Improvement

A magnetic sheet indicating the control set points is prepared for each type of production. When changing the production type, the magnetic sheet indicating the correct control settings is placed near the control switch. The controls are set using the values on the magnetic sheet. Other operators can tell whether the settings are right or wrong by looking at the magnetic sheet without needing a copy of the daily report.

These changes eliminate dependence on memorization and locate the information adjacent to the point of action.

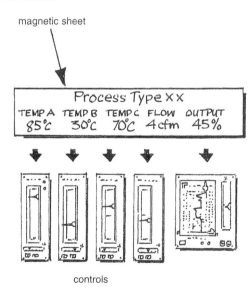

Misadjustment

Process	Torque nuts with pneumatic power wrenches
Problem	Drops in pneumatic pressure cause insufficient torque
Solution	Conveyance linked to air-pressure sensor
Product	
Parts	Nuts, pneumatic power wrenches
Stage	1-Assembly 2-Fasten

Control Function								
	$\sim$		Poka-yoke			Simplify		
State	Adjustment	Setting	Warn	Shutdown	Control	Tools/Eqpt	Process	Product
Complexity								
Prevent Mistakes								
Detect Mistakes			X	X				
Detect Defects								
Variation								

Description of Problem: Nuts are tightened to a specified torque with a power wrench driver by pneumatic pressure supplied throughout the factory.

Before Improvement
If air-pressure dropped during tightening, no warning of the problem was given, and the conveyor continued to move. Therefore, bolts were tightened with insufficient torque.

tightening operation

After Improvement
An air-pressure meter was installed in the airline. A lamp blinks, an alarm rings, and the conveyor stops if the air pressure drops below a critical point.

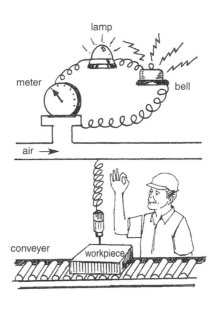

Process   Press fit cylindrical part into plate

Problem   Plug not pressed all the way

Solution   Gate prevents removal until plug travels the correct distance

Product

Parts   Plug, plate

Stage   1-Assembly
2-Insert part and press fit

Control Function							
∿		Poka-yoke			Simplify		
Adjustment	Setting	Warn	Shutdown	Control	Tools/Eqpt	Process	Product
State							
Complexity							
Prevent Mistakes							
Detect Mistakes							
Detect Defects			X				
Variation							

Description of Problem: Part A is set in a jig, and part B is pressed into the hole in part A.

Before Improvement

Workers were supposed to inspect the parts to make sure that insertion was sufficient, but often errors were overlooked due to operator carelessness.

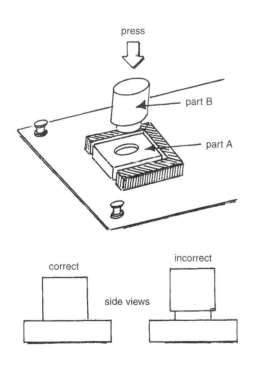

After Improvement

A gate was installed on the jig. If part B is not inserted sufficiently, it strikes against the gate, preventing the operator from removing the workpiece from the jig.

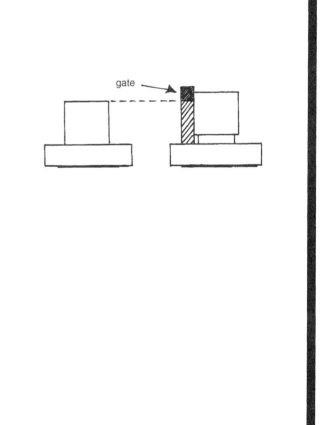

Misadjustment

	Process	Machine-stepped disks
Process		Machine-stepped disks
Problem		Incorrect dimensions
Solution		Out-of-tolerance part catches on mechanical inspection system
Product		
Parts		Round bars
Stage		1-Fabrication 2-Inspection

Control Function

State	Adjustment	Setting	Warn	Shutdown	Control	Tools/Eqpt	Process	Product
Complexity	▩		▩			▩		
Prevent Mistakes	▩					▩	▩	
Detect Mistakes	▩					▩		
Detect Defects	▩				X	▩		
Variation			▩	▩	▩	▩	▩	

Description of Problem: Steps are machined onto round brass bar stock, to the shape shown in the drawing. Because of possible variations in machining, it is necessary to check the finished dimensions of each step when it is completed.

Before Improvement
The dimensions of the bars were checked manually with gages.

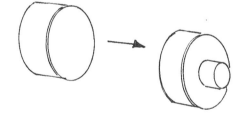

After Improvement
An inclined chute with a guide was installed, and the completed bars now are rolled along the guide. Interference plates mounted on the guide detect dimensional irregularities in the machined steps.

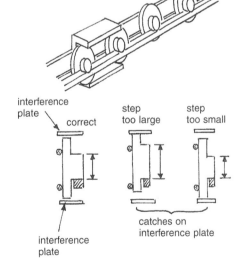

interference plate

correct

step too large

step too small

catches on interference plate

interference plate

Misadjustment

Example MD-16

Process	Pin formation	
Problem	Diameter on some pins is wrong	
Solution	Gates separate out bad pins	
Product	Drive pins	
Parts	Drive pins	
Stage	1-Fabrication 2-Inspection—roll forming	

Control Function							
	∿		Poka-yoke			Simplify	
State	Adjustment	Setting	Warn	Shutdown	Control	Tools/Eqpt	Process	Product
Complexity							
Prevent Mistakes							
Detect Mistakes							
Detect Defects			X	X			
Variation							

Description of Problem: Drive pins are processed in a high-volume manufacturing process.

Before Improvement

Occasionally the equipment is adjusted incorrectly and pins of the wrong diameter are produced. When this happens, numerous bad parts are produced before the problem is detected. In addition, pins of the wrong diameter from the previous batch sometimes get mixed with good parts.

When customers try to use drive pins that are too large, they can damage expensive products. If the pins are too small, they may wear too quickly or fall out, causing safety problems or product failures.

After Improvement

Immediately after fabrication, the pins slide past "gates" that separate the pins by diameter. Only pins of the proper diameter reach the finished stock. If an oversize or undersize pin is in the stream, sensors shut down the process and trigger an alarm. The operator can immediately eliminate the mixed parts or adjust the machine before additional defects are produced.

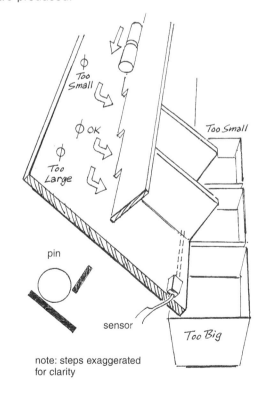

note: steps exaggerated for clarity

196

MISTIMED OR RUSHED (MT)

The operator does not have sufficient time to execute a process correctly, or does not respond at the appropriate time.

Principles that Eliminate Mistimed or Rushed Events   **Examples**

1. Where possible, make the "tact" time for all workstations in a sequence the same.

2. Processes are designed to be "Standard Operations."

3. Redesign the product or process so that the task is easier and can be done faster.

    a. Design assembly to be top-down or from the side.

    b. Avoid, where practical, the use of thin or flexible parts.

    c. Avoid, where practical, small parts (<0.040" (2mm)).

    d. Avoid parts that nest or tangle or maintain separation between them.

    e. Avoid, where practical, parts that are heavy, delicate, or require two hands to handle.

    f. Avoid, where practical, the need to add and remove fixtures.

4. Reduce the task difficulty for the allowed time:

    a. Eliminate unnecessary material from the work location with red tags,

    b. Eliminate or simplify decisions,   MT-2

    c. Organize the work environment using the 5S method, or

    d. Use Visual Control signboards to make the location of supplies obvious.

5. Vary production line speed, or change the task per station so that the operator has:

    a. More time per task where the operator is rushed (setup changes).   MT-1

    b. Less time per task where the workers are bored.

Principles that Eliminate Mistimed or Rushed Events   **Examples**

6. Prepare setup changes in advance.

   a. Select tools and parts needed for changeovers in advance.

   b. Move changeover tools to the production station before the changeover starts.

   c. Perform all possible setup operations before the changeover starts.

   d. Use settings rather than adjustments for every possible setup operation.

   e. Return changeover tools to storage after production has restarted.

7. Mistake-proof timing.

   a. One touch sets the timer duration.   MT-3

Process	Label and stamp products in small lots	
Problem	Insufficient setup time between changes led to various errors	
Solution	Vary conveyor speed so operator has time for setup changes	
Product		
Parts	Equipment for labeling and stamping	
Stage	1-Assembly 2-Setup	

Control Function

State	Adjustment	Setting	Warn	Shutdown	Control	Tools/Eqpt	Process	Product
	∿		Poka-yoke			Simplify		
Complexity					X		X	
Prevent Mistakes					X			
Detect Mistakes								
Detect Defects								
Variation								

Description of Problem: The production line changed from a mass-production facility where packaged parts were marked with labels to a small-lot production facility where packages are marked with either labels or stamps. One worker sets up and operates both a labeling machine and a rubber stamp station.

Before Improvement

No problems occurred in the past on the mass-production manufacturing line when all marking was done with labels. As small-lot production increased, errors began to occur. Because packaged parts could be marked either by stamping or by labeling, the number of setup operations increased. This lead to errors such as stamps too thinly inked, misaligned labels, and labels attached with insufficient paste. Time and effort were expended to correct these errors.

After Improvement

Research showed that problems were caused because the packed boxes were labeled on a conveyor moving at a constant speed that did not allow enough time to change setups. It was determined that varying the speed at which the packages are fed into the marking process would eliminate the labeling errors. A short conveyor with variable speed controls was installed between the chute and labeling machine. Now the operator can make visual checks of the labeling process until it is clear that the stamps are inked sufficiently or that the labels are pasted in the correct position with sufficient paste. The labeling and pasting errors are eliminated.

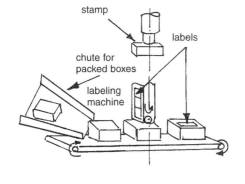

stamp
labels
chute for packed boxes
labeling machine

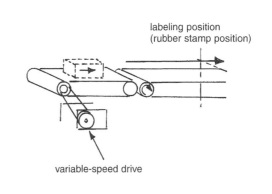

labeling position (rubber stamp position)
variable-speed drive

Process Insert components on circuit board

Problem Parts put in the wrong location

Solution Laser points to location

Product Circuit board assembly

Parts Circuit boards, discrete components

Stage 1-Insert components on circuit board
2-Insert part

	Control Function							
	∿		Poka-yoke			Simplify		
State	Adjustment	Setting	Warn	Shutdown	Control	Tools/Eqpt	Process	Product
Complexity							X	
Prevent Mistakes			X					
Detect Mistakes								
Detect Defects								
Variation								

Description of Problem: Circuit boards for modern consumer products are often very complex. Many of the parts, such as computer chips, are installed using automated equipment. However, discrete components, such as capacitors and transformers, may be installed manually.

Before Improvement
Operators are expected to install as many as 20 parts in less than a minute. The operation is complicated by the fact that each worker may have to install a variety of different components. Mounting points are similar, and components are often placed in the wrong location.

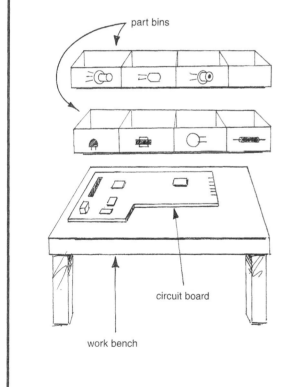

part bins

circuit board

work bench

After Improvement
"Smart" part bins are used to guide part selection, as described in other examples. An overhead low-power laser is linked to the "smart" part bin. The laser beam is aimed at the proper location for inserting the drawn part. If the discrete part requires a special orientation, the laser can trace a shape that outlines the proper orientation to help the operator assemble the component properly.

Since the worker does not need to make as many decisions, the task is easier to complete in the time allotted, and assembly errors are eliminated.

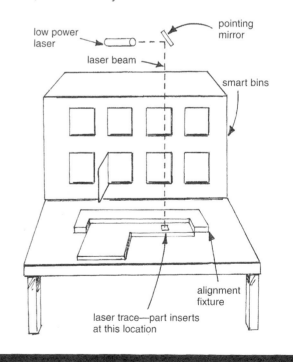

low power laser

pointing mirror

laser beam

smart bins

alignment fixture

laser trace—part inserts at this location

Mistimed, Misadjust, Inadequate Warning

Process	Oven cure
Problem	Product left in the oven too long
Solution	Replace timer
Product	Syntactic foam
Parts	Timer, oven, foam parts
Stage	1-Fabrication 2-Forming and curing

Control Function

		Poka-yoke			Simplify		
State	Adjustment	Setting	Warn	Shutdown	Control	Tools/Eqpt	Process	Product
Complexity								
Prevent Mistakes			X					
Detect Mistakes								
Detect Defects								
Variation								

Description of Problem: Syntactic foam parts need to be placed in an oven to cure for a brief period of time.

Before Improvement

The timer is not set properly, so the expected warning is not given at the right time. The mechanical timer must be turned past 15 minutes before it can be set to time events less than 15 minutes. The operator, who was not familiar with the timer, set it to 10 minutes. The alarm never sounded, and the parts were left in the oven too long, ruining them.

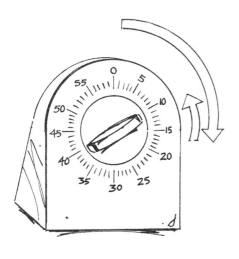

After Improvement

Timing errors can frequently be traced to problems in setting the timer. The cost of a good timer is generally trivial compared to the cost of a single wasted batch. Where the duration of each event has the same constant value, the best timer is one having preset timing initiated by pressing a single button. For events of variable duration, use timers where the duration can be set directly, without intermediate operations. Where possible, use timers where the alarm cannot be disabled, or make it obvious that the alarm mode is on or off. Alarms should be easily audible, even if the operator is distracted, and continuous enough that the alarm cannot be ignored. The display should be visible from across the room.

Perhaps the best alternative would be a timer, worn by the operator, that vibrates at the set time.

ADDED PART OR MATERIAL (OA)*

The failure to remove material or a part, such as protective coverings, temporary fixtures, or parts from a mold; or the addition of extra parts, such as dropping a bolt into a cavity, resulting from causes other than counting errors.

Principles that Eliminate Added Part(s) or Material	Examples
1. Treat parts to prevent adhesion of undesirable material.	
2. Design temporary parts so they can only stay in place as long as they are held.	OA-2, OA-3
3. Assure electrical connections are broken before product is removed with interlocks.	OA-4
4. Design temporary tools, fixtures, and test equipment to interfere with the next assembly.	OA-1, OA-7, OA-8
5. Insertion of a temporary part turns on an alarm that continues until it is removed.	OA-6
6. Detection of a tool in its holder (chuck key, wrench) enables machine operation.	OA-5
7. Guide part selection using "smart" part bins.	OP-5
8. Provide counting aids. a. A lifting tool can't be installed if stack height is too high.	OP-9

9. Detect part removal or nonremoval.
   a. Detect ejected part and enable the next operation.
   b. Detect nonejected part and lockout the next operation.
	OA-9
	OA-10

10. Provide a protective barrier that prevents dropped parts from falling into the product.	WL-17

Includes parts intentionally added that are not removed when required.

Added Material or Part

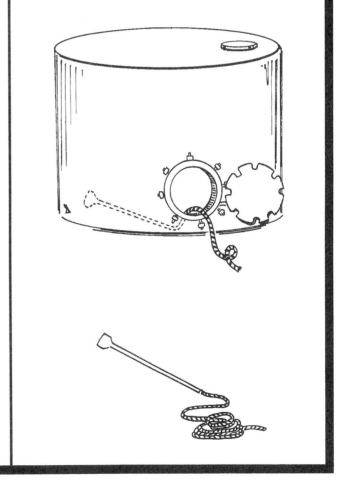

Example OA-1

Process   Clean storage tank

Problem   Cleaning tool is left in tank

Solution   Attach a rope to the tool

Product   Chemicals

Parts   Tank and tank cleaning tool

Stage   1-Maintenance
                 2-Clean tank

State	Control Function							
	Adjustment	Setting	Warn	Shutdown	Control	Tools/Eqpt	Process	Product
Complexity								
Prevent Mistakes					X			
Detect Mistakes								
Detect Defects								
Variation								

Control Function columns grouped: ∿ (Adjustment, Setting), Poka-yoke (Warn, Shutdown, Control), Simplify (Tools/Eqpt, Process, Product)

Description of Problem: Sediment in the bottom of a tank is removed with a cleaning tool.

Before Improvement
After cleaning the tank, the operator left the tool in the tank and closed the access port. When one operation was completed, attention focused on the next operation, and it was easy to forget a step in the previous operation.

After Improvement
A rope is attached to the cleaning tool. The cover of the access port cannot be closed until the rope and tool are removed from the tank.

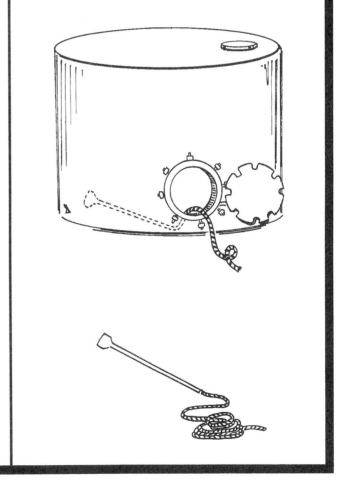

Added Material or Part

Process Remove handle from valve

Problem Handle not removed, valve accidentally opens

Solution Make handle an open-end wrench

Product Chemicals

Parts Valve and handle

Stage 1-Material production
2-Valve operation

Control Function							
∿		Poka-yoke			Simplify		
Adjustment	Setting	Warn	Shutdown	Control	Tools/Eqpt	Process	Product

State								
Complexity								
Prevent Mistakes					X			
Detect Mistakes								
Detect Defects								
Variation								

Description of Problem: The operator opens or closes a valve.

Before Improvement
The valve handle is in an area where individuals or equipment hit the handle. This can open or close the valve, causing defects in production. To avoid these problems, the operator is supposed to remove the valve after changing the valve setting. It is easy to forget to remove the handle at the end of the operation.

After Improvement
Change the valve handle design so that the handle will automatically come off the valve if the operator lets go of the handle. This can be accomplished in several ways. A taper-spring can be placed on the valve stem, or an open-end wrench could be used as a handle.

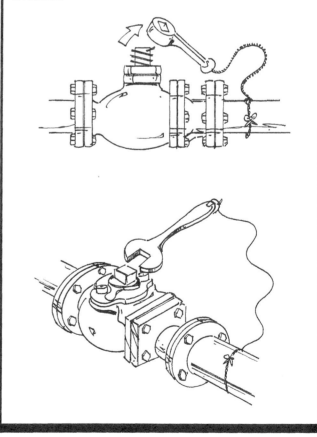

Process Fuel fill

Problem Operator drives away with the nozzle in the vehicle

Solution Alarm warns driver to remove nozzle

Product Automobile

Parts Automobile, gas pump, and fill nozzle

Stage 1-Stock management
2-Replenish fuel

State	Control Function							
	$\curvearrowright$		Poka-yoke			Simplify		
	Adjustment	Setting	Warn	Shutdown	Control	Tools/Eqpt	Process	Product
Complexity								
Prevent Mistakes					X			
Detect Mistakes				X				
Detect Defects								
Variation								

Description of Problem: Drivers insert the fill pump nozzle into the vehicle to transfer fuel to the vehicle.

Before Improvement

Occasionally the driver forgets to remove the nozzle from the vehicle before he or she drives away. This can damage the vehicle and do severe damage to the fuel pump. More importantly, the combination of gasoline and large mechanical forces poses a serious safety concern.

After Improvement

A weak or soft spring could be added to the dispensing nozzle. The operator must now hold the nozzle in place during the fueling process. Naturally, the nozzle must be able to shut off automatically if removed from the vehicle for safety reasons if this approach is used.

Although the spring solution may work in an industrial setting, the general public might resist because they want to do other things, such as wash the windows, while refueling. Although less effective and more expensive, a more acceptable long-term solution would be to have an audible warning to replace the nozzle after the pump shuts off. For distinction, the warning signal should come from the nozzle handle. This example illustrates the importance of designing mistake-proofing that users will accept.

Process   Die changeover for press setup

Problem   Detection cable on fixture broken because
                 operator forgot to remove it

Solution   Die transport will not operate while cable is
                 attached

Product

Parts   Press

Stage   1-Fabrication
                 2-Setup dies

	Control Function							
	$\sim$		Poka-yoke			Simplify		
State	Adjustment	Setting	Warn	Shutdown	Control	Tools/Eqpt	Process	Product
Complexity								
Prevent Mistakes					X			
Detect Mistakes								
Detect Defects								
Variation								

Description of Problem: When changing the setup on a large press, the old die moves out of the press and the new die moves in from the other side. This switch triggers a transport. Each die is also equipped with circuitry to detect the presence of the workpiece during processing, which is connected to the press controls by a cable. The cable must be disconnected before the dies are moved.

Before Improvement
When changing dies, the worker was to make a visual check of the cable. The standard procedure had instructions for this, but sometimes the cable was not removed before the die was moved. This snapped the cable or pulled and damaged the connecting terminals.

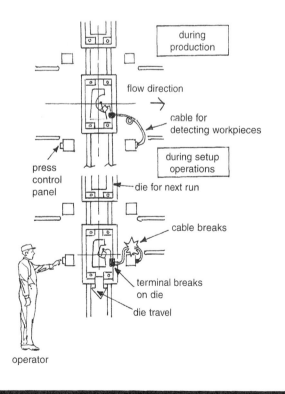

After Improvement
Two unused terminals in the terminal box on the die were jumpered. The switch operating the die transport mechanism now is interlocked with this circuit so that the transport switch does not operate while the cable is connected.

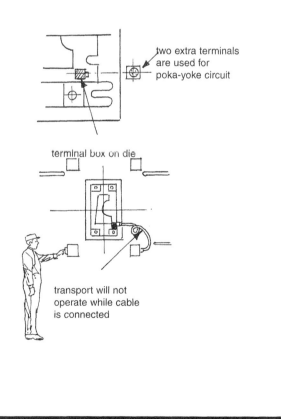

Added Material or Part

Example OA-5

Process	Bolt tightening
Problem	Wrench is not removed, damaging test assembly
Solution	Test cannot begin until wrench is returned to holder
Product	Engine test stand
Parts	Wrench
Stage	1-Assembly 2-Fasten

Control Function								
	$\curvearrowright$		Poka-yoke			Simplify		
State	Adjustment	Setting	Warn	Shutdown	Control	Tools/Eqpt	Process	Product
Complexity								
Prevent Mistakes				X				
Detect Mistakes								
Detect Defects								
Variation								

Description of Problem: A wrench is used to replace parts on a combustion engine test stand.

Before Improvement
Some parts on the test equipment must be replaced or cleaned often to obtain accurate test results. Consequently, the wrench is used frequently and is left on or near the test hardware for convenience during the maintenance activities. The wrench has accidentally been left in positions where the vibration of the engine during testing moved it, damaging expensive equipment by falling or banging into adjacent hardware. In some situations, the uncontrolled movement of such objects could also create hazardous conditions.

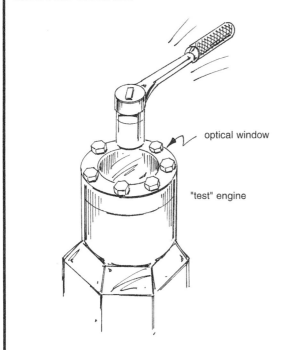

optical window

"test" engine

After Improvement
Operation of the engine is interlocked with a limit switch on a holster for the wrench. The wrench must be in the holster before the engine can be started. The same techniques used here for the wrench can be used to assure lathe chuck keys and milling head chuck keys are returned to holsters before lathe and milling operations are started. This prevents a serious safety problem—the chuck key is thrown across the room, potentially striking and injuring a worker.

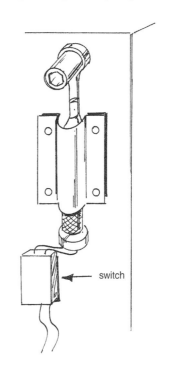

switch

Process	Remove heavy sample product from an assembly line
Problem	Auxiliary lifting jig not removed, stops line
Solution	Timer and alarm on jig reminds workers to remove jig
Product	
Parts	Sampling fixture
Stage	1-Assembly 2-Fixture removal

	Control Function							
	∿		Poka-yoke			Simplify		
State	Adjustment	Setting	Warn	Shutdown	Control	Tools/Eqpt	Process	Product
Complexity								
Prevent Mistakes			X					
Detect Mistakes								
Detect Defects								
Variation								

Description of Problem: A few times a day workers use a hand-operated lift to take products off the production line. For these special products, an auxiliary jig is put on the lift. After the products have been taken off the line, the auxiliary jig has to be removed before the product goes to the next process.

Before Improvement
The auxiliary jigs were mounted in a position where they were hard to see, and their color was the same as the surrounding objects. Because the operation took place only a few times a day, the worker sometimes forgot to remove the auxiliary jigs after the products had been taken off the production line, and the jigs moved on to the subsequent processes. To solve this problem, the auxiliary jigs were painted red to make them more noticeable, but there were still failures to remove the jigs.

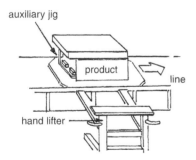

After Improvement
The process of mounting the auxiliary jig, taking the products off the line, and removing the auxiliary jig takes a very short time. Therefore a microswitch, battery, and buzzer were mounted on the auxiliary jig. The buzzer sounds as soon as the jig is set in place, and there is no time for the worker to get used to the sound and ignore it. Thanks to this improvement, workers no longer forget to remove the auxiliary jigs.

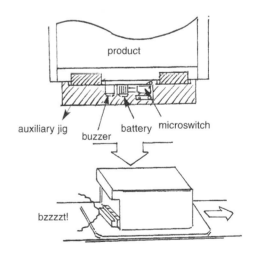

Added Material or Part

Process	Remove protective cover
Problem	Protective cover not removed
Solution	Next assembly prevented until lid is removed
Product	Pipe with bolt flange
Parts	Pipe, flange, and lid
Stage	1-Assembly 2-Remove part

	Control Function							
	∿		Poka-yoke			Simplify		
State	Adjustment	Setting	Warn	Shutdown	Control	Tools/Eqpt	Process	Product
Complexity								
Prevent Mistakes								
Detect Mistakes				X				
Detect Defects								
Variation								

Description of Problem: A protective cover or lid is put on the flange of new pipes to prevent foreign objects from entering them. The lid is to be removed for subsequent assembly.

Before Improvement
Connecting the pipes requires concentration. The operator often forgets to remove the lid when connecting pipes. Once assembled, the lid can block flow and become lodged at bends and valves, making it difficult to find the lid and remove it.

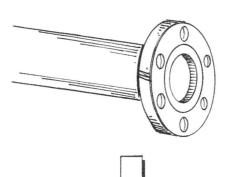

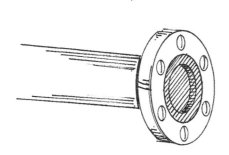

After Improvement
The flange on the lid is enlarged so that it partially covers the bolt hole pattern. If the lid is not removed, bolts cannot be installed in the next assembly step.

Complete correction of this problem required the cooperation of suppliers, who were asked to make the same change. Delivered pipes are checked to assure that the right lids were used on a large construction project.

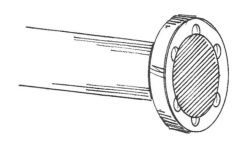

Added Material or Part

Example OA-8

Process   Remove test hardware

Problem   Test hardware not removed

Solution   Add a long "tail" to test hardware

Product   Electromechanical equipment

Parts   Product, connector tool, test equipment

Stage   1-Inspection
2-Remove hardware

	Control Function						
	∿		Poka-yoke			Simplify	
State	Adjustment	Setting	Warn	Shutdown	Control	Tools/Eqpt	Process	Product
Complexity								
Prevent Mistakes								
Detect Mistakes					X			
Detect Defects								
Variation								

Description of Problem: The product is given a comprehensive final inspection to assure delivery of a sound product. Operators can test each function by shutting down the appropriate product circuit. To do this, operators plug a connector into the product circuit breaker.

Before Improvement

At the conclusion of the test, operators are supposed to remove the circuit breaker connector tool and replace the cover. However, removing the tool is easy to forget. Once the cover is replaced, it is not obvious that the tool has been left in the product. When the tool is left in the product, the product does not work correctly for the customer.

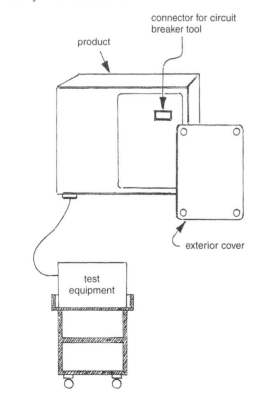

product

connector for circuit breaker tool

exterior cover

test equipment

After Improvement

A long cloth tape is attached to the circuit breaker connector tool. If the circuit breaker connector tool is not removed, the product cover cannot be replaced.

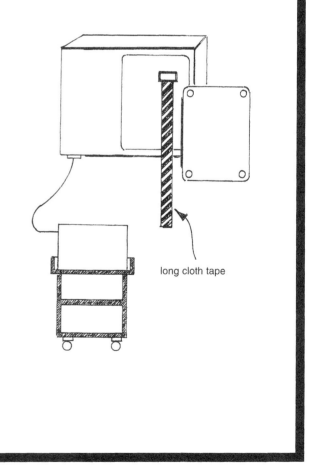

long cloth tape

Added Material or Part

Process   Trim small metal parts on a punch press

Problem   Errors in detection of ejected parts with magnetic detector

Solution   Channel parts through window in magnetic detector

Product

Parts   Small metal parts

Stage   1-Fabrication
2-Setup

Control Function							
$\bigwedge\!\!\bigvee$	Poka-yoke				Simplify		
Adjustment	Setting	Warn	Shutdown	Control	Tools/Eqpt	Process	Product
State							
Complexity							
Prevent Mistakes							
Detect Mistakes			X				
Detect Defects							
Variation							

Description of Problem: Small metal parts are trimmed in a punch press. After punching, the part is blown out of the die and through a magnetic detector. If the detector confirms that the previous part is out of the die, the press is reloaded and the process begins again.

Before Improvement

The sensitivity of the magnetic detector varies between the central section and the outer edges. For small, thin parts, the detector cannot be adjusted to detect parts passing through the central section, nor for parts passing near the outer edges.

If the outer edges were adjusted properly, parts passing through the central section were not detected; if the central section was adjusted properly, spurious detections were made by the outer edges. In either case, operations were held up and could produce improperly trimmed parts.

In addition, the turbulent air used for ejecting the parts sometimes caused spurious detection errors.

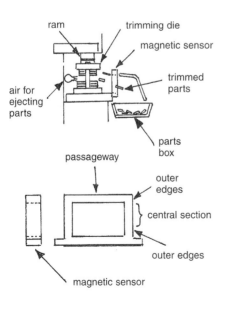

After Improvement

Guides for the ejected parts were improved so that the small, ejected parts can only pass through the sensitive bottom edge of the detector. The detector now can be adjusted to prevent spurious detection. Plastic, not sensitive to magnetism, is used in the new guide to prevent detection errors. In addition, the outlet guide has many small holes to improve the flow of air through the detector. These small holes are shaped so the parts will not cling to them.

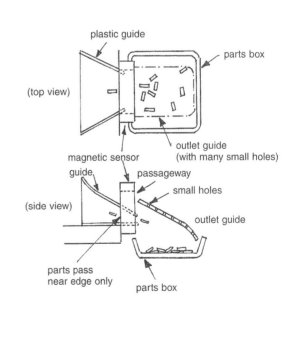

Added Material or Part

Process   Press mold parts

Problem   Damaged mold when parts left in press

Solution   Photoelectric detection of part removal

Product   Injection-molded plastic parts

Parts   Molded part

Stage   1-Fabrication
2-Remove finished part

State	Control Function							
	∿		Poka-yoke			Simplify		
	Adjustment	Setting	Warn	Shutdown	Control	Tools/Eqpt	Process	Product
Complexity								
Prevent Mistakes								
Detect Mistakes				X				
Detect Defects								
Variation								

Description of Problem: Products molded on a press.

Before Improvement
Sleepy night-shift operators sometimes forgot to remove molded products before operating the press again. Because correct operation relied on the workers' vigilance, die failures or defective products occurred about once a month.

After Improvement
A photoelectric switch is used to detect the presence of molded products. If a molded product remains in the press, the operation switch is disabled and the press cannot be operated. Smashing of molded products and die failures are completely eliminated.

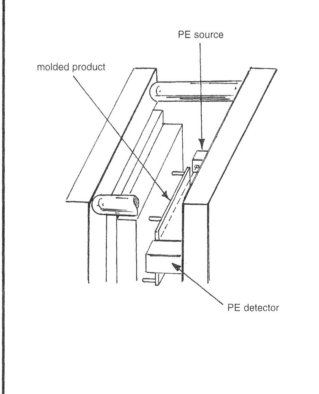

COMMIT PROHIBITED ACTION (OC)

Performing an action that is not allowed or desired. *Examples: Dropping a part, or turning on power to an electrical panel where another person is working.*

Principles that Eliminate Prohibited Action	Examples
1. Redesign the product or process to eliminate opportunities for prohibited actions.	
a. Redesign prevents flipped parts in transport.	OC-11
b. Design parts so that they cannot be used as handholds or footholds.	
2. Block access path between product and prohibited materials or environments.	
a. Timer closes access doors at the end of the access period.	OC-1
b. Guide prevents tool slip, protects parts.	OC-2
c. Part selection enables unique electrical interconnect.	OC-4
d. Magnetic caps keep paint out of holes.	OC-6
e. Protective cover prevents handling damage.	OC-9
f. Collar on grease brush prevents application in wrong location.	OC-10
g. Leaded fuel nozzle does not fit in gas stem of unleaded cars.	*MD-1*
h. Spilled fuel drained away from painted area.	*MD-1*
3. Guide prevents undesirable deformation during processing.	
4. Interconnect or interlock related or sequential operations.	
a. Mechanical interconnection.	OC-3, OC-7
b. Electrical interlocks.	
c. Electromechanical interlocks (automated lockout tag out).	OC-14
5. Temporary restraint prevents damaging relative motion until assembly is secured.	OC-5
6. Limit use of control handle to one control at a time.	
a. Can only be placed on one control at a time.	OC-8
b. Control must be restored to default setting to remove handle.	OC-8

Principles that Eliminate Prohibited Action   **Examples**

7. Set values like elapsed time, voltage, or counter beforehand and prevent continued operation if values are exceeded.

8. Detect hazard or risk.
   a. Lockout prohibited action (moving library shelves).   OC-12
   b. Shut down or reduce power (lasers).   OC-13, OC-15

Commit Prohibited Action

Process	Rooftop maintenance operations
Problem	Worker exposed to hazards during operating hours
Solution	Timer releases and locks access door
Product	Repair and maintenance service
Parts	Access door lock
Stage	1-Maintenance 2-Hazard alarm

	Control Function							
	∿		Poka-yoke			Simplify		
State	Adjustment	Setting	Warn	Shutdown	Control	Tools/Eqpt	Process	Product
Complexity					X		X	
Prevent Mistakes					X			
Detect Mistakes								
Detect Defects								
Variation								

Description of Problem: Maintenance and repair workers gain key-controlled access to the roof during non-operating hours. If the roof access door closes, the workers must get key service to unlock the door, so they prop the door open to avoid inconvenience. Because the door is propped open, workers can go back up on the roof after operation has resumed and hazardous materials are being vented to the roof.

Before Improvement

Roof access doors are normally locked during operating hours to prevent exposure to hazards. However, during maintenance and repair periods, workers frequently must retrieve parts and tools, making it difficult to keep the door locked. When operations resume, workers forget to close and lock the access doors, allowing workers to enter a hazardous environment.

roof access

"kicking wedge"

After Improvement

When the roof access door is opened, a latch catches and holds the door open during maintenance hours, eliminating the need for workers to prop the door open. An alarm on the roof alerts workers when operations are resuming and warns them to leave the roof area. An inexpensive water sprinkler timer actuates a solenoid that releases the door, which is then closed by a spring at the time operations in the building are to resume.

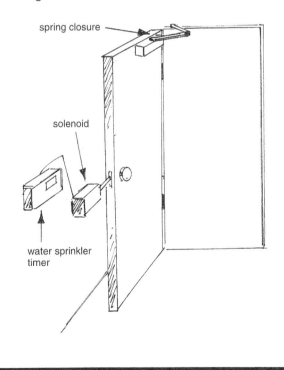

spring closure

solenoid

water sprinkler timer

Commit Prohibited Action

Process   Assembly

Problem   Circuit board cut by screwdrivers

Solution   Use protective guide

Product   Circuit board assembly

Parts   Circuit boards, screws, and screwdriver

Stage   1-Assembly
             2-Insert part and fasten

Control Function							
	∿	Poka-yoke			Simplify		
State	Adjustment	Setting	Warn	Shutdown	Control	Tools/Eqpt	Process	Product
Complexity								
Prevent Mistakes					X			
Detect Mistakes								
Detect Defects								
Variation								

Description of Problem: Six screws are used to attach a circuit board to a product. The screws are inserted and tightened with an air-driven screwdriver.

Before Improvement

If the operator slips while inserting the screws, the screw and screwdriver can cut the pattern on the circuit board, destroying the part. This problem may not be discovered until later in the assembly, when rework or repair is more difficult.

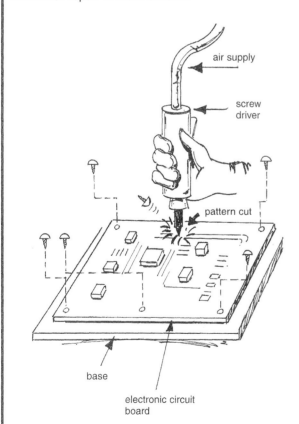

After Improvement

After locating the circuit board in the product, a guide is placed over the circuit board. The guide has clearance holes that are just large enough for the screws. With the guide in place, the screwdriver does not slip off the screw, and other irregular movements cannot damage the board.

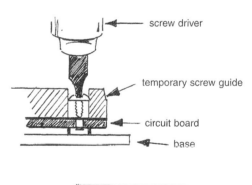

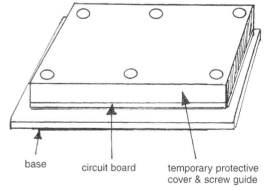

Commit Prohibited Action

Example OC-3

Process	Drain reacted materials
Problem	Chemicals drained before reaction is complete
Solution	Prevent key access until process completed
Product	Chemicals
Parts	Valves, tank, lock and key
Stage	1-Material production 2-Mix and drain

Control Function

State	Adjustment	Setting	Warn	Shutdown	Control	Tools/Eqpt	Process	Product
Complexity								
Prevent Mistakes					X			
Detect Mistakes								
Detect Defects								
Variation								

Description of Problem: Chemicals are mixed in a tank. These chemicals react and should never be drained from the tank until the process is complete. To prevent this from happening, the valve is locked during the reaction.

Before Improvement

The operator unlocked the valve and transferred the material before the reaction was complete. Although a key was used to prevent transfer, there was no indicator for the operator when it would be OK to open the valve. The reaction is controlled on the second floor, but the valve is opened on the first floor, making communication difficult.

After Improvement

The key for the operation was originally stored in the control room, but is now placed on the reaction tank. The key cannot be retrieved without opening an access port that is always opened after the reaction is complete.

Note: This same type of access control could be achieved with electrical interlocks.

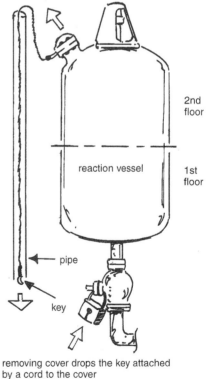

access cover- removed when reaction is done

2nd floor

reaction vessel

1st floor

pipe

key

removing cover drops the key attached by a cord to the cover

217

Commit Prohibited Action, Wrong Location

Example OC-4

Process   Exchange computer hard disks

Problem   Proprietary data transferred to open environment

Solution   LAN connection linked to hard disk

Product   Computer connection

Parts   Computer hard disks and local area networks (LAN)

Stage   1-Setup
2-Mate electrical connectors

State	Adjustment	Setting	Warn	Shutdown	Control	Tools/Eqpt	Process	Product
Complexity					X		X	
Prevent Mistakes					X			
Detect Mistakes								
Detect Defects								
Variation								

Control Function — (~) | Poka-yoke (Warn, Shutdown, Control) | Simplify (Tools/Eqpt, Process, Product)

Description of Problem: Two LAN computer connections are provided for each computer. One network is for open communication to networks and computers outside of the company; the other is for company proprietary data. To prevent proprietary data from inadvertently being released, there are two removable hard disks for each computer, an open hard disk and proprietary hard disk. The computer cannot be connected to the open network when the proprietary hard disk is installed, or vice-versa.

Before Improvement

Operators must change LAN connections when changing the hard disks in the machines. A checklist is used, but operators occasionally forget to switch connectors. If the operators do not change the LAN connections, proprietary data may be inadvertently available on the open network or inappropriately downloaded onto a hard disk that should not contain such information. Serious errors have occurred, with the potential for grave harm to the company.

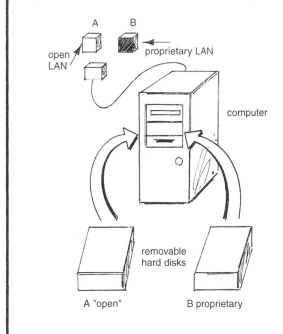

After Improvement

The LAN connectors are mounted side by side on the computer, and the hard disks have a bar attached to them that covers the inappropriate LAN connector. The hard disks cannot be exchanged without breaking the LAN connection, and once a hard disk is installed, the computer can only be connected to the appropriate LAN connection, completely eliminating the opportunity for LAN connection errors.

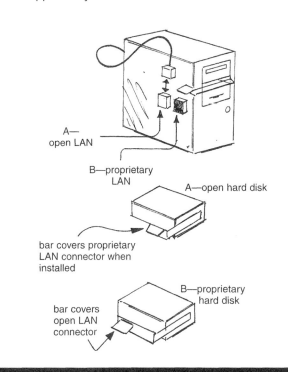

218

	Control Function							
	∿		Poka-yoke			Simplify		
State	Adjustment	Setting	Warn	Shutdown	Control	Tools/Eqpt	Process	Product
Complexity								
Prevent Mistakes					X			
Detect Mistakes								
Detect Defects								
Variation								

Process	Product assembly	
Problem	Cable damaged by cable guide	
Solution	Tape cable guide in place during assembly	
Product	Aerospace product	
Parts	Flat flex cable and foam blocks	
Stage	1-Assembly	
	2-Insert part	

Description of Problem: Two flat flex cables are routed between two foam blocks that protect the cables. The top foam block is held in place by gravity until another part is attached.

Before Improvement

The ends of the flat flex cable extend into the assembly workspace. If the ends of the flat flex cables are bumped during assembly, the foam cover, which is very lightweight, can be easily knocked out of the slot. As the next part in the sequence is lowered into place, the installer cannot see that the foam cover block has moved because visual access is restricted. If the next part is installed when the cover is not seated in the groove, the cover can be crushed, and the part that is intended to protect the cable will damage the cable.

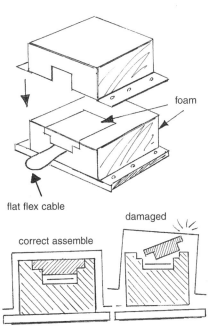

foam

flat flex cable

correct assemble

damaged

After Improvement

A piece of tape holds the block in place while the next part is installed. Bumping the flat flex cables cannot move the cover out of its place, and unseen damage to the cable is completely eliminated.

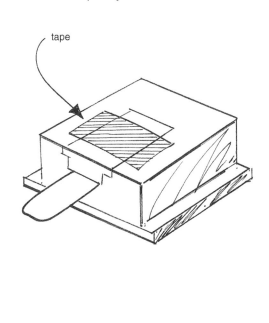

tape

219

Commit Prohibited Action

Example OC-6

Process Paint cylindrical brackets

Problem Paint deposited on inside of brackets

Solution Redesign holding rack

Product

Parts Axisymmetric brackets

Stage 1-Production preparation
2-Design paint fixture

State	Control Function							
	∿		Poka-yoke			Simplify		
	Adjustment	Setting	Warn	Shutdown	Control	Tools/Eqpt	Process	Product
Complexity								
Prevent Mistakes					X			
Detect Mistakes								
Detect Defects								
Variation								

Description of Problem: Brackets were placed in holding racks to have their outsides spray-painted.

Before Improvement
Paint was sometimes deposited accidentally on the inside of the brackets where it should not have gone. These brackets had to be discarded.

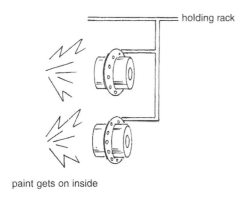

paint gets on inside

holding rack

After Improvement
A new rack was devised that sandwiches the bracket between a bottom plate and a magnetic cap to keep paint from getting on the inside.

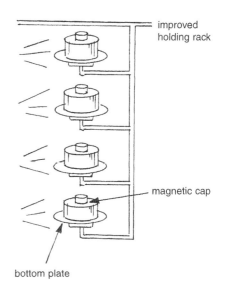

improved holding rack

magnetic cap

bottom plate

220

Commit Prohibited Action

Process	Filling gas or opening side door
Problem	Doors damaged by interference
Solution	Mechanically interlock doors
Product	Van
Parts	Gas cover door, sliding door
Stage	1-Use 2-Open doors

	Control Function							
	∿		Poka-yoke			Simplify		
State	Adjustment	Setting	Warn	Shutdown	Control	Tools/Eqpt	Process	Product
Complexity								
Prevent Mistakes					X			
Detect Mistakes								
Detect Defects								
Variation								

Description of Problem: With sliding doors on both sides of a van, it is almost impossible to position a side-mounted fuel fill port that does not interfere with opening the sliding side door of the van. Opening a sliding door while filling the van with gas will damage the sliding door or gas cover door and may present a serious safety hazard if a discharging fuel nozzle is knocked out of the fuel tank inlet.

Before Improvement

Passengers in the van are unlikely to realize that opening the side sliding door will impact the fuel door. This creates a hazard during refueling. In addition, the gas cover door or sliding door can be damaged if the sliding door impacts the fuel door.

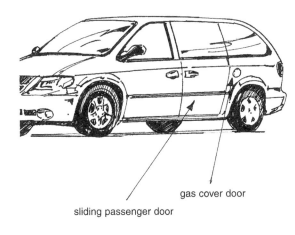

gas cover door

sliding passenger door

After Improvement

The sliding door and fuel cover door are interlocked. If the fuel door is opened, the sliding door cannot be opened. If the sliding door is opened, the gas cover door cannot be opened. Fueling hazards and errors in opening both doors at once are completely eliminated.

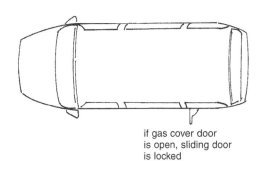

if gas cover door
is open, sliding door
is locked

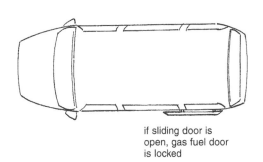

if sliding door is
open, gas fuel door
is locked

Process	Replenish raw materials
Problem	Valves to tank A & B open—only A should be open
Solution	Only one valve at a time can be opened
Product	Chemicals
Parts	Manifold pipe with valves, tanks
Stage	1-Stock management
	2-Replenish raw materials

Control Function							
∿		Poka-yoke			Simplify		
Adjustment	Setting	Warn	Shutdown	Control	Tools/Eqpt	Process	Product
State							
Complexity							
Prevent Mistakes				X			
Detect Mistakes							
Detect Defects							
Variation							

Description of Problem: A pipe supplies raw material to three different tanks (A, B, C). When tank A is being filled, the valves to the other tanks should be closed.

Before Improvement
The operator accidentally opened valve B while putting material in tank A. There was nothing in place to prevent the valves from being open at the same time.

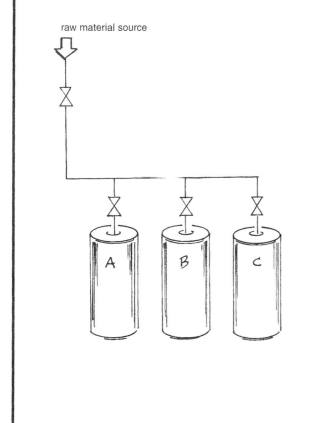

raw material source

After Improvement
An open-end wrench does not solve the problem, since a single handle could still open all valves. In addition, a spanner wrench in this application could cause injuries. A guard is designed that fits on each valve. When the valve is open, the handle cannot be removed. The valve must be closed to remove the handle and use it to open one of the other valves.

Another option would be to design covers that must be kept on two of the three valves and only fit if the valve is closed.

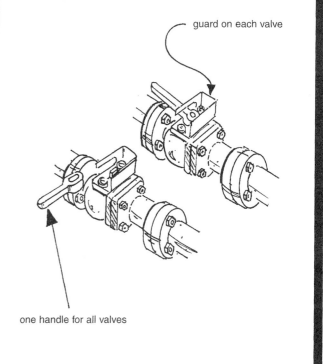

guard on each valve

one handle for all valves

Commit Prohibited Action

		Handling and insertion
Process		Handling and insertion
Problem		Tubing on HVAC unit does not align in next assembly
Solution		Cover prevents damage during handling
Product		Automobile
Parts		Heating, ventilating, and air conditioning (HVAC) assembly
Stage		1-Transportation and handling

Control Function

State	Adjustment	Setting	Warn	Shutdown	Control	Tools/Eqpt	Process	Product
			Poka-yoke			Simplify		
Complexity								
Prevent Mistakes					X			
Detect Mistakes								
Detect Defects								
Variation								

Description of Problem: The HVAC unit is a complex assembly that is flipped over several times during assembly. Copper tubing on the HVAC unit must be in proper alignment for insertion into the vehicle.

Before Improvement

The tubing on the HVAC frequently did not line up properly during insertion into the vehicle. This resulted in costly assembly delays, part shortages on the assembly line, and a large number of units returned to the supplier for repair.

Inspection showed that the tubing was installed correctly on the HVAC unit. It was then recognized that handling damaged the tubes after installation. Small bumps were bending the tubes, but this damage was not easy to detect.

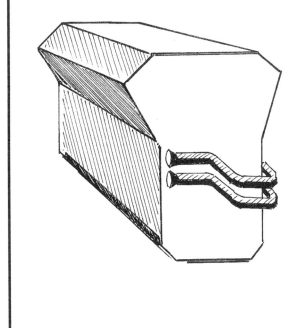

After Improvement

A temporary cover was made to protect the tubes. This cover was installed as soon as the tubes were installed and removed just before installing the HVAC unit in the vehicle. The problem was completely eliminated.

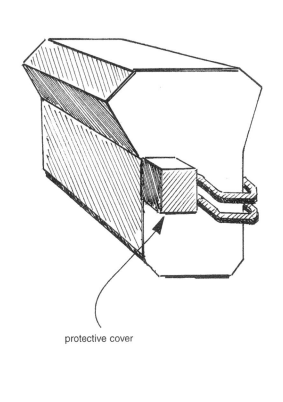

protective cover

223

Commit Prohibited Action

Example OC-10

Process   Grease ground fixture on cassette decks

Problem   Grease on pulley belt results in failures

Solution Stopper on grease brush prevents brush from reaching pulley

Product   Cassette deck

Parts   Grounding fixture

Stage   1-Assembly
              2-Setup

	Control Function							
	∿		Poka-yoke			Simplify		
State	Adjustment	Setting	Warn	Shutdown	Control	Tools/Eqpt	Process	Product
Complexity								
Prevent Mistakes					X			
Detect Mistakes								
Detect Defects								
Variation								

Description of Problem: A ground fixture on a cassette deck mechanism is greased with white grease, applied with a brush. However, if grease accidentally gets on the nearby pulley belt, the auto-stop mechanism will not work.

Before Improvement
Despite the vigilance of skilled workers, grease sometimes got on the pulley belt, causing defects.

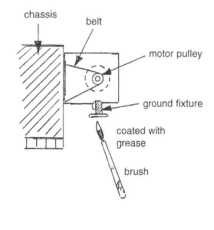

After Improvement
The brush was outfitted with a stopper, so that now it cannot reach all the way to the belt. Grease no longer gets on the belt, and auto-stop failures are completely eliminated. The addition of the stopper makes it possible for experienced workers and novices to do the work equally well.

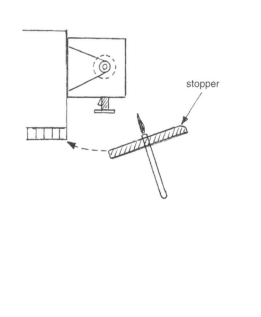

224

Process   Automated part feed—groove cutting machine

Problem   Parts flip upside down

Solution   Improve shutters

Product

Parts   Shaft with ring

Stage   1-Transportation and handling
2-Automatic feeder

State	Control Function							
	∿		Poka-yoke			Simplify		
	Adjustment	Setting	Warn	Shutdown	Control	Tools/Eqpt	Process	Product
Complexity					X		X	
Prevent Mistakes					X			
Detect Mistakes								
Detect Defects								
Variation								

Description of Problem: Parts are fed individually by an automatic feeder to a process for cutting grooves on shafts.

Before Improvement

The shutters for individual feed on the shaft chutes were poorly designed, and shafts in the chutes sometimes flipped upside down due to impact with the shutter. The grooves were then cut in the wrong end of the part, and no grooves were cut where they were needed.

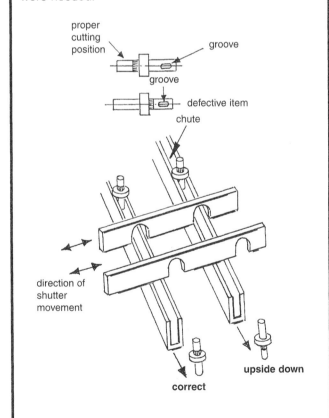

After Improvement

The shutters were redesigned to move the shafts gently down the chute, preventing them from flipping due to impact.

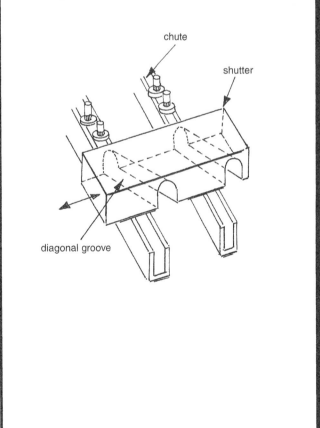

Commit Prohibited Action

Process   Move shelves to reach books

Problem   Bookshelves are moved with someone between stacks

Solution   Sensor locks out bookshelf movement

Product   Library

Parts   Moveable library shelves

Stage   1-Use
2-Move library shelves

	Control Function							
	∿		Poka-yoke			Simplify		
State	Adjustment	Setting	Warn	Shutdown	Control	Tools/Eqpt	Process	Product
Complexity								
Prevent Mistakes					X			
Detect Mistakes								
Detect Defects								
Variation								

Description of Problem: Archived books are accessed only infrequently. To reduce the storage volume, motorized, rolling shelves have been developed. The bookshelves are moved to create an aisle to reach any desired book in the archive.

Before Improvement

In a collection of moving bookshelves, there can be several aisles between the stacks. Opening one aisle could close an aisle where an unseen individual is standing. Even if a check is made before moving the stacks, someone could enter an aisle from the opposite side before the stacks are moved. Since the books are very heavy, the forces used in moving the books are large and pose a significant hazard.

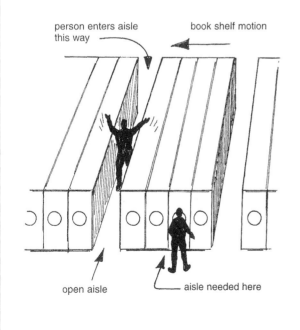

person enters aisle this way

book shelf motion

open aisle

aisle needed here

After Improvement

Sensors detect any individual in an aisle of the stacks, and movements that would close the aisle are locked out.

sensor detects person in aisle

prevents aisle closure

OK

open aisle

aisle needed here

Commit Prohibited Action

Example OC-13

	Process	Experimental laser operation
Process		Experimental laser operation
Problem		Operators burn eyes when adjusting setup
Solution		Pressure-sensitive mat turns power down
Product		Laser research
Parts		Lasers, lenses, mirrors, filters
Stage		1-Setup 2-Adjust mirror alignment

Control Function							
$\curvearrowright$		Poka-yoke			Simplify		
Adjustment	Setting	Warn	Shutdown	Control	Tools/Eqpt	Process	Product

State	Adjustment	Setting	Warn	Shutdown	Control	Tools/Eqpt	Process	Product
Complexity								
Prevent Mistakes				X				
Detect Mistakes								
Detect Defects								
Variation								

Description of Problem: Aligning a laser beam on an optical bench is a common activity required in many research settings.

Before Improvement

Operators adjust mirrors, filters, beam splitters, and lenses to control the laser beams. Adjusting laser beams can be very difficult, particularly if the laser power is turned off during the adjustment process. However, laser power is typically so high that it can cause serious eye damage. Even though operators know they are supposed to turn the lasers off during laser adjustment for safety, the rule is commonly ignored because of the difficulty of executing the task with the laser turned off. During adjustments there are many near misses and occasional eye injuries, even with protective eyewear.

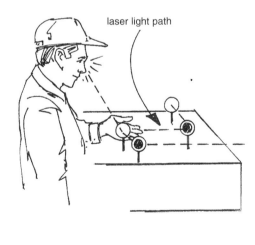

laser light path

After Improvement

The default laser power level is set below the threshold for eye damage. The high operating power is only enabled when pressure-sensing mats do not detect an operator within a few feet of the optical bench. As an alternative, the mat sensors could switch between two separate lasers, one high power and one low power, that are aligned on the same optical path. The operators can safely and easily adjust the beam, but the risk of eye injury is virtually eliminated.

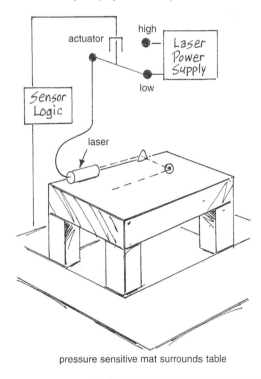

pressure sensitive mat surrounds table

227

Process	Inspect overhead crane
Problem	Crane could be operated while inspector was on crane
Solution	Interlock crane ladder step to operating circuit
Product	
Parts	Overhead crane
Stage	1-Inspection 2-Start

	Control Function							
	∿		Poka-yoke			Simplify		
State	Adjustment	Setting	Warn	Shutdown	Control	Tools/Eqpt	Process	Product
Complexity								
Prevent Mistakes				X				
Detect Mistakes								
Detect Defects								
Variation								

Description of Problem: Cranes must be given daily, monthly, and annual inspections. The inspectors work on the crane, using a ladder to climb up onto the crane structure. The other workers cannot see the inspectors when they are on the crane.

Before Improvement
Operators sometimes started up the crane without realizing that an inspector was at work on it. Fortunately, no accidents resulted, but the situation presented a serious safety risk.

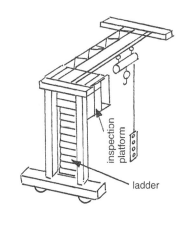

After Improvement
The ladder used to climb onto the crane has folding rungs, which are normally raised so no one can climb the crane. However, when the inspector lowers the rungs, a limit switch interlocked with the controls of the crane is tripped, preventing the crane from operating and assuring the inspector's safety.

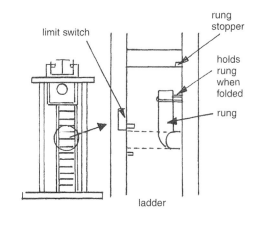

Process Load and unload analyzer

Problem Operator reaches into the equipment while moving

Solution Sensor shuts down motion

Product Clinical chemistry analysis

Parts Blood specimen vials

Stage 1-Inspection
2-Insert and remove part

		Control Function						
		〜		Poka-yoke		Simplify		
State	Adjustment	Setting	Warn	Shutdown	Control	Tools/Eqpt	Process	Product
Complexity								
Prevent Mistakes								
Detect Mistakes			X	X				
Detect Defects								
Variation								

Description of Problem: Operators frequently load and unload blood specimens from blood analyzer equipment. A carousel in the machine moves the specimen to various points for analysis.

Before Improvement

Operators who reach into the machine while the carousel is moving may be injured or damage the equipment. Since the carousel holds potentially hazardous blood samples, even a minor physical injury can be serious. A small hazard light warns the operator when reaching into the machine should be avoided, but this light can be easily covered or overlooked.

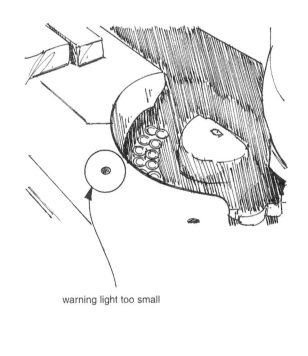

warning light too small

After Improvement

An infrared sensor that detects hands entering the loading and unloading space immediately stops the carousel motion. A large light warns the operator when loading or unloading operations might impede efficient operation.

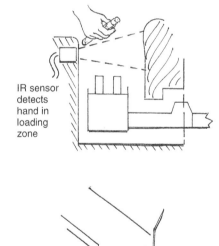

IR sensor detects hand in loading zone

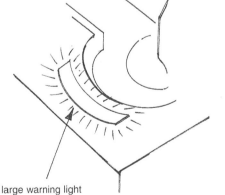

large warning light

OMITTED OPERATIONS (OO)

Failure to perform a required operation.

Principles that Eliminate Omitted Operations	Examples
1. Eliminate the need for the operation.	
a. By simplifying the product or process.	OO-1, OO-4
b. Equipment reverts to default state unless switch or control is held.	OO-9
2. Automate the execution (fan operation check, timer start).	*IW-6*
3. Detect the start of an operation.	
a. Automate subsequent operation.	
i. Start automated execution based on timeout.	OO-5
ii. Start automated execution based on counter.	OO-6
b. Shut down the operation or prevent part removal until operation is completed.	OO-3
i. Sense data "clear."	OO-7
ii. Sense shape, length, weight, stroke, stroke count, or duration.	
c. Interlock adjacent or related operations.	OO-11
4. Detect the completion of an operation.	
a. Automate equipment shutdown (heater).	OO-10
b. Interlock the next operation.	OO-2
5. Use methods for controlling the number of operations.	
a. Counter method.	
i. Counter verifies that the correct number of operations (automated counter).	OO-13
ii. The operator signals the start and checks counter for completion.	OO-14
6. Tag out an operation until the previous operation is completed.	OO-8
7. Wear a reminder (sash or badge, rope tied to ripcord).	OO-9, *WO-2*
8. Set a timer as a warning for a subsequent operation.	OO-9

9. Make omitted operations visible and obvious.   OO-12, OO-15

    a. Detect omission of an operation by comparison to correctly completed items.

        i. Compare grooves in cylinders or backlight translucent parts.

10. Interference reveals an unprocessed part downstream.

    a. Material that has not been removed.

        i. Pin in a hole or slot.   OO-17, OO-18, *MA-8*

           Diameter, clearance, groove interference, taper, bevel

    b. Next part cannot be inserted because fastener is not tightened.   *OP-8*

    c. Lack of interference when material is not added.

11. Detect a physical change caused by the process and provide an indicator of the
change. (centrifuge, magnetism).   OO-16, OO-19

12. Create and use an operation checklist.

13. Prepare standard procedure charts.

Process	Adjusting mirror angle of reflection
Problem	Loose screws due to omitted or insufficient adhesive
Solution	Screws are precoated with adhesives
Product	Electromechanical product
Parts	Mirror, adjustment screw
Stage	1-Setup 2-Adjustment

	Control Function							
	〜	Poka-yoke				Simplify		
State	Adjustment	Setting	Warn	Shutdown	Control	Tools/Eqpt	Process	Product
Complexity								
Prevent Mistakes					X			
Detect Mistakes								
Detect Defects								
Variation								

Description of Problem: After adjusting the angle of a reflecting mirror, the operator squirts an adhesive on the screw to prevent loosening. This process must be done correctly on each product, or the product will fail in use.

Before Improvement
The operator forgets to apply the adhesives. Even when applied, the adhesive may be uneven or is applied to the wrong area. The area where the adhesive is applied is difficult to check because it is hard to see.

After Improvement
The adjustment screw is precoated with adhesives by the screw supplier. This eliminates the need to apply adhesives during assembly. There is no unevenness of the adhesives or spraying in the wrong area. The need for checking the adhesive application is eliminated.

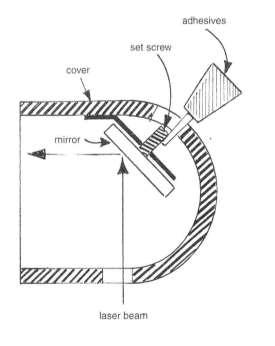

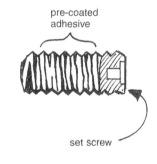

Process	Injection molding		
Problem	Mold broken when ejector does not reset		
Solution	Interlock mold closure with ejector reset		
Product	Injection molded plastic parts		
Parts	Injection mold, limit switch		
Stage	1-Fabrication 2-Molding		

	Control Function							
	$\curvearrowright$		Poka-yoke			Simplify		
State	Adjustment	Setting	Warn	Shutdown	Control	Tools/Eqpt	Process	Product
Complexity								
Prevent Mistakes					X			
Detect Mistakes								
Detect Defects								
Variation								

Description of Problem: At the completion of a molding cycle, the injection mold opens and an ejector pushes the finished resin or plastic parts out of the mold. After ejecting finished parts, return springs push the ejector back to its original position, and the mold is closed to form the next part.

Before Improvement
Sometimes the ejectors do not return to their original, pre-ejection position. If the mold is closed before the ejectors are retracted, the mold is broken.

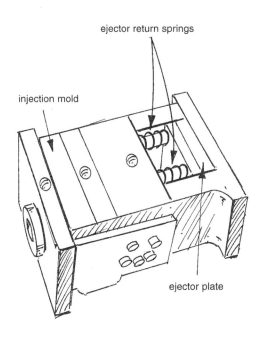

ejector return springs

injection mold

ejector plate

After Improvement
A limit switch is attached to the mold that detects if the ejectors have been properly reset. The mold closure is interlocked with this switch, so the mold cannot close if the ejectors are not in the proper position. Problems with broken molds are eliminated.

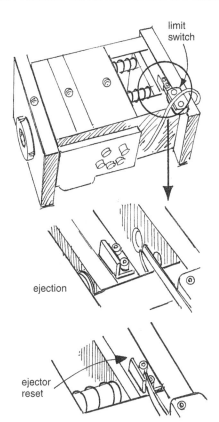

limit switch

ejection

ejector reset

Process	Secure door latch and safety catch
Problem	Operator forgets to secure safety catch
Solution	A key reminds user to secure safety catch
Product	Rental truck
Parts	Roll-up door latch, safety catch
Stage	1-Use 2-Set Safety catch

	Control Function							
	∿		Poka-yoke			Simplify		
State	Adjustment	Setting	Warn	Shutdown	Control	Tools/Eqpt	Process	Product
Complexity								
Prevent Mistakes					X			
Detect Mistakes								
Detect Defects								
Variation								

Description of Problem: The operator closes the truck roll-up door securing the latch but not the safety catch. Vibrations open the door during travel, and home furnishings fall from the truck.

Before Improvement

An owner rents a truck to move home furnishings. After loading the truck, the roll-up door is closed and secured properly.

The driver stops to get gas and opens the truck roll-up door to retrieve some items. The door is closed and the latch secured, but the driver forgets to secure the safety latch.

Vibration frees the door latch and the door bounces open. Furnishings are destroyed as they fall from the truck, creating a hazard for other drivers.

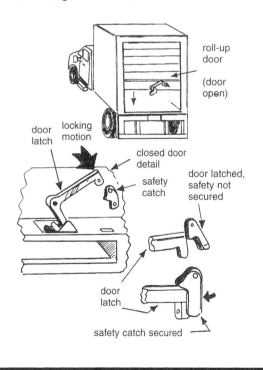

After Improvement

A key is used to set and release the safety catch. The key can only be removed from the safety catch when it is properly secured.

A warning on the truck dashboard reminds the driver not to travel until the safety catch is set and the safety catch key is returned to the dash, where it covers the warning.

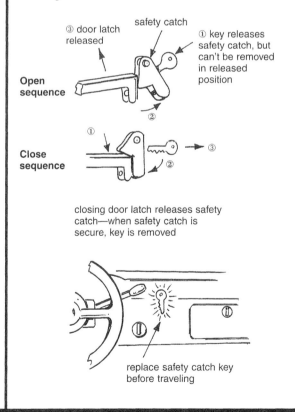

		Control Function						
		⌇	Poka-yoke			Simplify		
State		Adjustment	Setting	Warn	Shutdown	Control	Tools/Eqpt	Process	Product
Complexity						X		X	
Prevent Mistakes						X			
Detect Mistakes									
Detect Defects									
Variation									

Process   Punch and countersink radiator plates

Problem   Omitted countersink

Solution   Combine punch and countersink operation

Product   Radiator

Parts   Plate

Stage   1-Fabrication
2-Countersink

Description of Problem: Countersinking is specified for holes punched in radiator plates.

Before Improvement
After punching, the holes were countersunk with a drill press, but there were variations in the dimensions and the processing was sometimes omitted.

After Improvement
The punch was remodeled to punch and countersink the hole in one operation. Dimensional variations and omissions have been eliminated completely, and the processing time shortened, killing two birds with one stone. The only costs are for remodeling the punch.

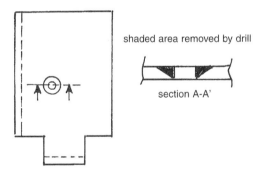

shaded area removed by drill

section A-A'

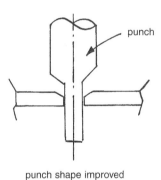

punch

punch shape improved

Omitted Operation

Example OO-5

Process	Turn on centrifuge to start spin cycle
Problem	Operator forgets to turn on centrifuge
Solution	After the lid is closed, a timer automatically starts the centrifuge
Product	Separation process for chemical analysis of blood
Parts	Centrifuge
Stage	1-Use 2-Startup centrifuge

	Control Function							
	∿	Poka-yoke				Simplify		
State	Adjustment	Setting	Warn	Shutdown	Control	Tools/Eqpt	Process	Product
Complexity					X		X	
Prevent Mistakes					X			
Detect Mistakes								
Detect Defects								
Variation								

Description of Problem: Clinical chemists execute other tasks while blood products are being centrifuged.

Before Improvement
Occasionally, operators forget to turn on the centrifuge after closing the lid. They do not realize that the centrifuge was not started until they check at the expected completion of the operation. Critical time is lost, and a full production cycle is wasted in time-urgent health care applications.

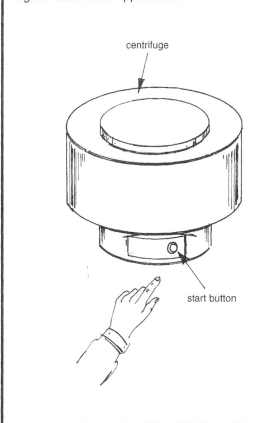

centrifuge

start button

After Improvement
An interlock senses the lid closure. If the centrifuge is loaded, the operation cycle is automatically started after a few seconds.

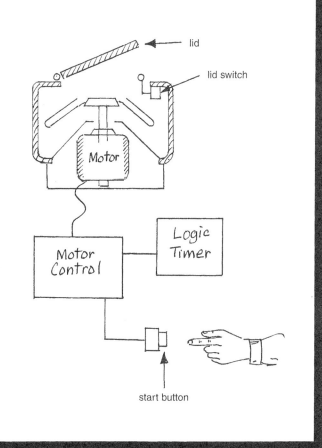

lid

lid switch

Motor

Logic Timer

Motor Control

start button

236

	Cast metal parts on an automated line
Process	Cast metal parts on an automated line
Problem	Dies deformed when cooling water is not turned on after startup
Solution	Automate water-cooling supply
Product	Cast metal parts
Parts	
Stage	1-Fabrication 2-Startup metal casting

	Control Function							
	∩∪		Poka-yoke			Simplify		
State	Adjustment	Setting	Warn	Shutdown	Control	Tools/Eqpt	Process	Product
Complexity								
Prevent Mistakes					X			
Detect Mistakes								
Detect Defects								
Variation								

Description of Problem: On a fully automated casting line using casting robots, each operator is assigned to more than one machine. The dies must be cooled, and the valve for the cooling water must be opened after three casting cycles when starting up the casting process.

Before Improvement
At about the third shot after the beginning of casting, the operator was to open the master valve for the water to cool the interior of the die. When the operator forgot to open the valve, problems sometimes ensued, such as the casting sticking to the dies or the dies becoming deformed by the heat.

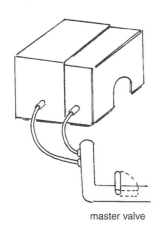

master valve

After Improvement
A solenoid-controlled valve and a counter were added to the process. The counter counts three shots after the beginning of casting and then signals the solenoid to open the water valve.

solenoid valve on water supply

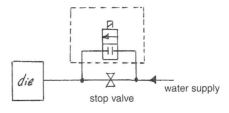

die — stop valve — water supply

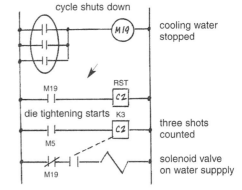

cycle shuts down

M19 — cooling water stopped

M19 — RST C2

die tightening starts K3 — C2 — three shots counted

M5

M19 — solenoid valve on water suppply

237

Process   Final inspection

Problem   Forget to clear register

Solution   Prevent data printout until register is cleared

Product   Electromechanical equipment

Parts   Product, test equipment

Stage   1-Inspection
                2-Final

	Control Function							
	∿		Poka-yoke			Simplify		
State	Adjustment	Setting	Warn	Shutdown	Control	Tools/Eqpt	Process	Product
Complexity								
Prevent Mistakes				X				
Detect Mistakes								
Detect Defects								
Variation								

Description of Problem: At the final inspection, a tester is connected to the product and values for each test on it are displayed. The data is also electronically passed to the test equipment. At the conclusion of the test, operators clear the displayed data by setting the displayed values to "0," turn off the product, and print the test data. The printed data is attached to the product, and the unit is shipped.

Before Improvement

Operators turn off the power and ship the product before clearing the data. When the customers receive products that have not been cleared, they are confused by the display and have difficulty getting the product in the correct mode of operation.

Step 1: obtain test data

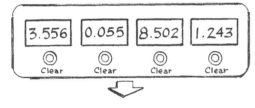

Step 2: print data

Step 3: clear data to "0"

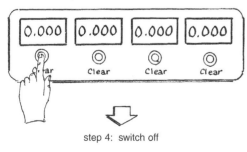

step 4: switch off

step 5: pack & ship

After Improvement

The program for the test equipment is changed so that the product data cannot be sent to the printer until the data registers are cleared.

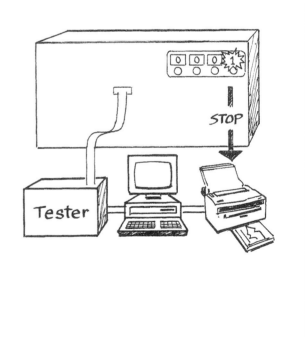

238

Omitted Operation

Process	Inspection of raw material
Problem	Omitted inspection
Solution	Tag-out product use until inspected
Product	Chemicals
Parts	Raw material in a tank
Stage	1-Inspection 2-Raw material sampling

Control Function

State	$\sim$		Poka-yoke			Simplify		
	Adjustment	Setting	Warn	Shutdown	Control	Tools/Eqpt	Process	Product
Complexity								
Prevent Mistakes					X			
Detect Mistakes								
Detect Defects								
Variation								

Description of Problem: After raw material is placed in a tank, operators are to conduct an inspection of the material before using it.

Before Improvement
The inspection is sometimes forgotten. At the time the material is released for processing, the operator has no way of knowing whether or not the material has been checked.

push button switch releases
raw material for production

After Improvement
A tag is created that is placed in front of the switch that releases the product for use. Before inspection, the tag blocks access to the switch. After inspection, the tag is repositioned to indicate the material is ready to use.

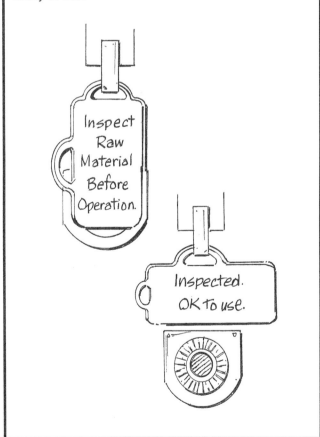

	Process	Close valve

Process   Close valve

Problem   Operator forgets to close valve

Solution   Automatic valve is only open while switch is held

Product   Chemicals

Parts   Valve

Stage   1-Material production
2-Valve operation

	Control Function							
	∿		Poka-yoke			Simplify		
State	Adjustment	Setting	Warn	Shutdown	Control	Tools/Eqpt	Process	Product
Complexity								
Prevent Mistakes			X		X			
Detect Mistakes								
Detect Defects								
Variation								

Description of Problem: After entering raw material into a process tank, the operator is supposed to close the supply valve.

Before Improvement
The operators are distracted as they turn their attention to other tasks. It is easy to forget to close the valve.

Note: The following situations can also apply to opening valves.

After Improvement
A spring can be used to automatically close small valves when the handle is released. For larger valves, an automatic valve is used that is controlled by a switch. The switch is spring loaded so that the valve automatically closes when released.

As an alternative, the operator could set a timer when the valve is opened that sounds an alarm when it is time to close the valve. If the operation is repeated on a daily basis, the alarm can be set for specific times.

Other alternatives would be to tag out a subsequent operation until the valve is closed, or to have the operator wear a sash with a reminder tag until the valve is closed.

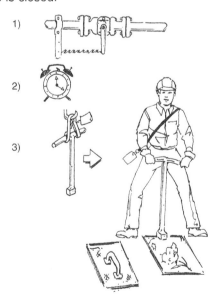

Process	Bond test pieces in heating-bonding machine

Problem — Heater not turned off, creates fire hazard

Solution — Press retraction trips limit switch, automatically turning heater off

Product

Parts

Stage — 1-Process control
2-Equipment shutdown

	Control Function							
	∿	Poka-yoke				Simplify		
State	Adjustment	Setting	Warn	Shutdown	Control	Tools/Eqpt	Process	Product
Complexity							X	
Prevent Mistakes				X				
Detect Mistakes								
Detect Defects								
Variation								

Description of Problem: A heating-bonding machine is used to bond together two test pieces. The test pieces are pressed down by the upper head and then heated. After bonding, the head is raised and the heating switch is turned off.

Before Improvement

Several different people used some machines that did not have single operators assigned exclusively to them. The various switches on these machines are sometimes not turned off. Failure to turn off the heaters is a particularly serious fire hazard. Such errors absolutely must be prevented.

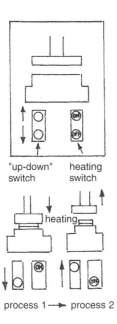

"up-down" switch   heating switch

process 1 → process 2

After Improvement

A boss was mounted on the strut of the upper head. When the head goes all the way up, the boss trips a limit switch, turning off the heating switch. Failure to turn off the heating switch is prevented.

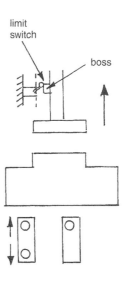

limit switch

boss

241

Process	Machine operations

Problem	Operations omitted

Solution Adjacent machine interlocks, does not allow one machine to start until other has started

Product

Parts

Stage 1-Fabrication
2-Sequential operations

Control Function								
	∿		Poka-yoke			Simplify		
State	Adjustment	Setting	Warn	Shutdown	Control	Tools/Eqpt	Process	Product
Complexity								
Prevent Mistakes				X				
Detect Mistakes								
Detect Defects								
Variation								

Description of Problem: A worker operates a number of machines arranged into a U-shaped processing line. After setting a workpiece in the jig of one machine and starting the processing there, the worker moves to the next operation, sets it up, and starts it.

Before Improvement
The worker sometimes forgot to start an operation after setting the workpiece on the jig. Delays or omitted processing resulted.

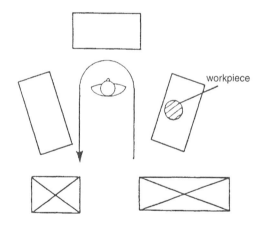

After Improvement
Limit switches were mounted on the jigs so the process power circuits can be interlocked. It is now impossible to turn on the switch for one machine until the start button for the preceding operation has been pressed.

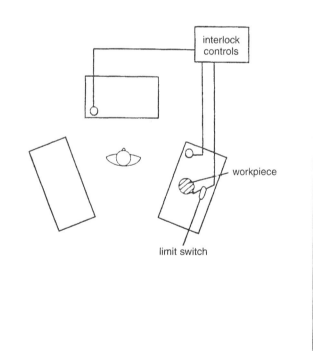

Omitted Operation

Process	Assembly
Problem	Fasteners not tightened
Solution	Convert bottom-up to top-down assembly
Product	Aerospace product
Parts	Pressure vessel and brackets
Stage	1-Assembly 2-Fasten

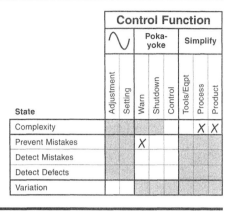

Control Function							
	∿		Poka-yoke			Simplify	
State	Adjustment	Setting	Warn	Shutdown	Control	Tools/Eqpt	Process	Product
Complexity							X	X
Prevent Mistakes			X					
Detect Mistakes								
Detect Defects								
Variation								

Description of Problem: In the complex assembly of a pressure vessel, some fasteners and parts are inserted from the bottom.

Before Improvement
Omitted parts are not always obvious with bottom-up assembly. An even bigger problem is that inserted fasteners are frequently not tightened because the worker forgets to check.

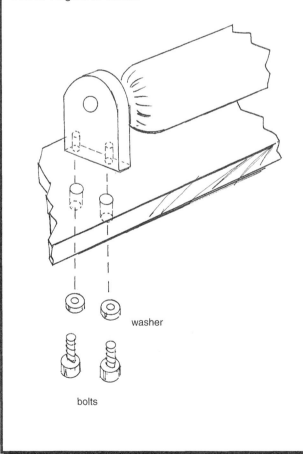

washer

bolts

After Improvement
The design is changed so that all parts are inserted either top-down (preferred) or from the side. Being able to see the parts provides a visual reminder, or warning, that fasteners must be tightened. Assembly is faster, and mistake rates are cut dramatically.

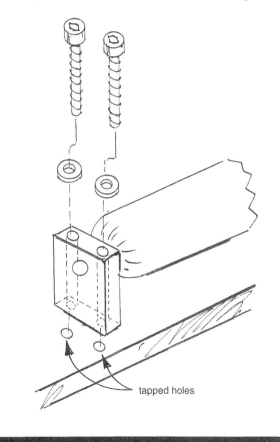

tapped holes

Process	Forming process
Problem	Perform process on only 1 of 2 required ends
Solution	Completion linked to counter
Product	Tube or pipe
Parts	Tube
Stage	1-Fabrication 2-Tube forming

	Control Function							
	∿		Poka-yoke			Simplify		
State	Adjustment	Setting	Warn	Shutdown	Control	Tools/Eqpt	Process	Product
Complexity								
Prevent Mistakes								
Detect Mistakes			X					
Detect Defects								
Variation								

Description of Problem: Both ends of each pipe are to be machine processed.

Before Improvement
Sometimes only one end is processed and sent to the next operation.

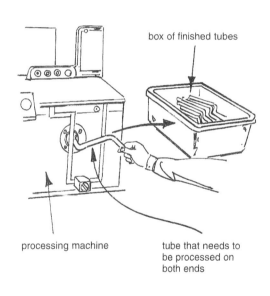

processing machine   tube that needs to be processed on both ends

box of finished tubes

After Improvement
A light sensor is added to the machine that detects when the operator moves the finished part to the box of processed parts. This sensor is linked to a counter. If the operator puts a pipe in the box of processed parts without operating the machine twice, an alarm sounds and a light turns on.

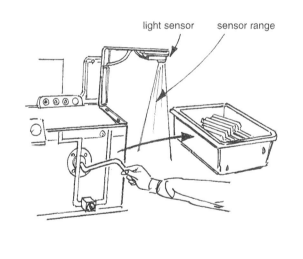

light sensor   sensor range

Omitted Operation

Process	Spot weld sheet metal
Problem	Omitted welds (wrong count)
Solution	Electronic counter(s)
Product	
Parts	
Stage	1-Assembly 2-Join with spot weld

	Control Function							
	∿	Poka-yoke			Simplify			
State	Adjustment	Setting	Warn	Shutdown	Control	Tools/Eqpt	Process	Product
Complexity								
Prevent Mistakes								
Detect Mistakes			X	X				
Detect Defects								
Variation								

Description of Problem: Spot welding is performed on a number of different components, each of which requires numerous welds. Several identical components are often processed in sequence in a batch.

Before Improvement

A work instruction sheet for welding each component specifies the number, location, and types of welds required. Workers were responsible for remembering the number of welds while processing subsequent components in the same batch. Occasionally the number recalled by the worker would be wrong, and welds were omitted. If the omitted welds were not discovered in subsequent processes, the defective items went on to the assembly line.

The workers also counted the number of items processed, and time was required to recheck the number of units processed after they were put on pallets.

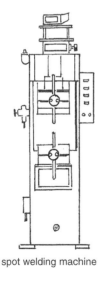

spot welding machine

After Improvement

A digital counter was added to the spot welding machine. The worker sets the required number of welds on the counter, which then counts the welds as they are made. The weld counter is interlocked with the foot switch used by the operator to perform the welds. Specifications of the counter panel include the following:

1. One digital preset counter for counting the number of items processed.
2. One or two buzzers, set for the number of each type of weld (some models have two series of welds).
3. A snap switch, display lights, etc., for setting the number of items to be processed and the number of welds on each item.

If 50 items are to be processed and each piece has 10 welds, a buzzer rings after the tenth weld, and the item counter is incremented. The weld counter is reset automatically. The spot welding machine shuts down after 50 pieces have been processed. In cases where there are two series of welds on the same item, both numbers are input to the weld counter and then output to the item counter. Welds are no longer omitted. The worker no longer needs to count the number of welds, and the count of items processed is more accurate. The amount of work completed can be checked at any time.

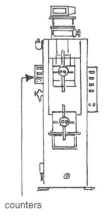

counters

Process   Packaging for shipment

Problem   Operations and paperwork omitted

Solution   Labels positioned for easy visibility

Product   Printed foil

Parts   Packing materials

Stage   1-Pack
2-Insert part and inspect

Control Function								
	∿		Poka-yoke			Simplify		
State	Adjustment	Setting	Warn	Shutdown	Control	Tools/Eqpt	Process	Product
Complexity								
Prevent Mistakes								
Detect Mistakes			X					
Detect Defects								
Variation								

Description of Problem: Printed rolls of material are prepared for shipment. The individual preparing the shipment counts the rolls and verifies that every roll has been individually labeled.

Before Improvement

Occasionally the packer forgets to count the parts or check the lay up. The toughest job is making sure that every roll has been marked. These problems result in customer complaints.

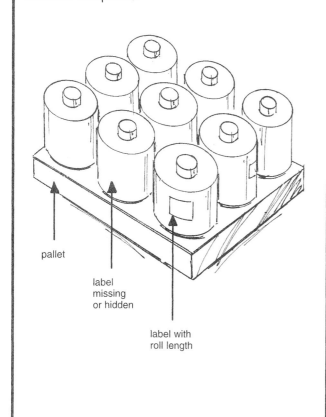

pallet

label
missing
or hidden

label with
roll length

After Improvement

The label marking is moved from a tag on the outside diameter of the printed roll to a ring around the core of the role. At a glance, the inspector can quickly identify the rolls that have not been properly marked, virtually eliminating marking omission errors.

missing label easy to spot
incorrect wind "stands" out

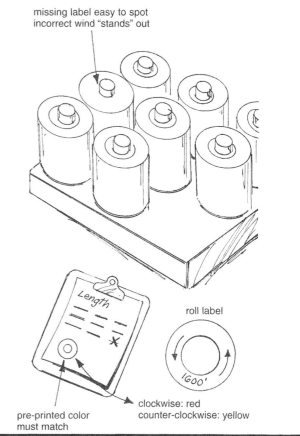

pre-printed color
must match

roll label

clockwise: red
counter-clockwise: yellow

Omitted Operation, Inadequate Warning

Process	Centrifuge
Problem	Blood that has not been centrifuged clogs analyzer
Solution	Sensor strip shows centrifuged samples
Product	Clinical chemistry specimen analysis
Parts	Blood specimen vial
Stage	1-Material production 2-Startup

	Control Function						
	∿		Poka-yoke			Simplify	
State	Adjustment	Setting	Warn	Shutdown	Control	Tools/Eqpt	Process	Product
Complexity							X	
Prevent Mistakes								
Detect Mistakes			X					
Detect Defects								
Variation								

Description of Problem: Blood is placed in a centrifuge to separate serum for analysis.

Before Improvement

Operators may forget to start the centrifuge or think a specimen has been centrifuged when it has not. Separated blood can be easily distinguished by observation, but essential labels conceal the blood. Thus, the cap must be removed to check the blood, unnecessarily exposing the lab workers to hazardous blood products.

When a sample that has not been centrifuged is passed to the analyzer, it clogs the machine, requiring time-consuming maintenance and possibly delaying lifesaving information in urgent situations.

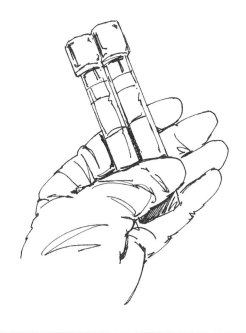

After Improvement

A strip filled with a suspension is attached to the specimen label. When centrifuged, the suspension separates, allowing the operator to easily detect specimens that have been centrifuged without opening the vials. Health risks are eliminated, and productivity is improved because operators do not need to constantly open and close vials.

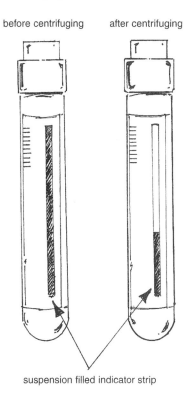

before centrifuging   after centrifuging

suspension filled indicator strip

Omitted Operation, Defective Material

Example OO-17

	Control Function							
	∿		Poka-yoke			Simplify		
State	Adjustment	Setting	Warn	Shutdown	Control	Tools/Eqpt	Process	Product
Complexity								
Prevent Mistakes								
Detect Mistakes								
Detect Defects					X			
Variation								

Process   Drill bearing holes and bend plate

Problem   Omitted hole drilling

Solution   Plate does not fit on bend fixture if holes are not drilled

Product

Parts   Plate

Stage   1-Fabrication
2-Insert workpiece and drill

Description of Problem: Bearings are drilled and then bent. If the bearings are bent first, it is impossible to drill the holes afterwards.

Before Improvement
Correct operations relied entirely on worker vigilance. However, workers sometimes inadvertently bent the bearings before they were drilled, creating a defective piece that had to be scrapped.

incorrect sequence

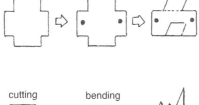

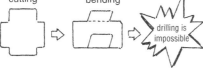

After Improvement
Pins were added to the bending die, making it impossible to set the bearings in place before they are drilled. Drilling omissions are completely eliminated.

correct sequence

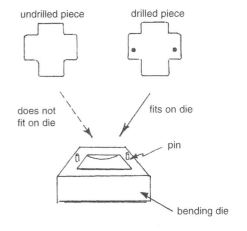

248

					Control Function						
							Poka-yoke		Simplify		
State					Adjustment	Setting	Warn	Shutdown	Control	Tools/Eqpt	Process	Product
Complexity												
Prevent Mistakes												
Detect Mistakes												
Detect Defects									X			
Variation												

Process — Pierce hole in die cast part

Problem — Products not pierced

Solution — Pin on downstream process checks piercing

Product —

Parts — Die cast parts

Stage — 1-Fabrication
2-Piercing

Description of Problem: Products are die cast and then pierced.

Before Improvement
Visual checks for piercing were performed in the final inspection before the products were shipped, but customers still discovered some products that had not been completely pierced.

correct

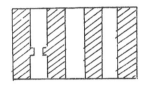

cross-section of part

not pierced

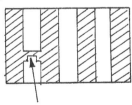

material to be removed

After Improvement
A pin was mounted on the jig of a process following the die casting, where the part is drilled. If the part has not been pierced, the pin prevents the part from seating correctly on the jig and omission of piercing is detected. This completely eliminates further processing of unpierced parts.

correct

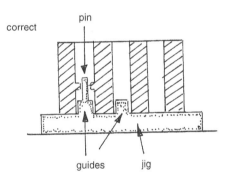

guides   jig

not pierced

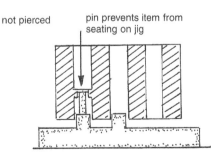

Process — Insert and torque crankcase bolts in motorcycle engines

Problem — Omitted or torqued bolts

Solution — Current and limit switches detect omissions and loose bolts

Product —

Parts — Crankcase bolts

Stage — 1-Assembly
2-Insert parts and fasten

	Control Function							
	～		Poka-yoke			Simplify		
State	Adjustment	Setting	Warn	Shutdown	Control	Tools/Eqpt	Process	Product
Complexity							X	
Prevent Mistakes								
Detect Mistakes								
Detect Defects				X				
Variation								

Description of Problem: In motorcycle engine assembly, crankcase bolts are inserted by an operator and tightened by an automated machine.

Before Improvement

The crankcase continued to move down the line, whether or not the operator inserted the bolts or the machine tightened them. Visual checks and other tests were performed to discover these abnormal items. Because this resulted in the performance of unnecessary operations, it led to increased work hours and burdened the operators.

After Improvement

A device was developed to test automatically for missing or untightened bolts. The device has several rods mounted to a circuit board, and the whole assembly is moved up and down with a pneumatic cylinder. The number and position of the rods correspond to those of the bolts. In use, the rods are supplied with 6V. The device can distinguish between three states:

1. When the bolts are inserted correctly and tightened, the rods contact the bolts (and allow current to flow between the rods) at the same time that limit switches 1 and 2 are actuated by the positioning of the circuit board assembly.
2. If the bolts have not been tightened, current flows through the rods before the circuit board has come into position to actuate the switches.
3. If the bolts have not been inserted, current will not flow even after switch 1 has been actuated by the circuit board. With this device in use, the number of work hours required for checks is reduced, and defective items are no longer sent on to the subsequent processes.

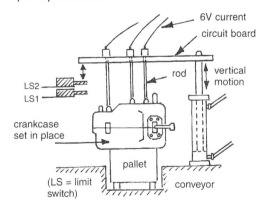

Omitted Operation

Example OO-20

Process Magnetize flywheels

Problem Process omitted

Solution Detect magnetization with proximity switch

Product

Parts Flywheels

Stage 1-Fabrication
2-Magnetize

Control Function	∿		Poka-yoke			Simplify		
State	Adjustment	Setting	Warn	Shutdown	Control	Tools/Eqpt	Process	Product
Complexity								
Prevent Mistakes								
Detect Mistakes								
Detect Defects			X					
Variation								

Description of Problem: Passing the parts through a magnetizing machine individually magnetizes each flywheel.

Before Improvement

The worker placed a flywheel in the magnetizing machine, magnetized the flywheel, and then placed it on a table for temporary storage. After the worker processed 20 pieces, the flywheels were checked with a screwdriver to make sure each was magnetized. Sometimes the worker inadvertently skipped the magnetizing process and did not detect the unmagnetized flywheels with the screwdriver test.

magnetizing line

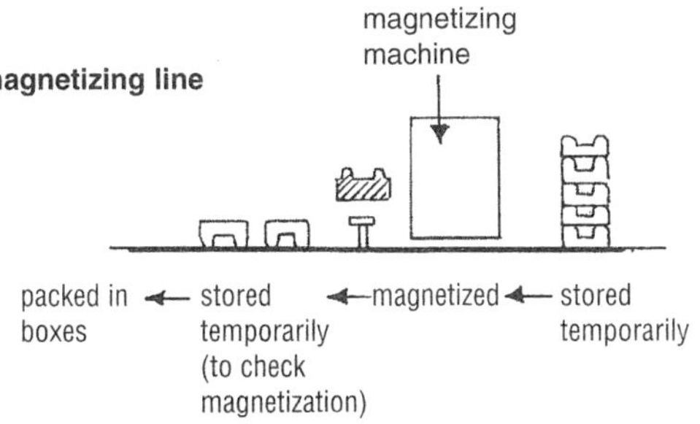
magnetizing machine
packed in boxes
stored temporarily (to check magnetization)
magnetized
stored temporarily

checking magnetization with a screwdriver

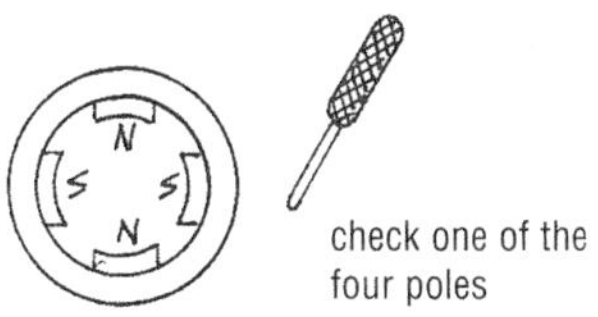
N
S
S
N
check one of the four poles

After Improvement

A proximity switch that detected magnetization on the conveyor belt eliminated the screwdriver test and temporary storage on the table. The items are passed one by one under the detector, and a warning light turns on if an unmagnetized flywheel is detected, alerting the operator.

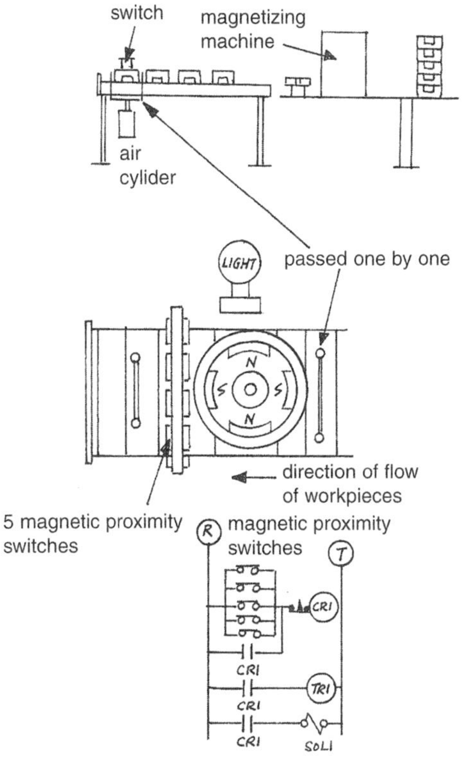
switch
magnetizing machine
air cylider
LIGHT
passed one by one
N
S
S
N
direction of flow of workpieces
5 magnetic proximity switches
R
magnetic proximity switches
T
CR1
CR1
TR1
CR1
CR1
SOL1

OMITTED PARTS AND COUNTING ERRORS (OP)

A missing part, or the wrong number of parts resulting from a counting error.

Principles that Eliminate Omitted Parts and Counting Errors	Examples
1. Eliminate parts by combining functions with other parts.	OP-1, OP-4
2. Visual Control signs and signboards assure that parts are available when needed.	
3. "Smart" part bins guide selection and detect part draw.	
a. Door opens to reveal correct part; next door opens after draw.	OP-2, *MT-2*
b. Switch on door detects draw and enables next operation.	
c. Light signals correct bin, sensor detects part draw and proceeds or warns.*	OP-5
d. "Traveling" door on bench enables access to one part at a time.	
4. Make part omission errors and counting errors obvious.	
a. Provide counting aids (counting method).	
i. Automate counting.	OP-3
ii. Lifting tool can't be installed if stack height is too high.	OP-9
iii. Counting tray or table makes counting easy.	OP-12
iv. Compare stack height to standard dimension.	*IM-8*
v. Count by weight (when unit weight is a large fraction of total weight).	
b. Layout makes missing parts obvious (remainder method).	
i. Shadow boxes or part outlines.	OP-6, OP-10
ii. "Matrix" box for fastener tray.	OP-11
iii. Put labels on roll ends for visibility.	*OO-15*
5. Prevent an operation if a part is missing.	
a. Short "drive" feature in wrench prevents nut tightening if washer is missing.	OP-13, OP-14
b. Prevent setup for transportation if part is missing.	OP-7
6. Sensor detects missing part and shuts the operation down.	*MA-12*
7. Use an attachment (cord or rope) to secure a part to a product (gas cap).	*MD-1*

8. Prevent insertion of the next part if a part is missing (light cover).   OP-8

9. Detect missing parts.
   a. Prevent subsequent operation.
      i.   Interlock process operation with part detection.   OP-15
      ii. Air stream blows away empty boxes.
      iii. Parts required for setup in jig.
   b. Warn operator a part is missing.
      i.   Low air pressure signals missing part.   OP-16
      ii. Rod with limit switch detects missing bolt.   *OO-19*
      iii. Pin doesn't fit if part is present.

SmartBins is a trademark of SpeasTech.

Omitted Part or Counting Error

Example OP-1

Process   Assembly of LIGA parts

Problem   Extremely small parts omitted

Solution   Combine parts into a single piece

Product   Miniature machines

Parts   LIGA parts

Stage   1-Assembly
2-Select part

	Control Function							
	∿		Poka-yoke			Simplify		
State	Adjustment	Setting	Warn	Shutdown	Control	Tools/Eqpt	Process	Product
Complexity								X
Prevent Mistakes								
Detect Mistakes								
Detect Defects								
Variation								

Description of Problem: The LIGA (German acronym) process can make parts so small that they are difficult to see with the unaided eye. These parts are assembled to make miniature machines and mechanisms.

Before Improvement
LIGA parts are so small that they are easily moved by common air disturbances and frequently lost. Part omissions are difficult or impossible to detect without inspection under a microscope. Consequently, assembly errors can easily occur, increasing the cost of products.

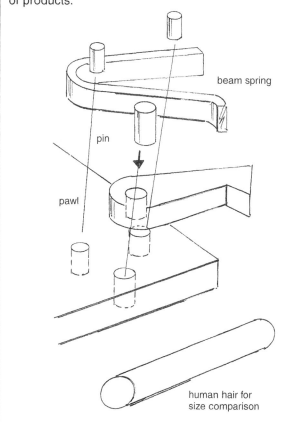

beam spring

pin

pawl

human hair for
size comparison

After Improvement
Combining multiple functions in a single part eliminates assembly operations. For example, instead of rotating bars about pinned joints, bars can flex about "living hinges" that act both as a pivot point and a spring. Where necessary, parts are separated after assembly with lasers. During assembly, parts are larger and easier to handle, eliminating many assembly and handling errors.

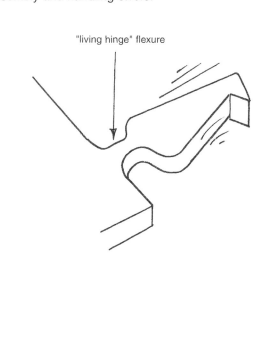

"living hinge" flexure

Omitted Part, Wrong Part

Process	Packaging for shipment
Problem	PC cards or other parts omitted
Solution	"Smart" part bins
Product	PC cards
Parts	PC card and packaging
Stage	1-Pack 2-Select and insert parts

	Control Function							
	⌒⌣	Poka-yoke				Simplify		
State	Adjustment	Setting	Warn	Shutdown	Control	Tools/Eqpt	Process	Product
Complexity					X		X	
Prevent Mistakes					X			
Detect Mistakes								
Detect Defects								
Variation								

Description of Problem: Manuals, cables, advertising, registration forms, and PC cards are boxed for shipment to customers. There are a wide variety of products being shipped. Operators must select the appropriate items for each package.

Before Improvement

To check the assembly, each package is weighed upon completion. However, many of the items are so small that the weight is not an accurate indicator. Many packages have been shipped with the wrong PC card, the wrong manual, or with missing PC cards. Customers are not happy, and resources are wasted correcting the problems.

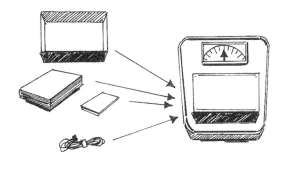

After Improvement

A door covers the access to each part. Based on the order, one door opens at a time to provide access to the correct part. The next door does not open until a part is removed from the open bin.

Packaging errors are eliminated. Each package contains all of the right parts assembled in the correct order. Productivity improves as operators spend less time making decisions and rechecking packaging mistakes.

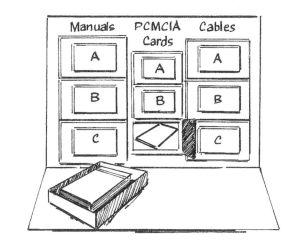

255

Process Packaging for shipment

Problem Manual counting errors

Solution Automate counting

Product Injection molded parts

Parts Shipping containers, parts

Stage 1-Pack
2-Count parts

State	Adjustment	Setting	Warn	Shutdown	Control	Tools/Eqpt	Process	Product
			Poka-yoke				Simplify	
Complexity							X	
Prevent Mistakes				X				
Detect Mistakes								
Detect Defects								
Variation								

Description of Problem: Operators manually count and pack acrylic products produced by injection-molding. The work is done manually, because the parts are fragile.

Before Improvement
Even though operators are careful, sometimes parts are not counted correctly.

36 or 37?

After Improvement
Since this is a high-volume process, the decision was made to use a sensor for counting the products. This was linked with a mistake-proofing device that automatically puts the right number of parts in each box. When box A is filled, a gate opens that routes parts to box B. When box B is filled, parts are routed to box C.

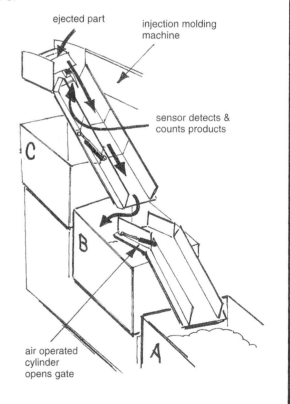

ejected part

injection molding machine

sensor detects & counts products

air operated cylinder opens gate

Omitted Part or Counting Error

Process — Bond information plate to timer lid

Problem — Plates omitted or bonded poorly

Solution — Mold information into lid

Product — Timer lid

Parts — Label (information plate)

Stage — 1-Assembly
2-Insert part and bond

State	Adjustment	Setting	Warn	Shutdown	Control	Tools/Eqpt	Process	Product
	Control Function			Poka-yoke			Simplify	
Complexity					X			X
Prevent Mistakes					X			
Detect Mistakes								
Detect Defects								
Variation								

Description of Problem: An information plate must be attached to the lid of the timer assembly.

Before Improvement

The information plate was bonded to the timer lid with an adhesive. However, there were variations in the bonding strength, and sometimes the plates were not mounted at all.

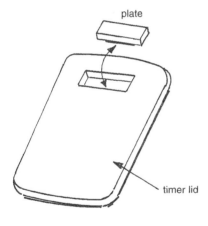

plate

timer lid

After Improvement

The bonding process itself has so many deficiencies that it is more efficient to use a different process for mounting the information plate. The solution is to make the label an integral part of the product from the beginning. Now the information plate is inserted in a die and molded into the timer lid. These integral plates cannot peel off, and mounting is never omitted.

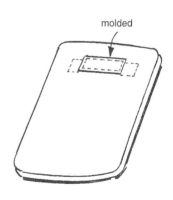

molded

Omitted Part, Wrong Part

Process   Pack part kits for succeeding processes

Problem   Wrong number or wrong parts packed

Solution   "Smart" parts bin

Product

Parts   Parts

Stage   1-Pack
2-Select and insert parts

Control Function								
	$\curvearrowright$		Poka-yoke			Simplify		
State	Adjustment	Setting	Warn	Shutdown	Control	Tools/Eqpt	Process	Product
Complexity								
Prevent Mistakes					X			
Detect Mistakes								
Detect Defects								
Variation								

Description of Problem: At a supply depot for a number of different processes, various parts are packed for delivery to the processes. Each process requires a specific number of different parts.

Before Improvement

For each process, the worker consulted an instruction sheet listing the number and types of parts that should be packed for the process. The worker took the parts from their bins one by one and packed them into boxes. Sometimes the parts were counted incorrectly, or the wrong parts were taken inadvertently.

After Improvement

Two goals were defined: (1) the parts needed and the quantities needed should be indicated mechanically; and (2) there should be a check that the number of parts packed is correct.

1. A "smart" parts rack was installed to achieve these goals. The worker inserts an instruction card for a given process into a card reader on the rack. A light goes on at the bin of the first part specified. When the worker has taken the correct number of parts, a buzzer sounds and a light goes on at the next part. The worker repeats this procedure for each process.

2. This new procedure has completely eliminated delivery of the wrong parts or the wrong number of parts, and has also tripled the worker's speed.

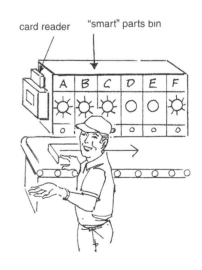

Process	Packing for travel
Problem	Omitted toiletry
Solution	Spray painted cloth reveals missing items
Product	Toiletries
Parts	Toothbrush, toothpaste, hairbrush, etc.
Stage	1-Pack 2-Select and insert parts

	Control Function						
	∿	Poka-yoke			Simplify		
State	Adjustment	Setting	Warn	Shutdown	Control	Tools/Eqpt	Process	Product
Complexity							X	
Prevent Mistakes			X					
Detect Mistakes								
Detect Defects								
Variation								

Description of Problem: Travelers must pack variety of toiletries for travel.

Before Improvement
Occasionally, a traveler may forget to pack a toothbrush, toothpaste, or another essential item. The problem may not be discovered until the next morning, when finding a suitable replacement becomes difficult.

After Improvement
Toiletry items are temporarily wrapped in cellophane and placed on a cloth or sheet of plastic. Spray painting the sheet with the wrapped items in place quickly produces an outline of the items needed for travel. By setting out the toiletry items on the sheet prior to travel, the traveler can quickly identify and procure missing items.

Process Assembly

Problem Omitted safety pin

Solution Pin must be in place to transport

Product Hand grenade

Parts Safety pin

Stage 1-Assembly
2-Insert part and inspect

	Control Function							
	∿		Poka-yoke			Simplify		
State	Adjustment	Setting	Warn	Shutdown	Control	Tools/Eqpt	Process	Product
Complexity								
Prevent Mistakes								
Detect Mistakes				X				
Detect Defects								
Variation								

Description of Problem: Safety pins are inserted into hand grenades during assembly. If the pin is left out, the grenade will detonate if dropped.

Before Improvement
Because of the severe safety hazard, two inspectors originally observed each safety pin insertion. Even with two inspectors, a safety pin was accidentally omitted and the grenade killed a worker when it was accidentally dropped.

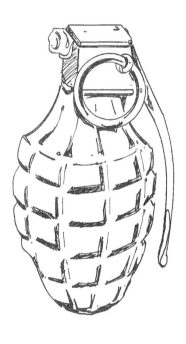

After Improvement
The holder for transporting the grenades to subsequent work areas was modified. Without the safety pin in place, it is impossible to load the grenade on the transport rack. Inspectors are no longer needed, and the hazard is eliminated. This concept was developed during World War II and is one of the earliest documented examples of mistake-proofing.

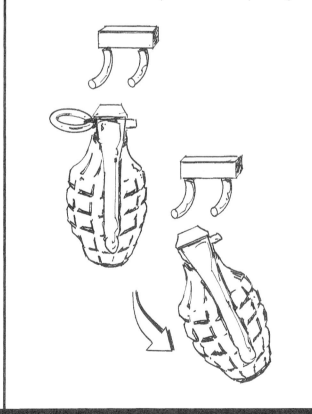

Omitted Part, Omitted Operation

Example OP-8

Process	Assembly
Problem	Omitted screw or spring
Solution	Screw must be installed for next assembly step
Product	Electronic product
Parts	Light cover, screw, and spring
Stage	1-Assembly 2-Insert part and fasten

Control Function

State	⌒⌣	Poka-yoke				Simplify		
	Adjustment	Setting	Warn	Shutdown	Control	Tools/Eqpt	Process	Product
Complexity								
Prevent Mistakes								
Detect Mistakes					X			
Detect Defects								
Variation								

Description of Problem: A light cover is attached to a baseboard with a screw. To prevent the lamp cover from rattling, a spring is placed between the baseboard and the light cover.

Before Improvement

The area is difficult to see, and it is easy for operators to forget to insert or tighten the screw. In addition, the spring is sometimes omitted and the light cover rattles.

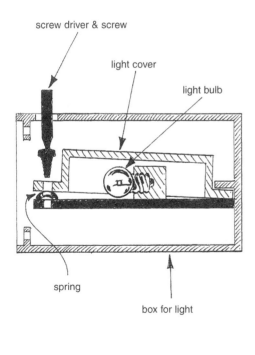

After Improvement

The baseboard is redesigned so that the spring completes that electrical circuit for the light. If the spring is missing, data measurements cannot be made in the next operation.

A protrusion is attached to the next part (a light barrier) added during assembly. If the screw has not been inserted and tightened, interference with the protrusion will prevent assembly.

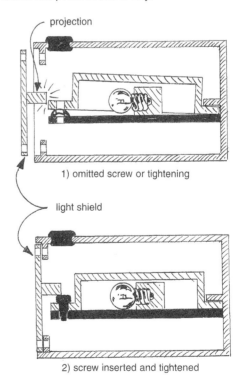

1) omitted screw or tightening

2) screw inserted and tightened

Omitted Part or Counting Error

Process Pack washers into delivery boxes

Problem Wrong number of parts

Solution Holding rods show too few washers, cannot be lifted if too many washers

Product

Parts Washer

Stage 1-Pack
2-Count parts

	Control Function							
	∿	Poka-yoke			Simplify			
State	Adjustment	Setting	Warn	Shutdown	Control	Tools/Eqpt	Process	Product
Complexity					X		X	
Prevent Mistakes								
Detect Mistakes					X			
Detect Defects								
Variation								

Description of Problem: Washers are packed into delivery boxes by threading 25 at a time onto rods, then packing four rods into each box, resulting in 100 washers per box.

Before Improvement
Sometimes the rods had 24 or 26 washers threaded on, and the boxes ended up with the wrong number of washers. In addition, the rods were hard to handle when they were loaded with washers.

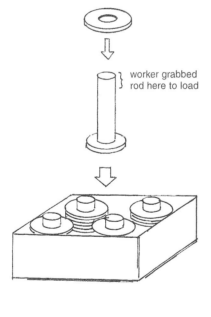

worker grabbed rod here to load

After Improvement
A mark is made on the rods at the level of the 25th washer so that too few washers can be detected. The rods are drilled so that a handle with a retaining pin can be inserted. If there are 26 washers, the hole will be blocked. The retaining pin thus prevents mistakes in counting the washers and makes the rods easier to handle.

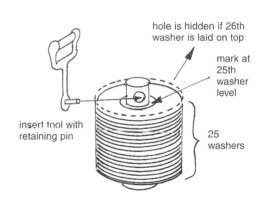

hole is hidden if 26th washer is laid on top

mark at 25th washer level

insert tool with retaining pin

25 washers

Omitted Part, Wrong Part

Process   Assembly

Problem   Omitted parts

Solution   Shadowbox part kits

Product   Aircraft engine parts

Parts   Part kits

Stage   1-Assembly
2-Setup

	Control Function						
	∿		Poka-yoke		Simplify		
State	Adjustment	Setting	Warn	Shutdown	Control	Tools/Eqpt	Process	Product
Complexity								
Prevent Mistakes								
Detect Mistakes			X					
Detect Defects			X					
Variation								

Description of Problem: Aircraft engines are complex assemblies that require many parts.

Before Improvement

During assembly, a missing part can shut down an expensive assembly operation. In addition, workers can easily forget to install a part because of the task complexity. Omitted parts may not be discovered until later in production, when expensive teardown is required.

Has anyone installed Z135485?

After Improvement

Parts required for assembly are arranged in shadowbox kits. In the box there is a sign for each needed part and a cavity by the sign that matches the shape of the part. The shadowbox is filled in preparation for assembly. If a part is not available, the empty space in the box is immediately recognized and the part can be procured. During assembly, parts are taken from the box. If the assembly is completed and parts remain in the shadowbox, it serves to warn operators that a part has been omitted in the assembly.

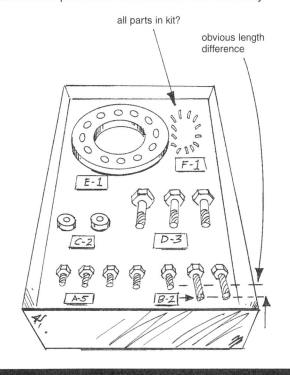

all parts in kit?

obvious length difference

263

Process   Bolt insertion

Problem   Bolts are omitted

Solution   A "matrix" block eliminates omitted fasteners

Product   Precision electronic manufacturing equipment

Parts   Bolts

Stage   1-Assembly
2-Insert part

	Control Function							
	〰		Poka-yoke			Simplify		
State	Adjustment	Setting	Warn	Shutdown	Control	Tools/Eqpt	Process	Product
Complexity								
Prevent Mistakes								
Detect Mistakes				X				
Detect Defects				X				
Variation								

Description of Problem: A variety of different bolts are needed at each assembly station in a low-volume production environment.

Before Improvement
Workers draw the parts for assembly from bins. Occasionally workers omit a bolt, and it is not discovered until late in the process when some disassembly is required. It is easy to omit a fastener or draw the wrong fastener from a bin.

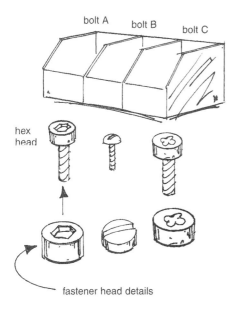

bolt A   bolt B   bolt C

hex head

fastener head details

After Improvement
A block is drilled that accepts the right quantity of each fastener for an assembly operation. Where possible, only the right fasteners fit in each drilled hole. Color bands help distinguish different fastener types. The block is filled prior to assembly. If a fastener is still in the block after assembly, the operator knows that a fastener has been omitted.

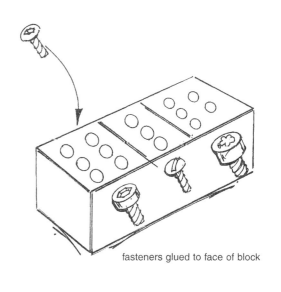

fasteners glued to face of block

Omitted Part or Counting Error

Example OP-12

Process	Counting
Problem	Wrong number of parts counted
Solution	Counting boxes and containers
Product	Small piece parts
Parts	Various small parts, counting boxes
Stage	1-Pack
	2-Count parts

Control Function

State	$\sim$		Poka-yoke			Simplify		
	Adjustment	Setting	Warn	Shutdown	Control	Tools/Eqpt	Process	Product
Complexity							X	
Prevent Mistakes								
Detect Mistakes			X					
Detect Defects								
Variation								

Description of Problem: Operators must count out a variety of small parts for packaging and shipment.

Before Improvement
Operators make many counting errors. It is very difficult to recognize when a counting error has occurred.

Have 35 or 45 parts been counted?

After Improvement
Counting boxes and platforms are used to facilitate counting. For oddly shaped items that are difficult to handle or orient, it may be helpful to divide sections of a platform or table with tape and place five items in each section, making it easy to confirm how many items are on the counting surface at once. Where items are easy to handle and orient, it is better to have boxes where only one part can fit in each location in a counting box or platform.

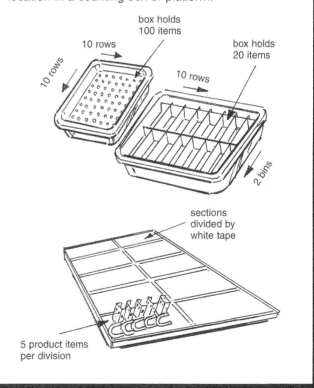

box holds 100 items

10 rows

10 rows

box holds 20 items

10 rows

2 bins

sections divided by white tape

5 product items per division

265

Omitted Part or Counting Error

Process   Assemble washer and nut, then torque nut

Problem   Missing washer

Solution   Modified nut driver will not drive nuts if washer is missing

Product

Parts   Washer, nut

Stage   1-Assembly
                2-Insert part

Control Function							
∿		Poka-yoke			Simplify		
Adjustment	Setting	Warn	Shutdown	Control	Tools/Eqpt	Process	Product
State							
Complexity							
Prevent Mistakes							
Detect Mistakes							
Detect Defects				X			
Variation							

Description of Problem: Nuts were tightened using an automatic nut driver.

Before Improvement
It was possible to tighten the nuts even if their washers were missing, and checking for the washers relied on worker vigilance. Defects occurred when nuts were tightened with their washers missing.

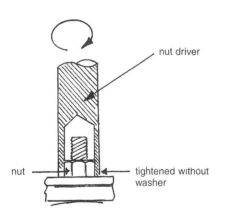

After Improvement
A stopper was built into the nut driver. If the washer is missing, the bolt strikes the stopper and prevents the driver from tightening the nut. Missing washers are completely eliminated. Note: For this poka-yoke to work, variations in length of the bolt must be very carefully controlled.

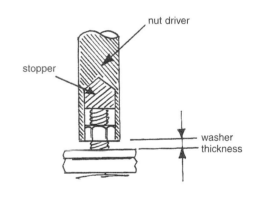

Omitted Part, Wrong Location

Process	Assemble spring washer and nut on shaft, then torque nut
Problem	Omitted washer
Solution	Modify nut so it cannot be tightened if washer is missing
Product	Shaft on rotor
Parts	Nut and washer
Stage	1-Assembly 2-Insert part

	Control Function							
	$\sim$	Poka-yoke			Simplify			
State	Adjustment	Setting	Warn	Shutdown	Control	Tools/Eqpt	Process	Product
Complexity	▨	▨			▨			
Prevent Mistakes	▨					▨	▨	
Detect Mistakes	▨							
Detect Defects	▨				X			
Variation				▨		▨	▨	

Description of Problem: Shafts are mounted onto rotors with a spring washer and nut, and tightened by an automatic torque wrench.

Before Improvement
The nut could be tightened onto the shaft even if the spring washer was missing. It was not possible to detect the omission after the nut was tightened.

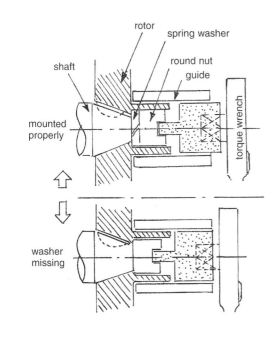

After Improvement
The screw tip of the torque wrench was improved by shortening it. Missing spring washers can now be detected because without them the nut cannot be tightened and the automatic wrench idles.

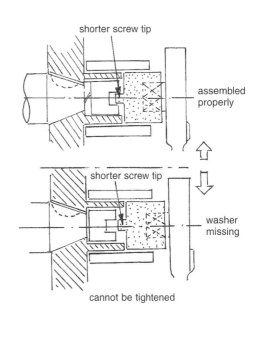

		Control Function						
		∿		Poka-yoke		Simplify		
State		Adjustment	Setting	Warn	Shutdown	Control	Tools/Eqpt	Process	Product
Complexity									
Prevent Mistakes									
Detect Mistakes									
Detect Defects				X	X				
Variation									

Process   Insert ring into cylinder of die-cast cup during die-casting

Problem   Omitted insert

Solution   Detector on deburring process checks for insert

Product

Parts   Ring, die-cast cup

Stage   1-Fabrication
2-Cast

Description of Problem: A certain part is inserted during the die-casting process.

Before Improvement
Because the insert is so critical to the correct operation of the part, 100 percent of the die-cast products were inspected visually and marked with a check. Despite this extensive inspection, customers still complained that insert parts had been omitted.

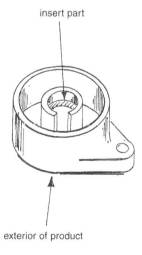

insert part

exterior of product

After Improvement
A sensor to detect the insert was mounted in the die for the deburring process that follows die-casting. The detector is interlocked with the press controls so the press will not operate if the insert is missing. In addition, a signal light and an alarm buzzer are triggered to inform the operator that the part is defective. The visual inspection process has been eliminated, and all defective parts are now detected.

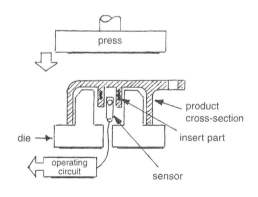

press

die →

operating circuit

product cross-section

insert part

sensor

Process   Assembly

Problem   Missing nozzles

Solution   Sensors detect missing nozzles

Product   Cylinder head

Parts   Nozzle, cylinder head

Stage   1-Assembly
2-Insert part, fasten, and inspect

	Control Function							
	∿		Poka-yoke			Simplify		
State	Adjustment	Setting	Warn	Shutdown	Control	Tools/Eqpt	Process	Product
Complexity							X	
Prevent Mistakes								
Detect Mistakes								
Detect Defects			X					
Variation								

Description of Problem: Flow restriction nozzles are installed in engine cylinder heads. After installing the nozzles, the operators would turn the head over and count the number of nozzles to assure that all nozzles had been installed.

Before Improvement
Sometimes nozzles were omitted without being detected. This resulted in defects that were difficult to detect in subsequent assemblies and potential problems for the user.

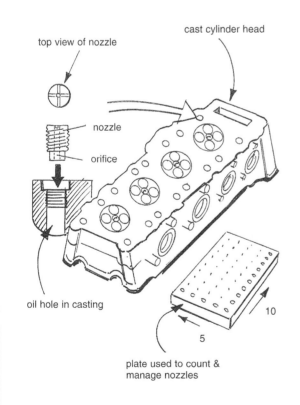

top view of nozzle

cast cylinder head

nozzle

orifice

oil hole in casting

10

5

plate used to count & manage nozzles

After Improvement
After the nozzles are installed, the cylinder head is placed on a tester that has pneumatic lines routed to each oil hole location. When a nozzle has been installed, the pressure in the line is 0.5 psig. However, if the nozzle is missing, the pressure in the line drops to 0.28 psig. Sensors detect any low-pressure conditions indicating missing nozzles and sound an alarm.

In addition to eliminating missing nozzles, the need to turn the head over for inspection is eliminated.

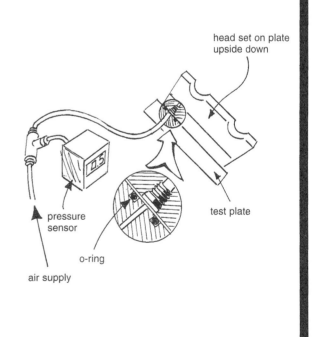

head set on plate upside down

test plate

pressure sensor

o-ring

air supply

WRONG CONCEPT OR MATERIAL (WC)

Design-decision errors resulting in incompatible materials, hazardous products, nonfunctional products, or any one of a wide range of problems. Such errors can also result in products that are subject to excessive wear, are not robust, are unreliable, or are unsatisfactory to customers.

Principles that Eliminate Wrong Concepts or Material   **Examples**

1. Develop and maintain design checklists unique to specific products.

   Examples of items that may be on a design checklist follow.

   Material Selection
   ☐ Compatible with adjacent materials
   ☐ Does not generate particles due to relative motion   WC-2
   ☐ Has adequate strength (at environmental extremes)
   ☐ Resists degradation due to aging
   ☐ Conductive (or nonconductive)
   ☐ Has adequate fatigue resistance
   ☐ Successive brazes on the same assembly are at lower temperatures than any previous braze

Design Concept

☐ Button and switch locations are easy to see, and labels are easy to read   WC-1

☐ Customer wants and needs have been assessed

☐ Customer feedback on the proposed concept predicts a successful product

☐ Parts have adequate constraints

☐ Wear will not expose electrical wiring or circuits   WC-3

☐ Fit is consistent with function

☐ Dimensions match interfaces with adjacent parts

☐ Environmental exposure is adequately defined

☐ The assembly has been analyzed to eliminate loose parts

☐ Parts are accessible for disassembly and maintenance

☐ Possible interference for the entire range of motion of the part is considered

Note: This list is not intended for any specific product, but is for illustrative purposes only. Naturally, design checklists for simple parts are likely to be longer than the one presented here. It should be noted that Toyota considers their design checklists among their most sensitive and highly valued corporate trade secrets.

Process   Using stereo

Problem   Poor contrast makes buttons hard to find

Solution   Review concepts for visibility and legibility

Product   Home stereo

Parts   Stereo control buttons

Stage   1-Use
2-Stereo equipment operation

Control Function							
∿		Poka-yoke			Simplify		
Adjustment	Setting	Warn	Shutdown	Control	Tools/Eqpt	Process	Product
State							
Complexity							
Prevent Mistakes				X			
Detect Mistakes							
Detect Defects							
Variation							

Description of Problem: Stereo equipment has a complex array of controls for tape decks, CD players, external audio signals, volume, balance, bass, treble, AM/FM, etc.

Before Improvement

The control buttons and knobs are black, and the surrounding case is charcoal gray. In poor lighting, the buttons virtually disappear except for a couple of controls that have lights. The labels associated with the controls have such a low contrast and such small lettering that they are almost unreadable.

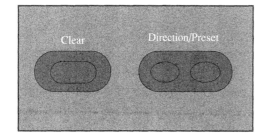

After Improvement

Stereo equipment is likely to be used at times when lighting levels are low. Although the selected color scheme would be difficult for anyone to use, it is particularly difficult for the elderly or those with visual disorders even when lighting levels are reasonable. One of the first steps in the design checklist should be to define and follow guidelines for contrast and legibility.

Similar problems are found in a variety of signs and controls in production environments. Signs, labels, buttons, and controls should have high contrast. Where color is used, make the message and the background differ as much as possible in hue, saturation, and brightness, and avoid contrasting hues from adjacent parts of the hue wheel.

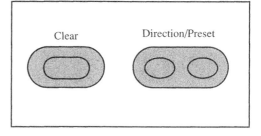

		Control Function							
		∿		Poka-yoke			Simplify		
State		Adjustment	Setting	Warn	Shutdown	Control	Tools/Eqpt	Process	Product
Complexity						X			X
Prevent Mistakes						X			
Detect Mistakes									
Detect Defects									
Variation									

Process   Customer use of cassette deck sliding control knobs

Problem   Metal on plastic slide creates dust

Solution   Change design so that plastic slides against plastic

Product   Cassette deck

Parts   Sliding control knob

Stage   1-Design
2-Material selection

Description of Problem: The cassette desk was designed with aluminum caps on the control knobs.

Before Improvement
Fine dust was created when the aluminum knob cap moved against the molded plastic guide. Applying grease was an unsatisfactory solution because it was black and took time to apply carefully.

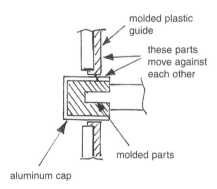

molded plastic guide

these parts move against each other

molded parts

aluminum cap

After Improvement
The shape of the knob and guide were changed so that only plastic parts move against each other. The dust is eliminated, and the greasing operation is not required.

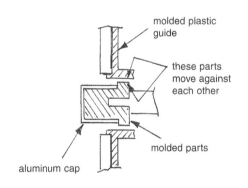

molded plastic guide

these parts move against each other

molded parts

aluminum cap

Wrong Concept or Material

Example WC-3

				Poka-yoke			Simplify		

Process Shield electrical lead terminals for a coil

Problem Short-circuit hazard from cable wear in vibration

Solution Reroute cables for safety

Product

Parts Coil cable

Stage 1-Design
2-Cable routing

State	Adjustment	Setting	Warn	Shutdown	Control	Tools/Eqpt	Process	Product
Complexity					X			X
Prevent Mistakes				X				
Detect Mistakes								
Detect Defects								
Variation								

Description of Problem: The lead terminals of induction coils are insulated with a protective tube.

Before Improvement

The plastic tube rested on the metal case of the product. If the tube was damaged by vibration, there was danger that the terminals would contact the metal case and cause short-circuits.

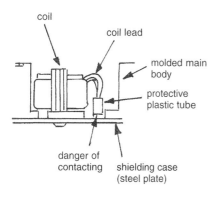

After Improvement

The shape of the molded plastic main body was changed to provide a niche for the plastic tube. The danger of short-circuits is completely eliminated. The expense for this improvement is the cost of remodeling the die for molding the main body.

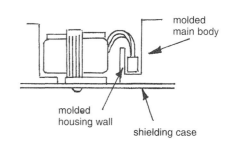

274

WRONG DESTINATION (WD)

After completing an operation, the product is sent to the wrong address or destination. *Examples: A good part is put in the "bad" bin, or HIV test results are sent to the wrong patient.*

Principles that Eliminate Wrong Destinations   **Examples**

1. Pick the right destination, not the location of easiest delivery.

   a. Coolant at drill tip.   WD-1

2. Automate sorting or counting and the assignment of destinations.   *WD-3, WD-4, OP-3*

3. Keep destination information linked with the product.

4. Make it easy to identify the correct destination.

   a. Symbol on specimen matches analytical equipment.   WD-2

   b. Use Visual Control signs and signboards to make the destination for fixtures
      and parts obvious.

   c. Use "airplane lights" to indicate the correct destination (light on at
      correct destination).

5. Print information once.

   a. Address appears through a window in an envelope.

Process	Drilling
Problem	Coolant does not reach tool tip
Solution	Coolant delivered through the drill
Product	Aircraft engines
Parts	Drilling machine, drills
Stage	1-Fabrication
	2-Drilling

Control Function							
∿		Poka-yoke			Simplify		
State	Adjustment	Setting	Warn	Shutdown	Control	Tools/Eqpt	Process	Product
Complexity								
Prevent Mistakes					X			
Detect Mistakes								
Detect Defects								
Variation								

Description of Problem: Deep holes are drilled in a variety of materials.

Before Improvement

Even though coolant is directed at the point that the drill enters the workpiece, the coolant cannot effectively circulate at the drill tip in deep holes. In some cases, the tool tip becomes so hot that the coolant can boil, preventing any coolant from reaching the cutting edge of the drill. This results in excessive tool wear and holes that are not straight, cylindrical, or of the correct diameter.

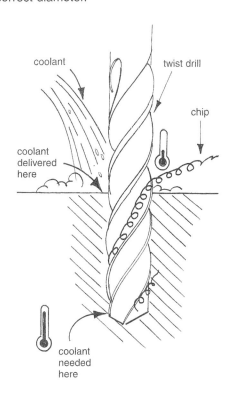

After Improvement

The use of coolant-fed drills assures that an adequate supply of circulating coolant is delivered to the place the coolant is needed, the drill tip. Coolant-fed drills have two small passages running through the flutes of the drill. Coolant is pumped through these holes, cooling the drill tip even while drilling deep holes.

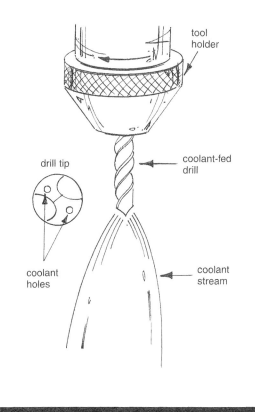

Wrong Destination

Process	Chemical analysis
Problem	Specimen is placed on the wrong machine
Solution	Symbol on label matches machine
Product	Blood analysis
Parts	Blood vials, blood analysis machines
Stage	1-Inspection 2-Setup chemical analysis

Control Function							
∿		Poka-yoke			Simplify		
Adjustment	Setting	Warn	Shutdown	Control	Tools/Eqpt	Process	Product
State							
Complexity				X		X	
Prevent Mistakes				X			
Detect Mistakes							
Detect Defects							
Variation							

Description of Problem: Similar clinical chemistry analytical machines are set up to perform different blood analysis operations.

Before Improvement
It is not obvious to the operator which clinical chemistry machine should be used to analyze the blood. The clinical chemist checks the computer records to determine which machine to use. It is not uncommon for the chemist to choose the wrong machine.

Searching the records to select the right equipment causes an unnecessary delay. In addition, putting the specimen on the wrong equipment can be a life-or-death error due to delay.

After Improvement
A visual code is printed on the vial label for the vial when the blood tests are requested. This code matches the machine that must be used for the blood analysis. The operator can quickly and accurately identify the proper clinical equipment. Unnecessary delays and errors are eliminated.

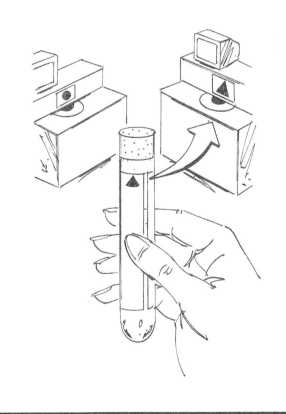

277

Process   Test and sort integrated circuits (ICs) based on test results

Problem   Defective ICs placed in "good" bin after testing

Solution   Electromechanical sorting discards bad ICs

Product

Parts   Integrated circuits

Stage   1-Inspection
             2-Sort

| | Control Function | | | | | | | |
| State | ∿ | | Poka-yoke | | | Simplify | | |
	Adjustment	Setting	Warn	Shutdown	Control	Tools/Eqpt	Process	Product
Complexity					X		X	
Prevent Mistakes					X			
Detect Mistakes								
Detect Defects								
Variation								

Description of Problem: An IC tester is used to measure the characteristic values of ICs against reference values. Those matching the reference values are put into a "good" box, while those deviating from the reference values are placed in a "defective" box.

Before Improvement
Because of operator error, some defective ICs were placed in the "good" box. When these ICs were used by customers the company received complaints.

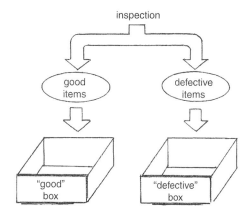

After Improvement
A sorting device was developed, as shown in the drawing. The gate to the "defective" and "good" boxes moves according to whether the IC has tested good or defective. The operator merely places the IC in the chute after testing, and the chute itself directs the IC to the appropriate box. Mix-ups between defective and good items are eliminated.

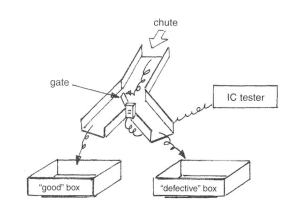

Wrong Destination

Process	Deburr and sort different molded parts
Problem	Similar parts not sorted correctly
Solution	Photoelectric detector used to sort
Product	
Parts	Molded parts
Stage	1-Fabrication 2-Sort

		Control Function					
		⌒⌄	Poka-yoke			Simplify	
State	Adjustment	Setting	Warn	Shutdown	Control	Tools/Eqpt	Process	Product
Complexity								
Prevent Mistakes								
Detect Mistakes			X					
Detect Defects								
Variation								

Description of Problem: Two similar parts are molded with a single die, then sorted and separated by hand during deburring.

Before Improvement
Because of inadvertent mistakes while sorting, the two parts were sometimes mixed together. Customers complained when they received the mixed-up parts in their deliveries.

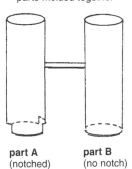

parts molded together

part A (notched)   **part B** (no notch)

After Improvement
A photoelectric detector was installed on the jig used in the deburring process. The parts are rotated, and if any light is detected, it is part A. If no light is detected, it is part B. The operator sorts the parts correctly with this device.

part A

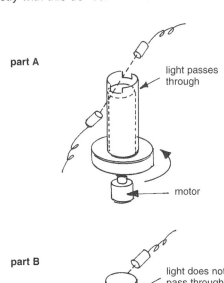

light passes through

motor

part B

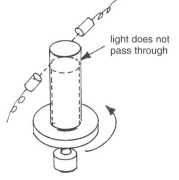

light does not pass through

Wrong Location (WL)

Part insertion or process execution in an incorrect location that is not the result of incorrectly orienting parts.

Principles that Eliminate Wrong Locations	Examples

1. Simplify the design to eliminate inserting (retrieving) parts or materials in the wrong location.
    a. Pre-apply material to a part before rather than after insertion. — *OO-1*
    b. Eliminate nonessential features that enable assembly in wrong location (extra holes). — WL-3
    c. Reduce the types of fasteners at each workstation to noninterchangeable sets. — WL-4
    d. Change the design so that one part fits all locations.
        i.   A single design is used for both right-hand and left-hand (multiple) functions. — WL-2
        ii. One spring type with different tensioning replaces multiple springs types. — *WP-2*
        iii. A part can be inserted in any location (PCI cards in computers).
    e. Eliminate wrong locations by removing nonessential parts with red tag tactics.

2. Multiple parts are inserted as an assembly and separated after insertion. — WL-6

3. Identical features on distinctly different parts enable a single setup configuration.
    a. Standard interface eliminates reference guide location adjustments. — WL-9

4. A notch on the part or carrier "sets" the location for drilling holes (or other process). — WL-11

5. Interference prevents insertion in the wrong location (shape or dimensions).

    a. Pins or ribs fit in mating holes, slots, grooves, or notch.   WL-5, WL-10, WL-14, WL-15

    b. Asymmetrical pin and hole pattern allows only one location.   WL-12

    c. Bend or fold in parts made from plate or sheet stock.   WL-1

    d. A variety of parts each have a unique shape and mating insertion feature.   WL-8, *WR-6*

    e. Selection of one part limits connector access for subsequent connection.   OC-4

6. A visual reference of correct location is placed at the work location.

    a. Visual Control signs and signboards make location of supply parts obvious.

    b. Wiring templates.   *WR-16*

    c. Make relationships between the controls, instruments, and equipment obvious.   *IA-4*

    d. Correct location is highlighted by a laser, light, or other visual indicator.   *MT-2*

    e. Holding tray provides visual reference and maintains correct lid locations.   WL-16

    f. Temporary fixture shows proper location.   WL-18

7. Use tactile feedback (shaped buttons) to facilitate selection of the correct hand placement.   *WO-6*

8. Interference detects defect.

    a. Insertion of a temporary fixture prevented if a part is in the wrong location.   WL-17

    b. Transportation prevented if a process is performed in the wrong location on a part.

Principles that Eliminate Wrong Locations	Examples
9. Different cable lengths on a wiring harness allow only correct connections.	WL-7
10. Diagonal markings reveal a part in the wrong location.	WP-12
11. A downstream process execution is interlocked with the detection of part location.	
12. Verify correct location by comparison.	
a. Matching tags at separated locations identify the correct valve to open.	WO-1
b. Access is unlocked when the raw material matches the material list for a scanned destination.	WP-5
c. Comparison with database catches typographical errors (hit wrong key).	WL-13

Process   Assemble bracket

Problem   Bracket assembled in wrong location

Solution   Bend prevents assembly error

Product   Aircraft engine part

Parts   Bracket, tube clamp, fasteners

Stage   1-Assembly
2-Insert part

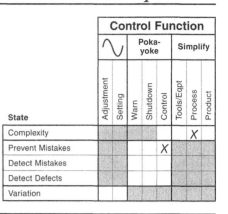

	Control Function							
	∿	Poka-yoke			Simplify			
State	Adjustment	Setting	Warn	Shutdown	Control	Tools/Eqpt	Process	Product
Complexity							X	
Prevent Mistakes				X				
Detect Mistakes								
Detect Defects								
Variation								

Description of Problem: A bracket is attached to the engine body to support tubing.

Before Improvement

The bracket can be installed in the wrong location and orientation. The tube holder can also be installed above and below the bracket. If the assembly is incorrect, the tubing may be unnecessarily stressed, or many parts may need to be disassembled to correct the assembly error.

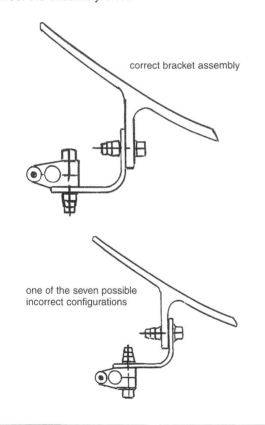

correct bracket assembly

one of the seven possible incorrect configurations

After Improvement

Simple bends on both ends of the bracket prevent assembly in any location or position except the correct one.

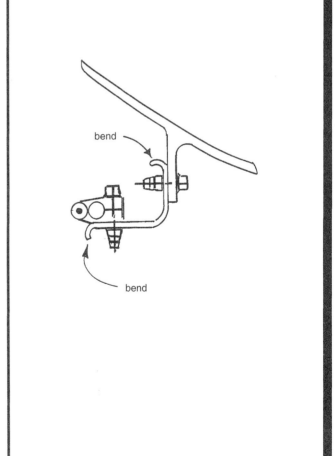

bend

bend

283

Wrong Location, Part, Orientation

Process	Assembly of shaft support
Problem	Right- and left-hand parts confused
Solution	One support works on both right and left end
Product	Mechanical device
Parts	Right- and left-hand shaft supports
Stage	1-Assembly 2-Insert part

	Control Function						
	∿		Poka-yoke			Simplify	
State	Adjustment	Setting	Warn	Shutdown	Control	Tools/Eqpt	Process	Product
Complexity								X
Prevent Mistakes					X			
Detect Mistakes								
Detect Defects								
Variation								

Description of Problem: Two shaft supports are attached to a base. The right- and left-hand shaft supports are different, but the differences are not obvious.

Before Improvement
Since the mounting features for the right- and left-hand shaft supports are identical, left-hand supports can be installed on the right, and right-hand supports can be installed on the left. In addition, both right- and left-hand supports can be assembled in the wrong orientation by rotating them 180 degrees about the axis of insertion.

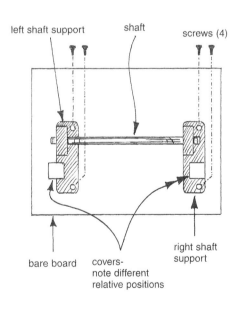

After Improvement
A minor redesign makes it possible to use the same part for both the right- and left-hand support, reducing product costs. The base of the support is also embossed, and clearance holes for the embossed features are added to the base. The embossed features and hole locations are asymmetrical relative to other mounting features, so each support can only be installed in one orientation.

This illustrates the value of using good assembly practices to mistake-proof the product design.

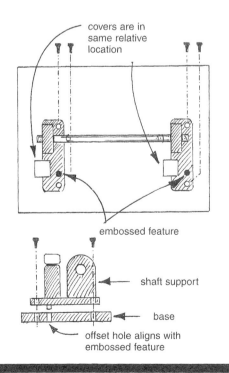

284

Wrong Location

Process	Insert plugs in circuit board holes
Problem	Plugs inserted in incorrect positions due to extra holes
Solution	Extra holes eliminated
Product	Circuit board
Parts	Hole plugs
Stage	1-Assembly 2-Setup

	Control Function							
	∿	Poka-yoke				Simplify		
State	Adjustment	Setting	Warn	Shutdown	Control	Tools/Eqpt	Process	Product
Complexity					X			X
Prevent Mistakes					X			
Detect Mistakes								
Detect Defects								
Variation								

Description of Problem: Plugs are inserted into holes in a circuit board.

Before Improvement

There were extra holes next to the correct plug holes on the circuit board. Plugs were inserted into them by mistake.

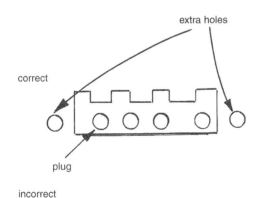

After Improvement

The extra holes were eliminated. Improper insertion of plugs is completely eliminated.

285

Process	Bolt insertion
Problem	Bolts are inserted in the wrong hole
Solution	Reduce the number of bolt types at each workstation
Product	Precision electronic equipment
Parts	Bolts
Stage	1-Assembly 2-Insert part

	Control Function							
	∿		Poka-yoke			Simplify		
State	Adjustment	Setting	Warn	Shutdown	Control	Tools/Eqpt	Process	Product
Complexity					X			X
Prevent Mistakes					X			
Detect Mistakes								
Detect Defects								
Variation								

Description of Problem: Occasionally, a worker inserts a bolt in the wrong hole when there are many dissimilar bolts installed at the same workstation.

Before Improvement

Some bolts are very similar. They may have the same thread pitch with different diameters, or be identical other than the length of the threaded portion. Installing the wrong bolt may damage the part. In addition, parts may not be restrained if the bolt is too long; or if it is too short, the bolt may not have adequate strength for the function.

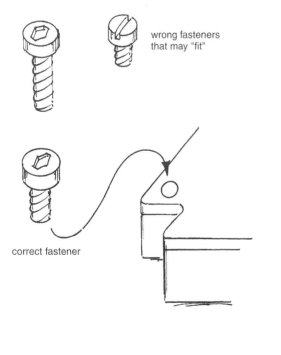

wrong fasteners that may "fit"

correct fastener

After Improvement

The bolts used at each assembly station are examined. Where possible, a single thread length, pitch, and head are used for each bolt diameter at a given station. The number of different bolt diameters is minimized. Bolts are selected so that small fasteners do not "thread" into larger threaded holes, and large bolts cannot "start" in smaller threaded holes.

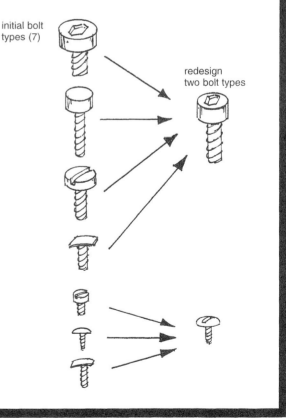

initial bolt types (7)

redesign two bolt types

Wrong Location

Example WL-5

Process   Install brackets into product

Problem   Brackets installed in wrong location

Solution   Brackets fit in unique locations using locating pins

Product   Component mounting

Parts   Brackets, bolt flange, cover

Stage   1-Assembly
2-Insert part

	Control Function							
	∿	Poka-yoke				Simplify		
State	Adjustment	Setting	Warn	Shutdown	Control	Tools/Eqpt	Process	Product
Complexity								
Prevent Mistakes					X			
Detect Mistakes								
Detect Defects								
Variation								

Description of Problem: Similar brackets are mounted on opposite sides of an axisymmetric assembly.

Before Improvement
Because the brackets are attached to a symmetric bolt-hole pattern, it is possible to put the brackets in the wrong location, or to get the brackets switched and installed on the wrong side of the assembly. Traditionally, fixtures have been used to assure that errors are not made in the orientation or location of the brackets. As a result, many parts that are not included in the final assembly are added and removed as the brackets are assembled. There are many opportunities for errors in setting up the fixtures; consequently, assembly errors are not entirely eliminated and assembly is difficult.

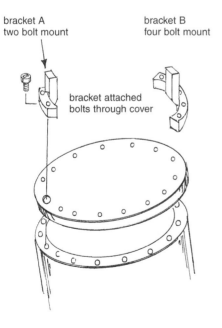

bracket A
two bolt mount

bracket B
four bolt mount

bracket attached
bolts through cover

After Improvement
Pins of different sizes are inserted in the brackets and matching holes are drilled in the cover plate. If the operator tries to install a bracket on the wrong side of a product, bolts cannot be installed to mount the brackets. Each bracket can now only be installed in one unique location and orientation. The need for fixtures is completely eliminated, and brackets are more accurately located than was possible with fixtures. In addition to eliminating assembly errors, this dramatically reduces assembly time and difficulty and is a good example of mistake-proofing the product.

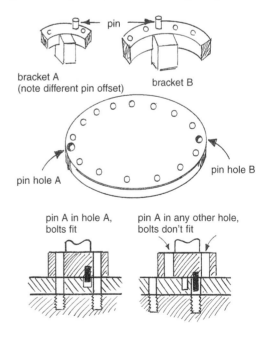

pin

bracket A
(note different pin offset)

bracket B

pin hole A

pin hole B

pin A in hole A,
bolts fit

pin A in any other hole,
bolts don't fit

287

Process	Assemble control units of cassette decks
Problem	Order of items was confused
Solution	Group as one part until after assembly
Product	Cassette decks
Parts	Levers, control
Stage	1-Assembly 2-Insert parts

Control Function							
	∿		Poka-yoke			Simplify	
State	Adjustment	Setting	Warn	Shutdown	Control	Tools/Eqpt	Process	Product
Complexity					X		X	X
Prevent Mistakes				X				
Detect Mistakes								
Detect Defects								
Variation								

Description of Problem: The levers for control units of cassette decks are assembled.

Before Improvement

Levers A, B, C, and D were each assembled separately. It was difficult to differentiate these parts without paying considerable attention, and defects occurred when parts were confused.

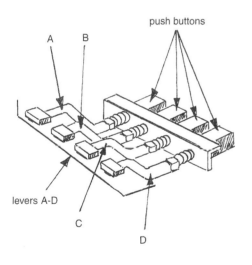

After Improvement

The four levers that were confused when handled separately are now grouped together. The levers are combined into one unit by means of coupling part. After assembly into the tape deck, the coupling part is broken off. Assembly errors are completely eliminated. Only one part number is needed, and the number of work hours has been reduced.

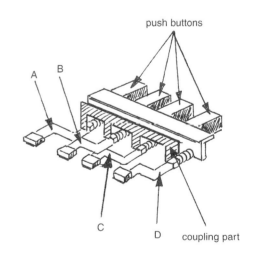

Wrong Location

Process	Assembling connector
Problem	Connector attached to the wrong actuator
Solution	Short cable reaches a single actuator
Product	Aerospace product
Parts	Actuator connectors
Stage	1-Assembly 2-Insert part

	Control Function							
	∿	Poka-yoke				Simplify		
State	Adjustment	Setting	Warn	Shutdown	Control	Tools/Eqpt	Process	Product
Complexity								
Prevent Mistakes					X			
Detect Mistakes								
Detect Defects								
Variation								

Description of Problem: A cable with multiple branches connects to two actuators with identical connectors.

Before Improvement

Occasionally operators switch connectors, connecting each actuator to the wrong branch of the cable. When this happens, the device will not function properly. Since the actuators have identical electrical interfaces, electrical checks do not detect this error. Using different connectors for the two actuators is not a practical solution.

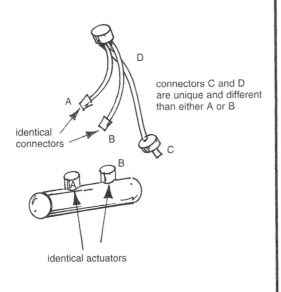

connectors C and D are unique and different than either A or B

identical connectors

identical actuators

After Improvement

One branch of the cable assembly is shortened so that it will just reach one of the actuators. It is impossible to attach this connector to the wrong actuator, eliminating assembly errors.

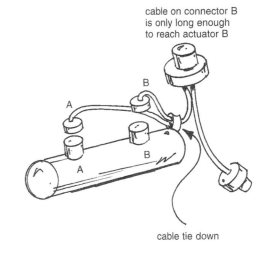

cable on connector B is only long enough to reach actuator B

cable tie down

Wrong Location

Example WL-8

Process	Inserting ink "blocks" in printer
Problem	Blocks inserted in the wrong receptacle
Solution	Ink blocks given unique shape
Product	High-resolution color printer
Parts	Printer and ink "blocks"
Stage	1-Use 2-Insert ink blocks

Control Function

State	Adjustment	Setting	Warn	Shutdown	Control	Tools/Eqpt	Process	Product
Complexity					X			X
Prevent Mistakes				X				
Detect Mistakes								
Detect Defects								
Variation								

Description of Problem: Four "blocks" of ink (magenta, cyan, yellow, and black) are used in a new color printing technology. If an ink block is loaded in the wrong receptacle, the ink block will melt and mix with existing colors, creating a serious problem that is very difficult to correct.

Before Improvement
During product development, the potential for inserting an ink block in the wrong slot is identified, and the consequence of such errors is quickly recognized.

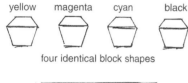
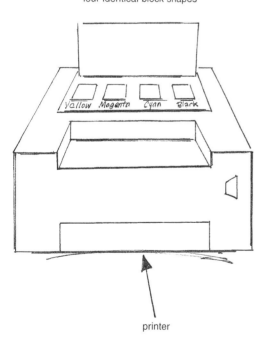

After Improvement
Ink blocks for each color are given a unique shape. Receptacles for each ink color match the shape of the ink blocks. Ink blocks cannot be inserted in the wrong receptacle (without intentionally cutting up the ink). The shape on each ink block is symmetric so that it can be inserted in either of two orientations.

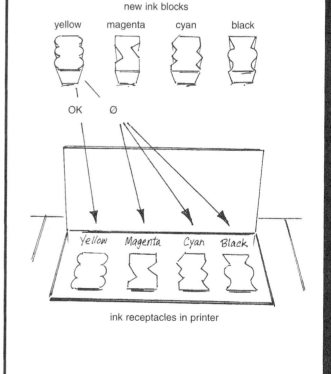

ink receptacles in printer

290

Wrong Location, Misalignment

Process   Setup plates of various sizes on a single machine for processing

Problem   Positioning and setup errors

Solution   One-step setup for all plates (reference pins)

Product

Parts   Plates, large

Stage   1-Fabrication
                2-Insert workpiece

Control Function							
	∿	Poka-yoke			Simplify		
State	Adjustment	Setting	Warn	Shutdown	Control	Tools/Eqpt	Process	Product
Complexity					X		X	
Prevent Mistakes					X			
Detect Mistakes								
Detect Defects								
Variation								

Description of Problem: A number of different sizes of plates are processed using one jig.

Before Improvement

The edges of the plates were used as positioning references. Reference positioning had to be redone for each different size, and setup errors resulted.

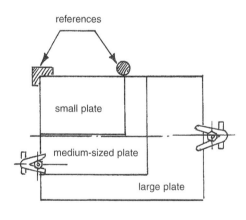

references

small plate

medium-sized plate

large plate

upper edge was used as a positioning reference

After Improvement

The process and materials were modified so that only one setup is needed for all the plates, regardless of their sizes. Locator pins built into the jig correspond to double holes drilled in the center of every plate so that all sizes of plates are automatically positioned correctly by merely setting them on the jig. Processing errors are completely eliminated.

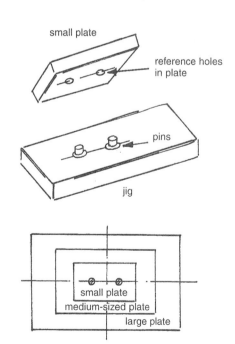

small plate

reference holes in plate

pins

jig

small plate
medium-sized plate
large plate

291

		Control Function								
		$\curvearrowright$		Poka-yoke			Simplify			
State		Adjustment	Setting	Warn	Shutdown	Control	Tools/Eqpt	Process	Product	
Complexity										
Prevent Mistakes						X				
Detect Mistakes										
Detect Defects										
Variation										

Process Assemble railings

Problem Railings attached in the wrong location

Solution Interference prevents assembly in wrong location

Product Electronic product

Parts Mounting board and railings

Stage 1-Assembly
2-Insert part

Description of Problem: Three different railings are attached to a product. These railings are distinguished by slots that are the same size and shape but in different locations on the three railings. These unique slots mistake-proof subsequent assembly when the railings are in the proper location.

Before Improvement
Unfortunately, because the alignment features for installing the railings are identical, each type of railing can be installed in any of the railing positions. Because the differences between the railings are subtle, such errors are easy to make.

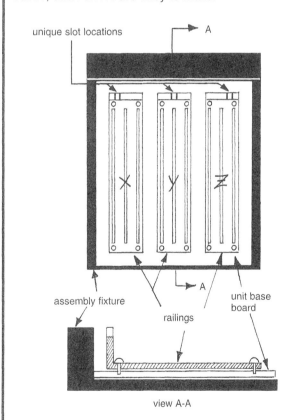

unique slot locations

view A-A

assembly fixture

railings

unit base board

After Improvement
Pins are added to the assembly fixture that align with the slots of the railings when the railings are in the proper locations. If the operator tries to put a railing into a location where is should not be used, interference with the pin prevents assembly.

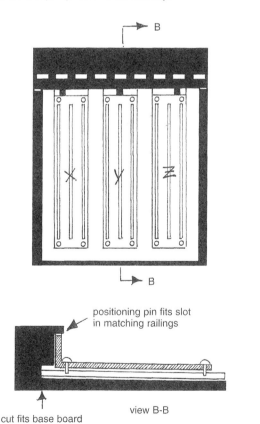

positioning pin fits slot in matching railings

cut fits base board

view B-B

Process	Drill a variety of different parts with a multispindle machine
Problem	Errors made setting up drill for different workpieces
Solution	Eliminate setups
Product	
Parts	Variety of parts
Stage	1-Fabrication 2-Setup drill

	Control Function							
	∿	Poka-yoke				Simplify		
State	Adjustment	Setting	Warn	Shutdown	Control	Tools/Eqpt	Process	Product
Complexity					X	X	X	
Prevent Mistakes					X			
Detect Mistakes								
Detect Defects								
Variation								

Description of Problem: Four mounting holes are drilled in many different types of plates. The holes are all equally spaced in one dimension, but are spaced differently along the other axis, depending on the size of the plate.

Before Improvement

The holes were drilled with a four-spindle drill press, which required setup for each different type of plate. When the number of types of plates increased, time required for setup increased as well, and setup errors increased, resulting in incorrectly drilled holes.

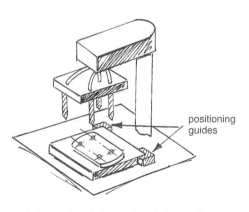

positioning guides

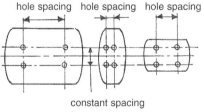

hole spacing   hole spacing   hole spacing

constant spacing

After Improvement

A new method for drilling the mounting plates was developed that makes setup operations unnecessary and completely eliminates defects in hole spacing. A two-spindle drill press is set to the constant hole spacing used in all the plates. A stop block is located on the drill press table in line with the spindles, and the jigs for the different plates now have notches at each hole position. The block fits into the notch in the jig as each plate is fed in. It is now possible to continuously feed the workpieces and position them accurately.

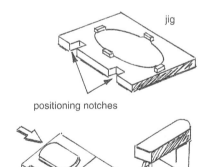

jig

positioning notches

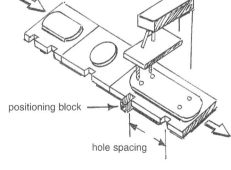

positioning block →

hole spacing

Wrong Location, Part

Example WL-12

Process	Insert right- and left-hand covers on a jig
Problem	Right and left covers interchanged in process
Solution	Jig modified to guarantee correct positioning
Product	
Parts	Covers, left and right
Stage	1-Fabrication 2-Insert workpiece—right- and left-hand parts

Control Function

State	Adjustment	Setting	Warn	Shutdown	Control	Tools/Eqpt	Process	Product
			Poka-yoke				Simplify	
Complexity					X		X	
Prevent Mistakes					X			
Detect Mistakes								
Detect Defects								
Variation								

Description of Problem: Left and right covers are mounted at the same time on the same jig. The covers are exactly symmetrical left to right, centering on A, with the exception of the long hole at position 2.

Before Improvement

It was possible to set the right and left covers in either position on the jig, and sometimes they were mounted in reverse inadvertently.

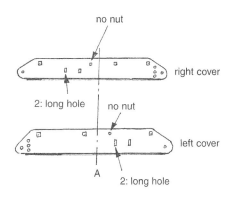

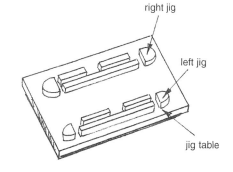

After Improvement

Target pins were mounted on the jig, so it is now impossible to mount the covers in reverse. Processing defects due to incorrect mounting are eliminated completely.

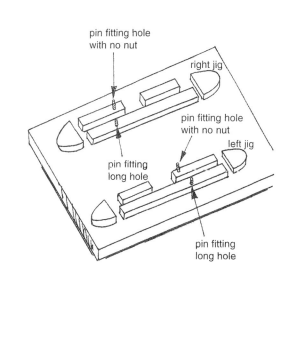

294

	Process	Programming
	Problem	Variable name not typed correctly
	Solution	Automate variable entry and checking
	Product	Software
	Parts	Software development tools
	Stage	1-Development
		2-Writing code

Control Function

State	Adjustment	Setting	Poka-yoke Warn	Poka-yoke Shutdown	Poka-yoke Control	Simplify Tools/Eqpt	Simplify Process	Simplify Product
Complexity								
Prevent Mistakes					X			
Detect Mistakes				X				
Detect Defects								
Variation								

Description of Problem: Software developers use functions, commands, and variables to create software.

Before Improvement

Although significantly improved, most programming applications are not mistake-proofed. Programmers can make simple errors, such as transposing letters in a variable name. These errors prevent the program from running or can cause hidden problems that are difficult to debug, wasting time and resources.

The programmer intended to type a variable name as:

Event_1

Here the last character is a numeric "one"

But accidentally typed:

Event_l

Here the last character is a lowercase letter "L."

The error is difficult to find and correct.

After Improvement

In the programming mode, the computer constantly compares the data entered against a list of commands, functions, and variables, including those created in the current program. Whenever a unique set of alphanumeric characters identifies a command, function, or variable, the programmer has the option of completing the name using an autotext mode, eliminating many typing errors. The description of the variable or function and its format is displayed in the bar at the bottom of the window.

After the first few variables have been created, if the alphanumeric characters do not match any on the program list, a window pops up and asks if the programmer is creating a new variable or function. If the programmer intended to use an existing variable, he is immediately alerted to the typographical error.

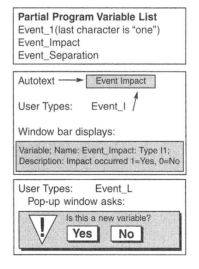

Partial Program Variable List
Event_1(last character is "one")
Event_Impact
Event_Separation

Autotext ⟶ Event Impact

User Types: Event_I

Window bar displays:

Variable: Name: Event_Impact: Type I1;
Description: Impact occurred 1=Yes, 0=No

User Types: Event_L
Pop-up window asks:

Is this a new variable?
Yes   No

Process	Insert cassette deck control buttons
Problem	Keycaps mistakenly reversed
Solution	Pins in different positions and matching holes on control panel mistake-proof assembly
Product	Cassette deck
Parts	Keycaps on control panel
Stage	1-Assembly 2-Setup

Control Function

State	Adjustment	Setting	Warn	Shutdown	Control	Tools/Eqpt	Process	Product
Complexity					X			X
Prevent Mistakes					X			
Detect Mistakes								
Detect Defects								
Variation								

(Poka-yoke: Warn, Shutdown, Control; Simplify: Tools/Eqpt, Process, Product)

Description of Problem: Keycaps are attached to cassette deck control buttons during control panel assembly. Four kinds of keycaps are bonded to the control buttons.

Before Improvement
The keycaps and control buttons all had the same shape and were interchangeable. Correct assembly relied exclusively on worker vigilance.

After Improvement
Poka-yoke pins were added in different positions to each keycap, and matching holes were added to the control buttons. Errors are completely eliminated. This solution can be applied in the future to new models of similar products.

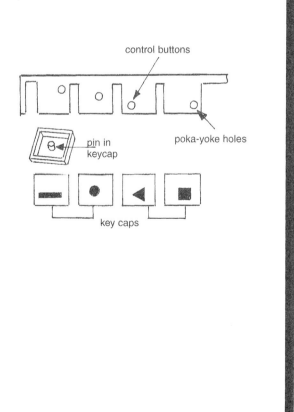

control buttons

pin in keycap

poka-yoke holes

key caps

Process	Setup transfer press
Problem	Feed bar fingers installed in wrong slots
Solution	Pin & slots make fingers non-interchangeable
Product	
Parts	Transfer press
Stage	1-Setup 2-Insert feed bar fingers

Control Function

State	∿		Poka-yoke			Simplify		
	Adjustment	Setting	Warn	Shutdown	Control	Tools/Eqpt	Process	Product
Complexity								
Prevent Mistakes					X			
Detect Mistakes								
Detect Defects								
Variation								

Description of Problem: Part of the process of setting up the transfer press is to replace the 24 left and right feed bar fingers in a particular pattern.

Before Improvement
The sockets in the feed bar all had the same dimensions, and the fingers could be mounted in the wrong order.

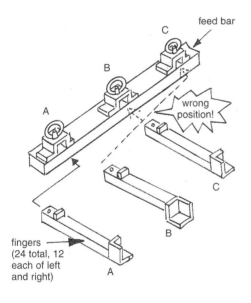

After Improvement
Notches were made in the mounting end of the left fingers, and poka-yoke pins were mounted in the corresponding sockets of the feed bar so that right fingers could not be mounted there. It is now impossible to mount the fingers in the wrong position on the feed bar.

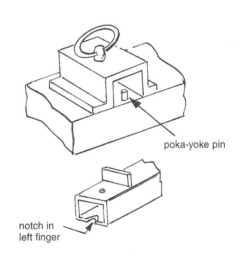

Process	Disassembly and assembly
Problem	Caps put on the wrong tank
Solution	Container maintains correct location
Product	Electromechanical product
Parts	4 tanks and caps
Stage	1-Inspection 2-Disassemble and reassemble

Control Function							
∿		Poka-yoke			Simplify		
Adjustment	Setting	Warn	Shutdown	Control	Tools/Eqpt	Process	Product
State							
Complexity							
Prevent Mistakes							
Detect Mistakes		X					
Detect Defects							
Variation							

Description of Problem: Operators remove four caps from four different tanks. After removing a material sample from each tank for quality assurance, the caps are replaced. Each of the four caps has a different color that matches the color of the tank.

Before Improvement
Because each cap has the same shape, caps can be placed on any tank, and errors sometimes occur even with the color matching.

four interchangeable caps on four tanks

product

delivery cart

railings prevent product from falling off the cart

After Improvement
A box is made that temporarily holds the caps while they are removed from the tanks. The box is color-matched with the lids and maintains the same relative order, so that the lids can be easily located when they are replaced.

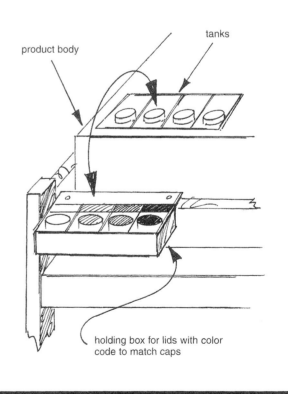

product body

tanks

holding box for lids with color code to match caps

298

	Process	Assemble exhaust pipes
	Problem	Exhaust pipes assembled in the wrong location
	Solution	Tool detects assembly errors
	Product	Internal combustion engine in a car
	Parts	Exhaust pipes and engine block
	Stage	1-Assembly 2-Insert part and fasten

Control Function

State	Adjustment	Setting	Warn	Shutdown	Control	Tools/Eqpt	Process	Product
			Poka-yoke			Simplify		
Complexity								
Prevent Mistakes								
Detect Mistakes								
Detect Defects			X					
Variation								

Description of Problem: Three different exhaust pipes are attached to each side of a six-cylinder engine. The bolt pattern for mounting each exhaust pipe is identical, but each exhaust pipe has slightly different bend angles and lengths.

Before Improvement
Because the exhaust pipes are similar, it is easy to make an assembly error. Even though an inspection is done at a later process, errors are sometimes overlooked and are found in finished cars.

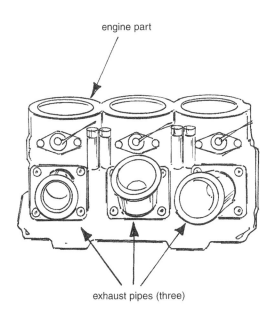

engine part

exhaust pipes (three)

After Improvement
An acrylic tool is made for each side of the engine. The acrylic tool will fit on the unattached ends of the exhaust ports only if the correct exhaust port has been installed in each location. The operator can detect and correct assembly errors immediately.

The tool also covers the exhaust ports and prevents objects, such as bolts and washers, from being dropped into the engine.

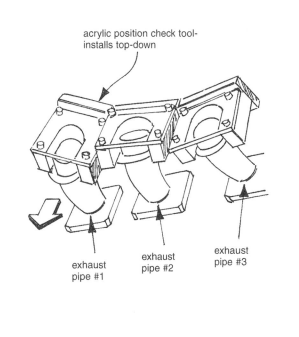

acrylic position check tool-installs top-down

exhaust pipe #1

exhaust pipe #2

exhaust pipe #3

Wrong Location *Example WL-18*

Process	Labeling
Problem	Labels placed in incorrect position
Solution	Label positioning template
Product	Electrical box
Parts	Label and electronic component cover
Stage	1-Assembly 2-Position and insert part

Control Function								
	$\sim$		Poka-yoke			Simplify		
State	Adjustment	Setting	Warn	Shutdown	Control	Tools/Eqpt	Process	Product
Complexity								
Prevent Mistakes								
Detect Mistakes				X	X			
Detect Defects								
Variation								

Description of Problem: Several warning and instruction labels must be attached to an electrical control box. The labels are attached at various production stages and vary according to the electrical configuration.

Before Improvement
It is easy to locate the label in the wrong location on the surface. If one of the labels is misplaced, subsequent labels that are required by law may not fit. Although the labels are a relatively low-cost part of a complex product, removing and replacing them is a difficult and time-consuming process that can halt or slow down production.

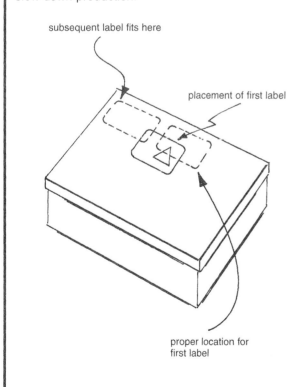

subsequent label fits here

placement of first label

proper location for first label

After Improvement
A template is use to locate each label. The templates have a label attached in the correct orientation, so the operator has a quick visual confirmation that the correct template has been selected to guide label placement.

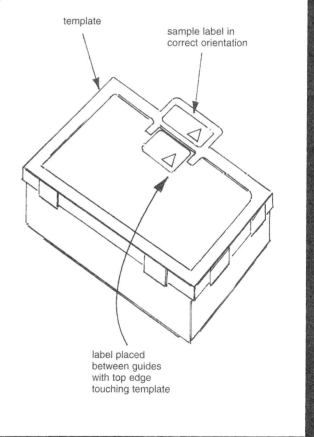

template

sample label in correct orientation

label placed between guides with top edge touching template

WRONG OPERATION (WO)

An operation is executed, but the wrong operation is used. *Example: a right-hand process is used on a left-hand part.*

Principles that Eliminate Wrong Operations   **Examples**

1. Mistake-proof the selection of instruction and have only one instruction visible at a time.   WO-4

2. Prevent incorrect operation on mirror image (right- and left-hand) parts.
    a. Jig that flips like a page in a book jig for right- and left-hand parts.   WO-3
    b. Mirror-image hole pattern is used to assure part is set up for the correct operation.   *WL-12*
    c. A single design is used for both right- and left-hand parts.   *WL-2*
    d. Eliminate left-hand threads.

3. Interlock the selection of the operation with detection of product type.

4. Make the selection of the wrong operation obvious.
    a. Matching tags at separated locations identify the correct operation.   WO-1
    b. Redesign makes the control setting easy to read.   WO-5
    c. Shaped buttons facilitate selection of correct operations (tactile feedback).   WO-6
    d. "Airplane light" indicates the location of the correct operation.
    e. Use kanban cards to make the selection of the next operation obvious.

5. Rope tied to ripcord reminds parachutist of the correct operation.   WO-2

6. Standard procedure chart guides selection of correct operation.

Wrong Operation, Location

Process   Valve opening and closing

Problem   Wrong valve opened

Solution   Matching tags on paired valves confirm operation

Product   Chemicals

Parts   Tanks and valves

Stage   1-Material production
               2-Valve operation

Control Function							
	∿	Poka-yoke			Simplify		
State	Adjustment	Setting	Warn	Shutdown	Control	Tools/Eqpt	Process	Product
Complexity							X	
Prevent Mistakes					X			
Detect Mistakes								
Detect Defects								
Variation								

Description of Problem: A separate pair of valves controls the material flow into each of three separate tanks. To fill tank A, the operator must open valves 1 and 4. Tank B is filled by opening valves 2 and 5, and the flow into tank C is controlled by valves 3 and 6.

Before Improvement

The distance between the valve pairs is substantial, and the pipe routings are complicated. It is difficult to correctly pick the right pair of valves, and errors such as opening valves 1 and 6 are not uncommon.

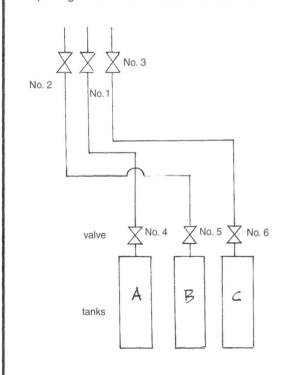

After Improvement

Three different sets of paired tags are created. The shape and color of each pair match, but are distinctly different from each of the other two sets. Matching tags are attached to the valves near the tanks, and the appropriate pair at the remote location. When the valve near the tank is opened, the tag on the open valve is removed. The operator selects the remote valve to be opened by comparing the remote tags with the removed tag.

The removed tag reminds the operator to close the valve pairs, and it is replaced at the tank valve when both valves have been closed.

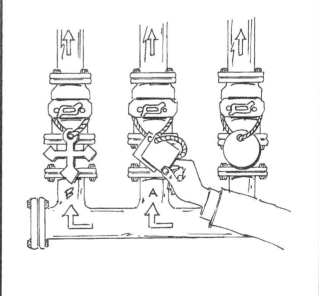

Wrong Operation, Omitted Operation

Process	Pulling ripcord
Problem	Ripcord not pulled
Solution	Standardize ripcord position and pull process
Product	Parachute
Parts	Ripcord, parachute
Stage	1-Use (recreation) 2-Pull parachute ripcord

Control Function							
	⌒⌣		Poka-yoke			Simplify	
State	Adjustment	Setting	Warn	Shutdown	Control	Tools/Eqpt	Process	Product
Complexity							X	X
Prevent Mistakes					X			
Detect Mistakes								
Detect Defects								
Variation								

Description of Problem: Five "base jumpers" planned to parachute from El Capitan in Yosemite National Park to demonstrate that jumping from a cliff with a parachute is safe.

Before Improvement

Knowing that park rangers would confiscate the parachutes because base-jumping is banned, one jumper did not use her regular parachute. This parachutist had safely completed over 3,000 jumps. Her regular chute had the ripcord on the back; however, the chute for this jump had the ripcord on the leg. The jumper fell to her death when she was unable to pull the ripcord.

In high-stress situations, individuals revert to practiced behavior, and "operational paradigms."

ripcord handle

After Improvement

When a change in equipment operation cannot be avoided, operation should be practiced many times before use. For this "one-time" event, tying the parachutist's hand to the ripcord handle could have prevented the mistake, while allowing normal hand movement during the jump. Because parachute changes are inevitable, the location of the ripcords on all parachutes should be standardized.

Many industrial accidents and deaths have resulted from this same type of problem. Pulling the control lever backwards should not move equipment forward, nor should moving the control to the right cause equipment to move to the left.

tie a rope from the hand to the ripcord handle

Wrong Operation

Example WO-3

Process   Attach drawer side rails to cabinet sides

Problem   Right rails on left side and vice-versa

Solution   "Page" jig guarantees correct positioning

Product   Cabinet

Parts   Drawer rails, right and left

Stage   1-Assembly
             2-Setup

Control Function							
∿		Poka-yoke			Simplify		
Adjustment	Setting	Warn	Shutdown	Control	Tools/Eqpt	Process	Product
State							
Complexity							
Prevent Mistakes				X			
Detect Mistakes							
Detect Defects							
Variation	X						

Description of Problem: Drawer rails are mounted on cabinet sides using one jig for both left and right sides.

Before Improvement

Mounting errors had been quite noticeable. Slippage of the mounting jig caused errors in some cases. In other cases, the operator forgot to reverse the mounting jig when changing between left and right cabinet sides. Misalignment of the drawer rails resulted in faulty operation of the drawers, or made it impossible to mount the drawers at all.

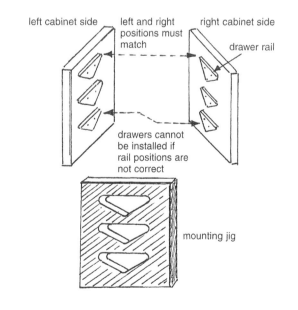

After Improvement

The drawer rail-mounting jig now is set into a workbench so it cannot slip. The mounting method also ensures that the jig is correctly positioned for mounting rails on either the left or right cabinet sides. Errors in mounting the drawer rails no longer occur.

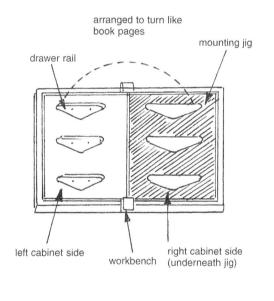

Wrong Operation, Ambiguous Information

Process	Read instructions	
Problem	Following wrong process	
Solution	Instruction charts reorganized—only one visible at a time	
Product		
Parts	Instructions	
Stage	1-Data management 2-Read instructions	

	Control Function							
	∿		Poka-yoke			Simplify		
State	Adjustment	Setting	Warn	Shutdown	Control	Tools/Eqpt	Process	Product
Complexity								
Prevent Mistakes					X			
Detect Mistakes								
Detect Defects								
Variation								

Description of Problem: Ten operations are covered by a group of instruction charts. The operator performs processing while consulting the dimensions listed for each operation.

Before Improvement

The operator was able to read instructions for the other operations while performing a given operation, since the instruction charts just sat on the workbench. Mistakes sometimes occurred because the operator accidentally followed the instructions for a different operation, such as using the dimensions for Step 2 while performing Step 1.

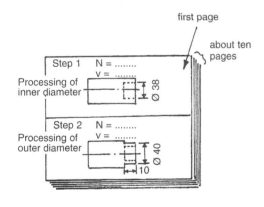

After Improvement

The instruction charts were bound into a single file so the operator can see only the instructions for the operation being performed. The cover of the file is attached to a plate so the file can be propped open at an angle on the bench. To go on to the next process, the operator turns the page in the direction indicated by the arrow. Defects have been completely eliminated.

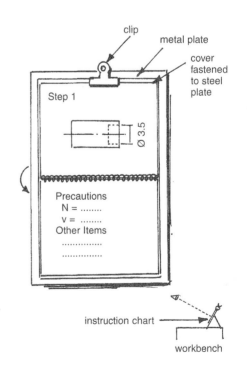

Wrong Operation

Process	Opening and closing valves
Problem	Turning the valve the wrong way breaks it
Solution	Marking shows when the valve is open
Product	Chemicals
Parts	Valve, handle, and stem
Stage	1-Material production 2-Valve operation

Control Function								
	$\sim$		Poka-yoke			Simplify		
State	Adjustment	Setting	Warn	Shutdown	Control	Tools/Eqpt	Process	Product
Complexity								
Prevent Mistakes			X					
Detect Mistakes								
Detect Defects								
Variation								

Description of Problem: Operators must open and close valves during a process.

Before Improvement
It is difficult to know whether or not a valve is open or closed because there are no physical indicators. The operator tried to open a valve that was already open, breaking it.

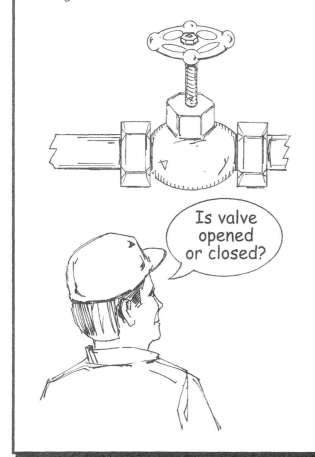

After Improvement
Although a reversible "open/closed" card could be used to show the valve setting, it is better to use the valve directly to indicate the open or closed state. One way that this can be done is to open the valve as far as possible and paint the valve stem red. Next, close the valve and spray the valve stem black. Now, whenever the red paint is visible, the operator knows the valve is open.

Another approach would be to remove the handle and slide a tight-fitting hose over the stem until it touches the valve bonnet with the valve closed. If the valve is opened, there is an apparent gap between the hose and bonnet.

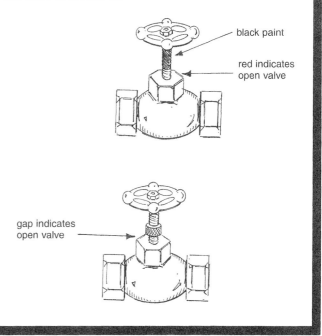

	Process	Machining
	Problem	Pressing the wrong switch destroys part
	Solution	Different switch shapes avoid confusion
	Product	Aircraft engine part
	Parts	Housing
	Stage	1-Fabrication 2-Machining

Control Function								
	∿		Poka-yoke			Simplify		
State	Adjustment	Setting	Warn	Shutdown	Control	Tools/Eqpt	Process	Product
Complexity								
Prevent Mistakes								
Detect Mistakes			X					
Detect Defects								
Variation								

Description of Problem: In complex, small-volume setups, the operator sometimes must move the machining tool close to or away from the part being machined. While watching the tool movement carefully, the operator may need to press a switch to stop the tool motion or change its path.

Before Improvement

Concentrating intently on the tool motion, the operator may inadvertently place his hand on the wrong button. When the wrong button is pressed, the equipment performs an unexpected operation, and the tool head may move toward the workpiece and damage or destroy the product before the operator has time to react.

Expensive parts requiring hundreds of hours of machine work can be completely scrapped by a single machining error. Since the operator cannot watch the machine motion and the switch at the same time, errors in pressing the wrong button can be made easily.

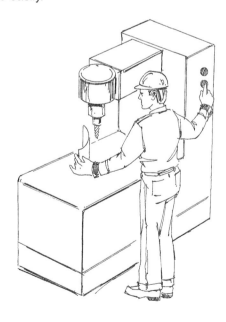

After Improvement

The button shapes for each switch are changed to be unique. The operator can tell which button he is touching without having to take his gaze off the tool path movement, eliminating errors in pressing the wrong switch.

307

WRONG PART (WP)

A part is selected, but it is the wrong part. *Examples: a red part is selected when green is required, or a 1″ long bolt is selected when a 2″ bolt is required.*

Principles that Eliminate Wrong Parts   **Examples**

1. Change design so that the same part can be used in right- and left-hand locations.   WP-1, WP-2

2. Look-alike parts at each work station are minimized, eliminated, or noninterchangeable.   *WL-4*
   a. All bolts, washers, and nuts in flange are identical.

3. Eliminate wrong parts in the production supply using shape, dimensions, or weight.
   a. Sort parts correctly.
   b. Jig for transport only holds correct parts.
   c. Conveyance equipment sorts similar parts.
   d. At changeovers, inspect for leftover parts in transport and process equipment.

4. Interference prevents assembly of similar but wrong part.
   a. Right- and left-hand jigs (brake cables).   WP-9
   b. Pins fit in mating holes.   WP-10, *WL-12*

5. A first-in first-out rack is used for parts drawn in a repeated sequence.   WP-8

6. A unique key from a remote location enables control of that location at control panel.   WP-4

7. Use "smart" part bins to control selection of parts and the selection sequence.
   a. "Smart" part bins with cover doors.   WP-3
   b. "Smart" part bins using rotating racks, sliding doors.
   c. "Smart" part bins with lights to indicate correct choice.   *OP-5*

   **"Smart" part bin setting or sequence based on detection of specific incoming product.*

8. A sensor detects the part (and mating parts).

   a. Access is unlocked when the raw material matches a material list for a scanned destination.   *WP-5*

   b. The process is shut down before processing if the wrong part is installed.   *DM-3*

   c. A mismatch of parts before assembly sounds an alarm.

9. Make the selection of the right part obvious.

   a. 5S's and kanban are used to simplify and assure the correct part selection.   *WP-6*

   b. Visual Control signs and signboards make the selection of the right supply part obvious.

   c. A printed banner facilitates rotary knife spacer selection.   *WP-7*

   d. Diagonal markings reveal incorrect parts.   *WP-12*

   e. Shadow box aids selection of correct part.   *OP-10*

   f. Matrix box aids in setup of small parts like fasteners.   *OP-11*

10. Insertion of a temporary fixture detects a wrong part.   *WL-17*

11. Sensor detects incorrectly mated parts after assembly and shuts down product flow.   *WP-11*

12. Identical parts made of dissimilar material are clearly marked.

Wrong Part, Orientation

Example WP-1

Process	Insert actuators on electronic components
Problem	Right and left actuators interchanged and misoriented
Solution	Eliminate the need for right- and left-hand actuators
Product	Aerospace product
Parts	Right- and left-hand actuators
Stage	1-Assembly 2-Select and insert parts

Control Function							
	∿	Poka-yoke			Simplify		
State	Adjustment	Setting	Warn	Shutdown	Control	Tools/Eqpt	Process	Product
Complexity					X			X
Prevent Mistakes					X			
Detect Mistakes								
Detect Defects								
Variation								

Description of Problem: Right- and left-hand actuators are made for electronic components. Either actuator can be attached in any of four orientations. Right- and left-hand components are made in pairs.

Before Improvement

Actuators are sometimes assembled in the wrong orientation. In addition, a right-hand actuator is sometimes assembled when a left-hand actuator is needed. Although errors are discovered quickly, correcting the error is time-consuming and expensive.

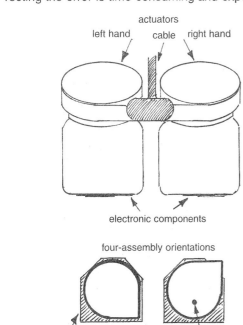

After Improvement

By simply making the cable slightly longer, it is possible to eliminate the need for both right- and left-hand actuators. All actuators can now be attached to the component using a single orientation controlled by a simple fixture. Actuator fabrication costs are reduced, right- and left-hand part selection errors are eliminated, and orientation errors are completely eliminated. This is an excellent example of mistake-proofing the product concept.

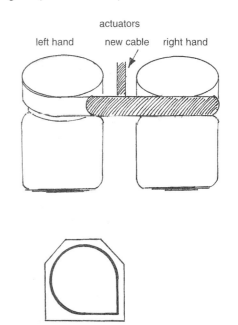

310

Wrong Part, Location

Example WP-2

Process	Insert springs
Problem	Wrong springs installed on a roller
Solution	Use the same spring on both ends
Product	Mechanical device
Parts	Pressure rollers and springs
Stage	1-Assembly
	2-Insert part

Control Function							
	∿	Poka-yoke			Simplify		
State	Adjustment	Setting	Warn	Shutdown	Control	Tools/Eqpt	Process	Product
Complexity								
Prevent Mistakes					X			
Detect Mistakes								
Detect Defects								
Variation								

Description of Problem: Operators attach different springs on opposite ends of a pressure roller to control roller pressure.

Before Improvement
Since the springs fit interchangeably on either end of the roller assembly, it is easy for operators to get confused and install the wrong springs. When this occurs the product may not function properly, and the error is difficult to detect before the product leaves the factory.

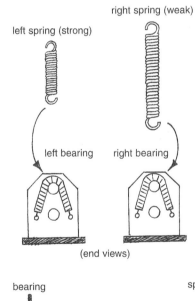

(end views)

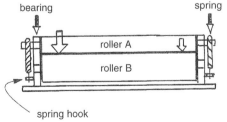

After Improvement
The product is redesigned so that identical springs are used on both ends of the roller assembly. To control the roller pressure, the spring attachment points are in different locations, so that the spring on one end must be stretched more than the one on the other end.

same spring is used on both bearings

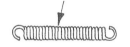

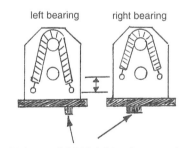

pins mistake-proof right & left bearing assembly

311

Process	Assemble products with different models on the same line								

Control Function

State	Adjustment	Setting	Warn	Shutdown	Control	Tools/Eqpt	Process	Product
	⌇⌇ (Adjustment/Setting)		Poka-yoke			Simplify		
Complexity						X		X
Prevent Mistakes					X			
Detect Mistakes								
Detect Defects								
Variation								

Problem Incorrect parts used

Solution Smart box

Product

Parts Part

Stage 1-Assembly
2-Select part

Description of Problem: Different models are manufactured on the same assembly line, and various similar parts are used on the different models.

Before Improvement
The parts belonging to different models were color-coded, and the operator selected and mounted parts according to the colors. However, errors still occurred fairly frequently.

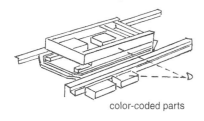

visually determine model

color-coded parts

After Improvement
A completely mistake-proof solution was devised on the process side, rather than the parts side:
1. Photoelectric switches detect which model is being assembled. A light comes on indicating the proper part. The operator watches for the light and selects the parts to mount accordingly.
2. The lids on the part boxes slide open and close automatically, allowing the operator to select only the correct parts for the given model. These improvements make it unnecessary for the operator to make any judgments, and the operator now can concentrate on operations and on reducing the number of assembly defects.

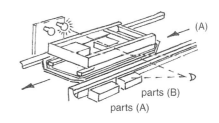

(A)

parts (B)
parts (A)

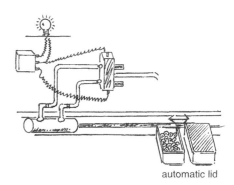

automatic lid

Wrong Part

Process	Clean fluid storage tanks
Problem	Clean wrong tanks, ruining good material
Solution	Non-interchangeable keys on tank required for cleaning
Product	Chemicals
Parts	Storage tank
Stage	1-Maintenance 2-Clean

Control Function							
∿		Poka-yoke			Simplify		
Adjustment	Setting	Warn	Shutdown	Control	Tools/Eqpt	Process	Product
State							
Complexity							
Prevent Mistakes				X			
Detect Mistakes							
Detect Defects							
Variation							

Description of Problem: Empty tanks are cleaned in place. A worker uses a control board to switch on the circuit for the tank to be cleaned.

Before Improvement
The operator visually determined which tank was to be cleaned, then made the connection on the control board. Sometimes the connection was inadvertently made to the circuit for the wrong tank. The nonempty tank would be filled with water by mistake, ruining the contents.

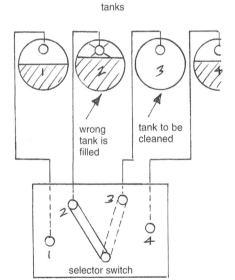

After Improvement
A key switch protects each connection on the control board. Each tank has its own key, marked with a distinctive shape and stored in a correspondingly shaped frame on the tank. The key will fit only its switch on the control board, and it cannot be put back on the wrong tank. To initiate the cleaning-in-place process, the worker takes the key from the tank to be cleaned and inserts it in the proper keyhole on the board. It is now impossible to clean the wrong tank.

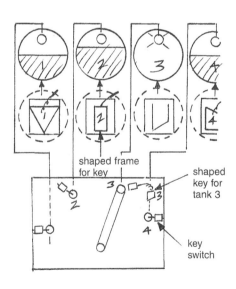

Process Putting raw materials into the tank

Problem The wrong raw materials are put in the tank

Solution Interlock tank lid release with bar code readings

Product Chemicals

Parts Tank and raw materials

Stage 1-Stock management
2-Replenish raw materials

	Control Function							
	∿		Poka-yoke			Simplify		
State	Adjustment	Setting	Warn	Shutdown	Control	Tools/Eqpt	Process	Product
Complexity								
Prevent Mistakes					X			
Detect Mistakes								
Detect Defects								
Variation								

Description of Problem: The operator puts 9 different kinds of raw materials into 26 different tanks. The raw materials are selected by visually reading the labels. Before adding the raw material to the tank, the operator compares the material label with appropriate raw material labels on the tank.

Before Improvement

Mistakes are made, and the wrong raw materials are put into the tank. When this occurs the batch of material is wasted, and the tank may require cleaning, unnecessarily wasting time and resources.

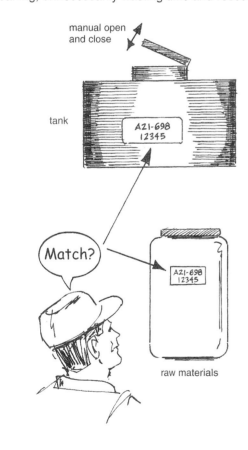

After Improvement

A computer-controlled lock is added to each tank lid. The barcodes on the raw materials are scanned when drawn from stores to replenish the tanks. The barcode on the tank must also be scanned. The computer does not unlock the tank lid unless the raw material is on the material list for the tank.

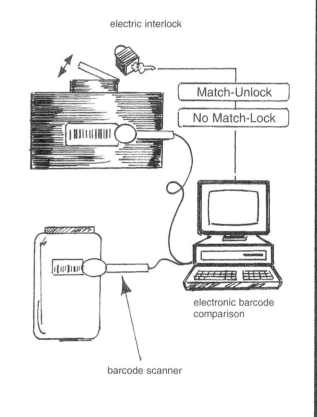

Process	Screening or sifting
Problem	Wrong wire mesh screens selected
Solution	Organize wire screens with kanban
Product	Sifted raw material
Parts	Various wire screens and mechanical sieve
Stage	1-Material production 2-Sort—sieve

	Control Function						
	$\curvearrowright$	Poka-yoke			Simplify		
State	Adjustment	Setting	Warn	Shutdown	Control	Tools/Eqpt	Process	Product
Complexity								
Prevent Mistakes					X			
Detect Mistakes								
Detect Defects								
Variation								

Description of Problem: Wire mesh screens are used to sift raw material. Because a variety of products require different particle sizes, the screens or sieves must be changed when there are changes in the product type.

Before Improvement

It is difficult to visually determine the hole sizes in the screens. As a result, the wrong wire mesh size is sometimes installed in the sieve. After the wire screens are assembled in the sieve, it is difficult to notice the error. Thus, when errors are made, a substantial amount of material may be processed before the problem is discovered and corrected.

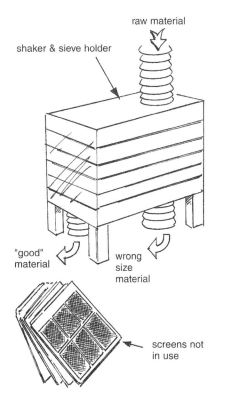

raw material

shaker & sieve holder

"good" material

wrong size material

screens not in use

After Improvement

It is best to eliminate actions that require thinking, searching, and calculating for operations that must be performed quickly. Therefore, 5S methods are used to organize, store, and mark wire screens that are not in use. Before the process changeover occurs, 5 screens of the appropriate mesh size are prepared near the sieve. After assembly into the sieve, a kanban card is posted to indicate the mesh size in use and facilitate replacement at the proper location.

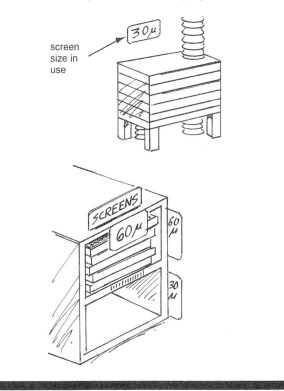

screen size in use

30µ

SCREENS

60µ

60 µ

30 µ

Wrong Part

Example WP-7

		Process	Cut rolled sheet, film, or foil into strips

Process   Cut rolled sheet, film, or foil into strips

Problem   Incorrect cutter spacing

Solution   Provide cutter selection guide and spacer setup check

Product   Printed foil or film wrapped on cores

Parts   Foil or film and core

Stage   1-Setup
2-Insert parts

Control Function							
	∿		Poka-yoke		Simplify		
State	Adjustment	Setting	Warn	Shutdown	Control	Tools/Eqpt	Process	Product
Complexity								
Prevent Mistakes			X		X			
Detect Mistakes			X		X			
Detect Defects								
Variation								

Description of Problem: The right combination of spacers is used to set the distance between rotary knives used for cutting foil into strips.

Before Improvement
Operators determine and select knife spacers. Observing the location of the cuts on the roll checks knife spacing. Occasionally the wrong spacers are selected, and the knives cut the sheet in the wrong place. When the cuts are in the wrong place, the entire setup must be torn down and rebuilt. Sometimes errors are not detected until a substantial amount of material has been wasted.

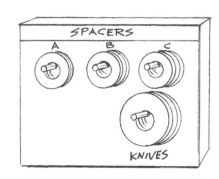
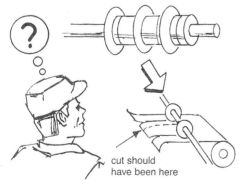

cut should have been here

After Improvement
A computer program determines the correct spacer combinations. A "banner" is printed showing spacer selection and knife spacing for each setup, allowing the operator to perform the setup more quickly and check the setup as it progresses.

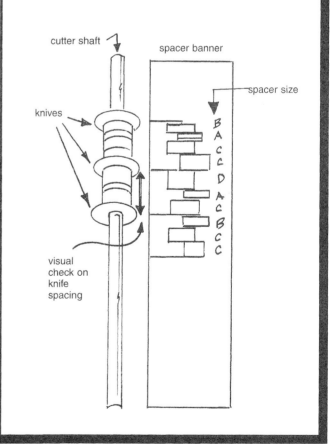

cutter shaft
spacer banner
knives
spacer size
visual check on knife spacing

316

Wrong Part

Process	Inspect cassette tape decks by playing several tapes
Problem	Tapes out of sequence
Solution	Use first-in, first-out tape rack
Product	Cassette tape decks
Parts	Inspection tapes
Stage	1-Inspection 2-Sequential operations

Control Function							
	∿	Poka-yoke			Simplify		
State	Adjustment	Setting	Warn	Shutdown	Control	Tools/Eqpt	Process	Product
Complexity					X		X	
Prevent Mistakes					X			
Detect Mistakes								
Detect Defects								
Variation								

Description of Problem: When a cassette deck is inspected, the inspector uses a series of cassette tapes to check the performance of the unit. It is important that the inspector perform the test in the proper sequence and that all the tests are performed.

Before Improvement
A slotted rack was used to store the tapes. If a tape was accidentally placed on the worktable or carried off, the inspector could lose track of how far inspection had gone. Errors might occur because the inspector thought that inspections had been performed that had not.

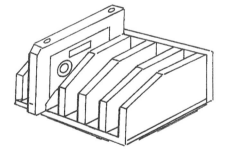

After Improvement
A new first-in, first-out rack was developed that dispenses the tapes only in the proper order for testing. When one tape is removed for use, the next tape slides down, ready for use. When a tape has been used, the inspector places it in the top of the rack, where it remains in the correct order. Errors in the testing sequence are completely eliminated.

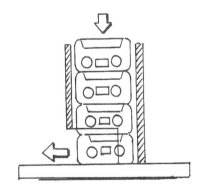

Process   Brake cable assembly

Problem   The wrong parts are used in assembly

Solution   Assembly to is modified to prevent using the wrong part

Product   Brake cables

Parts   Cables, and right- and left-hand cable covers

Stage   1-Assembly
2-Insert part and bond

	Control Function							
	∿		Poka-yoke			Simplify		
State	Adjustment	Setting	Warn	Shutdown	Control	Tools/Eqpt	Process	Product
Complexity								
Prevent Mistakes								
Detect Mistakes					X			
Detect Defects								
Variation								

Description of Problem: Right and left rubber covers are attached to brake cables.

Before Improvement
Even with caution, right- and left-hand parts are confused, and two to three incorrect assemblies are passed along to the customer each year.

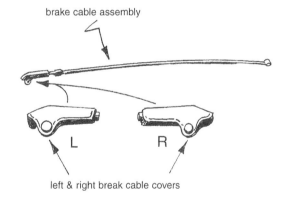

brake cable assembly

L   R

left & right break cable covers

After Improvement
Features are added to the assembly tool that prevent using a left-hand cover when a right-hand cover is needed, and vice-versa.
This example illustrates the importance placed on controlling infrequent errors by manufacturers that are achieving exceptionally low defect rates.

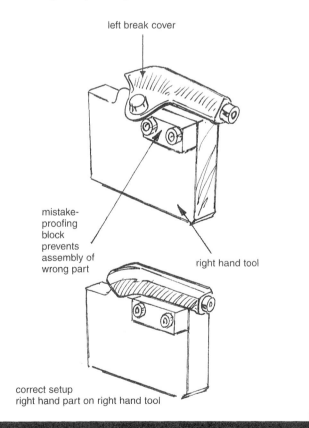

left break cover

mistake-proofing block prevents assembly of wrong part

right hand tool

correct setup
right hand part on right hand tool

Wrong Part

Example WP-10

Process — Attach floor and body with right- and left-hand steering features

Problem — Front panels and bodies for right and left side steering are matched incorrectly

Solution — Modify jig to prevent mismatched assembly

Product — Automobile

Parts — Front floor panels and chasis (right and left)

Stage —
1-Assembly
2-Join

	Control Function							
	∿	Poka-yoke				Simplify		
State	Adjustment	Setting	Warn	Shutdown	Control	Tools/Eqpt	Process	Product
Complexity								
Prevent Mistakes								
Detect Mistakes				X				
Detect Defects								
Variation								

Description of Problem: Front floors are mounted on automobile chassis. Different floors are used for cars with right-hand and left-hand steering mechanisms.

Before Improvement
A model to be made with left-hand steering was sometimes constructed with a front floor meant for a right-hand steering car.

After Improvement
A limit switch in the floor-mounting area detects the arrival of a left-hand steering car. This raises a pin mounted on an air cylinder in the position of the left-hand steering column hole. When the pin is raised, only a left-hand floor can be mounted on the chassis.

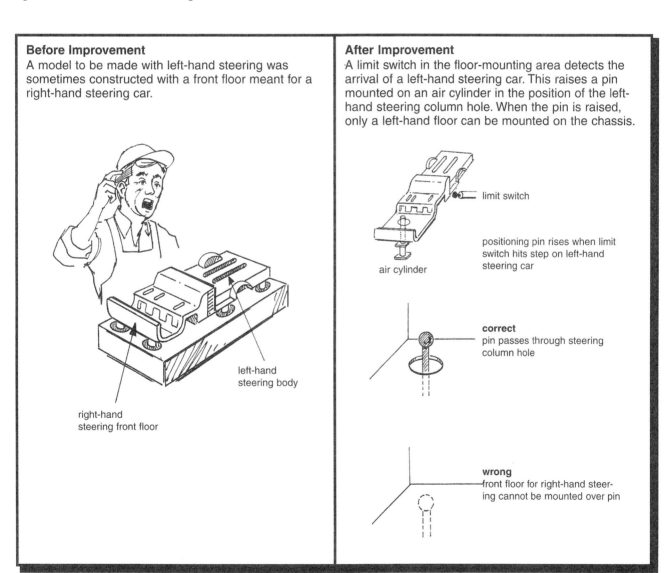

left-hand steering body

right-hand steering front floor

limit switch

air cylinder

positioning pin rises when limit switch hits step on left-hand steering car

correct
pin passes through steering column hole

wrong
front floor for right-hand steering cannot be mounted over pin

Process	Attach back lids to camera bodies
Problem	Bodies and back lids matched incorrectly
Solution	Add assembly check into automatic focusing check
Product	Camera
Parts	Back lids, body
Stage	1-Assembly 2-Setup

Control Function								
	∿		Poka- yoke			Simplify		
State	Adjustment	Setting	Warn	Shutdown	Control	Tools/Eqpt	Process	Product
Complexity								
Prevent Mistakes								
Detect Mistakes								
Detect Defects			X					
Variation								

Description of Problem: In a camera assembly process, camera lids are attached to the main camera bodies. Sometimes a back lid with dating functions is attached to a regular unit, or a regular back lid is attached to a body with dating functions.

Before Improvement
The workers in a subsequent process made visual checks to see whether the cameras were assembled with the correct bodies and lids, and they rejected those that did not match. The checks depended entirely on the workers' vigilance. Inadvertent errors resulted, and some defective units moved along the line.

After Improvement
Since the process of mounting the back lids is combined with the process of checking the automatic focusing, the automatic focusing device was improved so the shutter does not operate during the check if there are lid assembly mistakes. This makes it possible to detect mismatched lids perfectly during the mounting process.

	Body	Back Lid	Pass/Fail	Switch		Shutter
1	regular body	regular lid	O	body off	back lid OFF	release
2	regular body	dating function lid	X	OFF	ON	can't release
3	dating function body	regular lid	X	ON	OFF	can't release
4	dating function body	dating function lid	O	ON	ON	release

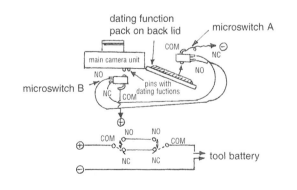

dating function pack on back lid
microswitch A
main camera unit
microswitch B
pins with dating fuctions
tool battery

Process — Load slides into carousel

Problem — Slides loaded in the wrong order

Solution — Mark slides to easily identify order

Product — Slide show

Parts — 35 mm slides

Stage — 1-Use
2-Assemble parts for slide show

	Control Function							
	∿		Poka-yoke			Simplify		
State	Adjustment	Setting	Warn	Shutdown	Control	Tools/Eqpt	Process	Product
Complexity								
Prevent Mistakes								
Detect Mistakes								
Detect Defects			X					
Variation								

Description of Problem: After preparing a slide presentation, the presenter takes slides to another location for the presentation. Slides are loaded in a carousel or tray for display.

Before Improvement

It is very easy to get the order of the slides confused. In addition, slides can be loaded into the tray in the wrong orientation and may display upside down or backwards, embarrassing the presenter. If a box of slides is dropped, setup errors are likely.

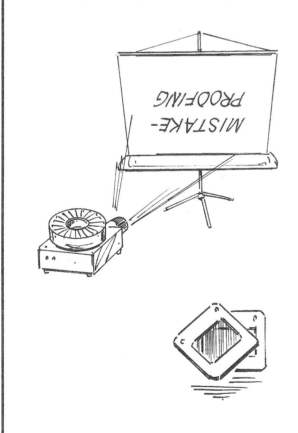

After Improvement

After the slides have been put in the proper order and the correct orientation verified, the slides are marked with a diagonal line across the top and another mark down one edge. A single diagonal line is not a sufficient indicator of correct sequence, because a slide that is flipped side-to-side would appear to fit in another location without the second mark. Now, if a slide is out of order or in the wrong orientation, the error is obvious.

Diagonal markings can be used in a wide number of applications to clarify proper assembly sequence.

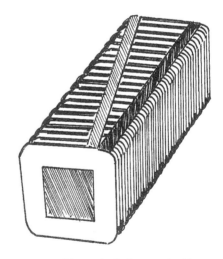

slides marked after organized in
correct orientation and proper order

WRONG ORIENTATION (WR)

A part is inserted in the correct location, but the part has the wrong orientation.

Principles that Eliminate Wrong Orientations   **Examples**

1. Where possible, make parts symmetric.

   a. End-to-end symmetry. Example: WR-1, WR-2

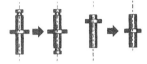

   b. Symmetry about insertion axis.

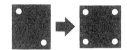

2. Change the correct orientation (single orientation for multiple parts).   *WP-1*

3. Electromagnet repels magnets inserted in the wrong orientation.   WR-15

4. Make parts asymmetric, and make the asymmetry obvious (shape/dimension), then apply principle 5 or 6.

Change that Makes Asymmetry Obvious	End-to-End Asymmetry	Asymmetry about the Insertion Axis
Change diameter of one end	WR-4	
Add a notch, hole, rib, groove, bend, or pin	*WL-1*, WR-9, WR-13,	*WL-1*, WR-8, 10, 13
Pin count per side is unequal		
Make pin/tab length unequal		WR-3
Change hole/feature location		
Pins of different diameters		
Other asymmetries		WR-5, WR-6, *WP-1*

5. Interference prevents setup or assembly of asymmetrical parts in the wrong orientation.

Interference that Prevents Wrong Setups or Assembly	End-to-End Asymmetry	Asymmetry about the Insertion Axis
Guide block, rib, or fill area	WR-12	WR-7, 14,16
Pin fits in hole or notch		WR-11
Other interferences		WR-17, WR-20

Principles that Eliminate Wrong Orientations

6. Detect the incorrect orientation of asymmetric parts during setup, then shut down or warn.

	End-to-End Asymmetry	Asymmetry about the Insertion Axis
Detect asymmetry	WR-18	

7. Interference or lack of interference in a subsequent process prevents setup if a part orientation is wrong.   WR-19

8. Provide a visual indicator of the correct orientation.   WP-12

   a. Fasten a part in the correct orientation to processing equipment.

9. Detect an incorrect orientation in a subsequent process, then shut down or warn.

Wrong Orientation

Process Stake a shaft to a plate

Problem Wrong orientation of shaft

Solution Make ends interchangeable

Product

Parts Shaft, plate

Stage 1-Assembly
2-Join by staking

	Control Function							
	∿		Poka-yoke			Simplify		
State	Adjustment	Setting	Warn	Shutdown	Control	Tools/Eqpt	Process	Product
Complexity					X		X	X
Prevent Mistakes					X			
Detect Mistakes								
Detect Defects								
Variation								

Description of Problem: A shaft is joined to a chassis by staking.

Before Improvement
One end of the shaft was grooved for an E-ring, while the other end had no groove. Aside from that difference, the shaft was symmetrical, and the operator could join the shaft to the chassis with either end free. This resulted in errors that made it impossible to mount the E-ring during later assembly.

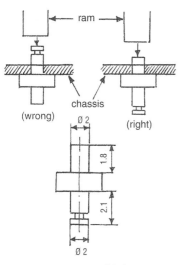

old shape – one groove

After Improvement
Both ends of the shaft are now grooved for an E-ring, so either end can be staked to the chassis without creating an error. The E-ring can always be mounted, and it is impossible to create a defect.

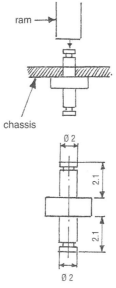

new shape – two grooves

Wrong Orientation

Example WR-2

Process	Inserting a gear on a spindle
Problem	Gear is installed in the wrong orientation
Solution	Put a pad on both sides of the gear
Product	Gear assembly
Parts	Gear and spindle
Stage	1-Assembly 2-Insert part

	Control Function							
	∿		Poka-yoke			Simplify		
State	Adjustment	Setting	Warn	Shutdown	Control	Tools/Eqpt	Process	Product
Complexity								X
Prevent Mistakes				X				
Detect Mistakes								
Detect Defects								
Variation								

Description of Problem: To prevent excessive wear, gears have a flat integral surface on one side that bears on a low-friction pad.

Before Improvement

The bearing pad on the gear is a subtle feature that installers can easily overlook. Occasionally the gear is installed with the pad on the wrong side. These defects are extremely difficult to detect. When the gear is installed on the wrong side, the equipment will fail prematurely.

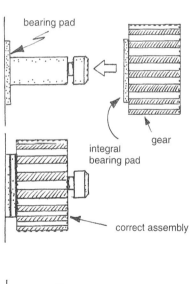

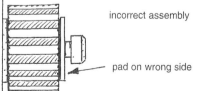

After Improvement

The gear is changed so that both of its sides have bearing pads. Assembly is faster because the operator does not have to concentrate on the correct orientation. Designing the product for ease of assembly would have prevented this problem during concept development.

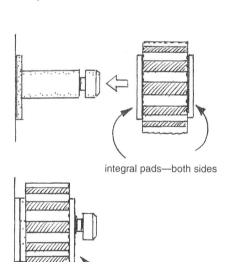

integral pads—both sides

gear assembles either end first

Wrong Orientation

Process	Part insertion
Problem	Insertion in the wrong orientation damages parts
Solution	Only one orientation possible through redesign
Product	Aerospace product
Parts	Mechanical cover
Stage	1-Assembly 2-Insert part

Control Function							
∿		Poka-yoke			Simplify		
Adjustment	Setting	Warn	Shutdown	Control	Tools/Eqpt	Process	Product
State							
Complexity							X
Prevent Mistakes				X			
Detect Mistakes							
Detect Defects							
Variation							

Description of Problem: A mechanical cover supports and protects an electronic component.

Before Improvement

If the cover is assembled in the wrong orientation, the supported component can be damaged when the cover is tightened into place. Since the interference that causes the damage is not visually accessible, the damage can occur without the assembler realizing that the damage has occurred.

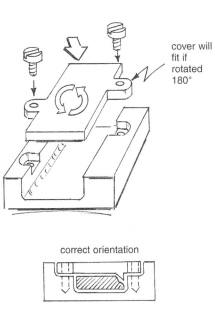

cover will fit if rotated 180°

correct orientation

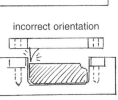

incorrect orientation

After Improvement

The cover is redesigned so that it can be installed only in one orientation, using non-axisymmetric assembly features. This illustrates the value of using good assembly practices to mistake-proof a product.

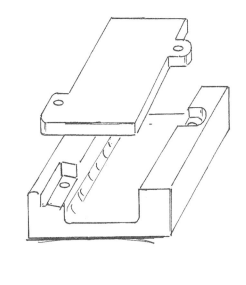

Process   Press fit shaft to a control arm

Problem   Wrong orientation of shaft

Solution   Make shaft fit only one way

Product

Parts   Shaft, plate (control arm)

Stage   1-Assembly
2-Insert part and press fit

Control Function							
∿		Poka-yoke			Simplify		
Adjustment	Setting	Warn	Shutdown	Control	Tools/Eqpt	Process	Product
State							
Complexity					X		X
Prevent Mistakes					X		
Detect Mistakes							
Detect Defects							
Variation							

Description of Problem: A shaft is pressed into a press hole in a control arm.

Before Improvement

The two ends of the shaft had the same diameter, and either end could be pressed into the hole. Shafts were often pressed into the hole backwards.

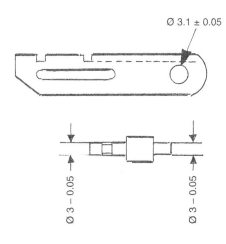

Ø 3.1 ± 0.05

Ø 3 − 0.05   Ø 3 − 0.05

After Improvement

The diameters of the press hole and the end of the shaft to be pressed were made smaller so that the other end does not fit the press hole. The danger of backward press fitting is completely eliminated.

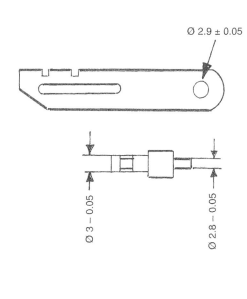

Ø 2.9 ± 0.05

Ø 3 − 0.05   Ø 2.8 − 0.05

Process	Resealing epoxy after use
Problem	Cap put on backwards
Solution	Obvious orientation and features assure correct assembly
Product	Two-part epoxy
Parts	Epoxy, dispenser, and cap
Stage	1-Assembly 2-Insert part

	Control Function							
	∿		Poka-yoke			Simplify		
State	Adjustment	Setting	Warn	Shutdown	Control	Tools/Eqpt	Process	Product
Complexity					X			X
Prevent Mistakes					X			
Detect Mistakes								
Detect Defects								
Variation								

Description of Problem: Epoxy comes in two parts, the epoxy resin and hardener. For convenience, these are packaged in two paired syringe tubes. When only a portion of the epoxy is used, a protective cap keeps the epoxy from oozing out and protects it for later use.

Before Improvement

If the cap is put on backwards, hardener and epoxy will mix in the cap during insertion, bonding the cap to the syringe and preventing subsequent use. In the initial designs, errors in inserting the cap were common. In the recent past, features on the cap have been used to prevent installation of the cap in the wrong orientation. In spite of these features, customers installed the caps backwards and were dissatisfied when the caps could not be removed or epoxy leaked out, ruining other items.

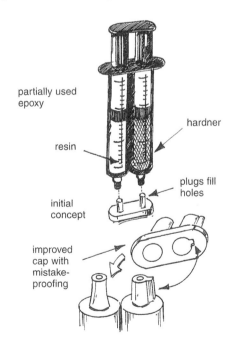

partially used epoxy

resin

hardner

plugs fill holes

initial concept

improved cap with mistake-proofing

After Improvement

The cap shape is changed so that the correct orientation is obvious, and it is impossible to install in the wrong orientation.

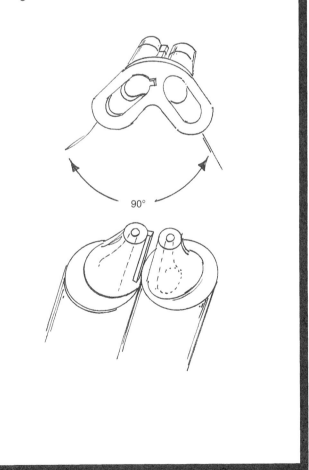

90°

Wrong Orientation

Process Connector insertion

Problem Connector plates inserted in the wrong orientation and location

Solution Connector plates changed to fit in only one orientation

Product Metal housing for aerospace product

Parts Electrical connectors, connector plates, and housing

Stage 1-Assembly
2-Insert part

	Control Function						
	∿	Poka-yoke			Simplify		
State	Adjustment	Setting	Warn	Shutdown	Control	Tools/Eqpt	Process	Product
Complexity								X
Prevent Mistakes				X				
Detect Mistakes								
Detect Defects								
Variation								

Description of Problem: A complex housing has many connectors. For assembly and shielding, the connectors are attached to a plate, which is then welded into the housing.

Before Improvement

The connector plates were symmetric and could be installed in the housing in two orientations. However, the "D" slot on each connector can only be oriented one way for the next assembly. One connector plate was welded into the housing in the wrong orientation. The problem was not discovered until the final assembly was complete, resulting in a very expensive repair.

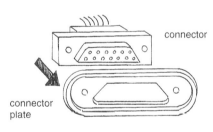

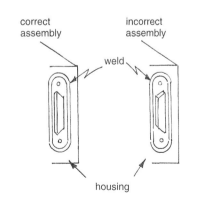

After Improvement

The connector plates and mating holes were redesigned so that they will fit only in one orientation. When the mistake occurred, it was also recognized that connector plates could be interchanged so that connectors could be welded in the wrong locations. Connector plates were changed. It is now impossible to insert a connector in the wrong location.

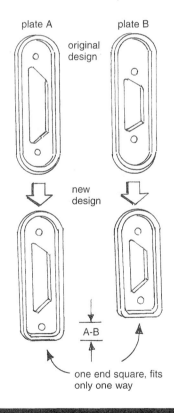

			Control Function							

Process   Connector installation in product

Problem   Connector installed in wrong orientation

Solution   Fixture prevents wrong insertion

Product   Electronic box for aerospace product

Parts   D-shaped connector

Stage   1-Assembly
              2-Insert part

	Control Function							
		Poka-yoke			Simplify		
State	Adjustment	Setting	Warn	Shutdown	Control	Tools/Eqpt	Process	Product
Complexity								
Prevent Mistakes					X			
Detect Mistakes								
Detect Defects								
Variation								

Description of Problem: A D-shaped connector prevents incorrect electrical connections.

Before Improvement
Occasionally the connectors are assembled in the housings in the wrong orientation. Even though the electrical connection is mistake-proofed, the mating cable cannot be connected because the connector is not oriented correctly. The problem is extremely difficult to repair if the housing is a welded or hermetic assembly, or if the electronic equipment in the housing must be potted for severe vibration environments.

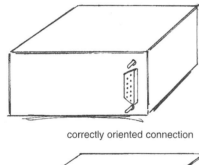

correctly oriented connection

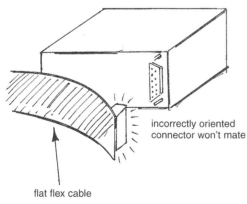

incorrectly oriented connector won't mate

flat flex cable

After Improvement
The connector features are used during assembly with simple fixtures to assure that the connector can only be installed in the housing in the correct orientation. Assembly errors are completely eliminated.

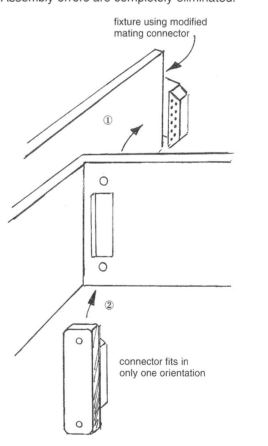

fixture using modified mating connector

①

②

connector fits in only one orientation

331

Wrong Orientation

Process	Stack circuit boards	
Problem	Inserting board in the wrong orientation activates battery	
Solution	Mounting feature assures board fits in a single orientation	
Product	Aerospace system telemetry	
Parts	Circuit boards	
Stage	1-Assembly 2-Insert part	

Control Function

State	Adjustment	Setting	Warn	Shutdown	Control	Tools/Eqpt	Process	Product
			Poka-yoke			Simplify		
Complexity								
Prevent Mistakes					X			
Detect Mistakes								
Detect Defects								
Variation								

Description of Problem: Electronic boards are stacked to make a sophisticated, modern telemetry system. The connectors between the boards are square and symmetric about the centerline.

Before Improvement

Because the electrical connectors between the boards are square and the mounting features are symmetric, boards can be assembled in the wrong orientation. As a result, an incorrect assembly was made, activating the telemetry battery and reducing its useful life. In addition, there were strong suspicions that telemetry components may have been damaged by excessive voltage being applied to some circuits. The telemetry had to be disassembled, and the circuit boards retested.

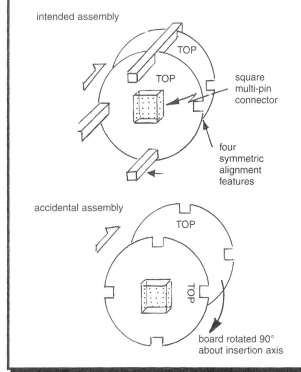

After Improvement

One of the mounting features is modified so that boards only fit together in one orientation. This makes it impossible to accidentally assemble the boards in the wrong orientation, actuate the telemetry batteries, or damage the boards by inadvertently applying too much power to critical circuits during assembly.

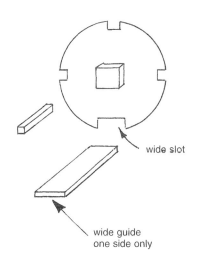

Wrong Orientation

Process	Press-bend sheet metal
Problem	Wrong side up
Solution	Change part and jig shape (notch) for asymmetry
Product	
Parts	Plate, punched sheet metal
Stage	1-Fabrication 2-Insert workpiece—press bend

State	Control Function							
	∿		Poka-yoke			Simplify		
	Adjustment	Setting	Warn	Shutdown	Control	Tools/Eqpt	Process	Product
Complexity								
Prevent Mistakes					X			
Detect Mistakes								
Detect Defects								
Variation								

Description of Problem: A punched piece of sheet metal is positioned in a jig and bent.

Before Improvement

It was possible to place the piece in the jig incorrectly with the burr side up, so that the rough edges were on the wrong side of the bend.

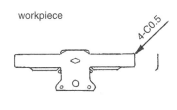

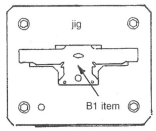

After Improvement

The shape of the piece and the jig were altered slightly in a nonfunctional area so that the piece cannot be placed into the jig the wrong way.

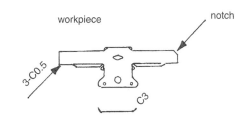

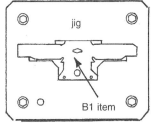

Wrong Orientation

	Process	Insert push buttons on cassette deck control levers
Problem		Buttons mounted upside down
Solution		Make insertion features asymmetrical
Product		Cassette deck
Parts		Push buttons on control levers
Stage		1-Assembly 2-Setup

Control Function							
	∿	Poka-yoke			Simplify		
State	Adjustment	Setting	Warn	Shutdown	Control	Tools/Eqpt	Process	Product
Complexity					X			X
Prevent Mistakes					X			
Detect Mistakes								
Detect Defects								
Variation								

Description of Problem: Push buttons are mounted onto cassette deck control levers.

Before Improvement

Because the top and bottom shapes were similar, it was difficult to tell the top of a button from the bottom, so push buttons were often mounted upside down.

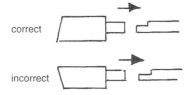

correct

incorrect

After Improvement

The button and control lever were redesigned using a mortise and tenon joint. It is impossible to mount the push button upside down, so defects no longer occur.

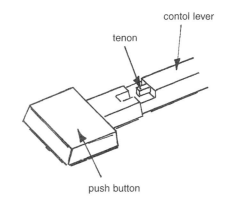

contol lever

tenon

push button

334

Wrong Orientation

Process	Drill multiple holes in plate
Problem	Workpieces set in wrong position
Solution	Add pin to jig
Product	
Parts	Plate
Stage	1-Fabrication 2-Insert workpiece and drill

Control Function

State	Adjustment	Setting	Warn	Shutdown	Control	Tools/Eqpt	Process	Product
	∿		Poka-yoke			Simplify		
Complexity								
Prevent Mistakes					X			
Detect Mistakes								
Detect Defects								
Variation								

Description of Problem: Workpieces have a set of holes punched by a turret punch press. They are then set up in a jig on a drill press, where more holes are drilled. It is easy to mistake the front of the workpiece for the back, or the left side for the right side.

Before Improvement
Workpieces were sometimes mounted in the drill press upside down or with right and left reversed, leading to holes drilled in the wrong place.

correctly mounted

first process
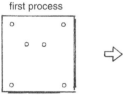

second process

incorrectly mounted

defectively drilled

After Improvement
A pin corresponding to one of the holes punched in the previous process was mounted on the jig. Only when the piece is mounted properly will it fit into the jig for drilling.

correctly mounted

pin prevents incorrect mounting

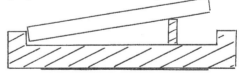

Process   Insert brackets into asymmetrical cases

Problem   Cases set in jig upside down

Solution   Guide on jig prevents upside-down setup

Product

Parts   Brackets, cases

Stage   1-Assembly
            2-Setup

Control Function							
	∿		Poka-yoke			Simplify	
State	Adjustment	Setting	Warn	Shutdown	Control	Tools/Eqpt	Process	Product
Complexity					X		X	
Prevent Mistakes					X			
Detect Mistakes								
Detect Defects								
Variation								

Description of Problem: Brackets are mounted on cases that are more or less symmetrical on top and bottom, except for a notch on the bottom.

Before Improvement
The cases were supposed to be inserted in the jigs with the notched side down. However, the operator sometimes mistakenly put the cases in position upside down before mounting the bracket, resulting in a defective product.

correct

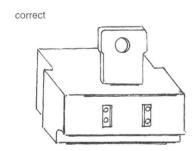

defective

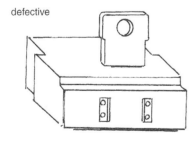

After Improvement
A guide was mounted on the jig so the cases do not fit in place upside down. This completely eliminated mounting errors.

correct   side view

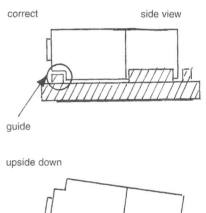

guide

upside down

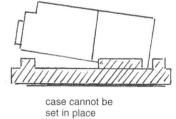

case cannot be
set in place

Process	Pressure vessel assembly
Problem	Pressure vessel installed in wrong orientation
Solution	Features create a unique mounting orientation
Product	Pressure system
Parts	Pressure vessel
Stage	1-Assembly 2-Insert part

	Control Function							
	∿		Poka-yoke			Simplify		
State	Adjustment	Setting	Warn	Shutdown	Control	Tools/Eqpt	Process	Product
Complexity					X		X	X
Prevent Mistakes					X			
Detect Mistakes								
Detect Defects								
Variation								

Description of Problem: A pressure vessel is installed into an aerospace system.

Before Improvement

The original concept had identical mounting features on both ends of the pressure vessel. Because the features were identical, the vessel could be flipped end-to-end during installation, or rotated about the axis of the vessel. When these problems were discovered, the vessel would have to be removed and reinstalled, causing unnecessary delay.

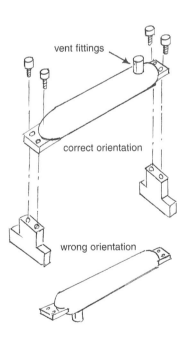

vent fittings

correct orientation

wrong orientation

After Improvement

The mounting features on each end were changed so that it is impossible to flip the vessel end-to-end during insertion. A pin was also added to the mounting bracket, and a matching hole drilled in the mounting flange of the pressure vessel. Interference prevents assembly unless the pressure vessel is also in the correct rotational position. Assembly errors are eliminated by mistake-proofing the product.

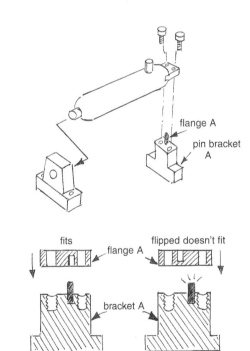

flange A

pin bracket A

fits — flange A — flipped doesn't fit

bracket A

Process	Weld plate to workpiece
Problem	Block setup backwards
Solution	Interference block on jig prevents backward setup
Product	
Parts	Plate, block
Stage	1-Assembly 2-Join

	Control Function							
	∿		Poka-yoke			Simplify		
State	Adjustment	Setting	Warn	Shutdown	Control	Tools/Eqpt	Process	Product
Complexity					X		X	
Prevent Mistakes					X			
Detect Mistakes								
Detect Defects								
Variation								

Description of Problem: A workpiece was placed on a jig for a plate to be welded to it.

Before Improvement
It was possible to unintentionally mount the workpiece on the jig backwards, leading to defects when the plate was welded to the wrong side.

correct

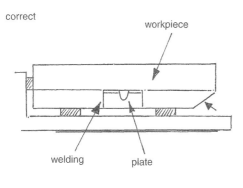

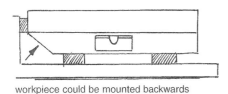

workpiece could be mounted backwards

After Improvement
A block was installed to prevent the workpiece from being mounted backwards. This eliminates defects.

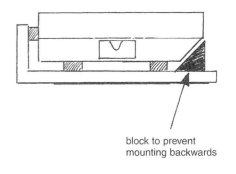

block to prevent mounting backwards

Wrong Orientation

Process	Motor magnet assembly
Problem	Magnets inserted with wrong polar orientation
Solution	Magnetic field prevents wrong orientation
Product	Motor
Parts	Magnets and magnet frame
Stage	1-Assembly 2-Insert part

	Control Function							
	∿	Poka-yoke				Simplify		
State	Adjustment	Setting	Warn	Shutdown	Control	Tools/Eqpt	Process	Product
Complexity								
Prevent Mistakes					X			
Detect Mistakes								
Detect Defects								
Variation								

Description of Problem: Magnets are removed from bin, oriented on layout table, and then inserted into a ring for motors. In this process, each magnet is handled twice.

Before Improvement
The pole orientation is a subtle feature that is time-consuming to properly orient. Occasionally an orientation error may be undetected, or the wrong pattern may be used. The magnetization pattern for each ring is checked (twice). Even with these checks, errors often result in expensive tear-down and rebuild activities when magnets are installed in the wrong orientation.

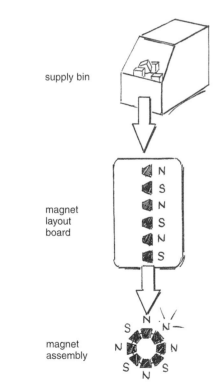

supply bin

magnet layout board

magnet assembly

After Improvement
A series of electrical coils wound to match the desired magnet pattern is placed under a nonmagnetic plate in a thin box (note that opposites attract). The magnets under the plate attract magnets being assembled if inserted in the proper orientation, and repel magnets that are in the wrong orientation, assuring that only correctly oriented magnets may be assembled into the ring.

To release a completed magnet assembly, power to the coils is turned off, allowing the worker to easily remove the completed rings.

Magnets are handled only once, a separate layout board is eliminated, "pattern" checks are no longer needed, and errors are completely eliminated.

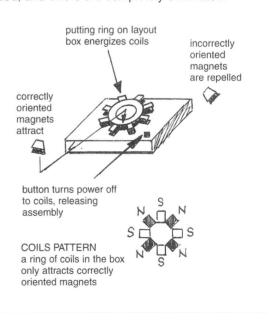

putting ring on layout box energizes coils

incorrectly oriented magnets are repelled

correctly oriented magnets attract

button turns power off to coils, releasing assembly

COILS PATTERN
a ring of coils in the box only attracts correctly oriented magnets

Wrong Orientation

Process   Wiring connector to components

Problem   Wiring is reversed

Solution   Mating connector holds connector in correct orientation

Product   Electronic component for aerospace product

Parts   Prewired connector

Stage   1-Assembly
                 2-Wiring

Control Function							
		Poka-yoke			Simplify		
State	Adjustment	Setting	Warn	Shutdown	Control	Tools/Eqpt	Process	Product
Complexity								
Prevent Mistakes					X			
Detect Mistakes								
Detect Defects								
Variation								

Description of Problem: Connectors come prewired, ready for connection to circuit boards and other devices.

Before Improvement

The connector was occasionally positioned in the wrong orientation during wiring. As a result, the wiring was done backwards. When this occurred, the problem was not detected until the product assembly was complete, resulting in a very expensive rework.

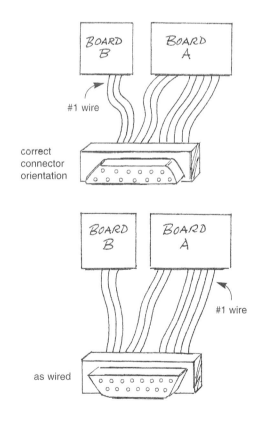

After Improvement

During wiring, the connector plugs into a mating connector. The connector can only be wired in the correct orientation, eliminating errors in wiring the connector backwards.

After temporarily mating the connector for correct orientation during wiring, the wires are fanned out through a layout block. Small wire samples by each slot in the layout block help assemblers quickly see the correct order and avoid routing a wire to the wrong connection point. Connection errors are virtually eliminated, and cable length consistency is improved.

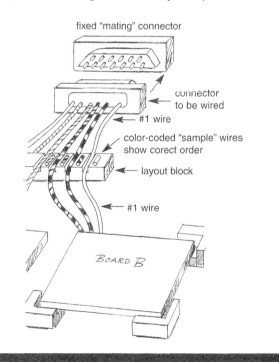

		Control Function							
		∿		Poka-yoke			Simplify		
State		Adjustment	Setting	Warn	Shutdown	Control	Tools/Eqpt	Process	Product
Complexity									
Prevent Mistakes						X			
Detect Mistakes									
Detect Defects						X			
Variation									

Process   Control rod processing

Problem   Product is set up in the wrong orientation

Solution   Block prevents orientation errors

Product   Control wire

Parts   Shaped control wire

Stage   1-Assembly
                 2-Insert workpiece and join

Description of Problem: A control wire is set up for processing. One end of the wire is wound in a loop, which must be oriented correctly or the process will produce a defect.

Before Improvement
Because of the complex shape of the wire loop, it is easy to set the parts up incorrectly. In addition, the wire wrap should be at least 1 1/2 turns, but some parts are defective because wire wrap is incomplete. These defects are often overlooked.

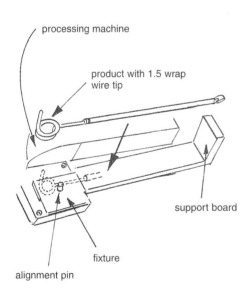

- processing machine
- product with 1.5 wrap wire tip
- support board
- fixture
- alignment pin

After Improvement
A mistake-proofing block is added to the setup that matches the shape of the wire loop. If the angle of wire wrap is not complete, or if the operator tries to set up the part in the wrong orientation for processing, the part will not fit and the process cannot be executed.

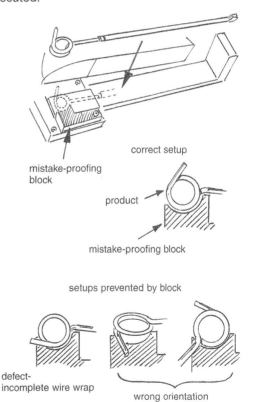

- mistake-proofing block
- correct setup
- product
- mistake-proofing block
- setups prevented by block
- defect-incomplete wire wrap
- wrong orientation

		Control Function							
		∿		Poka-yoke			Simplify		
State		Adjustment	Setting	Warn	Shutdown	Control	Tools/Eqpt	Process	Product
Complexity									X
Prevent Mistakes					X				
Detect Mistakes									
Detect Defects									
Variation									

Process   Press-fit globe-shaped part to shafts

Problem   Parts mounted upside down due to near symmetry

Solution   Difference in end-to-end features shuts down process when orientation is incorrect

Product

Parts   Globe-shaped part, shaft

Stage   1-Assembly
                2-Setup

Description of Problem: A globe-shaped part is mounted onto a shaft by press-fitting.

Before Improvement

The part is shaped symmetrically on top and bottom, and the end to be fitted to the shaft is almost the same size as the opposite end. Sometimes the parts were fitted onto the shaft upside down. The operator checked during the operation that the part was mounted correctly, but parts were still sometimes mounted upside down, resulting in problems in the following processes.

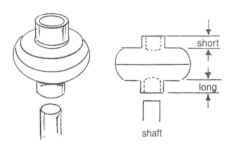

After Improvement

A detector was devised to alert the operator when a part has been mounted backwards, using the slight difference in lengths of the top and bottom. When a part is mounted backwards (with the longer part at the top), it forces the weight up, spreading the press collet. The press cannot be used for pressing until it is set up again; so the operator always notices incorrect mounting. A better solution would be to change the design so both ends are the same length.

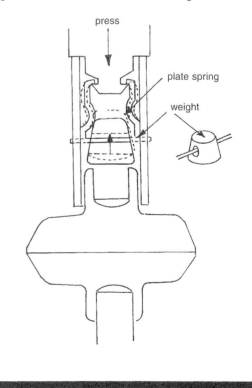

		Control Function							
		∿	Poka-yoke			Simplify			
State		Adjustment	Setting	Warn	Shutdown	Control	Tools/Eqpt	Process	Product
Complexity								X	
Prevent Mistakes									
Detect Mistakes						X			
Detect Defects									
Variation									

Process   Press fit oil seal into housing

Problem   Part is inserted in the wrong orientation

Solution   Seal falls off press tool in the wrong orientation

Product   Combustion engine subassembly

Parts   Oil seal and cast housing

Stage   1-Assembly
2-Insert part and press fit

Description of Problem: A press is used to insert an oil seal into a cast housing. To install the oil seal, it is first placed upside-down, with the flat surface up, on a press tool. This assembly is flipped over and installed on the press. The press then drives the oil seal into the housing.

Before Improvement

The assembly operation is identical whether or not the oil seal has been placed on the press tool correctly. As a result, there is no way to determine if the oil seal has been installed correctly. If the seal is not installed correctly, oil leaks occur, resulting in customer complaints.

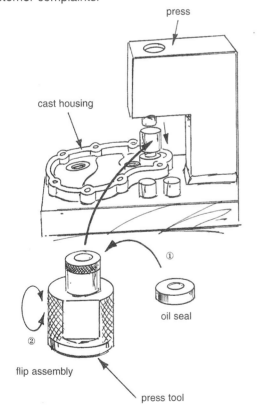

After Improvement

The press tool is modified by reducing the diameter of the tip. If the part is placed on the tool in the correct orientation, friction will hold the part on the tool until assembly is completed. However, if the seal is placed on the tool upside down, it will fall off the tool when the assembly is flipped over to be put on the press.

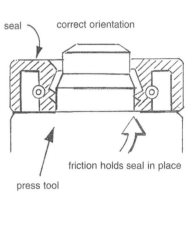

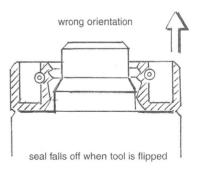

Process   Attaching label

Problem   Barcode put on upside down

Solution   Notch barcode and match to part shape

Product   Label attachment

Parts   Label and molded plastic cover

Stage   1-Assembly
2-Insert part

Control Function							
$\curvearrowright$		Poka-yoke			Simplify		
Adjustment	Setting	Warn	Shutdown	Control	Tools/Eqpt	Process	Product
State							
Complexity							X	
Prevent Mistakes								
Detect Mistakes				X				
Detect Defects								
Variation								

Description of Problem: Barcodes are attached to a part.

Before Improvement
It is difficult to see at a glance whether or not a barcode is upside down. This is particularly true when the barcode label does not have any letters or numbers. Some labels are installed upside down.

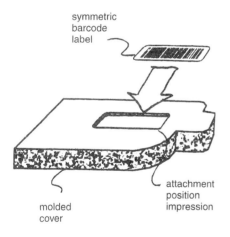

symmetric barcode label

molded cover

attachment position impression

After Improvement
One corner of the label is notched, and a matching notch is formed in the plastic parts. Now the correct orientation of the label is obvious, and errors are eliminated.

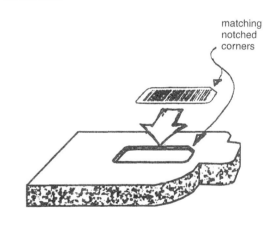

matching notched corners

APPENDIX B

WORKSHEETS

Permission is granted to copy the Worksheet Masters in Appendix B. Permission to copy the Worksheet Masters in Appendix B does not imply permission to copy or distribute any other material in this book.

QCC Assembly Time Factors for Worksheet

Instructions: Use this table to select operation time (in seconds) for each part or assembly operation. Enter the time into the QCC Worksheet. If a conditon does not apply, the cell may be blank, or the designer may enter more appropriate time factors that are not listed below. Time is in seconds.

A. End-to-End Alignment

Time	Condition
1.3	>1 end-to-end orientation (i.e., left figure below)
1.8	>1 end-to-end orientations — subtle feature
1.8	1 end-to-end orientation — obvious feature
2.3	1 end-to-end orientation — subtle feature

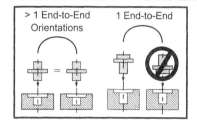

B. Rotational Alignment about Insertion Axis

Time	Condition
0.5	2 or 3 alignments — obvious feature
1.0	2 or 3 alignments — subtle feature
1.0	1 alignment — obvious feature
1.5	1 alignment — subtle feature

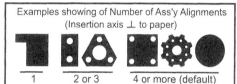

C. Thickness (Note: time · 2 if insertion orientations < 4)

Time	Part Thickness
0.0	> 2 mm
0.2	0.5 to 2 mm
0.5	< 0.5 mm

D. Size (Note: time · 2 if insertion orientations < 4)

Time	Part Size
0.0	> 12 mm
0.1	6 to 12 mm
0.4	2 to 6 mm
0.6	< 2 mm

E. Handling Conditions

Time	Part Condition
0.0	No special conditions
0.5	Heavy
1.0	Delicate
1.5	Nests/tangles
6.0	Severe nest/tangle
2.0	Tweezers req'd
3.5	Other tools req'd

Note: Times for each condition that apply are additive

F. Insertion Clearance Access

Time	Clearance	Time	Clearance
0.0	Very large	0.9	Small
0.3	Large	1.6	Very small

G. Insertion Direction

Time	Insertion Directions
0.6	Top down
1.4	From side
1.7	Diagonally or twist/turn/tilt
2.0	Up from bottom

Note: Times for each condition that apply are additive

H. Insertion Condition

Time	Insertion Condition
0	Self-aligning and align before mating
0.5	Self-aligning or aligns before mating
1.3	Constrained motion
1.4	Temporary hold down required
1.5	Two hands
2.3	Fixture or rotate
6.0	Flexible

Note: Times for each condition that apply are additive

I. Fastener

Time	Fastener Type
0.0	Washer
1.0	Pin
2.5	Retaining ring
4.0	Screw
5.0	Nut
6.0	Rivet

J. Fastening Process (Part not added):

Time	Type of Process
1	Snap or press fit
3	Bending or crimping
4	Screwing process
5	Polymer stake or weld
7	Solder
9	Weld/braze
11	Adhesive

K. Adjustments

Time	Type of Process
0.0	No adjustments
2.0	Adjustments converted to "settings"
15.0	Adjustments

Calculate Time to Complete Each Operation (Top)

$$T_{op} = A + B + C + D + E + F + G + H + I + J + K$$

QCC WORKSHEET

QCC Time Factors (seconds)

Ass'y/Subass'y Name

No.	Part/Op. Description	A End to End Orientation	B Rotational Alignment	C Part Size	D Part Thickness	E Handling Condition	F Insertion Clearance	G Insertion Direction	H Insertion Condition	I Fastener	J Fastening Process	K Adjustment	L Time/Each Operation (T_{op})	M Number of Repetitions (N_{rep})	N Repetition Time (L x M) (T_{rep})	O Insert Part (1 = Yes; 0 = No)	P No. of Parts/Operation (M x O)
1																	
2																	
3																	
4																	
5																	
6																	
7																	
8																	
9																	
10																	
11																	
12																	
13																	
14																	
15																	

TOP		TAT		NUP		NP	
C							
OR							

Step 1: Identify assembly sequence

Step 2: List parts & assembly operations in order of execution in top row of table

Step 3: Enter part/fastening times from QCC simplify time factor

Step 4: Enter sum of ass'y times A-K in column L

Step 5: Enter number of times each operation is repeated in column M. Enter T_{op} x N_{rep} in row N.

Step 6: Enter a 1 in column O if a part is inserted, a 0 otherwise

Step 7: Calculate summary statistics

NUP = Number of unique parts (column O sum)

TOP = Total number of operations (column M sum)

TAT = Total assembly time (column N sum)

NP = Number of parts = (column P sum)

C = Assembly complexity = TAT -2.4* TOP

OR = Operation difficulty rating = TAT /(2.4* TOP)

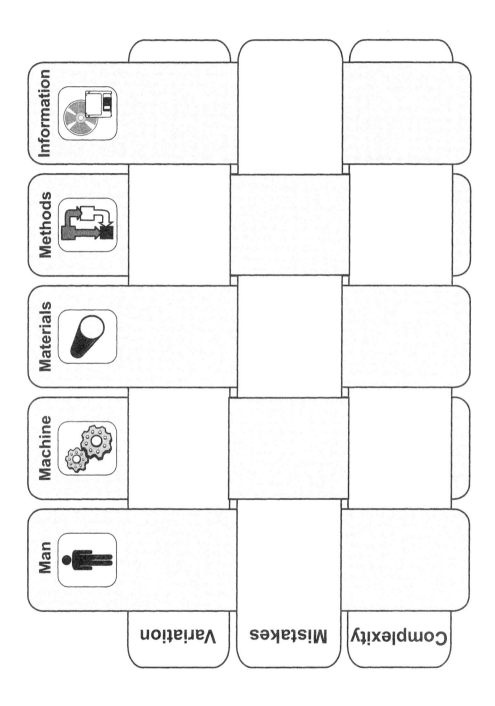

4M's and an I—CMV Matrix

QCM—Mistake-Proofing Example Worksheet

Classification   *Example No.*

Process _____

Problem _____

Solution _____

Product _____

Parts _____

Stage _____

Problem Urgency				Control Function							
				∿		Poka-yoke			Simplify		
Frequency:	Process Impact	Corporate Impact	Product:	Adjustment	Setting	Warn	Shutdown	Control	Tools/Eqpt	Process	Product
×	×	=									
Rate 1 to 3, 3 = Worst											
State											
Complexity											
Prevent Mistakes											
Detect Mistakes											
Detect Defects											
Variation											

Description of Problem:

Before Improvement	After Improvement

APPENDIX C

Mistake-proofing Devices, Sensors, and Suppliers

As previously noted, mistake-proofing, in general, must be inexpensive to be cost effective. Resources are wasted in the development of mistake-proofing if ineffective concepts or devices are selected. Even when a good mistake-proofing concept is developed, the implementation of the most effective devices may depend upon commercial products that are unfamiliar or not readily available to the developer. To reduce the time and cost required to implement mistake-proofing concepts, we will first provide a brief overview of mistake-proofing devices and sensors. Tables show the relative utility of these devices in mistake-proofing and clarify their various applications. A list of suppliers of products useful for mistake-proofing is also supplied, along with a table that summarizes the type of products available from the listed suppliers.

Devices

Many devices that do not depend upon sensor technology are useful in mistake-proofing. Counting boards and trays, and checklists are just a few examples of such devices that have been described in the text and examples of this book. Following is a summary of common mistake-proofing devices, illustrating their variety and utility. An asterisk(*) in the heading indicates that the devices are frequently used in mistake-proofing, or are particularly effective mistake-proofing devices.

*Counters and Timers

Counters track the number of events that have occurred, and are one of the more common and most effective mistake-proofing tools. They can be mechanical devices, like odometers, or electrical devices like quartz crystal clocks that count the units of time that have passed. Many electromechanical counters also exist. In some cases, the counting is performed mechanically, but an electrical output signal is provided. In other cases, the counting may actually be done electrically, but the display may be mechanical.

WARNING DEVICES

Warning devices attract the attention of the operator, and inform them regarding the required action if properly design. Warning devices alert the operator by light, sound, tactile sensations, by odors (in rare cases), or by a combination of these methods. A warning device may indicate that:

- Stock needs replenished,
- It is time to perform a planned operation,
- A wrong or defective part is in the production stream,
- A problem with the production equipment needs correction, or
- Emergency conditions exist.

Warning devices may also be used to indicate the status of the production line or sensors, or inform regarding the progress of an operation.

*Visual

Lights are the most commonly used warning devices. For emergencies or conditions requiring urgent response, flashing or spinning lights are appropriate. Lights may be separate devices or imbedded in switches or controls. Lights are most effective when visual access is not obscured, and when located to visually indicate where action is required, like the call lights in a airplane that show the attendant the row where attention is required by the passenger. Lights should have sufficient brightness to readily attract attention, but should never be so bright or cast a color so intense that vision is impaired. Colors can be used effectively with lights to clarify function, but caution should be used to consider color blindness. Lights behind translucent materials can display information essential to the correct execution of the task.

Other methods for visually displaying warnings include television screens, computer monitors, liquid crystal displays (LCD), and light emitting diodes (LED). Some devices like LCDs and LEDs may be difficult to read when the ambient lighting is poor, and may not provide sufficient warning in some applications.

*Aural

Whistles, sirens, horns, bells, and chimes are common audio warning devices. Loud whistles, and sirens should only be used for emergencies and extremely urgent conditions. Even in these conditions, the sound should not be so loud or last so long that it makes the execution of the correct urgent response difficult. Speakers can provide the most flexible warning, allowing a variety of distinctly different audio signals for different problems. With speakers, a wide range of recorded and simulated sounds can be projected, and the sound volume can be adjusted. Although vocal warnings or instructions can be given with recordings or simulations, voice warnings should be used with caution. Unexpected voice warnings can be so startling that workers are unnerved, responding in unexpected ways that may cause defects or dangerous situations.

Tactile

In noisy environments or visually "busy" locations, audio and visual warnings may not attract the attention of workers. In these situations, tactile warning devices, such as vibrators, will be more effective. Vibratory warnings may also be helpful in situations where only one worker needs to receive a warning that could be distracting to other workers. Tactile warning devices can be passive. For example, heavy burlap or sisal wall coverings can be applied to surfaces that workers should not regularly touch. The rough texture, and prickly feel is so uncomfortable that workers quickly learn not to touch the surface. Similarly, rough floors or ground treatments discourage foot traffic in areas where it is not appropriate.

Shaped control buttons, or knobs are another form of tactile warning. An octagonal shaped button, for example, can warn the operator that this button will stop the machine if pressed. These warning devices can be very important when the operator must operate a variety of controls while looking at the operation rather than the controls. Similarly, a reminder sash is both a tactile and visual reminder that an operation must be performed.

*Human Barriers

Where practical, barriers are highly effective mistake-proofing devices. A barrier can be something as simple as a door that only opens when the operator is to reach for an object behind the door. Unlike many other mistake-proofing devices that can be purchased, barriers generally require custom design. Caution must be used to assure that movement of barriers is safe and does not pose any hazards or risks. Barriers are particularly important in safety applications, where workers may ignore warnings or instructions.

Lockout/Tag out procedures developed for personnel safety represent one form of barrier that provides both a visual and tactile or physical barrier.

Olfactory

To detect leaks of gaseous or liquid materials, odorants are often added to fluids such as natural gas. Odorants are not used frequently, but are particularly important in application where fluids are odorless, or difficult to detect, and hazardous.

PROCESS CONTROL DEVICES—SWITCHES AND VALVES

Modern products and industrial production rely heavily on a broad array of control devices. Pneumatic, hydraulic, and electromechanical control systems are common. Actuators, motors, and switches are typical devices used to perform the control functions. Controllers can sequence a wide range of complex operations virtually error free. Sophistication and automation do not assure, however, that control systems and their operation are mistake-proofed. Frequently, errors occur at the operator to equipment interface due to the incorrect operation of switches and valves.

Interlocks

Mechanical and electrical interlocks are essential for preventing prohibited actions, like opening a valve before pressure is relieved in a tank. Interlocks can also enable an operation. Interlocks can be electrical, mechanical, or electromechanical.

Hold to Operate Switches and Valves

When filling a tank an operator can forget to turn off a fill valve, or forget to turn off a heater at the end of a process cycle. By selecting a valve or switch that automatically resets to the off or closed setting as soon as it is released these errors are eliminated. Alternatively, sensors could be used to detect completion of the cycle, and provide a signal the resets the switch or valve.

One Key or Handle for Multiple Switches or Valves

Errors can also easily occur where only one of many valves should be open (or closed) at a time, like the valves on a manifold for filling a tank with chemicals from a variety of sources. A single unique handle or key that operates all valves or switches solves this problem. To make the mistake-proofing complete, removal of the operating key from any switch (or valve) should be prevented until the switch is reset to the normally closed position.

Matching Tags

Operators can easily operate the wrong switch or valve when coordinated operations are required at isolated locations. A shaped, color-coded tag picked up when operating the first valve or switch that matches unique markings on a control at the remote location helps the operator quickly select the correct action.

Remote Unique Key

In some facilities, there are multiple sets of identical equipment that operate independently. When operated remotely, it is easy for operators to startup or shutdown an operation on the wrong set of equipment. For example, an operator could initiate a cleaning cycle on the wrong tank, ruining a tank full of raw materials instead of cleaning an empty tank. After inspecting the tank to assure that it is empty, a unique key with a tag that matches unique tank and control panel markings could be carried from the tank to the control point. This key only enables the cleaning cycle for empty tank, and is carried back to the tank when the cleaning cycle is completed.

Temporary Covers for Non-critical Controls

Some control panels provide such a wide array of information to the operator that the information becomes confusing during complex operations or operations that are not performed frequently. In these circumstances, the operator may respond to signals that appear to be alarms but are the normal part of unique process cycles. To prevent these errors, a temporary cover can be placed over controls that should not be touched during the operation. On computers, the display of unessential information can be blocked out. This allows the operator to focus on the information that is essential and blocks the operations that should not be executed.

PART SELECTION AND INVENTORY CONTROL DEVICES

If a part is not available when needed in production, significant delays that are very costly will occur. Having the wrong part is just like having no part at all. Thus, selecting the right part is an important element of inventory control and supply chain management, as well as the final assembly process.

*Smart Part Bins

Smart part bins are one of the most effective ways to control the selection of products, but are only practical for volume production. Smart part bins prevent the selection of the wrong part, or parts in the wrong sequence. They can be constructed in a variety of ways. One approach is to control access to parts with doors. The correct door opens for the next part based on identification of the assembly or the selection of the previous part. When the selection is only between two sets of parts, a sliding door can cover the incorrect set.

For parts that must always be picked in the same sequence, an opening can slide sequential past the correct bins, or the bins can be moved past a single opening. Naturally safety is an important consideration with sliding doors and bins.

As an alternative, a variety of sensors can be used to detect when a person reaches into a bin. This can be linked to a program, that signals the bin location where the next part is to be drawn with "airplane" lights. If a part is drawn from the wrong bin, an alarm sounds, and if the correct part is drawn, the light at the next part location turns on. Commercial products can be purchased that provide these functions. Smart part dispensing methods can also dispense the correct number of fasteners or small parts, if multiple parts are needed.

*Kanban

Kanban is an invaluable tool in controlling inventory. The same technique can be used to guide complex operations that must be executed in a variety of locations around a facility. At the location of the first operation (Point A) is a tag (Tag A) that shows the location of the next operation (Point B). The operator takes Tag A to Point B and follows the instructions for the operation printed on the tag. When the operation is completed, Tag A is turned over and placed at Point B. Tag B is then pulled, which guides the operator to the next operation point (Point C), and so forth until the operation is completed. When the operation is reversed, the cards are returned to the original location as instructed on the back side of the card, setting up the operation for the next cycle.

Kanban is also a valuable technique for assuring that tools and fixtures are returned to the correct storage location after use on the production floor. This technique can be particularly important for correct placement of items that are so similar visually that they can be readily confused.

*Shadowboxes and Matrix Boxes

For small volume production, shadowboxes and matrix boxes aid part selection in several ways. First, these boxes aid in the selection of the correct parts by providing a place to put each part. Ideally, needed parts will only fit in one location in the box, or, if a part fits in the wrong location, the difference in the cavity and part shape or size will make the error obvious. Labels adjacent to each cavity in the box identify the parts that are to be placed in the cavity. Finally, the number of cavities in each box matches the number of parts that need to be placed in the kit. If there is a blank space in the box, the operator can see immediately that the right number of parts has not been selected, and if there are parts left in the box at the end of assembly, the operator knows that the right number of parts have not been assembled in the product.

*Counting Boxes, Trays, and Aids

Frequent errors are made in counting out the number of parts or assemblies. Counting boxes and trays allow the placement of the same small number of parts in each divided section of the box or tray. Missing parts are obvious, and the box or tray contains a fixed number of parts when filled, virtually eliminating counting errors.

Parts can be counted by weight if the variation in weight for a collection of parts is less than the smallest weight of any individual items. However, weighing methods are not particularly good for counting assembled parts in applications where there are a variety of parts that differ significantly in weight. To illustrate, weighing a package to determine if a PC Card has been inserted may lead to the wrong conclusion because the PC Card is such a small part of the total package weight.

Stack height can also be an effective counting method when parts have uniform dimension, and can be stacked.

*Sorting Devices

Sorting devices separate dissimilar parts or good parts from bad parts. They generally separate by physical differences such as dimension or shape or by weight. They may also separate parts by center of gravity. These devices can be particularly useful in separating right and left hand parts. Eliminating the wrong part from the production stream, is one of the most valuable tools in mistake-proofing. A single bad bolt in the production stream can shutdown automated assembly equipment and cost several thousand dollars.

First-in, First-Out Rack

If inventory is loaded and drawn from the same direction, the product in the storage location may become "stale" if the bin is never emptied. Old product may lose its value from deterioration, like food products, or iron products that rust in the storage environment. A first-in, first-out rack assures that the product is consumed in the order that the storage location is filled. It can be as simple a storage rack where parts are removed from the front, but replenished from the rear.

In some situations, test equipment must be used in a specific repeated sequence for evaluating the product. In such applications, a first-in, first-out rack can be very helpful. It assures that the test equipment can only be used in the same consistent sequence with each part.

INFORMATION DISPLAY AND CONTROL DEVICES

Although modern technology has enabled graphic displays of remarkable sophistication, many production processes depend upon simple written or printed instructions. Both methods of communications have strengths and weaknesses. Mistake-proofing devices have been developed for both technologies.

*Checklists

Checklists help operators to perform the operations in the correct manner and sequence while avoiding easily forgotten actions. Checklists slow down process execution. As a result, operators often become casual about reading and following checklists for frequently repeated activities. In addition, there are more effective tools for mistake-proofing operations. Consequently, checklists are most appropriate for infrequent operations of low volume production.

Ideally, checklists and instructions should only allow one instruction to be visible at a time, since reading the wrong instructions on a page causes many errors. Where a matrix chart contains instructions for a variety of operating conditions, a cover sheet with windows that allow the operator to see only the critical information for the specific product can double as a checklist.

*Signs and Signboards

Signs and signboards assure that each part is stored by address in a location that is easy to find. Signboards communicate where needed supplies may be obtained, and the quantity of material that must be delivered. Signboards may also indicate the status of the production line.

*Mirrors

Many errors are committed simply because the operator cannot or does not see a defect causing condition. Mirrors make it possible for operators to easily see defect causing conditions that may otherwise be missed. Care must be taken when using mirrors because of the reversal of the image, which can result in misinterpretation.

*Visual References

It is very difficult for anyone to determine without other aids whether a rod is within an eighth of an inch of its intended one-foot length. Measurements with a ruler, measuring tape, caliper, or scale are sufficiently accurate, but are time consuming and very prone to measurement errors. When parts do not require tight tolerances, out of tolerance parts can be detected visually. The ability to distinguish defective or out of tolerance parts is greatly enhanced by a visual reference. If the same foot long rod is placed in a groove and slid to a stop at one end, operators can quickly detect with remarkable accuracy and consistency whether the rod is longer or shorter than marks on the tray indicating the maximum and minimum length allowable. The tray, in this case, is a mistake-proofing device that provides a visual reference for the length. In a similar way, a red line can be painted on the wall to indicate the maximum stack height for the inventory control of bags of raw material.

Visual references are critical in eliminating gage-reading errors. A mark on a dial face at the correct value makes the correct gage setting obvious. When parts are being weighed, the pan weights can be adjusted so that the correct scale reading is exactly the same for all products being measured. With this approach, a single mark on the scale makes it possible to weigh all products without errors.

Often, the same production equipment is used to manufacture a variety of products. Different gage settings are required at the controls for each product. Operators can become confused when the instructions are not located adjacent to the control devices and sensor readings. Changeable overlays the mark scale readings and indicate appropriate settings for each specific product eliminate many adjustment errors.

Visual references are one of the least expensive yet most effective mistake-proofing devices. A painted valve stem can provide a visual indicator of whether a valve is open or closed. By painting a diagonal stripe on the outside diameter of an assembly of stacked cylinders, it is very easy to disassemble them and determine if they are reassembled in the same order just by checking to see that the stripe on the reassembled product is continuous. A white box can also be painted on the floor to designate a storage location.

Drawings, Pictures, and Videos

Traditionally, production information has been communicated in text and drawings. The preparation of assembly or operating instructions using these techniques can be expensive, and is often difficult to interpret. The development of the digital camera and video equipment provides opportunities for capturing information faster, at lower cost, and in a less ambiguous manner than can be represented in drawings. This is particularly true for operations that are only repeated occasionally. For the most complex operations, video recordings of properly executed operations may communicate the correct operation in the least ambiguous manner.

PART AND MATERIAL DISTINCTION DEVICES

Where differences in parts are small, or tolerances are tight, differences between correctly processed parts and defective or wrong parts cannot be detected visually. In such situations the desired parts must be distinguished from undesirable parts using mechanical methods or functional test equipment requiring sensors.

*Barriers, Covers, and Guides

If a process flattens a metal disk, a barrier could be setup that allows processed parts to slide under the barrier, while blocking the passage of unprocessed parts. By setting the barrier at an angle to the direction of disk travel, the barrier could move or guide unprocessed parts or wrong parts out of the production stream without blocking the production flow. Barriers block the movement of parts or material, but guides move defective or wrong parts out of the production stream. Barriers and guides are most useful in continuous production, and typically require custom designs. Guides can sort parts by orientation, center of gravity, shape, or dimension.

Barriers and guides can be inert or part of an active sensor system. When an unprocessed electrically conductive part makes contact with a barrier, it can complete a low voltage electrical path, triggering an alarm or shutting down the process until the production problem that caused the defect is corrected. In such applications, the barrier becomes part of the sensor system, detecting out of tolerance parts.

Barriers can have a variety of forms. They can be simple guards that keep a paint brush from reaching places that should be not touched, a protective cover that prevents tubes from being damaged, or a plastic sheet that keeps paint or plastic from being scratched.

*Templates, Fixtures, and Jigs

Templates, fixtures, and jigs are most useful where parts are setup and removed one at a time, as opposed to continuous processing. These devices are typically used to correctly position parts or equipment for processing. Fixtures that incorporate mistake-proofing may detect a wrong or defective part, prevent its setup or removal, or detect or prevent the setup of a part in the wrong position or orientation. Jigs and fixtures can be adaptable for processing similar parts on the same equipment, and can be made like a page of a book for processing right and left hand parts.

Templates, fixtures, and jigs typically require custom design. While jigs and fixtures can be quite expensive for precision operations, the incremental cost for incorporating mistake-proofing may be small as long as the mistake-proofing is implemented as the concept is developed. Interference is the best method for making setup or removal of defective or wrong parts impossible.

Fixtures and jigs can be used in conjunction with other sensors to detect parts with incorrect dimensions, shapes, or features. For example, a fixture could have a spring-loaded pin that fits into a hole in a correctly fabricated part. If the hole is too small, or in the wrong location, the pin will be depressed when a part is inserted, making an electrical contact that shuts down the operation. Thus, the fixture becomes part of the sensing system.

MISTAKE-PROOFING DEVICE SUMMARY

Table C-1 illustrates the application of a wide variety of mistake-proofing devices and summarizes their value in measuring, detecting, or controlling mistakes.

TABLE C-1

Mistake-proofing devices and their value in preventing mistakes by category

Key:
◉ High Value
○ Moderate Value

Column groups under **Mistake-Proofing Application**:
- **Information Errors**: Ambiguous Information, Incorrect Information, Misread/measure/interpret, Omitted Information, *Inadequate Warning* (Visual, Aural, Tactile, Olfactory)
- **Misalign, Adjust, Time**: Misaligned Parts, Misadjustments, Mis-timed or Rushed
- **Omission or Commission**: Added Material or Part, Commit Prohibited Action, Omitted Operations, Omitted Parts/Counting Error
- **Selection Errors**: Wrong Concept or Material, Select Wrong Destination, Select Wrong Location, Select Wrong Operation, Select Wrong Part, Select Wrong Orientation

Mistake-proofing devices	MP Value	Process Controls	Defective Materials	Ambiguous Info	Incorrect Info	Misread/measure	Omitted Info	Visual	Aural	Tactile	Olfactory	Misaligned Parts	Misadjustments	Mis-timed/Rushed	Added Material/Part	Commit Prohibited	Omitted Operations	Omitted Parts/Count	Wrong Concept/Material	Wrong Destination	Wrong Location	Wrong Operation	Wrong Part	Wrong Orientation
Counting Devices																								
Counters	◉															◉	◉	◉						
Timers	◉													◉			◉							
Warning Devices																								
Lamp, flasher, LCD,	◉							◉						◉						○	○	○	○	
Monitor and screen	○			◉				◉						◉			○			○	○	○	○	
Airplane light	◉			◉		◉		◉						◉			○			○	○	○	○	
Bell, whistle, siren, chime	◉								◉								○			○	○	○		
Audio Speaker	○								◉								○			○	○	○		
Lockout/tag out	◉	◉						○		◉							○							
Operator barrier, door	◉	◉		◉				○		◉					○	○	○			○	○			○
Reminder sash	○							◉		◉				◉			○							
Shaped button, handle	○									◉							○					○	○	
Vibrator	○									◉				◉			○							
Odorant	○										◉			◉	○									
Switches, Valves																								
Interlock	◉	◉															◉							
Hold to operate switch	○	◉											◉				◉	◉						
1 key for multiple switch	○	◉						◉		◉							◉	◉				◉	◉	
Matching tags	○	◉						◉														◉	◉	
Remote unique key	○	◉						◉		◉							◉					◉	◉	
Cover for non-crit. control	○	◉				◉								○			◉							
Selection & Sorting Devices																								
Smart part bin	◉	◉						◉		○					◉	○		◉						◉
Kanban	○	◉		○			○	○									◉	◉		◉	◉	◉	◉	◉
Shadowbox & matrix box	○	○		○		○	○	○							◉			◉						◉
Counting box and tray	○	○						○							◉			◉						◉
Sorting Devices	◉		○																					◉
First-in first-out rack	○	○															○							◉
Info. Display & Control																								
Checklist	○	◉		◉		◉	◉	○									○	○	○	○	○	○	○	
Signs and signboard	◉	◉		◉	◉	◉	◉	◉									○	○	○	○		○		
Mirrors	◉			◉		○	◉	◉									○							
Visual reference	◉					◉		◉					○				○							○
Fixed value mark on scale	○					◉		◉					○											
Red line	○	○				◉	◉	◉							○			○						○
White line	○	○					◉	◉													○	○		○
Diagonal line	○	○		◉		◉		◉				○										○		○
Changeable signs	○	○		◉	◉	◉		○					○									○	○	
Picture, video, drawing	○	○		◉	◉	◉	◉	◉				○	○									○	○	○
Barrier, Template, Guide																								
Barrier, cover, guide, & stop	◉		◉			◉	◉					○			◉	◉					◉	◉	◉	◉
Template and jig	◉		◉			◉	◉					◉	◉		○	◉					◉	○	◉	◉

SENSORS

Sensor technology is rapidly improving, with the addition of many new technologies and devices every year. The cost of sensors is dropping, while the accuracy, reliability, and effectiveness of sensors is improving. As a result, sensors are playing an increasingly important role in mistake-proofing. Due to the rapid expansion of sensor technology, it is virtually impossible to provide a comprehensive summary of sensors that may be useful in mistake proofing. The following information on mistake-proofing sensors is provided simply to help the reader identify a few of the more common device options that might be useful in mistake-proofing. As in the previous sections, asterisks indicate devices that are particularly popular or useful in mistake-proofing.

*LOCATION, POSITION, AND DISPLACEMENT SENSORS

Rectilinear position and location measurements are among the most important mistake-proofing tools. Position measurements can determine where a part is located, the shape or dimension of a part, or whether or not a part is present. Lengths, such as height, width, or thickness, can be measured with a single sensor if one of the surfaces of the part being measured rests against a reference surface. As an alternative, lengths can be measured by the difference between two simultaneous measurements with separate sensors. By measuring the location of a feature before and after it is moved, the displacement of the feature can be determined.

Position measurements using one or more sensors can be used to measure attributes of a surface such as flatness, run out, roundness, straightness, and eccentricity. Multiple sensors that detect surface position or location can also be used to check relationships between surfaces or features such as relative location, perpendicularity, parallelism, and concentricity. This section describes devices useful in measuring rectilinear position, and location, or characteristics derived from such measurements.

Linear Displacement or Position Sensors and Switches

Where the position of an object needs to be determined, or the stroke of equipment measured, limit switches at positions of the maximum and minimum linear travel are one of the most inexpensive solutions. Linear variable differential transformers (LVDTs) are also relatively cost effective for measuring displacements up to 20 inches. For larger displacements, optical encoders can be used to measure position over the range of several feet. Traditionally, optical encoders for displacement measurements have been quite expensive, but Hewlett Packard inkjet printers are using very inexpensive and effective optical encoders for accurately controlling print head motions. Cables connected to rotary encoders are available for displacements up to 10 feet or more. Where precision and accuracy are not essential, ultrasonic gages are very inexpensive, but these can only be used where the object is large enough and sufficiently planer to reflect sound waves.

Proximity Sensors and Switches

Proximity measurements are a special class of linear measurements, where the position of an object is measured only if the object is very close to the intended position. Thus, proximity measurements are commonly used to determine whether or not a part or subassembly is present, and in the correct position. Proximity measurements are often used a "go" or "no go" linear measurement, and are among the easiest types of devices to interlock with equipment operation. Proximity measurements can be made with contacting or non-contacting devices. Non-contacting proximity devices include Hall effect transducers, capacitance gages, and differential transformers.

*Limit Switches and Microswitches

Microswitches or limit switches are the most common type of contacting proximity switches and the most frequently used mistake-proofing detection device. Microswitches come in a wide variety of configurations. For the greatest positional accuracy, the object should directly push on the microswitch pin or push-button. However, this type of microswitch requires the greatest forces for operation, and may be damaged by objects moving perpendicular to the stroke of the microswitch pin. To decrease the actuation force, hinged levers or leaf springs are added to the microswitch. While decreasing the force required for actuation, these levers also increase the motion required to actuate the switch. With rollers attached to the pin or the lever arms, objects can slide across the contact point (in one direction) without damaging the microswitch. Leaf springs or coil springs provide restoring forces at the contact point that allows the microswitch to follow cams and dogs.

*Touch Sensors and Switches

One extremely accurate and very inexpensive technique for measuring position on precision parts is based on conductive pins. Naturally, this technique is only useful if the workpiece is electrically conductive. Pins, surrounded by electrically insulating material are bonded into fixtures before the final machining of the fixture surfaces. The final machining operations cut these pins flush with the fixture surfaces that will be used to control the workpiece setups. A low voltage is applied to the pins and the fixture is grounded. A current is conducted through each pin only if the workpiece makes contact with each pin and the fixture. With precision ground surfaces on the fixture, this technique can verify position within 5 millionths of an inch.

Thickness and Dual Surface Transfer Sensors

Material thickness and uniformity can be a critical property for materials processed as sheets or films, or for coatings like paint. Thin materials, like sheets of paper, plastic films, thin pouches, or circuit boards, are also moved along in production streams where electrostatic forces can cause thin parts to adhere to each other. Thickness measurements are required in both cases, either to control layer thickness of processed materials or to determine if the number of layers being transported is correct. By using two sensors, on opposite surfaces, the thickness of the material or number of layers can be measured. In some special circumstances, thickness can be measured from a single surface. For example, a capacitance gage can measure the thickness of nonconductive paint on a conductive surface.

Rotary Displacement and Position Sensors and Switches

Angular measurement sensors detect the rotation of an object. Electrical or optical encoders are used for accurate angle measurements about a fixed axis.

Pressure Sensitive Mats and Screens

Areal sensors determine the location of an object on a plane. Video monitor touch screens are one type of areal sensor. Safety mats that detect the presence and location of a person standing on the mat are another type of areal sensor.

Spatial Measurements

Spatial sensors determine the location and orientation of an object within a volume. Spatial sensors can be based on triangulation using ultrasonic or electromagnetic waves, or inertial navigation units. Spatial sensors tend to be relatively expensive, and are rarely necessary or cost effective for mistake-proofing.

Tip, Tilt, and Inclination

Some objects may be damaged if turned upside-down during transportation. Simple tip sensors can detect and record these harmful events. If the package is turned upside down, a colored weight drops behind a translucent window and is locked into place, providing a permanent visual indicator that the product was mishandled. Other sensors can actively detect tilt or changes in inclination. Mercury in a glass vial will complete an electrical path between two leads when tipped sufficiently.

DYNAMIC MEASUREMENTS

Velocity, acceleration, shock and vibration measurements are needed to understand product or equipment motions. Devices that measure these attributes are being used more frequently in mistake-proofing to detect the start or end of a process, to assure that process or transport parameters are within limits, or to detect if a product has been moved or ejected.

Motion and Velocity Sensors

Velocity is a description of how fast an object is moving and the direction of motion. Velocity is rarely measured directly, but is generally derived from other measurements such as linear displacements or accelerations. An object can have both linear and angular velocity.

Accelerometers and Tachometers

Accelerometers detect the response of a body to an applied force. Typically, most accelerometers have a mass and sensing element. The accelerating force is transmitted to the mass through the sensing element that detects the amount of force required to move the mass. Since the force is proportional to the acceleration (Force = mass times acceleration), the acceleration is proportional to the measured force. Common sensing elements for accelerometers are made of piezoelectric or piezoresistive materials, or strain gages. Measuring acceleration typically requires expensive gages and equipment. Consequently, accelerometers are generally not practical for most mistake-proofing applications.

Acceleration can also be derived from changes in displacements (second derivative). Since there are many inexpensive linear transducers, accelerations derived from linear measurements can sometimes be used in mistake-proofing.

The change in the spin rate of a body is a function of angular or rotational acceleration. The methods of measuring rotational acceleration are similar to the methods for measuring linear accelerations. For objects that rotate about a fixed axis, a stationary sensor can be used to detect the number of times a feature on the shaft passes the sensor in a given time interval. From this the rotational acceleration and spin rate can be determined.

Vibration, Hit, and Shock Sensors

Vibration and shock sensors are used to measure dynamic response. The design of these sensors is similar to the design of accelerometers, except that vibration and shock sensors typically are selected to measure higher frequencies and larger accelerations. Due to the higher frequency responses being measured, vibration and shock measurements commonly require higher sampling rates than accelerometers. Shock and vibration measurements can be expensive, and are therefore generally used for prototype development. In the recent past, there has been increased interest in using such devices to detect machine wear that may signal the need for equipment repair or replacement.

*Hit sensors are a special type of vibration and shock gage that can detect when an object strikes a surface. Hit sensors can be used with counters to count parts, or may distinguish between good and bad parts by differences in the trajectories of the parts. Hit sensors are inexpensive enough that they can be useful mistake-proofing devices.

FORCE AND STRAIN SENSORS

The force or load applied to an object, and the reaction of an object to a force can reveal defects, or defect causing conditions. On a press, for example, an unusually high force may indicate a problem in the setup and can be interlocked to shut down the operation before extensive damage is done to the product or the press. Special force measuring devices have been developed to measure torque, shear, tensile forces, and compressive forces. Forces can be measured by piezoelectric or piezoresistive gages. Forces may also be measured by the deflection or distortion of a spring when subjected to a load.

A thin resistive material is etched or deposited on a non-conductive material to form a strain gage. Stretching the strain gage thins the conductive material increasing its resistance. When the strain gage is bonded to a structure, changes in the resistance of the gage can then be used to measure strains in the structure. Stress, or the force per unit area, is typically derived from strain measurements.

*OPTICS AND PHOTO ELECTRIC SENSORS

One advantage of photoelectric and optical sensors is that they make measurements without physical contact with the parts. This avoids damage to fragile or flexible parts. In addition, optical sensors can make measurements at the speed of light, enabling measurements to be made more quickly than is possible with mechanical sensors. As a consequence, optical devices are likely to grow in popularity in their role in mistake-proofing.

*Photo-electric Sensors

There are two basic types of photoelectric sensors—transmission and reflectance. The photodetector and light source are in two separate devices in the transmission type of system. An opaque object passing between the light source and the photodetector blocks the light, which is sensed by the photodetector. The light source and detector are in a single device for the reflectance photoelectric detectors. If an object passes in front of the reflectance type of photoelectric device, the amount of light reflected from the source increases, as sensed by the photodetectors. Photoelectric detectors are used to verify that parts are present, count parts or features, and register parts.

A light curtain is a special class of transmission photoelectric detectors. The light source and detectors are arranged in linear arrays, making it possible to detect the width of the interrupted light. This type of sensor can measure the dimension of a part or identify the location of the break in the light path.

Fiber optics can be use with photoelectric sensors to detect objects and object properties in tightly focused areas. For example, fiber optic sensors can detect unthreaded bolts, unknurled shafts, broken wires, or parts that are the wrong length. Fiber-optic photoelectric systems can also detect through holes, registration marks, or missing parts.

*Color Property Measurements (Luminance, Reflectance, Hue, Saturation): One advantage of optical detection systems is that they can be configured to look for specific colors, hue, saturation, reflectance, or luminance. Taking advantage of these features, it is possible to identify the presence or absence of parts, labels, and markings and to determine if a part is or is not in the correct orientation.

*Scanners

Scanners are used to automatically read coded information. The most common scanners are barcode scanners. Scanners have significant value in mistake-proofing because they can nearly eliminate errors in identifying parts and transposition errors in recording information that must be read. Barcode scanners use a laser light that sweeps across the barcode, and a photodetector reads the pattern of the reflected light.

The newest coding, called Data Matrix, uses a pattern of squares in a square array. Rather than using lasers that sweep the image, the pattern is recognized with Charge Couple Devices (CCDs) such as those found in standard video cameras. The advantages of the matrix symbology is that more information can be contained in the code, the codes can be printed on smaller labels suitable for smaller parts, and the matrix information contains error correction data that would not fit in on a standard barcode label.

CCD and Video Sensors

Images captured with charge coupled devices (CCDs) or video equipment are being used more and more frequently in inspection and have potentially significant application opportunities in mistake-proofing. Captured images are compared against electronically defined standards, enabling the detection of missing or out of tolerance parts.

SOUND TRANSDUCERS AND SENSORS

Microphones have been used in a few applications to detect unusual sounds associated with abnormal operating conditions. In these situations, sounds beyond the range of hearing warn the operators when equipment must be fixed or repaired to avoid serious damage. Hydrophones detect sounds transmitted in liquids.

Ultrasonic

Ultrasonic devices emit high frequency chirps, above the frequency of human hearing. These sounds are reflected off the closest objects in the foreground. By measuring the elapsed time between the chirp and reflected wave, the distance to the nearest object can be determined. These devices are relatively inexpensive, and have been used in cameras to set the focus, and are often used in tanks to measure the fluid level. Although, effective, ultrasonic distance measurements are not highly accurate.

FLUID MEASUREMENTS

Pressure and Vacuum Sensors

Controlling pressure in hydraulic, pneumatic, or other pressurized systems can be critical to safe and proper operation. Fortunately, there are a wide variety of inexpensive and effective pressure sensing and control devices. Even inexpensive compressors for home use have controls that turn the compressor on and off at preset minimum and maximum pressures. These inexpensive controls can be purchased separately and used to interlock or enable other actions or equipment.

Dial pressure gages generally have a tube or diaphragm that expands or changes shape when pressurized. This change in shape is mechanically linked to control a pointer position. In high quality pressure gages with electrical outputs, the deflection of a thin diaphragm is measured with strain gages arranged in a wheatstone bridge. Pressure relief valves can be used to "set" the downstream pressure for a wide range of upstream pressures.

Level and Depth Sensors

When liquids are stored in vessels or tanks, the quantity of liquid in the tank generally must be known or determined. The simplest method for determining the liquid level is to make the tank out of a translucent or transparent material, so that operators can see the liquid levels directly. A transparent vertical tube mounted externally to the tank with hydraulic connections can perform the same function. In translucent tanks, the liquid may not provide enough contrast to make the fluid level readily apparent. In these cases, a brightly colored float may make it possible to observe the fluid level.

Large hydrostatic forces or material incompatibilities may require the use of opaque materials for storage vessels. Even if the tank is translucent, many mistakes may be avoided if some operations are interlocked with the quantity of fluid in the tank. For example, some cars have sensors that shut down the engine, avoiding expensive damage, if the quantity of lubricating oil drops too low. Floats can be mechanically or electrically linked to display tank fluid levels or perform functions like shutting off the flow of water in a toilet tank when the fluid reaches a desired level.

In some applications, ultrasonic sensors can be used effectively to measure fluid level. Pressure gages and liquid surface sensors are also used to measure fluid quantities. Naturally, where the shape of the tank is irregular, nonlinear conversions from fluid levels or depth to fluid volumes may be required.

Flowmeters and Leak Detectors

Flow meters can determine the rate of fluid movement, or by integration the quantity of fluid moved. Flow meters can be based on nutating disks (liquids, water meters), rotating propellers or vanes, hot wire anemometers (gases), or venturi tubes. For gases or clear liquids, a "floating" ball in a conical tube is sometime used. As the ball rises in the transparent tube, the flow area around the ball increases decreasing the upward drag on the ball. The ball rises upward in the tube until the upward drag on the ball balances gravitational forces. The vertical position of the ball is read on a scale that is calibrated in terms of flow rate.

Leak detectors measure the amount of material escaping from a confined volume. Leak detectors are essential in preventing costly losses, or unintended exposure to hazardous materials.

Fluid Property Measurements

Turbidity, viscosity, density, and pH are among the many fluid properties that need to be known to control some processes. Measurements of fluid properties have become so inexpensive that domestic washing machines and automobiles have multiple fluid property sensors. Some sensors measure the constituents of a fluid, such as oxygen. Fluid property measurements are likely to be used in mistake-proofing more frequently, particularly in controlling raw material purity.

*Weight Measurements

Weight and mass are among the most important physical properties measured for mistake-proofing. Weight can be used to count the number of parts, measure out a quantity of bulk material, or to determine the quantity of fluid added or removed from a product. It can also be used to distinguish between individual parts.

Weight can be measured with balances, or scales. In a balance, the object is weighed using counterbalancing weights. In scales, the counterbalancing force may be springs or weights. Some modern electronic scales use force transducers instead of counterbalancing forces.

Electrical and Magnetic measurements

Electrical measurements are the bases of virtually all sensor technologies—the output of the device is converted to an electrical signal that is proportional to the detected property. Voltage, current, power, frequency, phase, continuity, resistance, capacitance, and inductance are typical electrical properties that are measured.

Electromagnetic Field Measurements and Metal Detection

Measurements of the strength of an electrical field or variations in frequency or amplitude of an electrical field can also be use for mistake-proofing devices. For example, a coil with hole through its center can be electrically energized. If a metal part is thrown or passed through the center of the coil it changes the strength of the electrical field, since the passing part acts like "core" in the electrical field. The change in the electric field can be used to count metal parts or to assure that a part is ejected from a machine before the next cycle begins.

Electromagnetic field measurement can also be use to determine whether or not a part has been magnetized or to measure the strength of a magnetic field.

Environmental Sensors

Temperature Sensors

Temperature measurements are normally made with thermocouples or thermisters. Thermocouple materials are selected based on the temperature that must be measured, response time, compatibility with the media, and the desired accuracy of measurement. Thermisters are less expensive than thermocouples, but are generally less accurate and can only measure temperatures up to the range of high temperature electronics devices. The highest temperatures are determined using optical systems that measure the spectrum of emitted light. Bimetallic coils are used effectively to measure temperatures in many inexpensive devices such as home thermostats, and mercury or other expanding liquids are still used in thermometers. Temperatures can also be measured with infrared detectors.

Detection of undesired temperatures can be critical in preventing serious product failures. To illustrate, infrared detectors that identified hot bearings on the wheels of trains provided a major breakthrough in preventative maintenance for the railroad industry.

Humidity and Moisture Measurements

Moisture and humidity can damage or destroy some products, such as electronic devices. In other cases, the product may be ruined if the environment becomes too dry. In either situation, the environment must either be controlled, or the user must be warned if critical limits have been exceeded. Humidity and moisture sensors are essential in these applications.

Environment Logging Devices

The temperature of some products must be maintained within defined control limits throughout the useful life of the product. Produce and certain organic chemicals must be kept cool to prevent deterioration, during transportation or storage. On the other hand, asphalt and sulfur must be heated to keep them in liquid state. Some products are irreversibly damaged if heated or cooled beyond defined limits.

Inexpensive sensors are available for logging environmental conditions. Labels with wax based markings that melt at defined temperatures can reveal when products have reached too high a temperature. Temperature logging devices that can accurately measure and record temperatures every few minutes for a period of several months are now available and relatively inexpensive. While these devices do not prevent mistakes, they can detect mistakes that occur when a product is outside of the immediate control of the manufacturer.

MISTAKE-PROOFING SENSOR SUMMARY

Table C-2 illustrates the application of a wide variety of mistake-proofing sensors and summarizes their value in measuring, detecting, or controlling mistakes.

SUPPLIERS

In general, the goal should be to create mistake-proofing devices from tools, scrap, hardware, and equipment that are at hand and relatively inexpensive. However, commercial products are sometimes necessary. To help the reader quickly identify potential resources for mistake-proofing, a list of suppliers is provided, with the goal of reducing the time it takes individuals to find the mistake-proofing device they need. The suppliers listed here, range from large organizations representing dozens of manufacturers, to small companies that produce a very narrow range of products. In general, the goal has been to select industry leaders or manufacturers of products uniquely suited to mistake-proofing. Naturally, many outstanding suppliers and products may not be represented due to the limited scope of this book.

Table C-3 summarizes the products available from each listed source. Following this table the contact information for each supplier is provided. Most of these companies have excellent catalogs on the Internet for reviewing their product offerings. The robustness or fitness-for-use of the products offered by these suppliers have not been evaluated for specific applications. Thus, the publisher and author provide the information in this section without warranty.

TABLE C-2

Mistake-proofing sensors and their value in preventing mistakes by mistake category.

Key:
- ⊙ High Value
- ○ Moderate Value

Mistake-proofing sensors	Mistake-Proofing Value	Defective Materials	Information Errors: Ambiguous Information	Incorrect Information	Misread, measure, interpret	Omitted Information	Inadequate Warning	Misalign, Adjust, Time: Misaligned Parts	Misadjustments	Mis-timed or Rushed	Omission or Commission: Added Material or Part	Commit Prohibited Action	Omitted Operations	Omitted Parts, Counting Error	Selection Errors: Wrong Concept or Material	Select Wrong Destination	Select Wrong Location	Select Wrong Operation	Select Wrong Part	Select Wrong Orientation
Location, Position Sensors																				
Limit, microswitches	⊙	⊙			⊙			⊙	⊙			⊙	○	⊙			⊙	⊙	⊙	⊙
Touch sensors, switches	⊙	⊙			⊙			⊙	⊙			⊙	○	⊙			⊙	⊙	⊙	⊙
Proximity sensors, switches	⊙	⊙			⊙			⊙	⊙			⊙	○	⊙			⊙	⊙	⊙	⊙
Linear displacement, position	○				⊙			⊙				⊙				○				
Rotary displacement, position	○				⊙			⊙				⊙								○
Pressure sensitive mat/screen	○				⊙							⊙				⊙		⊙		
Thickness, dual surface xfer	○	⊙			⊙			○			⊙	○		⊙					⊙	
Tilt, tip, inclination	○				⊙			○				○								○
Accel., Vibration, and Shock																				
Accelerometers, tachometers									○	⊙		⊙						○	○	
Vibration, motion	○	⊙							○	⊙		⊙	⊙					○	○	○
Hit & shock	○	⊙								⊙		⊙	⊙						○	
Force or Strain Sensors																				
Force, torque	○				⊙				⊙			○	⊙	⊙			○	⊙	○	
Strain gauges	○				⊙				⊙			○	⊙				○	⊙	○	
Optical Sensors																				
Photoelectric transmission	⊙	⊙			⊙	○		⊙	⊙		⊙	○	○	⊙			⊙		○	○
Fiber-optic	⊙	⊙			⊙	○		⊙	⊙		⊙	○	○	⊙			⊙		○	○
Light curtain	⊙	⊙			⊙	○		⊙	⊙		⊙	○	○	⊙			⊙		○	○
Photoelectric reflectance	⊙	⊙			⊙	⊙		⊙	⊙		⊙	○	○	⊙			⊙		⊙	○
Fiber-optic	⊙	⊙			⊙	⊙		⊙	⊙		⊙	○	⊙	⊙			⊙		⊙	○
Light properties (hue, sat.)	⊙	⊙			⊙	⊙		⊙	⊙		⊙	○	⊙	⊙			⊙		⊙	○
Barcode scanners	⊙		⊙		⊙					⊙						⊙	⊙	⊙	⊙	
Imaging, CCD/video	⊙	⊙	⊙		⊙					⊙	⊙	⊙	⊙	⊙		⊙	⊙	⊙	⊙	⊙
Optical encoders	○							⊙	⊙			○								
Sound Transducers and Sensors																				
Micro/hydrophones, acoustics		○					⊙				⊙	⊙		⊙						
Ultrasonics	⊙	⊙			⊙				⊙		⊙			⊙						
Fluid sensors																				
Pressure, vacuum	⊙	○			⊙				⊙	⊙	⊙									
Level, depth	⊙	○			⊙				⊙	⊙	⊙									
Flowmeter, leak	○	○			⊙				⊙	⊙	⊙									
Fluid properties	○	⊙			⊙				⊙											
Weight Measuring Sensors	⊙	⊙			⊙				⊙		⊙		⊙	⊙	○			⊙	⊙	
Electromagnetic Sensors																				
V, A, power, frequency, phase	○	⊙			⊙			⊙	⊙		○	○	○	○			⊙	⊙	⊙	⊙
Resistance, cap., inductance	○	⊙			⊙			⊙	⊙		○	○	○	○			⊙	⊙	⊙	⊙
Continuity	⊙	⊙			⊙			⊙	⊙		○	○	○	○			⊙	⊙	⊙	⊙
Electromagnetic field	○	⊙			⊙						○			○						
Environmental Sensors																				
Temperature, infrared	⊙	○				⊙			⊙			⊙			⊙					
Humidity, moisture	○	○				⊙			⊙			⊙			⊙					
Data loggers	⊙	○				⊙			⊙			⊙								

TABLE C-3A

Mistake-proofing sensors and devices available by supplier or manufacturer.

Key:
X Supplies this type of product

Section	Product	AA Electric	ACT Liquid Level Sensors	AGM Container Controls	American Aerospace Controls	American Electronic Components	Applied Physics Systems	Balluff	Banner Engineering	Baumer Electric Ltd.	Bruel & Kjaer	Burkert Contromatic USA	Clarostat Sensors and Controls	Columbia Research Labs	Control Devices	Control Systems Engineering	Custom Sensors	Davis Instruments	DEEM Controls	Dialight	Durham Instruments	Edwards Signalling	Endevco	Energy Science
Number of Product Categories		30	6	3	1	7	1	11	10	12	3	7	4	5	11	6	1	15	2	2	10	2	3	1
Devices	Counters	X																			X			
Devices	Timers	X	X															X			X			
Warning Devices	Lights, flashers																			X		X		
Warning Devices	Audio devices											X										X		
Warning Devices	Vibrators																							
Warning Devices	Smart part bins							X																
Warning Devices	Switches	X	X			X						X				X					X			
Location, Position	Limit, microswitches	X						X																
Location, Position	Proximity sensors, switches	X				X		X	X	X											X			
Location, Position	Touch sensors, switches																							
Location, Position	Linear displacement, position	X				X		X	X	X			X								X			
Location, Position	Rotary displacement, position					X				X			X											
Location, Position	Pressure sensitive mat/screen	X														X	X							
Location, Position	Thickness, dual surface xfer	X																						
Location, Position	Tip, tilt, inclination					X								X		X					X			
Dynamic	Accelerometers, tachometers	X				X					X			X		X		X					X	
Dynamic	Vibration, motion	X				X					X			X				X						
Dynamic	Hit, shock			X																			X	
Force, Strain	Force, torque	X												X				X			X			
Force, Strain	Strain gages													X				X			X			
Optical	Photoelectric transmission	X						X	X	X					X									
Optical	Fiber-optic	X						X	X	X														
Optical	Light Curtain	X							X	X						X								
Optical	Photoelectric reflectance	X						X	X	X					X									
Optical	Fiber-optic	X						X	X	X														
Optical	Light properties (hue, bright.)	X						X	X	X								X						
Optical	Barcode Scanners	X						X																
Optical	CCD/Video	X																						
Optical	Optical encoders	X													X					X				
Sound	Micro/hyrophones, acoustics										X							X						
Sound	Ultrasonics	X							X	X		X				X					X			
Fluid	Pressure	X	X							X		X			X			X			X		X	
Fluid	Level, depth	X	X									X			X			X	X					
Fluid	Flowmeters, leak	X										X			X			X	X					
Fluid	Fluid properties	X	X												X			X						
Sensors	Weight Measurements																	X						
Electro-magnetic	V, A, power, frequency, phase	X			X																			X
Electro-magnetic	Resistance, cap., inductance	X							X	X			X		X									
Electro-magnetic	Electromagnetic field	X					X	X							X									
Environmental	Temperature, infrared	X	X									X	X		X			X						
Environmental	Humidity & moisture sensors	X		X														X						
Environmental	Data loggers			X											X			X						

TABLE C-3B

Mistake-proofing sensors and devices available by supplier or manufacturer.

Key:
X Supplies this type of product

Table columns (Company): Entran Devices (4), Fiber Dynamics (7), Flow Technology (2), Flowline Components (5), Gama Electronics (2), H. F. Jensen (3), Highly Electric (3), **Honeywell** (20), HTM Electronics Industries (9), Impact Register (4), ITT Cannon (1), Ixthus Instrumentation (6), **Keyence of America** (11), Kistler Instruments (6), Knowles Electronics (5), Korea Partner IIndustry (1), Korry Electronics Co (1), Ktech (2), Lucas Nova Sensor (5), Mass Products (4), Mettler Toledo (6), Miller Edge (3), Nonvolatile Electronics (2)

Category	Entran Devices	Fiber Dynamics	Flow Technology	Flowline Components	Gama Electronics	H. F. Jensen	Highly Electric	Honeywell	HTM Electronics Industries	Impact Register	ITT Cannon	Ixthus Instrumentation	Keyence of America	Kistler Instruments	Knowles Electronics	Korea Partner IIndustry	Korry Electronics Co	Ktech	Lucas Nova Sensor	Mass Products	Mettler Toledo	Miller Edge	Nonvolatile Electronics
Number of Product Categories	4	7	2	5	2	3	3	20	9	4	1	6	11	6	5	1	1	2	5	4	6	3	2
Devices — Counters									X			X									X		
Devices — Timers									X			X											
Warning Devices — Lights, flashers																							
Warning Devices — Audio devices																							
Warning Devices — Vibrators																X							
Warning Devices — Smart part bins																							
Warning Devices — Switches					X		X		X		X						X						
Location, Position — Limit, microswitches					X		X	X															
Location, Position — Proximity sensors, switches		X				X	X	X	X			X	X							X			X
Location, Position — Touch sensors, switches																						X	
Location, Position — Linear displacement, position								X					X						X				
Location, Position — Rotary displacement, position																			X				
Location, Position — Pressure sensitive mat/screen																						X	
Location, Position — Thickness, dual surface xfer																							
Location, Position — Tip, tilt, inclination										X									X				
Dynamic — Accelerometers, tachometers	X							X		X				X					X				
Dynamic — Vibration, motion		X		X										X	X								
Dynamic — Hit, shock										X				X								X	
Force, Strain — Force, torque	X							X						X									
Force, Strain — Strain gages	X	X																	X				
Optical — Photoelectric transmission								X	X				X										
Optical — Fiber-optic		X						X	X				X										
Optical — Light Curtain													X										
Optical — Photoelectric reflectance								X	X				X										
Optical — Fiber-optic		X						X	X				X										
Optical — Light properties (hue, bright)													X										
Optical — Barcode Scanners													X										
Optical — CCD/Video												X	X										
Optical — Optical encoders									X														
Sound — Micro/hyrophones, acoustics															X					X			
Sound — Ultrasonics			X					X				X								X			
Fluid — Pressure	X	X				X		X				X	X					X					
Fluid — Level, depth		X				X		X							X					X			
Fluid — Flowmeters, leak		X						X															
Fluid — Fluid properties								X							X						X		
Weight Measurements														X	X						X		
Electro-magnetic — V, A, power, frequency, phase		X						X															
Electro-magnetic — Resistance, cap., inductance		X	X									X											
Electro-magnetic — Electromagnetic field								X													X		X
Environmental — Temperature, infrared		X						X										X			X		
Environmental — Humidity & moisture sensors								X													X		
Environmental — Data loggers								X		X													

TABLE C-3c

Mistake-proofing sensors and devices available by supplier or manufacturer.

Key:
X Supplies this type of product

	NTE International	Omega Engineering	Omron (OMCA)	Pace Scientific	Paroscientific	Patriot Sensors and Controls	Photo Vision Systems	Schaevitz Sensors	Setra Systems	Sick	Speastech	Spectec	Supreme Exim	Syscan	The Fredricks Company	Trans-tek	Turck USA	Vatell	Vibration Sensing Devices	Western Sensor	Wolo Manufacturing
Number of Product Categories	1	11	18	6	5	5	1	7	3	12	1	2	2	2	2	3	6	1	5	4	1
Devices — Counters		X	X																		
Devices — Timers		X	X												X						
Warning Devices — Lights, flashers																					
Warning Devices — Audio devices																					X
Warning Devices — Vibrators																					
Warning Devices — Smart part bins											X										
Warning Devices — Switches												X									
Location, Position — Limit, microswitches	X	X									X										
Location, Position — Proximity sensors, switches		X						X									X		X		
Location, Position — Touch sensors, switches																					
Location, Position — Linear displacement, position		X				X		X	X							X	X		X		
Location, Position — Rotary displacement, position		X						X								X					
Location, Position — Pressure sensitive mat/screen																					
Location, Position — Thickness, dual surface xfer		X																			
Location, Position — Tip, tilt, inclination								X							X						
Dynamic — Accelerometers, tachometers						X		X													
Dynamic — Vibration, motion						X				X							X		X		
Dynamic — Hit, shock																					
Force, Strain — Force, torque								X	X												
Force, Strain — Strain gages								X													
Optical — Photoelectric transmission		X								X											
Optical — Fiber-optic		X								X											
Optical — Light Curtain										X											
Optical — Photoelectric reflectance		X								X											
Optical — Fiber-optic		X								X											
Optical — Light properties (hue, bright.)		X	X							X										X	
Optical — Barcode Scanners		X								X				X							
Optical — CCD/Video	X	X					X							X						X	
Optical — Optical encoders		X				X															
Sound — Micro/hyrophones, acoustics												X									
Sound — Ultrasonics		X		X								X					X				
Fluid — Pressure		X	X	X	X	X		X	X								X			X	
Fluid — Level, depth		X	X																		
Fluid — Flowmeters, leak		X		X						X							X				
Fluid — Fluid properties		X		X						X											
Weight Measurements									X												
Electro-magnetic — V, A, power, frequency, phase			X																		
Electro-magnetic — Resistance, cap., inductance		X															X				
Electro-magnetic — Electromagnetic field																				X	
Environmental — Temperature, infrared		X	X																X	X	
Environmental — Humidity & moisture sensors		X	X	X																	
Environmental — Data loggers		X	X														X				

Supplier Contact Information

The following list contains the contact information for the suppliers in Table C-3. The list is organized alphabetically by the supplier's name, and provides the street, email, and Internet addresses, as well as phone and fax numbers, where available.

AA Electric, Inc
P.O. Box 325
1220 Washington Avenue
Cedarburg, WI 53012
Phone: (800) 558-7033   FAX: (800) 638-4969
Internet: www.aa-electric.com
email: info@aa-electric.com

ACT Liquid Level Sensors
7050 East Highway 101
Shakopee, MN 55379
Phone: (877) 800-8820   FAX: (612) 890-3644
Internet: www.actsensors.com/index.html
email: info@actsensors.com

AGM Container Controls, Inc.
P.O. Box 40020
3526 East Fort Lowell Road
Tucson, AZ 85717-0200
Phone: (800) 995-5590   FAX: (520) 881-4983
Internet: www.agmcontainer.com/
email: sales@agmcontainer.com

American Aerospace Controls Inc.
570 Smith Street Farmingdale
New York, NY 11735-1115
Phone: (888) 873-8559   FAX: (631) 694-6739
Internet: www.a-a-c.com/
email: info@a-a-c.com

American Electronic Components, Inc.
P.O. Box 280
23590 County Road 6
Elkhart, IN 46515
Phone: (219) 264-1116   FAX: (219) 264-4681
Internet: www.aeciusa.com
email: Marketing@AEC-Echlin.com

Applied Physics Systems
1245 Spacepark Way
Moutain View, CA 94043
Phone: (650) 965-0500   FAX: (650) 965-0404
Internet: www.appliedphysics.com
email: aps2g@appliedphysics.com

Balluff, Inc.
8125 Holton Drive
Florence, KY 41042
Phone: (800) 543-8390   FAX: (859) 727-4823
Internet: www.balluff.com/
email: balluff@balluff.com

Banner Engineering Corporation
P.O. Box 9414, Dept. 101
9714 Tenth Avenue North
Minneapolis, MN 55440
Phone: (763) 544-3164   FAX: (763) 544-3213
Internet: www.bannerengineering.com
email: sensors@baneng.com

Baumer Electric Ltd.
122 Spring Street C-6
Southington, CT 06489
Phone: (800) 937-9336   FAX: (860) 628-6280
Internet:
    www.baumerelectric.com/baumer/boxe.html
email: sales.us@baumerelectric.com

Bruel & Kjaer Inc.
2815 Colonnades Court, Building A
Norcross, GA 30071-1588
Phone: (800) 332-2040   FAX: (800) 870-6157
Internet: www.bkhome.com/
email: BKinfo@SpectrisTech.com

Burkert Contromatic USA
2602 McGaw Avenue
Irvine, CA 92614
Phone: (949) 223-3100   FAX: (949) 223-3198
Internet: www.burkert-usa.com/

Clarostat Sensors and Controls, Inc.
12055 Rojas Drive, Suite K
El Paso, TX 79936
Phone: (800) 872-0042   FAX: (800) 223-5138
Internet: www.clarostat.com/

Columbia Research Labs, Inc.
1925 Macdade Blvd.
Woodlyn, PA 19094
Phone: (800) 813-8471   FAX: (610) 872-3882
Internet: www.columbiaresearchlab.com/

Control Devices, Inc.
11182 US Hwy 69
North Tyler, TS 75706
Phone: (903) 882-3161
Internet: www.control-devices.com
email: sales@control-devices.com/contact.htm

Control Systems Engineering, Inc.
P.O. Box 187
6 Liljegren Rd
South Woodstock, CT 06267
Phone: (800) 927-2980   FAX: (860) 928-4254
Internet: www.controlsrus.com/
email: cse@controlsrus.com

Custom Sensors, Inc.
30 York Street
Auburn, NY 13021
Phone: (315) 252-3741   FAX: (315) 253-6910
Internet: www.csensors.com/index_d.html
email: info@csensors.com

Davis Instruments
4701 Mount Hope Drive
Baltimore, MD 21215
Phone: (800) 368-2516   FAX: (800) 433-9971

Internet: www.DavisOnTheWeb.com
email: sales@davisontheweb.com

DEEM Controls, Inc.
Port Huron, MI
Phone: (800) 411-9666
Internet: www.deemencoders.com
email: info@deemencoders.com

Dialight Corporation
1913 Atlantic Avenue
Manasquan, NJ 08736
Phone: (732) 223-9400   FAX: (732) 223-8788
Internet: www.dialight.com/

Durham Instruments
1400 Bayly Street Unit 23
Pickering, Ontario L1W 3R2
Canada
Phone: (888) 819-0491   FAX: (905) 839-4325
Internet: www.disensors.com/
email: sales@disensors.com

Edwards Signalling
90 Fieldstone Court
Cheshire, CT 06410-1212
Phone: (203) 699-3300   FAX: (203) 699-3365
Internet: www.edwards-signals.com/index.htm

Endevco Corporation
30700 Rancho Viejo Road
San Juan Capistrano, CA 92675
Phone: (800) 982-6732   FAX: (949) 661-7231
Internet: www.endevco.com/
email: applications@endevco.com

Energy Science Corp.
P.O. Box 152
Goleta, CA 93116
Phone: (805) 964-9119   FAX: (805) 967-8789
Internet: www.amploc.com
email: sales@amploc.com

Entran Devices Inc.
10 Washington Avenue
Fairfield, NJ 07004-3877
Phone: (973) 227-1002   FAX: (973) 227-6865
Internet: www.entran.com/
email: sales@entran.com

Fiber Dynamics Corporation
909 Industrial Blvd.
Bryan, TX 77803
Phone: (405) 775-2093   FAX: (409) 775-5177
Internet: www.fiberdynamics.com/
email: sales@fiberdynamics.com

Flow Technology, Inc.
4250 East Broadway Road
Phoenix, AZ 85040
Phone: (800) 528-4225   FAX: (602) 437-4459
Internet: www.ftimeters.com/
email: ftimarket@ftimeters.com

Flowline Components, Inc.
10500 Humbolt Street
Los Alamitos, CA 90720
Phone: (562) 598-3015   FAX: (562) 431-8507
Internet: www.flowline.com/
email: US.sales@flowline.com

Gama Electronics
P.O. Box 1488
Chrystal Lake
Crystal Lake, IL 60039
Phone: (815) 356-9600   FAX: (815) 356-9603
Internet: www.gamainc.com/
email: GAMA@GAMAInc.com

H. F. Jensen
Emdrupvej 70
DK-2400 København,
NV
Phone: (453) 953-6040   FAX: (453) 953-6048
Internet: www.hfjensen.dk/
email: info@hfjensen.dk

Highly Electric Co., Ltd.
782 Heritage Drive
Ft. Lauderdale, FL 33326
Phone: (954) 349-1203   FAX: (954) 349-9172
Internet: www.highly.com/

Honeywell
101 Columbia Road
Morristown, NJ 07962
Phone: (800) 537-6945
Internet:
    content.honeywell.com/sensing/sitemap/
email: info@corp.honeywell.com

HTM Electronics Industries
8651 Buffalo Avenue
Niagara Falls, NY 14304
Phone: (800) 644-1756   FAX: (888) 283-2127
Internet: www.htm-optex.com/
email: custserv@htm-optex.com

Impact Register, Inc.
1870 Starkey Rd. Suite A
Largo, FL 33771
Phone: (727) 585-8572   FAX: (727) 586-0532
Internet: www.impactregister.com/
email: info@impactregister.com

ITT Cannon
8081 Wallace Road
Eden Prairie, MN 55344
Phone: (612) 934-4400   FAX: (612) 934-9121
Internet: www.ittcannon.com

Ixthus Instrumentation Ltd.
P.O. Box 6176
Whitchurch, Hampshire RG25 3RJ
UK
Phone: 44 1256 771166   FAX: 44 1256 771616
Internet: www.chamois.net/ixthus/index1.htm
email: sales@ixthus.co.uk

Keyence Corp. of America
50 Tice Blvd.

Woodcliff Lake, NJ 07675
Phone: (201) 930-0100   FAX: (201) 930-0099
Internet: www.keyence.com
email: keyence@keyence.com

Kistler Instruments Corporation
75 John Gleen Dr.
Amherst, NY 14228-2119
Phone: (888) 547-8537   FAX: (716) 691-5226
Internet: www.kistler.com/
email: kicsales@kistler.com

Knowles Electronics Inc.
1151 Maplewood Drive
Itasca, IL 60143
Phone: (630) 250-5100   FAX: (630) 250-0575
Internet: www.knowlesinc.com

Korea Partner Industry Co., Ltd.
25-2, Songkok-Ri, Hyangnam-Myun
Hwasung-Gun, Kyunggi-do
Korea
Phone: 82-31-352-0062   FAX: 82-31-352-0061
Internet: kpi@kpi.co.kr
email: jwchoi@kpi.co.kr

Korry Electronics Co
901 Dexter Avenue North
Seattle, WA 98109
Phone: (800) 257-8921   FAX: (206) 281-1365
Internet: www.korry.com
email: info@korry.com

Ktech
2201 Buena Vista SE, Suite 400
Albuquerque, NM 87106-4265
Phone: (505) 998-5830   FAX: (505) 998-5850
Internet: www.ktech.com
email: sensors@ktech.com

Lucas Nova Sensor
1055 Mission Street
Fremont, CA 94539-8203
Phone: (510) 661-6000   FAX: (510) 770-0645

Internet: www.novasensor.com
email: Karen.Siebe@trw.com

Mass Products Corporation
280 Lincoln Street
Hingham, MA 02043-1796
Phone: (800) 962-7543   FAX: (781) 740-2045
Internet: www.massa.com/
email: mpc@massa.com

Mettler Toledo
1900 Polaris Parkway
Columbus, OH 43240
Phone: (800) 638-8537   FAX: (614) 438-4900
Internet: www.mt.com/home/mettlertoledo.asp
email: leads@mt.com

Miller Edge, Inc.
P.O. Box 159
Rt. 796 & Woodview Road
Jennersville, PA 19390
Phone: (800) 887-3343
Internet: www.milleredge.com
email: info@milleredge.com

Nonvolatile Electronics, Inc.
11409 Valley View Park
Eden Prairie, MN 59344-3617
Phone: (800) 467-7141   FAX: (612) 996-1600
Internet: www.nve.com/
email: info@nve.com

NTE International Co., Ltd.
Rm 907, Fook. Hong Ind. Bldg.19 Sheung
    Yuetrd.
Kowloon Bay, Kowloon,
Hong Kong
Phone: 852-8206-9212   FAX: 852-8206-9252
Internet: www.nteco.com/
email: nteinternati@ismart.net

Omega Engineering Inc.
One Omega Drive
Stamford, CT 06907-0047
Phone: (800) 872-9436
Internet: www.omega.com
email: sales@omega.com

Omron Management Center of America,inc.
  (OMCA)
1300 Basswood, Suite 100
Schaumburg, IL 60173
Phone: (800) 556-6766   FAX: (847) 843-7787
Internet: oeiweb.omron.com/oei/

Pace Scientific Inc.
6407 Idlewild Road, Suite 2.214
Charlotte, NC 28212
Phone: (704) 568-3691   FAX: (704) 568-0278
Internet: www.pace-sci.com
email: sales@pace-sci.com

Paroscientific, Inc
4500 148th Avenue N.E.
Redmond, WA 98052
Phone: (425) 883-8700   FAX: (425) 867-5407
Internet: www.paroscientific.com/
email: support@paroscientific.com

Patriot Sensors and Controls Corp.
1644 Whittier Avenue
Costa Mesa, CA 92627-4115
Phone: (949) 642-2400   FAX: (949) 642-9490
Internet: www.xducer.com/

Photo Vision Systems LLC
P.O. Box 509
Cortland, NY 13045
Phone: (607) 756-5200   FAX: (607) 756-5319
Internet: www.photon-vision.com/
email: sales@photo-vision.com

Schaevitz Sensors
1000 Lucas Way
Hampton, VA 23666

Phone: (757) 766-1500   FAX: (757) 766-4297
Internet: www.schaevitz.com/

Setra Systems, Inc.
159 Swanson Rd.
Boxborough, MA 01719
Phone: (800) 257-3872
Internet: www.setra.com/
email: transducer.sales@setra.com

Sick, Inc.
6900 West 110th Street
Bloomington, MN 55438
Phone: (612) 941-6780   FAX: (612) 941-9287
Internet: www.sickoptic.com/
email: info@sickoptic.com

Speastech
1527 Bowman Road, Suite F
Little Rock, AR 72211
Phone: (888) 377-6766   FAX: (501) 219-9995
Internet: www.speastech.com/
email: rgartley@speastech.com

Spectec
P.O. Box 360
Emigrant, MT 59027
Phone: (406) 333-4967   FAX: (406) 333-4259
Internet: www.spectecsensors.com/
email: info@spectecsensors.com

Supreme Exim Corporation
P.O. Box: 50-70
Taipei City,
Taiwan, R.O.C.
Phone: 886-2-2597-3458 FAX: 886-2-2597-2008
Internet: www.supreme-
    exim.com.tw/switch.htm
email: supreme8@ms34.hinet.net

Syscan
1851 Zanker Road
San Jose, CA 95112
Phone: (888) 298-0498   FAX: (408) 436-6151

Internet: www.syscaninc.com/
email: sales@syscaninc.com

The Fredricks Company
P.O. Box 67
2400 Philmont Avenue
Huntingdon Valley, PA 19006-0067
Phone: (215) 947-2500   FAX: (215) 947-7464
Internet: www.frederickscom.com/
email: sensors@frederickscom.com

Trans-tek, Inc.
P.O. Box 338
Route 83
Ellington, CT 06029
Phone: (800) 828-3964   FAX: (860) 872-4211
Internet: www.transtekinc.com
email: transtekct@aol.com

Turck Inc. USA
3000 Campus Drive
Minneapolis, MN 55441
Phone: (763) 553-7300   FAX: (763) 553-0708
Internet: www.turck.com/

Vatell Corporation
240 Jannelle Road
Christianburg, VA 24073
Phone: (540) 961-2001
Internet: www.vatell.com
email: mkt@vatell.com

Vibration Sensing Devices
217 Cedar Street
Somerville, MA 02145
Phone: (617) 776-8068   FAX: (617) 776-1470
Internet: www.vsdco.com/
email: DVR@VSDCO.COM

Western Sensor, Inc
P.O. Box 1658
Hayden, ID 83835
Phone: (208) 722-3291   FAX: (208) 722-4471
Internet: www.dmi.net/ir-sensor

email: WSI@MMI.Net

Wolo Manufacturing Corp.
1 Saxwood Street
Deer Park, NY 11729
Phone: (800) 645-5808   FAX: (631) 242-0720
Internet: www.wolo-mfg.com/index.html
email: wolo@worldnet.att.net

BIBLIOGRAPHY

Adler, Paul S. "Time and Motion Regained," *Harvard Business Review*, January-February 1993, pp. 97–108.

Adler, Paul S. and Robert E. Cole. "Designed for Learning: A Tale of Two Auto Plants," *Sloan Management Review*, Spring 1993, pp. 85–94.

American Society of Quality. "About ASQ—Genichi Taguchi." February 16, 2000. ASQ. www.asq.org/about/history/taguchi.html.

AT&T. "AT&T Quality—Our Quality Heritage—Quality History 1877–Divestiture." June 22, 2000. AT&T. http://www.att.nl/quality/timeline.html.

Assembly View™—Design for Assembly Analysis for the Macintosh, User Manual, 1989. Sapphire Design Systems.

The Associated Press. "Lockeford boy loses cancer battle." Stockton: *The Record*, March 7, 1998.

The Associated Press. "Space shuttle workers afraid to report errors, study finds." Modesto: *The Modesto Bee*, July 27, 1993.

Barnes, Ralph M. *Motion and Time Study-Design and Measurement of Work*, Seventh Edition (New York: Wiley & Sons, 1980), pp. 12–21, 63, 361–388.

Boothroyd Dewhurst, Inc. Advertisement for the "1993 International Forum on DFMA," Wakefield, 1993.

Boothroyd, G. and P. Dewhurst. *Product Design for Assembly*, Section 2. Kingston: Boothroyd Dewhurst, Inc., 1985.

Buckley, Shawn and Phil Barkan. Conversation at Stanford, 1994.

Card, S., W. English, and B. Burr. "Evaluation of mouse, rate-controlled isometric joystick, step keys and text keys for test selection on a CRT," *Ergonomics*, 21(8), 1978, pp. 601–613.

Chase, Richard B., and Douglas M. Stewart. "Make Your Service Fail-Safe," *Sloan Management Review*, Spring 1994, pp. 35–44.

French, Howard W. "Accident at nuclear fuel plant releases radiation over Japan—Response delay is criticized." Pleasanton, Livermore, Dublin: *New York Times* article carried in *The Valley Time* 115(274), October 1, 1999, p. A1.

Frye, Ralph. Discussions regarding the observed impact of Smart Bins (and mistake-proofing) on productivity. Employee of SpeasTech, Inc. Little Rock. AR, 1997.

Gebala, Dave, telephone conversation, 1996.

Guwande, Atul. "Annals of Medicine—When Doctors Make Mistakes." *New Yorker* LXXIV(44), February 1, 1999, pp. 40–55.

Harris, Douglas H., and Frederick B. Chaney. *Human Factors in Quality Assurance* (New York: Wiley, 1969), p. 9.

Harry, Mikel J., and Reigle Stewart. *Six Sigma Mechanical Design Tolerancing*. Scottsdale: Motorola Publication No. 6s-2–10/88, 1988.

Hinckley, C. Martin. *A Global Conformance Quality Model—A New Strategic Tool for Minimizing Defects Caused by Variation, Error, and Complexity*. Stanford: Dissertation submitted to the Department of Mechanical Engineering and the Committee of Graduate Studies of Stanford University, 1993, pp.8–9, 26, 79–80, 136.

Hinckley, C. Martin, and Philip Barkan. "The Role of Variation Mistakes and Complexity in Producing Non-conformities." *Journal of Quality Technology* 27(3), July 1995, pp. 242–249.

Hirano, Hiroyuki, editor-in chief. *JIT Factory Revolution—A Pictorial Guide to Factory Design of the Future* (Portland: Dr. J. T. Black, ed. English Edition, Productivity Press, 1988).

Hirano, Hiroyuki. *Poka-yoke—Mistake-Proofing for Zero Defects* (New York: PHP Institute, Inc., 1994).

Ishii, Kosuke, and ME217 Teaching Team. *Design for Manufacturability: Product Definition— Course Reader for ME217A, Dept of Mechanical Engineering at Stanford University*. Stanford, 1997, pp. 6.1–4, 6.1–5.

Ishikawa, Kaoru. *Guide to Quality Control*, Seventh Printing (Tokyo: Asian Productivity Organization, 1990).

Juran, J. M., editor-in chief; Frank M. Gryna, associate editor. *Juran's Quality Control Handbook*, Fourth Edition (New York: McGraw-Hill, 1988), p. 24.6.

Kohn, Linda T., Janet M. Corrigan, and Molla S. Donaldson, Editors. *To Err Is Human: Building a Safer Health System* (Washington: Committee on Quality of Health Care in America, Institute of Medicine, National Academy Press, 2000), p. 26.

MacKenzie, Scott, Abigail Sellen, and William Buxton. "A Comparison of Input Devices in Elemental Pointing and Dragging Tasks," *Human Factors in Computing Systems-Reaching Through Technology, CHI 1991 Conference Proceedings*, April 27–May 2, 1991. Edited by Scott P. Robertson, Gary M. Olson, and Judith S. Olson (Reading: Addison Wesley Publishing Co.), pp. 161–166.

Pemberton, Mary. "Missing bolts identified as cause of stealth crash." Associated Press. Athens Daily News. *Athens Banner Herald*, December 13, 1997.

Nikkan Kogyo Shimbun/Factory Magazine, ed. *Poka-yoke: Improving Product Quality by Preventing Defects* (Portland: Productivity Press, 1988).

Rook, L. W., Jr. *Reduction of Human Error in Production*. Albuquerque. Sandia National Laboratories SCTM 93–62(14), Division 1443, June 1962.

Ross, Phillip J. *Taguchi Techniques for Quality Engineering* (New York: McGraw-Hill, 1988).

Sawyer, Kathy. "Conversion Error Sank Mars Probe." Pleasanton, Livermore, Dublin: *Washington Post* article carried in *The Valley Time* 115(274), October 1, 1999, p. A1.

Seidenstein, Sidney. (Undated materials). Presentation for Lockheed Missiles & Space Company, Inc., Sunnyvale, CA.

Shaffer, R. H. and H. A. Thomson. "Successful change programs begin with results," *Harvard Business Review* 70, January-February 1992, pp. 80–89.

Shingo, Shigeo. *A Revolution in Manufacturing: The SMED System.* (Portland: English translation, Productivity Press, 1985).

Shingo, Shigeo. *Zero Quality Control: Source Inspection and the Poka-yoke System.* (Portland: English translation, Productivity Press, 1986).

Smith, Bill. "Making a War on Defects-Six Sigma Design," *IEEE Spectrum*, September 1993, pp. 43–47.

Student report submitted for ME217A at Stanford University, December 1992.

Sturges, Robert. "A Quantification of Manual Dexterity: The Design for an Assembly Calculator," *Robotics and Computer-Integrated Manufacturing* 6(3), 1989, pp. 237–252.

Swain, A. D. and H. E. Guttmann. *Handbook of Human Reliability Analysis with Emphasis on Nuclear Power Plant Applications.* Albuquerque: Sandia National Laboratories, NUREG/CR-1278, SAND80–0200, RX, AN, August, 1983.

Stalk, George Jr., and Thomas M. Hout. *Competing Against Time—How Time-Based Competition Is Reshaping Global Markets* (New York: The Free Press, 1990).

Tavormina, Joseph J,. and Shawn Buckley. "Automatic 3–Dimensional Inspection Using Sensor Fusion." Presentation at the 25th Annual IICIT Connector and Interconnection Symposium, September 1992.

Wiggs, Gene, discussions regarding GE Aircraft Engine's research on the link between fabrication time and part complexity, 1997.

Womack, James P., Daniel T. Jones, and Daniel Roos. *The Machine that Changed the World.* (New York: Rawson Associates, 1990).

General Index

MISTAKE-PROOFING PRINCIPLES AND EXAMPLES INDEX

T - #0043 - 230425 - C0 - 280/208/24 [26] - CB - 9781563272271 - Gloss Lamination